The NT Desktop

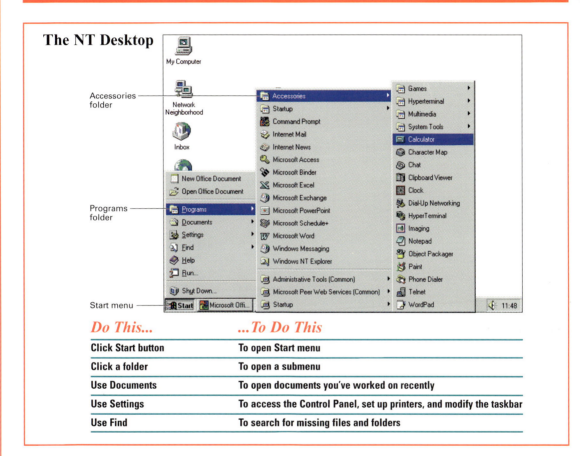

Do This...	...To Do This
Click Start button	To open Start menu
Click a folder	To open a submenu
Use Documents	To open documents you've worked on recently
Use Settings	To access the Control Panel, set up printers, and modify the taskbar
Use Find	To search for missing files and folders

The Windows NT Explorer Window

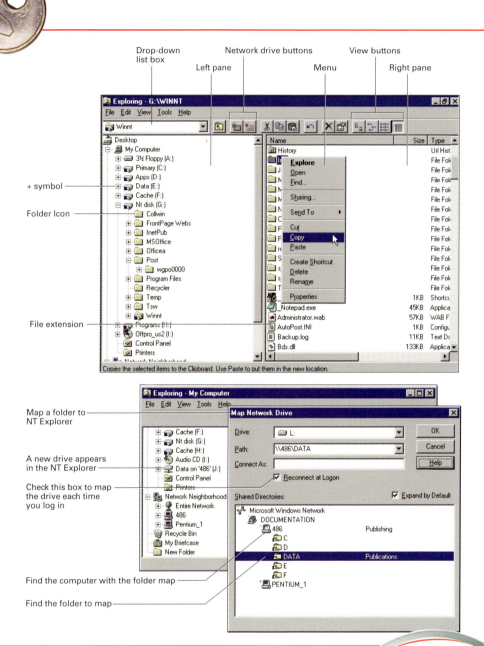

Copyright © 1997 IDG Books Worldwide. All rights reserved.
For more information about IDG Books call **1-800-762-2974**.
ISBN 0-7645-8025-6

DISCOVER WINDOWS NT® WORKSTATION 4.0

DISCOVER WINDOWS NT® WORKSTATION 4.0

BY PETER KENT

IDG BOOKS WORLDWIDE, INC.

AN INTERNATIONAL
DATA GROUP COMPANY

FOSTER CITY, CA • CHICAGO, IL •
INDIANAPOLIS, IN • SOUTHLAKE, TX

Discover Windows NT® Workstation 4.0

Published by
IDG Books Worldwide, Inc.
An International Data Group Company
919 E. Hillsdale Blvd., Suite 400
Foster City, CA 94404

http://www.idgbooks.com (IDG Books Worldwide Web site)

Copyright © 1997 IDG Books Worldwide, Inc. All rights reserved. No part of this book, including interior design, cover design, and icons, may be reproduced or transmitted in any form, by any means (electronic, photocopying, recording, or otherwise) without the prior written permission of the publisher.

Library of Congress Catalog Card No.: 96-79767

ISBN: 0-7645-8025-6

Printed in the United States of America

10 9 8 7 6 5 4 3 2 1

1IPC/RU/QT/ZX/FC

Distributed in the United States by IDG Books Worldwide, Inc.

Distributed by Macmillan Canada for Canada; by Contemporanea de Ediciones for Venezuela; by Distribuidora Cuspide for Argentina; by CITEC for Brazil; by Ediciones ZETA S.C.R. Ltda. for Peru; by Editorial Limusa SA for Mexico; by Transworld Publishers Limited in the United Kingdom and Europe; by Academic Bookshop for Egypt; by Levant Distributors S.A.R.L. for Lebanon; by Al Jassim for Saudi Arabia; by Simron Pty. Ltd. for South Africa; by Pustak Mahal for India; by The Computer Bookshop for India; by Toppan Company Ltd. for Japan; by Addison Wesley Publishing Company for Korea; by Longman Singapore Publishers Ltd. for Singapore, Malaysia, Thailand, and Indonesia; by Unalis Corporation for Taiwan; by WS Computer Publishing Company, Inc. for the Philippines; by WoodsLane Pty. Ltd. for Australia; by WoodsLane Enterprises Ltd. for New Zealand. Authorized Sales Agent: Anthony Rudkin Associates for the Middle East and North Africa.

For general information on IDG Books Worldwide's books in the U.S., please call our Consumer Customer Service department at 800-762-2974. For reseller information, including discounts and premium sales, please call our Reseller Customer Service department at 800-434-3422.

For information on where to purchase IDG Books Worldwide's books outside the U.S., please contact our International Sales department at 415-655-3172 or fax 415-655-3295.

For information on foreign language translations, please contact our Foreign & Subsidiary Rights department at 415-655-3021 or fax 415-655-3281.

For sales inquiries and special prices for bulk quantities, please contact our Sales department at 415-655-3200 or write to the address above.

For information on using IDG Books Worldwide's books in the classroom or for ordering examination copies, please contact our Educational Sales department at 800-434-2086 or fax 817-251-8174.

For press review copies, author interviews, or other publicity information, please contact our Public Relations department at 415-655-3000 or fax 415-655-3299.

For authorization to photocopy items for corporate, personal, or educational use, please contact Copyright Clearance Center, 222 Rosewood Drive, Danvers, MA 01923, or fax 508-750-4470.

LIMIT OF LIABILITY/DISCLAIMER OF WARRANTY: AUTHOR AND PUBLISHER HAVE USED THEIR BEST EFFORTS IN PREPARING THIS BOOK. IDG BOOKS WORLDWIDE, INC., AND AUTHOR MAKE NO REPRESENTATIONS OR WARRANTIES WITH RESPECT TO THE ACCURACY OR COMPLETENESS OF THE CONTENTS OF THIS BOOK AND SPECIFICALLY DISCLAIM ANY IMPLIED WARRANTIES OF MERCHANTABILITY OR FITNESS FOR A PARTICULAR PURPOSE. THERE ARE NO WARRANTIES WHICH EXTEND BEYOND THE DESCRIPTIONS CONTAINED IN THIS PARAGRAPH. NO WARRANTY MAY BE CREATED OR EXTENDED BY SALES REPRESENTATIVES OR WRITTEN SALES MATERIALS. THE ACCURACY AND COMPLETENESS OF THE INFORMATION PROVIDED HEREIN AND THE OPINIONS STATED HEREIN ARE NOT GUARANTEED OR WARRANTED TO PRODUCE ANY PARTICULAR RESULTS, AND THE ADVICE AND STRATEGIES CONTAINED HEREIN MAY NOT BE SUITABLE FOR EVERY INDIVIDUAL. NEITHER IDG BOOKS WORLDWIDE, INC., NOR AUTHOR SHALL BE LIABLE FOR ANY LOSS OF PROFIT OR ANY OTHER COMMERCIAL DAMAGES, INCLUDING BUT NOT LIMITED TO SPECIAL, INCIDENTAL, CONSEQUENTIAL, OR OTHER DAMAGES.

TRADEMARKS: ALL BRAND NAMES AND PRODUCT NAMES USED IN THIS BOOK ARE TRADE NAMES, SERVICE MARKS, TRADEMARKS, OR REGISTERED TRADEMARKS OF THEIR RESPECTIVE OWNERS. IDG BOOKS WORLDWIDE IS NOT ASSOCIATED WITH ANY PRODUCT OR VENDOR MENTIONED IN THIS BOOK.

 is a trademark under exclusive license to IDG Books Worldwide, Inc., from International Data Group, Inc.

ABOUT IDG BOOKS WORLDWIDE

Welcome to the world of IDG Books Worldwide.

IDG Books Worldwide, Inc., is a subsidiary of International Data Group, the world's largest publisher of computer-related information and the leading global provider of information services on information technology. IDG was founded more than 25 years ago and now employs more than 8,500 people worldwide. IDG publishes more than 275 computer publications in over 75 countries (see listing below). More than 60 million people read one or more IDG publications each month.

Launched in 1990, IDG Books Worldwide is today the #1 publisher of best-selling computer books in the United States. We are proud to have received eight awards from the Computer Press Association in recognition of editorial excellence and three from *Computer Currents'* First Annual Readers' Choice Awards. Our best-selling *...For Dummies*® series has more than 30 million copies in print with translations in 30 languages. IDG Books Worldwide, through a joint venture with IDG's Hi-Tech Beijing, became the first U.S. publisher to publish a computer book in the People's Republic of China. In record time, IDG Books Worldwide has become the first choice for millions of readers around the world who want to learn how to better manage their businesses.

Our mission is simple: Every one of our books is designed to bring extra value and skill-building instructions to the reader. Our books are written by experts who understand and care about our readers. The knowledge base of our editorial staff comes from years of experience in publishing, education, and journalism — experience we use to produce books for the '90s. In short, we care about books, so we attract the best people. We devote special attention to details such as audience, interior design, use of icons, and illustrations. And because we use an efficient process of authoring, editing, and desktop publishing our books electronically, we can spend more time ensuring superior content and spend less time on the technicalities of making books.

You can count on our commitment to deliver high-quality books at competitive prices on topics you want to read about. At IDG Books Worldwide, we continue in the IDG tradition of delivering quality for more than 25 years. You'll find no better book on a subject than one from IDG Books Worldwide.

John Kilcullen
CEO
IDG Books Worldwide, Inc.

Eighth Annual Computer Press Awards ≥1992

Ninth Annual Computer Press Awards ≥1993

Tenth Annual Computer Press Awards ≥1994

Eleventh Annual Computer Press Awards ≥1995

IDG Books Worldwide, Inc., is a subsidiary of International Data Group, the world's largest publisher of computer-related information and the leading global provider of information services on information technology. International Data Group publishes over 275 computer publications in over 75 countries. Sixty million people read one or more International Data Group publications each month. International Data Group's publications include: **ARGENTINA:** Buyer's Guide, Computerworld Argentina, PC World Argentina; **AUSTRALIA:** Australian Macworld, Australian PC World, Australian Reseller News, Computerworld, IT Casebook, Network World, Publish, Webmaster; **AUSTRIA:** Computerwelt Osterreich, Networks Austria, PC Tip Austria; **BANGLADESH:** PC World Bangladesh; **BELARUS:** PC World Belarus; **BELGIUM:** Data News; **BRAZIL:** Annuário de Informática, Computerworld, Connections, Macworld, PC Player, PC World, Publish, Reseller News, Supergamepower; **BULGARIA:** Computerworld Bulgaria, Network World Bulgaria, PC & MacWorld Bulgaria; **CANADA:** CIO Canada, Client/Server World, ComputerWorld Canada, InfoWorld Canada, NetworkWorld Canada, WebWorld; **CHILE:** Computerworld Chile, PC World Chile; **COLOMBIA:** Computerworld Colombia, PC World Colombia; **COSTA RICA:** PC World Centro America; **THE CZECH AND SLOVAK REPUBLICS:** Computerworld Czechoslovakia, Macworld Czech Republic, PC World Czechoslovakia; **DENMARK:** Communications World Danmark, Computerworld Danmark, Macworld Danmark, PC World Danmark, Techworld Denmark; **DOMINICAN REPUBLIC:** PC World Republica Dominicana; **ECUADOR:** PC World Ecuador; **EGYPT:** Computerworld Middle East, PC World Middle East; **EL SALVADOR:** PC World Centro America; **FINLAND:** MikroPC, Tietoverkko, Tietoviikko; **FRANCE:** Distributique, Hebdo, Info PC, Le Monde Informatique, Macworld, Reseaux & Telecoms, WebMaster France; **GERMANY:** Computer Partner, Computerwoche, Computerwoche Extra, Computerwoche FOCUS, Global Online, Macwelt, PC Welt; **GREECE:** Amiga Computing, GamePro Greece, Multimedia World; **GUATEMALA:** PC World Centro America; **HONDURAS:** PC World Centro America; **HONG KONG:** Computerworld Hong Kong, PC World Hong Kong, Publish in Asia; **HUNGARY:** ABCD CD-ROM, Computerworld Szamitastechnika, Internetto online Magazine, PC World Hungary, PC-X Magazin Hungary; **ICELAND:** Tolvuheimur PC World Island; **INDIA:** Information Communications World, Information Systems Computerworld, PC World India, Publish in Asia; **INDONESIA:** InfoKomputer PC World, Komputek Computerworld, Publish in Asia; **IRELAND:** ComputerScope, PC Live!; **ISRAEL:** Macworld Israel, People & Computers/Computerworld; **ITALY:** Computerworld Italia, Macworld Italia, Networking Italia, PC World Italia; **JAPAN:** DTP World, Macworld Japan, Nikkei Personal Computing, OS/2 World Japan, SunWorld Japan, Windows NT World, Windows World Japan; **KENYA:** PC World East African; **KOREA:** Hi-Tech Information, Macworld Korea, PC World Korea; **MACEDONIA:** PC World Macedonia; **MALAYSIA:** Computerworld Malaysia, PC World Malaysia, Publish in Asia; **MALTA:** PC World Malta; **MEXICO:** Computerworld Mexico, PC World Mexico; **MYANMAR:** PC World Myanmar; **NETHERLANDS:** Computer! Totaal, LAN Internetworking Magazine, LAN World Buyers Guide, Macworld Netherlands, Net, WebWereld; **NEW ZEALAND:** Absolute Beginners Guide and Plain & Simple Series, Computer Buyer, Computer Industry Directory, Computerworld New Zealand, MTB, Network World, PC World New Zealand; **NICARAGUA:** PC World Centro America; **NORWAY:** Computerworld Norge, CW Rapport, Datamagasinet, Financial Rapport, Kursguide Norge, Macworld Norge, Multimediaworld Norge, PC World Ekspress Norge, PC World Nettverk, PC World Norge, PC World ProduktGuide Norge; **PAKISTAN:** Computerworld Pakistan; **PANAMA:** PC World Panama; **PEOPLE'S REPUBLIC OF CHINA:** China Computer Users, China Computerworld, China InfoWorld, China Telecom World Weekly, Computer & Communication, Electronic Design China, Electronics Today, Electronics Weekly, Game Software, PC World China, Popular Computer Week, Software Weekly, Software World, Telecom World; **PERU:** Computerworld Peru, PC World Profesional Peru, PC World SoHo Peru; **PHILIPPINES:** Click!, Computerworld Philippines, PC World Philippines, Publish in Asia; **POLAND:** Computerworld Poland, Computerworld Special Report Poland, Cyber, Macworld Poland, Networld Poland, PC World Komputer; **PORTUGAL:** Cerebro/PC World, Computerworld/Correio Informático, Dealer World Portugal, Mac*In/PC*In Portugal, Multimedia World; **PUERTO RICO:** PC World Puerto Rico; **ROMANIA:** Computerworld Romania, PC World Romania, Telecom Romania; **RUSSIA:** Computerworld Russia, Mir PK, Publish, Seti; **SINGAPORE:** Computerworld Singapore, PC World Singapore, Publish in Asia; **SLOVENIA:** Monitor; **SOUTH AFRICA:** Computing SA, Network World SA, Software World SA; **SPAIN:** Communicaciones World España, Computerworld España, Dealer World España, Macworld España, PC World España; **SRI LANKA:** Infolink PC World; **SWEDEN:** CAP&Design, Computer Sweden, Corporate Computing Sweden, Internetworld Sweden, it.branschen, Macworld Sweden, MaxiData Sweden, MikroDatorn, Natverk & Kommunikation, PC World Sweden, PCAktiv, Windows World Sweden; **SWITZERLAND:** Computerworld Schweiz, Macworld Schweiz, PCtip; **TAIWAN:** Computerworld Taiwan, Macworld Taiwan, NEW ViSiON/Publish, PC World Taiwan, Windows World Taiwan; **THAILAND:** Publish in Asia, Thai Computerworld; **TURKEY:** Computerworld Turkiye, Macworld Turkiye, Network World Turkiye, PC World Turkiye; **UKRAINE:** Computerworld Kiev, Multimedia World Ukraine, PC World Ukraine; **UNITED KINGDOM:** Acorn User UK, Amiga Action UK, Amiga Computing UK, Apple Talk UK, Computing, Macworld, Parents and Computers UK, PC Advisor, PC Home, PSX Pro, The WEB; **UNITED STATES:** Cable in the Classroom, CIO Magazine, Computerworld, DOS World, Federal Computer Week, GamePro Magazine, InfoWorld, I-Way, Macworld, Network World, PC Games, PC World, Publish, Video Event, THE WEB Magazine, and WebMaster; online webzines: JavaWorld, NetscapeWorld, and SunWorld Online; **URUGUAY:** InfoWorld Uruguay; **VENEZUELA:** Computerworld Venezuela, PC World Venezuela; and **VIETNAM:** PC World Vietnam.

2/14/97

Welcome to the Discover Series

Do you want to discover the best and most efficient ways to use your computer and learn about technology? Books in the Discover series teach you the essentials of technology with a friendly, confident approach. You'll find a Discover book on almost any subject — from the Internet to intranets, from Web design and programming to the business programs that make your life easier.

We've provided valuable, real-world examples that help you relate to topics faster. Discover books begin by introducing you to the main features of programs, so you start by doing something *immediately*. The focus is to teach you how to perform tasks that are useful and meaningful in your day-to-day work. You might create a document or graphic, explore your computer, surf the Web, or write a program. Whatever the task, you learn the most commonly used features, and focus on the best tips and techniques for doing your work. You'll get results quickly, and discover the best ways to use software and technology in your everyday life.

You may find the following elements and features in this book:

Discovery Central: This tearout card is a handy quick reference to important tasks or ideas covered in the book.

Quick Tour: The Quick Tour gets you started working with the book right away.

Real-Life Vignettes: Throughout the book you'll see one-page scenarios illustrating a real-life application of a topic covered.

Goals: Each chapter opens with a list of goals you can achieve by reading the chapter.

Side Trips: These asides include additional information about alternative or advanced ways to approach the topic covered.

Bonuses: Timesaving tips and more advanced techniques are covered in each chapter.

Discovery Center: This guide illustrates key procedures covered throughout the book.

Visual Index: You'll find real-world documents in the Visual Index, with page numbers pointing you to where you should turn to achieve the effects shown.

Throughout the book, you'll also notice some special icons and formatting:

A Feature Focus icon highlights new features in the software's latest release, and points out significant differences between it and the previous version.

Web Paths refer you to Web sites that provide additional information about the topic.

Tips offer timesaving shortcuts, expert advice, quick techniques, or brief reminders.

The X-Ref icon refers you to other chapters or sections for more information.

Pull Quotes emphasize important ideas that are covered in the chapter.

Notes provide additional information or highlight special points of interest about a topic.

The Caution icon alerts you to potential problems you should watch out for.

The Discover series delivers interesting, insightful, and inspiring information about technology to help you learn faster and retain more. So the next time you want to find answers to your technology questions, reach for a Discover book. We hope the entertaining, easy-to-read style puts you at ease and makes learning fun.

Credits

ACQUISITIONS EDITOR
John Osborn

DEVELOPMENT EDITOR
Barbra Guerra

TECHNICAL EDITOR
Cary Torkelson

COPY EDITOR
Nate Holdread

PROJECT COORDINATOR
Katy German

GRAPHICS AND PRODUCTION SPECIALIST
Ritchie Durdin

QUALITY CONTROL SPECIALIST
Mick Arellano

PROOFREADERS
Desne Border
Andrew Davis
Stacey Lynn
Candace Ward
Anne Weinberger

INDEXER
Elizabeth Cunningham

BOOK DESIGN
Seventeenth Street Studios
Phyllis Beaty
Kurt Krames

About the Author

Peter Kent has been testing and installing software and hardware, training users, and writing computer books and documentation for 15 years. He's the author of *Discover FrontPage 97* (IDG Books), the best-selling *Complete Idiot's Guide to the Internet* (Que), and around thirty other computer and Internet-related books. His work has appeared in a variety of publications, including the *Manchester Guardian, Internet World, Windows User,* and the *Dallas Times Herald.* Peter's books have been translated into over a dozen languages.

Peter spent about 10 years selling his technical writing services to anyone who would pay, but now mostly sits at home in monkish isolation writing computer books. Well, not quite monkish; he lives with his wife and two boys in Denver, Colorado, 50 minutes from the nearest ski slopes (which he plans to visit far more often once he slows down and writes fewer books). He can be reached at pkent@arundel.com.

FOR CHRISTOPHER

PREFACE

Welcome to *Discover Windows NT Workstation 4.0*. This book provides step-by-step instructions for working in Windows NT Workstation. It's designed for the average user who needs to know this operating system quickly and work with NT programs right away. You learn how to get things done quickly and easily — from opening programs to making tape backups and from switching between program windows to setting up a phone connection to an Internet service provider or another NT computer.

Here are just a few of the things you'll learn:

* How to quickly open programs using the Start button, desktop icons, the Run command, and so on.

* How to customize the NT desktop to suit your needs (for example, how to add items to the Start menu and create your own desktop icons).

* How to use Windows NT Explorer, a file-management program, and the My Computer folder windows.

* How to install and manage printers.

* How to secure your data by defining which other users, if any, may work with your files and what exactly they may do with them.

* How to connect to other computers on the network and how to share your data with other network users.

* How to use the NT accessory applications to work with text files, write letters and memos, swap data between programs, and select special characters for use in your documents.

* How to work with multimedia to play your audio CDs and MIDI, video, animation, and sound files.

* How to create and modify bitmap pictures and how to annotate scanned documents.

* How to back up data onto a tape drive so that you don't lose all your data in the event of computer damage or theft.

* How to work on the Internet using Microsoft Internet Explorer.

* How to customize dozens of different NT characteristics to suit the way you work.

Discover Windows NT Workstation 4.0 is a no-nonsense guide to getting started with NT Workstation, so turn to the first chapter . . . and get started!

CONTENTS AT A GLANCE

Preface, xi

QUICK TOUR   1

PART ONE—YOUR FIRST LOOK AT NT

1   WHAT WINDOWS NT CAN DO FOR YOU   9

2   STARTING WINDOWS NT 4.0   19

3   STARTING PROGRAMS   39

4   CUSTOMIZING THE DESKTOP   61

5   WORKING WITH FILES IN NT EXPLORER   75

6   MORE FILE PROCEDURES — NT EXPLORER AND MY COMPUTER   95

7   USING PRINTERS AND FONTS   115

8   PROTECTING YOUR WORK — PROFILES AND SECURITY   141

PART TWO—NT'S ACCESSORIES

9   TEXT AND NUMBERS — WORDPAD, NOTEPAD, CALCULATOR, & MORE   165

10	WORKING WITH PICTURES — PAINT AND IMAGE	189
11	USING MULTIMEDIA IN WINDOWS NT	207
12	KEEPING YOUR DATA SAFE — BACKUP	225
13	SIMPLE COMMUNICATIONS — HYPERTERMINAL & PHONE DIALER	239

PART THREE — NETWORKING, THE INTERNET, AND INTRANETS

14	USING THE NETWORK NEIGHBORHOOD AND NETWORK UTILITIES	259
15	CORRESPONDING WITH E-MAIL	277
16	COMPUTING ON THE ROAD AND ON THE INTERNET	297
17	WORKING ON THE WEB — USING INTERNET EXPLORER	319

PART FOUR — GETTING UNDER THE HOOD

| 18 | CUSTOMIZING YOUR SYSTEM | 333 |
| 19 | MAINTAINING AND FIXING WINDOWS NT | 353 |

Discovery Center, 365
Visual Index, 415
Index, 417

CONTENTS

Preface, xi

QUICK TOUR, 1

PART ONE—YOUR FIRST LOOK AT NT, 7

1 WHAT WINDOWS NT CAN DO FOR YOU, 9
   What's an Operating System?, 11
     Using NT's security, 11
   Windows NT Workstation's Features, 12
   What Is Windows NT Server?, 16
   What Windows NT Won't Do, 17
   Summary, 18

2 STARTING WINDOWS NT 4.0, 19
   Booting NT, 20
     Dual-boot computers, 20
     The Hardware Profile/Last Known Good Menu, 21
     Logging on, 22
   Understanding the Windows NT Desktop, 23
     The desktop icons, 27
   Using the Taskbar, 28
     Starting programs with the Start button, 29
     Customizing the taskbar, 30
     Using the tray, 33
   Using Folders and Directories, 34
   Locking and Closing Windows NT, 35
   More Ways to Shut Down NT, 36

Add Volume Control to the Taskbar, 37

Sort Your Icons, 37

Viewing the Desktop Contents, 38

Summary, 38

3 STARTING PROGRAMS, 39

Starting Programs, 39
- Starting programs from the menu, 40
- Starting programs using the desktop icons, 42
- Starting programs with the document menu, 42
- Starting programs using the Run command, 43
- After they're running: All about multitasking, 44

Managing Windows, 45
- Sizing the window, 48
- Using the taskbar to manage windows, 48

Switching between Windows, 49
- Managing windows with Task Manager, 51

Finding, Opening, and Saving Files, 53

Closing Programs, 56

The Keyboard Accelerators, 57

A Congested Menu Rx, 57

A Few Quick Tips , 58
- Closing document windows, 58
- Running a program, 58
- Opening a file, 59
- Reaching the Task Manager , 59

Summary, 59

4 CUSTOMIZING THE DESKTOP, 61

Creating Your Own Menu Options, 61
- Adding menu options, 62
- Removing menu options, 63
- And all the rest — advanced modifications, 63

Creating Desktop Shortcuts, 65

Creating Folders, 66

Managing Shortcuts and Folders, 67

Creating Desktop Files, 69

Installing New Programs, 70

A Word about User Profiles, 71
Right-Click the Start Button, 73
Adding Options to the Menu, 73
Summary, 74

5 WORKING WITH FILES IN NT EXPLORER, 75

Opening Explorer, 75

Moving Around in the Directory Tree, 78

Configuring NT Explorer, 79

Working with Files, 81
    Multiple file operations, 83
    Different Explorer views, 84

Finding File and Folder Information, 86
    Viewing drive information, 89
    Compressing drives, folders, and files, 89

Using the Toolbar, 90

Quickly Open a Folder, 92

Different Explorers for Different Occasions, 92

Modifying Shortcut Icons, 93

Send To a Common Folder, 93

Summary, 94

6 MORE FILE PROCEDURES — NT EXPLORER AND MY COMPUTER, 95

Disk Utilities — Formatting, Copying, and More, 96
    Formatting disks, 96
    Copying disks, 98
    Checking for disk errors, 99
    Backing up disks, 99
    Defragmenting disks, 100

Associating Files with Applications, 100

Using My Computer, 104
    Setting up the folder windows, 105

Finding Stuff with Find and Go To, 105
    Saving a search, 109
    A direct path to a directory, 110

Deleting (and Retrieving) Files, 110
    Configuring the Recycle Bin, 112

What are all these *.TMP Files?, 113

Quickly Open README Files, 113

Summary, 114

7 USING PRINTERS AND FONTS, 115

Installing a Printer, 116
    Multiple drivers for one printer?, 120
    What about network printers?, 120

Using Your Printer, 121

Managing Printers, 123

Modifying Printer Properties, 124
    The printer properties, 124
    The document properties, 128

Font Management, 129
    Viewing fonts, 129
    Installing new fonts, 131
    Removing fonts, 132

Picking Special Characters, 133

Creating Print Files, 135

Fonts Come in Different Forms, 137

Instant Character Map, 138

Summary, 139

8 PROTECTING YOUR WORK — PROFILES AND SECURITY, 141

Creating a User Account, 142

All About Groups, 144
    What's the point?, 145
    Creating a new group, 146

Assigning a User to a Group, 148

Determining Overall Account Policies, 148

What Can Users Do?, 150
    Assigning rights to a group or user, 150
    Restricting access to resources, 151
    Who owns this, anyway?, 153

Big Brother's Watching! How to Audit, 154
    System auditing, 154
    Watching folders, files, printers, and fonts, 155
    Viewing the audit trail, 157

Work on Several Users at Once, 159

Copying Profiles and Accounts, 159

Setting up the User's Environment, 161

Setting up Dialin Access, 161

Summary, 162

PART TWO—NT'S ACCESSORIES, 163

9 TEXT AND NUMBERS — WORDPAD, NOTEPAD, CALCULATOR, & MORE, 165

Copying Data — Using the Clipboard, 166

Working with a ClipBook, 169
  Using a ClipBook page, 169

Word Processing for the Masses — WordPad, 171
  Opening a document, 173
  Working with text, 174
  Changing the look with fonts, 175
  Changing the look with paragraphs, 177
  Using tabs, 177
  Finding and replacing text, 179
  Printing and previewing, 179
  Saving your work, 180
  Setting up WordPad options, 181

A Simple Text Editor — NotePad, 182

Figuring Numbers — Calculator, 183

Working with "Objects" and OLE, 185

Summary, 187

10 WORKING WITH PICTURES — PAINT AND IMAGE, 189

Starting Microsoft Paint, 190
  Opening an existing image, 192

Working with the Tools, 192
  The tool options, 193
  Entering text, 194
  Opaque versus transparent, 195

Working with Colors, 196
  Changing views, 198
  Advanced commands, 199

Opening Imaging for Windows NT, 199

Making Annotations, 201
    Setting properties, 202
    More imaging commands, 203

Working with Wallpaper, 205

Create Your Own Rubber Stamps, 205

Summary, 206

11 USING MULTIMEDIA IN WINDOWS NT, 207

Preparing for Sound, 208

Playing Your CDs, 211
    All about the Play List, 213
    Setting the options, 214

Playing Sounds with Sound Recorder, 215
    Recording sounds, 215
    Editing sounds, 216

Video and More with Media Player, 217
    Media Player's options, 219

Controlling the Volume, 220

Marking and Copying Media Player Selections, 222

Don't Be Selfish! Share Your Music!, 223

Summary, 223

12 KEEPING YOUR DATA SAFE — BACKUP, 225

Setting Up the Tape Drive, 226

Making Backups, 227

Picking a Backup Type, 231

Your Backup Strategy, 232

Getting the Data off the Tape — Restoring, 233

Tape Maintenance, 235

Scheduling Backups, 236

Summary, 238

13 SIMPLE COMMUNICATIONS — HYPERTERMINAL & PHONE DIALER, 239

Preparing Your Modem, 240

Working with HyperTerminal, 244

Working Online, 246
    Downloading files, 248

Setting Up a New Connection, 250

Using the Phone Dialer, 250

Setting Up Long Distance Services and Calling Cards, 252

Summary, 255

PART THREE—NETWORKING, THE INTERNET, AND INTRANETS, 257

14 USING THE NETWORK NEIGHBORHOOD AND NETWORK UTILITIES, 259

Preparing Your Network Connection, 260

Using Network Neighborhood, 262
    Finding the data you need, 263
    A shortcut — mapping a drive, 264
    Find the computer you need, 266

Sharing Your Information on the Network, 267

Accessing the Network Throughout NT, 269

Immediate Messaging — Using Chat, 270
    Setting up your chat window, 271

Installing a Network Card, 272

Summary, 276

15 CORRESPONDING WITH E-MAIL, 277

Setting Up Windows Messaging, 277

Opening Windows Messaging and Sending E-mail, 282

Retrieving and Reading E-mail, 284

Using Remote Mail to Grab E-mail, 288

Using the Address Book, 289
    Sending e-mail to an existing address, 289
    Adding names to the address book, 290

Much, Much, More, 292

Setting Up a Postoffice, 293
Adding User Accounts, 294
Summary, 295

16 COMPUTING ON THE ROAD AND ON THE INTERNET, 297

Setting Up Dial-Up Networking, 298
    Installing Dial-Up Networking, 298
    Setting up your first connection, 300

Dialing into Your New Connection, 303
    Closing your connection, 305
    Keeping the monitor handy, 306

Taking Files on the Road with Briefcase, 307
    Packing files in the briefcase, 308
    Using the briefcase, 308
    Checking your files, 309

Working with Hardware Profiles, 311

MultiLink Connections, 315

Briefcase too Big for a Floppy?, 316

Summary, 317

17 WORKING ON THE WEB — USING INTERNET EXPLORER, 319

Getting Started with Internet Explorer, 320

Upgrading Internet Explorer, 321

Moving Around on the Web, 323
    Click a link, 323
    Type a URL, 323
    Select from the Favorites, 324
    Select from the history list, 325

Searching for What You Need, 326

Finding Your Way Back, 327

More Internet and Intranet Stuff, 328

Summary, 329

PART FOUR—GETTING UNDER THE HOOD, 331

18 CUSTOMIZING YOUR SYSTEM, 333

Setting Accessibility Options, 336
- Keyboard settings, 336
- Sound settings, 337
- Mouse settings, 337
- General settings, 339

Modifying the Date and Time, 340

Resolutions, Colors, and Wallpaper, 341
- Background, 341
- Screen Saver, 341
- Appearance, 342
- Plus!, 344
- Settings, 345

Configuring the Keyboard and Mouse, 346
- Keyboard settings, 346
- Mouse settings, 348

Audible Computing — Modifying Sounds, 349

What Happens During Startup?, 350

Summary, 352

19 MAINTAINING AND FIXING WINDOWS NT, 353

A Quick Look at the System — Task Manager, 355

Tracking System Performance, 357
- Alerts, logs, and reports, 359

Viewing Event Logs, 360

Finding System Information, 361

Your Basic Maintenance Schedule, 363

Summary, 364

Discovery Center, 365

Visual Index, 415

Index, 417

WINDOWS NT QUICK TOUR

PRACTICE USING THESE SKILLS

BOOTING UP NT   PAGE 1

STARTING A PROGRAM   PAGE 3

SAVING YOUR WORK   PAGE 5

SHUTTING DOWN NT   PAGE 6

Before we jump all the way into learning Windows NT Workstation, how about getting your feet just a little wet? In this Quick Tour, you'll see how to boot Windows NT, start a program inside NT, do a little work and save that work in a file, and then close down the operating system.

Booting up NT

1. Turn on your computer. If the computer is already on, and there's a dialog box with a Restart button on the screen, click Restart.

2. The computer begins its boot process. You may see a message similar to the following screen (otherwise, skip to Step 4):

```
Please select the operating system to start

 Windows NT Workstation Version 4.00 
Windows NT Workstation Version 4.00 [VGA mode]
Microsoft Windows
```

```
Use  ↑  and  ↓  to move the highlight to your choice.
Seconds until highlighted choice will be started automatically: 30
```

3. The first line of the message is highlighted and will automatically be accepted after the number of seconds shown on the last line. Make sure that Windows NT Workstation Version 4.00 is highlighted (use the arrow keys), and then press Enter to continue.

4. You'll see a number of text messages, which you can ignore.

5. After a few moments, you'll see a dialog box telling you to press Ctrl+Alt+Delete to log on. Press and hold all three of these keys at the same time.

6. The Logon Information dialog box opens. Type your account name into the first text box and your password into the second. (Your system administrator can give you your password. Or, if you installed Windows NT on this machine, the account name is Administrator, and the password is the password you entered during installation.)

7. You may also be able to enter a domain name (type the one given to you by your system administrator).

8. Click OK or press Enter. You may see a dialog box telling you to enter a new password. If so, type your password in both the *New Password* and *Confirm New Password* boxes (you won't see what you type — each character is replaced with a * symbol), and then click OK.

9. You are now logged onto Windows NT. You may see the Welcome to Windows NT dialog box, shown in the following figure. If so, click the Close button to remove it.

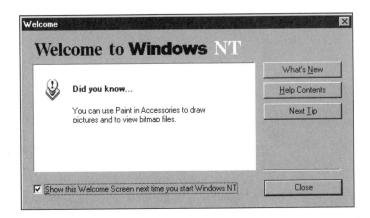

10. Now you'll see your Windows NT *desktop*, which is similar to the following figure. (If your system has been customized in some way, it

may look different — the bar with the Start button may be on a different edge of the screen, and there may be more icons on the desktop.)

Starting a Program

1. Click the Start button to open the Start menu. The menu shown in the following figure contains two entries at the top. These entries are not present on all NT systems, because this system also has Microsoft Office installed. All the other entries will be present on all NT systems.

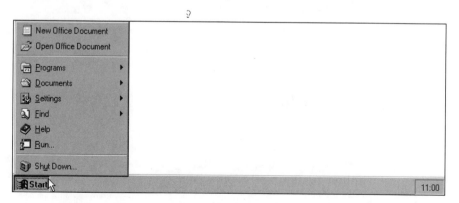

2. Move the mouse over the Programs entry and a submenu opens.

3. Move the mouse over the Accessories entry and another submenu opens.

4. Point at the WordPad entry at the bottom of the menu and click the mouse button. WordPad opens.

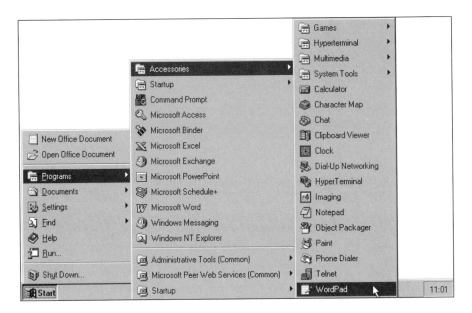

5. Type a few notes in WordPad. Then choose File→Exit.

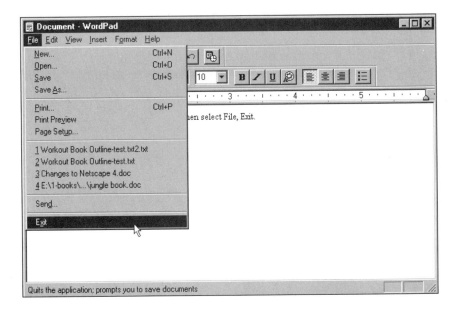

Saving Your Work

1. A messages box asks if you want to save the document. Click Yes.

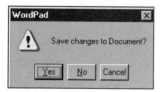

2. Click in the *Save in* drop-down list box, and then click the disk drive that Windows NT is stored on. (Your disk-drive icons may look different — the little hand means that the drive is available to other network users.)

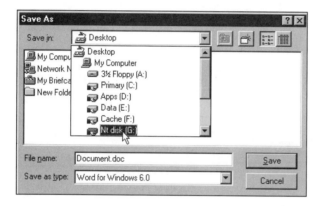

3. Double-click the Temp directory.

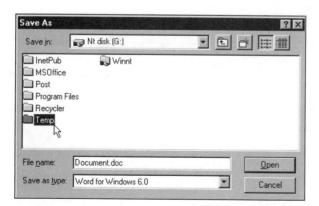

4. In the *File name* text box, double-click anywhere on Document.doc.

5. Type a filename, such as **Test Document**, and then press Enter. The document is saved, and WordPad closes.

Shutting Down NT

1. Click the Start button, then choose Shut Down.

2. Make sure *Shut Down the Computer* is selected, and then click Yes. Windows NT will close. In a few moments, you will see a small dialog box with the message *It is now safe to turn off your computer.* You can turn off the computer or click the Restart button to restart Windows NT.

That was pretty simple, wasn't it? Plus you've already learned some of the most basic procedures you will be using every day — revving up NT, starting programs, saving your work, and leaving NT. Of course there's more... plenty more. So turn to Chapter 1 to get started.

PART ONE
YOUR FIRST LOOK AT NT

THIS PART CONTAINS THE FOLLOWING CHAPTERS

CHAPTER 1 WHAT WINDOWS NT CAN DO FOR YOU

CHAPTER 2 STARTING WINDOWS NT WORKSTATION

CHAPTER 3 STARTING PROGRAMS

CHAPTER 4 CUSTOMIZING THE DESKTOP

CHAPTER 5 WORKING WITH FILES IN NT EXPLORER

CHAPTER 6 MORE FILE PROCEDURES — NT EXPLORER AND MY COMPUTER

CHAPTER 7 USING PRINTERS AND FONTS

CHAPTER 8 PROTECTING YOUR WORK — PROFILES AND SECURITY

NT means New Technology, and if you're upgrading from Windows 3.1, you may find it a little strange at first. Even if you've worked with Windows 95, you'll find plenty that's unfamiliar — such as all the security features. Read Part 1, however, and you'll soon feel at home.

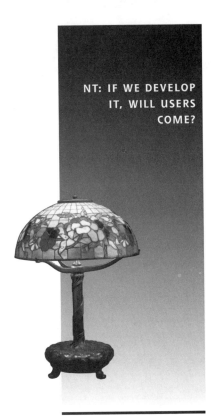

NT: IF WE DEVELOP IT, WILL USERS COME?

With the burgeoning popularity of PCs and UNIX workstations in the 80s, the general public and businesses alike started demanding user-friendly operating systems to perform simple to complex tasks. DOS — the most widely used system — was tedious at best, multiple PC and workstation platforms were rarely able to interact with one another, and processing was time consuming.

Thus, David Cutler, who helped launch Microsoft with Bill Gates, came up with a mission-critical plan to carry the young company through the long haul: develop a portable operating system, unlike UNIX, that could run on any microprocessing architecture while running higher-level, multiple projects simultaneously.

Christened *Windows New Technology,* this new operating system was "initially intended to support OS/2, along with 6-bit and 32-bit Windows products. Eventually, Windows NT became a 32-bit operating system that could run multiple tasks on any microprocessor," says Frank Antale, director of Windows NT program management.

By 1993, Windows NT was ready for the public. Now the big questions: Would they find it inviting and user-friendly? Would they prefer it to their Windows 3.1?

Microsoft's usability labs invited folks from a customer site to find out. "It was an adjustment for some to go from 3.1 to NT. It was funny to watch them try it for the first time," Antale laughs.

For example, with Windows 3.1, the testers were accustomed to performing only one task at a time, while NT is multitasking. When the hourglass icon appeared on screen indicating an operation in progress, "people literally stopped work," Antale notes, just as they had with 3.1. But when they moved the hourglass off the busy window onto the background, they were surprised that they could accomplish another task simultaneously.

Overall, companies find NT's user interface a refreshing change from command-driven operating systems. "We're seeing NT Workstation installations side by side with UNIX Workstations," contends Antale. "Our deployment strategy is to phase NT into major companies within 1 to 3 years. More companies are finding that a single NT operating system can drive costs down."

Antale adds, "As processor and memory caps grow larger, and with our adding plug and play, power management, and more reliability, NT is appearing on more machines targeted for home use. Now that it's been developed, will users come? Summed up by Antale, "As the Pentium Pro becomes the processor of choice, so will NT be the operating system of choice. It's the core of the Microsoft operating system business."

CHAPTER ONE
WHAT WINDOWS NT CAN DO FOR YOU

IN THIS CHAPTER YOU LEARN THESE KEY SKILLS

WHAT'S AN OPERATING SYSTEM?   PAGE 11
WINDOWS NT WORKSTATION'S FEATURES   PAGE 12
WHAT IS WINDOWS NT SERVER?   PAGE 16
WHAT WINDOWS NT WON'T DO   PAGE 17

Why are you using Windows NT Workstation? Why not use Windows 3.1 or Windows 95? Your company may have chosen NT for you, of course, but why? Because Windows NT has a variety of features that Windows 3.1 and Windows 95 *don't* have.

In particular, NT has several important characteristics:

* Security
* Stability
* Speed
* Network support
* Multi-platform support
* Multiple processors

Windows NT is a safe system (you can lock any system resource, from printers to files to fonts), it's stable (it rarely crashes or locks up), and it's fast when running on the newer Pentium and Pentium Pro computers. NT runs not only on Pentium computers but also on 486s, as well as on RISC-based computers (workstations with Alpha AXP, MIPS R4x00 or PowerPC processors).

Are you tired of all the crashes in Windows 3.1? Did you upgrade to Windows 95 because of those crashes, only to find that Windows 95 has its fair share, too? Well, NT is incredibly stable. Crashes are rare, and when they do occur, they generally affect only one program. It's rare to have NT lock up completely, and you almost never have to reboot.

NT can work with multiple processors and run faster than normal. Instead of having a single CPU (Central Processing Unit) chip in your computer, you may have two or more (Windows NT Workstation can work with one or two chips; Windows NT Server can work with up to 32 chips). More chips means more computer power, faster calculations, and faster operations.

Microsoft designed NT as a networked machine. The networking software you need is built-in (see Figure 1-1) and easy to use, too, as you learn in Chapter 14.

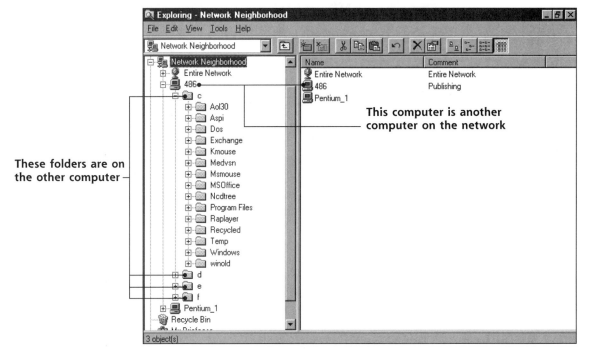

Figure 1-1   Treat data on other networked computers as if it were on your own hard disks.

  Visit http://www.microsoft.com/ntworkstation/ **on the World Wide Web for both general and technical information about Windows NT Workstation.**

This chapter gives you a quick overview of Windows NT Workstation and what it can do for you (and what it *can't* do for you, too).

What's an Operating System?

Windows NT is an *operating system*. An operating system is a special program or suite of programs used to communicate with the computer's hardware. The operating system works between the hardware and the programs you need to run.

A program, to be of any use, has to communicate with your computer's hardware in some way. It has to tell the video card what to display on your computer monitor, the sound card what sounds to play through your speakers, the communications ports what sort of data to send to the printer, and so on.

> **TIP** What does NT stand for? *New Technology*.

A program can talk directly to the hardware, which is how programs used to be written in the early days of computing (and still are, in some special cases). But there's a big problem with direct communication. Making the program speak to the hardware takes a great deal of work, and it's much more work creating a program that will work with all the thousands of different types of hardware, such as different video cards, different printers, different sound cards, and so on.

An operating system insulates software publishers from these communication problems. The publisher just has to ensure that the program works within the operating system and not worry about the hardware. The operating system takes information from the program and passes it on to the hardware, in a form that the hardware can understand. It also takes information from the hardware — from keyboards, mice, scanners, digitizing tablets, and other input devices — and passes it on to the program.

Windows NT actually takes the role of the operating system one step further. Not only does it sit between the hardware and the programs, but it's actually a barrier between the hardware and the programs. For security reasons, programs running in Windows NT cannot access the hardware, even if they want to — they must go through the operating system.

> **TIP** To find the latest updates to Windows NT — the "service packs" — use your Web browser to go to `ftp://ftp.microsoft.com/bussys/winnt/winnt-public/fixes/usa/nt40`. This is an FTP site; you'll probably find the service pack in a directory called `usspx`, where x is the service pack number. These service packs contain bug fixes, system improvements, and so on. Read the .txt and .htm files you find in the directories at the FTP site for more information.

Using NT's security

NT is a secure system. It was designed to satisfy the most demanding requirements for government and corporate use, allowing users and administrators complete control over all system resources. A user can define how others can use particular files and folders. An administrator can lock particular users out of areas of the hard disk, provide access to printers for some users and not for others, and even define who can use which fonts!

Just about anything can be locked or restricted in some manner. You can let some users view your documents, for example, but not modify them. You can restrict other users from even viewing your documents. Perhaps you want some users to be able to modify them, but not control them, and maybe you trust someone enough to allow him or her total control over the files, allowing and restricting access to the files at will. You have tremendous control over system resources, as you learn in Chapter 8.

NT can provide this degree of security because of its total control of the system hardware. If NT says a user or program can't touch a particular file, that's it — there's no way around it (see Figure 1-2).

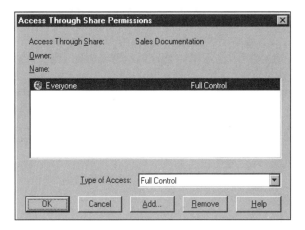

Figure 1-2 You can strictly control access to your data.

 TIP These security features work only if your hard disks are formatted as NTFS (NT File System) disks. NT can work with both NTFS and the older FAT (File Access Table) file systems used by Windows 3.1, Windows 95, and MS-DOS.

Windows NT Workstation's Features

Today's operating systems provide much more than an "environment" in which a program can run. Operating systems not only handle messages between hardware and software but also incorporate all sorts of programs that make working with a computer easier, from programs that enable you to copy and delete files to programs that enable you to send e-mail messages.

In this book, you look at the following features of Windows NT Workstation:

The taskbar, Start button, and desktop icons. These tools start and manage programs. See Chapter 3.

Windows NT Explorer. A file-management program used to move, copy, and delete files and folders; also provides other useful functions, such as formating floppy disks and testing hard disks. See Chapters 5 and 6.

My Computer and Folder windows. Folders used in a similar way to Windows NT Explorer; a simpler, yet less capable, way to manage files and folders. See Chapter 6.

Find. This nifty utility rapidly searches your hard disks for missing files and folders (see Figure 1-3). See Chapter 6.

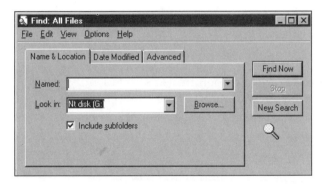

Figure 1-3 Find is a nice search tool for tracking down missing files and folders.

Printers folder. A special folder used to manage and install printer drivers, the software used to print your documents. See Chapter 7.

Fonts folder. A special folder used to install fonts. See Chapter 7.

User Manager. A program that you use to create user accounts so that different users can keep their data private and customize their desktops. See Chapter 8.

Permissions. You can set permissions on anything — files, folders, briefcases, printers, and fonts. In other words, you can define which users may work with these resources and what they may do. See Chapters 8 and 14.

Auditing. NT contains a system you can use to *audit* the use of system resources. You can see which users use files, folders, printers, and more, and when and how they use them. See Chapter 8.

Clipboard. A program you never see but which enables you to copy data — text, pictures, even sounds — between programs. See Chapter 9.

Clipbook. A program that enables you to see the contents of the Clipboard and to save information from the Clipboard for later use. See Chapter 9.

Object Packager. A little-used utility that helps you *package* data from one program and insert it into a document in another program. I won't spend a lot of time on Object Packager, but you will learn other, simpler methods for sharing data between programs in Chapter 9.

WordPad. A simple word processor you can use to write letters, memos, reports, and so on. See Chapter 9.

Notepad. A text editor program that enables you to write, but without any fancy formatting (bold, italic, bullet lists, and so on). See Chapter 9.

Calculator. Yes, a calculator. Simple addition, multiplication, division, and subtraction calculations, plus more complicated scientific and statistical calculations. See Chapter 9.

Character Map. This program helps you identify special characters that you can use in your programs. These characters include characters used in many languages, copyright and trademark symbols, currency symbols, and more. See Chapter 9.

MS Paint. A simple paint program that you can use to create and modify bitmap files (.BMP). See Chapter 10.

Imaging for Windows NT. A program designed for annotating files, such as text documents scanned into your computer. See Chapter 10.

CD Player. This essential utility turns your $4000 computer into the equivalent of a $50 CD player — listen to your favorite music while pretending to work. See Chapter 11.

Sound Recorder. Record sounds and place them inside word processing documents or use them as your system sounds. See Chapter 11.

Multimedia Player. This program plays sound, MIDI (Musical Instrument Digital Interface), animation, and video files. It also plays music through your CD player. See Chapter 11.

Volume Control. This program controls the sound volume of your computer speakers and the volume of input channels (your microphone, for example). See Chapter 11.

Windows NT Backup. This program copies data from your hard disks to a tape so that you can store your data safely. See Chapter 12.

HyperTerminal. A serial-communication program used to connect to BBSs (bulletin board systems). See Chapter 13.

Phone Dialer. A simple program that stores your most-used phone numbers and dials them at the click of a button. See Chapter 13.

Network Neighborhood. You can view Network Neighborhood in a typical file-folder window or within Windows NT Explorer so that you can see and work with files and folders stored on other computers connected to your network. See Chapter 14.

Chat. You can send *real-time* text messages to other network users. As you type the message, the other user instantly sees it, character by character. See Chapter 14.

Windows Messaging. An e-mail program. You can send and receive messages via a Microsoft Mail or Internet mail system. See Chapter 15.

Dial-Up Networking. You use this program to connect to other NT computers or an Internet service provider, across the phone lines. See Chapter 16.

Briefcase. Pack files you want to use on your business trip into a briefcase, and put the briefcase on your laptop. When you return, the briefcase can quickly tell you which files have changed and update the originals on your desktop computer for you. See Chapter 16.

Hardware Profiles. If you use a laptop in the office and on the road, you can create different hardware profiles and load the appropriate one. While traveling, for example, you can disable your networking hardware. See Chapter 16.

Internet Explorer. This program is a World Wide Web browser, and it will soon be a brand-new way to view data on your computer's hard disk. See Chapter 16.

Telnet. This program connects you across the Internet to a Telnet host. Once connected, your computer acts like a *dumb terminal* (a simple screen and keyboard) connected to that host. See Chapter 17.

Peer Web Services. You can turn your own computer into a mini Web server so that other intranet (and perhaps Internet) users can view your Web pages. See Chapter 17.

The Control Panel. This folder contains dozens of utilities used to configure your system, from Date/Time (set your system date, time, and time zone) to Display (pick a display resolution, colors, desktop decoration, and more); see Figure 1-4. I describe these utilities throughout the book where appropriate, or go to Chapter 18 for a list of the Control Panel icons.

Figure 1-4 The Control Panel provides more than two dozen utilities for customizing and controlling Windows NT.

Disk Administrator. Disk Administrator formats and partitions hard disks (if you're sure you know what you're doing!). See Chapter 19.

Event Viewer. View messages from the system about errors, auditing, security, and so on. See Chapter 19.

Performance Monitor. Use this program to view scores of different system performance measurements. See Chapter 19.

Task Manager. This program switches between and closes programs (see Chapter 3) and enables you to view performance information such as memory use (see Chapter 19).

Windows NT Diagnostics. This simple information box displays detailed data about your system, from disk-drive and network data to IRQ (Interrupt Request) and DMA (Direct Memory Access) information. See Chapter 19.

What Is Windows NT Server?

Windows NT comes in two flavors: Workstation and Server. This book covers the workstation, although the server is similar. The server simply has additional tools that enable it to work as a network *server* — a computer that provides services to other computers (the *workstations*).

The Workstation can function as a server to some degree, as you'll see in this book. Other network users can connect to a Workstation computer and use files, printers, folders, *briefcases,* and Web pages. But the Workstation software license limits such access to no more than 10 connections at a time (functionally, Workstation is capable of handling more connections; legally, according to the license, it can't). NT Server may have more connections, depending on the type of license purchased.

The base software used in NT Workstation and NT Server is exactly the same. There's simply a setting within NT Server that says "act like a server."

What Windows NT Won't Do

Two significant problems keep some users from converting to Windows NT. Although many users would love to have the speed and stability of NT, it comes at the price of reduced hardware and software compatibility. Because a scanner or video card or other piece of hardware works with Windows 3.1 or Windows 95 doesn't mean that it works with NT. You may run into programs that won't run on Windows NT, too.

Microsoft estimates that Windows 95 supports 1000 more device drivers than Windows NT Workstation (device drivers are programs designed to allow your software to work with hardware devices such as printers, scanners, video cards, and so on). Most popular devices are supported by Windows NT, but many are not.

As for software, some programs — even programs designed for Windows 95 — won't run in Windows NT. The security features that I discussed stop programs from communicating directly with the computer's hardware. All communications must go through NT. However, some programs attempt to work directly with the hardware. Many MS-DOS games, for example, access hardware directly.

If you want to see information about the differences between Windows NT and Windows 95, go to http://www.microsoft.com/ntworkstation/techdiff.htm.

The solution to this problem is for the application publisher to modify its software so that it does not attempt to access hardware directly. In many cases, publishers are doing that. The popularity of Windows NT guarantees that software compatibility will improve.

Other programs try to use Virtual Device Drivers (VxD), a special type of driver (a program used to interface between a program and a piece of hardware) used in other Windows operating systems. But Windows NT doesn't have VxDs, so these programs won't run. Some programs have been written incorrectly, in such a manner that they run okay in Windows 95 but won't run in Windows NT. Microsoft is testing large numbers of programs, however, and informing software publishers of problems. Windows NT 4.0 is becoming a popular operating system, and most software publishers are interested in making sure that their programs run properly. These problems should improve over time, but for now, the problems are a definite consideration, especially if you're a software hog who likes to download and use everything you can from the Internet. Much of what you download won't run!

WEB PATH **For a list of hardware tested with Windows NT Workstation, go to** `http://www.microsoft.com/hwtest/`. **For a list of software publishers supporting NT, go to** `http://www.microsoft.com/ntworkstation/Partners.htm`.

Also not present in Windows NT at the time of writing (although it will probably be added in the future) is Plug and Play. Plug and Play is a system introduced with Windows 95 that enables the operating system to recognize hardware devices that you install and automatically install drivers and set up the software so that the hardware operates correctly. Of course, this may not be much of a problem because many Windows 95 users complain that Plug and Play doesn't work well, anyway.

Summary

This chapter is a quick overview of Windows NT and what it can do for you. The list of features is a simple preview of what's to come: a secure, stable, and fast operating system. (If you're accustomed to Windows 3.1 and Windows 95 system crashes, you'll really love the stability of Windows NT.) But now it's time to get down to work. In the next chapter, you see how to start NT and move around a little. In the chapter after that, you see how to start your programs and switch between programs. The rest of the book explains all the fancy utilities and features that make NT such a great operating system.

CHAPTER TWO

STARTING WINDOWS NT 4.0

IN THIS CHAPTER YOU LEARN THESE KEY SKILLS

BOOTING NT PAGE 20

UNDERSTANDING THE WINDOWS NT
DESKTOP PAGE 23

USING THE TASKBAR PAGE 28

USING FOLDERS AND DIRECTORIES PAGE 34

LOCKING AND CLOSING WINDOWS NT PAGE 35

Before you really can understand how to use the programs you work with, you have to understand the operating system in which they work. (You learned what an operating system is in Chapter 1.) The operating system provides a set of rules by which your programs must function, so after you've learned the operating system, you've learned these important rules: how to open programs, how to switch between programs, how to handle windows and dialog boxes, and so on.

FEATURE FOCUS If you've used Windows 95, you'll find that Windows NT Workstation is similar (although with many significant differences that you'll discover in later chapters). If you've been using Windows 3.1, or some other operating system, you'll find that Windows NT is *extremely* different. This chapter introduces Windows NT Workstation and covers what you'll find when you first start Windows NT.

Booting NT

I'll begin right at the beginning: starting Windows NT. I assume that you've just arrived at your computer and found one of the two following situations:

* The computer is turned off.
* The computer is on, but there's a dialog box with a message saying *It is now safe to turn off your computer.*

If the computer is turned off, use the power switch to turn it on. If you see the dialog box, simply press Enter on the keyboard or click the Restart button with the mouse.

Your computer begins to *boot*. That's the term used to refer to the process by which the computer loads into memory all the information it's going to need to do its job. This loading may take a minute or two. However, in some cases you're given the opportunity to load a *different* operating system.

TIP   I use three basic mouse terms: *click, right-click,* and *double-click.* By default, most computer mice are set up so that the primary button is the left button. In other words, most mouse operations are carried out by clicking the left button. When I tell you to *click* the mouse button, I mean use the left mouse button; click the button and release. (Of course, if you have a special left-handed mouse, or you have configured your mouse so that the primary button is the right one, when I say *click,* you click your right button.) *Right-click* means press the other button, the one that is not the primary button — generally the right button. Finally, the term *double-click* means click the item twice in quick succession.

Dual-boot computers

Your computer may be capable of running two or more operating systems. For instance, it may be set up to run both Windows NT *and* Windows 95. If so, partway through the boot process you'll see a message such as the following on your screen (if you don't see this message, skip to the next section, "The Hardware Profile/Last Known Good Menu"):

```
Please select the operating system to start
{Windows NT Workstation Version 4.00}
  Windows NT Workstation Version 4.00 [VGA mode]
  Microsoft Windows
Use [↑] and [↓] to move the highlight to your choice.
  Seconds until highlighted choice will be started automatically: 30
```

The message may not look quite the same on your computer screen, depending on which systems you can boot and which system is the *default* system (the one that the computer loads if you take no action). Of course, you want to load Windows NT Workstation. In this case, you can simply press Enter, or you can wait until the counter on the bottom line (the number 30 counts down) gets to zero. In some cases, you may have to use the up arrow or down arrow keys to move the highlight to Windows NT Workstation Version 4.00, and then press Enter.

TIP   You can define which of the operating systems should open by default — that is, which system should open if you take no action — in the

The Hardware Profile/Last Known Good Menu

The boot procedure now continues. You'll see various text messages, which can be ignored in most cases. However, there is one you should know about: *Press spacebar NOW to invoke Hardware Profile/Last Known Good Menu*. What's this about? The Hardware Profile/Last Known Good menu allows you to choose either a hardware profile or the Last Known Good configuration. (You learn about hardware profiles in Chapter 16). The vast majority of users will never have more than one hardware profile, so they never need to use this menu to pick another profile. The Last Known Good configuration is like a safety net. If you install something in Windows NT that somehow stops you from booting into NT, you can use this menu to go back to the previous setup so that you can get into NT again.

SIDE TRIP

WHY TWO NT OPTIONS?

Why are there two Windows NT Workstation options in the screen you just saw? The first boots Windows NT using special software designed for your computer's *video card* — the computer card that sends information to the computer display. It uses the card's own video *drivers* to make the video card work. The other option is a sort of emergency entrance to NT. If, for some reason, your computer display is not displaying legible information after you boot into Windows NT, it may be because of a problem with these video drivers. Selecting *Windows NT Workstation Version 4.00 [VGA mode]* loads the generic VGA (Video Graphics Adapter) drivers. These drivers are much simpler and should work with any video card installed in a computer capable of working with Windows NT. In most cases, you won't have to use this option, loading the generic VGA drivers. After your video drivers are set up and working correctly, everything should be fine. Generally, you may run into a problem only when you change drivers or video cards.

Still, you may never have to use this menu option. In the vast majority of boot processes, most users simply ignore this message and continue.

Logging on

You'll soon see the Windows NT logo appear, and a few moments later you'll see a dialog box that says *Press Ctrl+Alt+Delete to log on*. DOS and other versions of Windows use this keyboard sequence to reboot or close the system. Windows NT, however, uses the sequence as a security measure. As you read in Chapter 1, Windows NT is a very secure system, and the Ctrl+Alt+Delete sequence is one more way that it protects itself. Ctrl+Alt+Delete does actually perform a sort of "mini" reset. It clears certain areas of memory and forces the operating system to start "clean" at the logon procedure. The sequence clears any unauthorized programs running in the background and stops other programs from watching a logon procedure and grabbing account names and passwords, the sort of trick used by people trying to break into computer systems.

Follow this procedure to log on:

1. Press and hold down the Ctrl, Alt, and Delete keys at the same time. You'll then see the Logon Information dialog box.

2. Type your account name into the first text box. Where do you get this? Your system administrator can give you your username (and password, too). If you installed NT yourself, the account name is *Administrator* (and the password is the password you entered during installation).

3. Type your password into the second text box.

4. There *may* be another box, the Domain drop-down list box. If so, select the network domain to which you want to be connected from the list box (if you are not sure which, ask your system administrator).

5. Click OK or press Enter.

Assuming you entered the correct information, you now are logged into Windows NT. What do you see? Well, that depends. I'm going to describe what you see if no one has logged on and changed things around, as if you are booting into the normal unchanged Windows NT. If you or someone else has customized Windows NT in some way, modifying the desktop and various configuration settings, what you see will look different from what I describe — although you should still be able to find your way around. I assume that one change *has* been made to your computer — that Microsoft Office has been installed. Many NT systems come with Office already installed.

You may see the Welcome to Windows NT dialog box, a Help box that opens each time you start NT and displays tips. If so, click the Close button to remove it.

TIP You may want to click the Show *This Welcome Screen Next Time You Start Windows* NT check box. Clicking this box clears it so that the Welcome to Windows NT box doesn't appear again. You can always open it again later if you want. Click the Start button and choose Run. When the Run dialog box opens, type **welcome** and press Enter.

Understanding the Windows NT Desktop

After typing **welcome** and pressing Enter, you now see something similar to Figure 2-1. Table 2-1 describes each item shown in Figure 2-1.

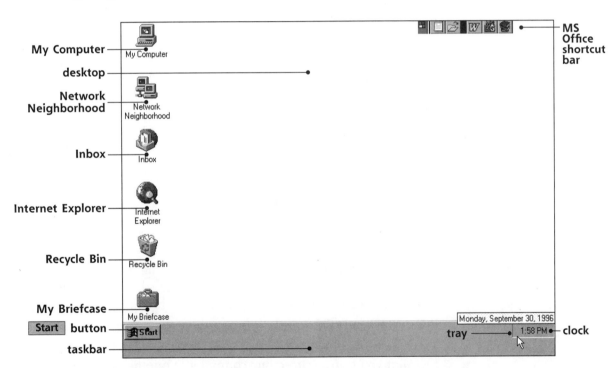

Figure 2-1 The Windows NT Desktop contains components that help you start your programs and run various utilities.

STARTING WINDOWS NT 4.0 **23**

TABLE 2-1 The Windows NT Desktop Components

Component	Description
DESKTOP	This large blank area is the desktop. You can think of all the other items as sitting on top of the desktop. When you run a program, it sits above the desktop.
TASKBAR	This bar contains the Start button and also displays a button for each running program. You use the taskbar to open and switch between programs.
Start	This opens the Start menu, which you use to start programs.
2:01 PM	This little area of the taskbar holds special utilities. Many programs put small icons in the tray that, when clicked, open a menu or dialog box.
CLOCK	Right now, the only thing held by the tray is a digital clock. Point at the clock and a small box appears, which shows the full date and time. Click with the right mouse button and a menu opens.
	This icon opens a folder in which you can view the contents of your disk drives, the Control Panel (see Chapter 18), the Printers folder (see Chapter 7), and the Dial-Up Networking folder (see Chapter 16).
	This icon opens the Network Neighborhood folder, which allows you to view directories on other computers connected to your corporate network. (see Chapter 14.)
	This icon opens Windows Messaging, the communications system built into Windows NT. It can be used to handle corporate and Internet electronic mail (or e-mail). (See Chapter 15.)
	This icon opens the Internet Explorer Web browser. (See Chapter 17.)
	This icon is sort of a trash can. Drag and drop files here to delete them, but you can still retrieve them later. There are actually two icons; if you can see paper inside the bin, the bin holds files. No paper means the bin is empty. (See Chapter 6.)
	This icon opens the Briefcase program, which is used to coordinate files that you transfer from one computer to another — generally from your desktop computer to your laptop. (See Chapter 16.)
	This taskbar isn't part of NT itself. It was installed by MS Office. You can open programs quickly by clicking a button on the taskbar.

SIDE TRIP

FOR WINDOWS 3.1 USERS

If you've been working with Windows 3.1, the Windows NT desktop can take a little getting used to because it works in such a different manner. In Windows 3.1, the desktop is not really "active." It's simply something that can contain a picture (known as *wallpaper*). When you first open Windows 3.1, you see Program Manager, which contains all the icons that start your programs. In Windows NT, however, the icons that open your programs are sitting directly on the desktop. There is no Program Manager to hold the program icons. And then there's the taskbar, something completely new, too. Table 2-2 shows the major differences between Windows 3.1 and Windows NT. (Of course, if you've never used Windows 3.1, the left column of this table won't be much help to you. The right column may still be useful, however.)

TABLE 2-2 Windows 3.1 Versus Windows NT

In Windows 3.1	In Windows NT
USE PROGRAM MANAGER TO START PROGRAMS	You'll mainly use the `Start` menu. Click the `Start` button to open the menu. Most programs are in the `Program` submenu. You can also add *shortcuts* to the desktop. (See Chapter 4.)
NEW PROGRAMS OFTEN CREATE NEW PROGRAM GROUPS	New programs may install an icon representing the program in the `Programs` menu. They also may create new submenus on the `Programs` menu, with their program icons within the submenus. If you upgraded from Windows 3.1 to Windows NT, each Program Manager program group is represented by a separate submenu.
MINIMIZED PROGRAMS ARE SHOWN AS DESKTOP ICONS	Each minimized program is represented by a button on the taskbar. Click the button to open the program. Right-click to see window controls and a Close command. The desktop icons in NT don't represent running programs.
START A PROGRAM AND THEN WAIT	You can start a program, and then start another, and then another. Windows NT is a true multitasking system, so you can do something, such as start a program, while a program is running in the background. Watch out, though. The first program may suddenly pop up when you're not expecting it! (See Chapter 3.)

(continued)

TABLE 2-2 Windows 3.1 Versus Windows NT (*continued*)

In Windows 3.1	In Windows NT
START PROGRAMS AUTOMATICALLY USING THE STARTUP GROUP	The Windows 3.1 Startup Program group is replaced by the `Startup` submenu. You can see the contents by choosing `Start` → `Programs` → `Startup`.
THE VARIOUS ACCESSORIES ARE IN AN ACCESSORIES GROUP	Choose `Start` → `Programs` → `Accessories`.
THE GAMES ARE IN THE GAMES PROGRAM GROUP	Choose `Start` → `Programs` → `Accessories` → `Games`.
USE FILE MANAGER TO SEE FILES AND DIRECTORIES	File Manager is replaced by Windows NT Explorer, which you can find by choosing `Start` → `Programs` → `Windows NT Explorer`. (See Chapter 5.)
OPEN CONTROL PANEL FROM PROGRAM MANAGER	Choose `Start` → `Settings` → `Control Panel`. (See Chapter 18.)
INSTALL NEW PROGRAMS USING THE RUN COMMAND	Install new programs by opening the Control Panel and double-clicking Add/Remove New Programs. (See Chapter 4.)
RUN PROGRAMS USING THE RUN COMMAND	Choose `Start` → `Run`.
USE WINDOWS SETUP TO CONFIGURE WINDOWS	Open the Add/Remove New Programs utility and click the Windows NT Setup tab.
CONFIGURE PRINTERS USING PRINT MANAGER	Choose `Start` → `Settings` → `Printers`. (See Chapter 7.)
GET TO DOS USING THE MS-DOS ICON	Choose `Start` → `Programs` → `Command Prompt`.
SWITCH BETWEEN PROGRAMS USING ALT+TAB	You still can use Alt+Tab (and Alt+Esc). You also can use the taskbar. (See Chapter 3.)
VIEW TASK MANAGER USING CTRL+ESC	Right-click the taskbar to see a menu that has some of the old Task Manager controls (and more). Choose `Task Manager` from the menu to see an advanced Task Manager.
GET HELP FROM THE PROGRAM MANAGER	Choose `Start` → `Help`.
CLOSE WINDOWS USING THE `File` ⇨ `Exit` COMMAND	Choose `Start` → `Shutdown`.

In Windows 3.1	In Windows NT
FINDING FILES CAN BE DIFFICULT	Choose `Start` → `Find`. NT searches your computer for particular files and directories or searches the network for a particular computer. (See Chapter 6.)
THERE IS NO DIRECT WAY TO OPEN A PRIOR DOCUMENT	Choose `Start` → `Documents`. You'll see a list of documents — pictures, word-processing files, text files, and so on — that you've opened in various programs. Click a document to launch a program and display the document.
USE ALT+TAB TO SWITCH TO PROGRAM MANAGER	Not being able to switch back to the desktop to start a program can be confusing. As most programs are started from the `Start` menu, switching back is not always a problem, but the desktop icons are not always represented by matching menu options. I'll explain a way around this problem at the end of the chapter.
PRESS CTRL+ALT+ DELETE TO IF A PROGRAM HAS FROZEN	If you press Ctrl+Alt+Delete in Windows NT, you'll see the Windows NT Security dialog box, which is used to lock the system or log off.

The desktop icons

The icons in Windows NT are different from the icons in the Windows 3.1 Program Manager. (Forget about the icons displayed on the desktop in Windows 3.1; these icons represented programs that were running but minimized. In Windows NT, minimized programs are represented by buttons on the taskbar.) Windows NT icons can represent several things, such as the following:

Files. You can save a file on the desktop — a document you've created or a file downloaded from the Internet, for example. An icon represents this file. If you double-click the icon, the file runs. If the file is a program file, then the program starts. If the file is a document file, then the program that uses that type of file opens and loads the file.

Shortcuts. You can create shortcut icons for convenience. You may want to place shortcut icons to your favorite programs on the desktop (I'll show you how in Chapter 4) so that you can quickly start the programs from there rather than working your way through the Start menu to find them. (The program icons in Windows 3.1 are, in effect, shortcuts.)

Folders. A folder is a "container" that can store other items, such as files and shortcuts. You can create folders on the desktop and then store other items inside them. Double-clicking a folder opens it.

The difference between the file and shortcut icons needs a little more explanation. A shortcut icon is a link from the desktop to a file somewhere on your hard disk. In effect, when creating a shortcut icon, you're telling the computer to create an icon on the desktop, but make it activate program xx in the xx directory.

A file icon, however, is not a link from the desktop to another place; it represents a real file stored on your desktop. What *is* the desktop, then, and how can it store files? The desktop is a special directory on your hard disk. This directory is even called Desktop, and you can view it after you've read Chapter 5 and know how to use Windows NT Explorer. (There are several different Desktop directories for different user profiles — you'll learn about profiles in Chapter 8. For example, the desktop shown for the Administrator's account is stored in the `/Winnt/Profiles/Administrator/Desktop/` directory.)

How can you tell the difference between these different types of desktop icons? Here's how:

Folder icons. These look like folders.

Shortcut icons. The little arrow in the bottom left corner of the icon indicates that it's a shortcut.

File icons. This icon doesn't have a little arrow, and it doesn't look like a folder, so it's a real computer file stored on the desktop.

What about the icons you see that are already installed by Windows NT — My Computer, Network Neighborhood, Inbox, Internet Explorer, Recycle Bin, and Briefcase? You can think of each of these icons as a sort of shortcut, really. They don't represent files stored in the Desktop directory. Rather, when you double-click one, a program stored somewhere else starts. However, these icons are not created in the same way as the shortcut icons that you can create; these icons are a special sort of shortcut "internal" to Windows NT.

Using the Taskbar

The next important component is the *taskbar*, which you can see in Figure 2-2.

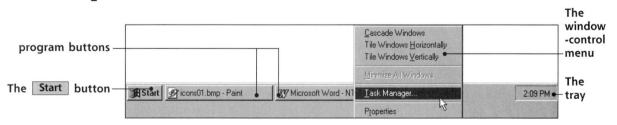

Figure 2-2 The Windows NT taskbar.

The taskbar holds four items:

Start Click this to open a menu from which you can choose a program you want to run.

Program buttons. Each program you run places a button on the taskbar. These buttons can be used to bring the program to the front and to view a list of window and exit commands.

The window-control menu. Right-click the taskbar to see a menu that's used to control the open program windows.

2:01 PM The little framed area on the right side of the taskbar — known as the *tray* — holds various utilities. By default, the tray holds a digital clock, which also can show the date (point at it). As you'll see in a moment, it can hold other items, too.

Starting programs with the Start button

Click the Start button. The Start menu pops up, as you can see in Figure 2-3.

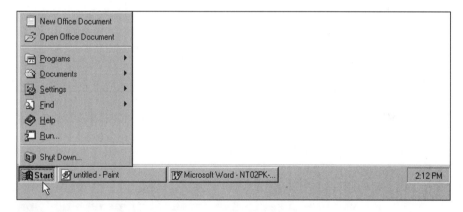

Figure 2-3 Click the Start button to open the Start menu.

A *menu* is a list of options from which you can make selections. The Start menu contains menu options that lead to other menus and that run programs. Here's an explanation of what you can see in my Start menu (yours may look a little different):

New Office Document. This menu option was installed by Microsoft Office. It opens a dialog box from which you can choose a document type to create. Other installation and setup programs may add options to the Start menu, too.

Open Office Document. This menu option was also placed here by Microsoft Office. It displays an Open dialog box from which you can choose an existing document.

Programs. This option leads to another menu (a *submenu*) from which you can start programs. Most installation programs add icons to the Programs menu (see Chapter 3).

Documents. This option displays a menu containing documents that you've worked with recently in various programs. Choose one to open a program and display the document.

Settings. This option opens a menu from which you can open the Control Panel folder (used to make various Windows NT settings; see Chapter 18), the Printers folder (used to install printers; see Chapter 7), and the Taskbar Properties dialog box, which is covered later in this chapter.

Find. This option opens a menu from which you can choose to search your computer for a file or folder or search the network for a particular computer (see Chapter 6).

Help. This option starts the Windows NT Help program.

Run. Select this option to start a program by typing its name or selecting it from a file and directory listing (see Chapter 3).

Shutdown. Select this option to close Windows NT.

Play around with the Start button to see how it works. Any menu option with a little black triangle on the right side opens a submenu (also known as a *cascading menu*). Click the Programs option, and another menu opens. Click the Accessories option, and you see yet another menu, as shown in Figure 2-4.

TIP   If you have a special keyboard designed for Windows 95 or Windows NT, you have a key that opens the Start menu. Simply press the key that has the Windows logo at any time, even if the taskbar is not visible, and up pops the taskbar and Start menu. If you don't have this key, you can press Ctrl+Esc.

Customizing the taskbar

You can use a number of methods to set up the taskbar, and I suggest that you experiment to find the method that works best for you. You can configure the taskbar using the Taskbar Properties dialog box. To display this dialog box, right-click an empty piece of the taskbar and a pop-up menu opens; click

Properties. Figure 2-5 shows the Taskbar Properties dialog box. The first two check boxes, *Always on top* and *Auto hide*, control the manner in which the taskbar works.

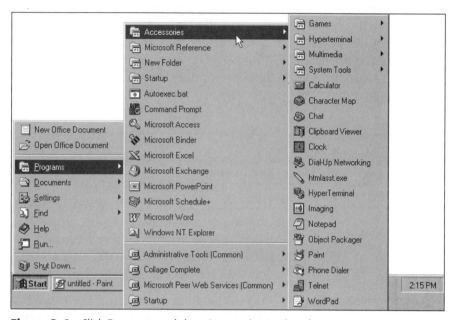

Figure 2-4   Click Programs and then Accessories to view the Accessory programs.

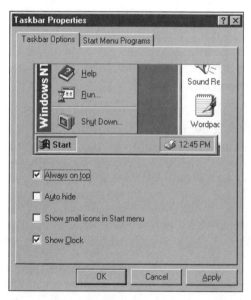

Figure 2-5   Use the Taskbar Properties dialog box to customize the taskbar.

Always on top means that the taskbar is always available to the mouse, even if you are working in another program. It *doesn't* necessarily mean that the taskbar is always visible, however, depending on the *Auto hide* check box. You use this check box to make the taskbar automatically disappear from your screen. To make the taskbar reappear, use the Windows logo key on your keyboard or move the mouse to the edge of the screen. (You'll notice a thin gray strip along the edge of the screen. When your mouse touches that strip, the taskbar opens.)

Now, combining these two options makes the taskbar work in different ways. These different ways are described in Table 2-3.

TABLE 2-3 Configuring the Taskbar

Always on top	Auto hide	The taskbar
ON	OFF	NT is set up this way when you first install it. The taskbar is always visible on your screen, which is nice, except that it reduces the amount of space you have available for your programs. Windows NT squeezes your program windows into the space not covered by the taskbar.
ON	ON	This is how I use my taskbar. The taskbar is not always visible, but I can quickly retrieve it by pressing the Windows logo key on my keyboard or by moving the mouse to the edge of the screen. The advantage? More space is available to my programs. The big disadvantage? The taskbar often pops up when I don't want it, because I've accidentally touched the edge of the screen. (As you'll see in a moment, however, you can move the taskbar to a different edge.)
OFF	ON	The taskbar is not always visible, and you can't easily retrieve it by moving the mouse to the edge of the screen, either. If you're working in another program, you have to use the Windows logo key on your keyboard or minimize the program you're in to get to the desktop. Then move the mouse to the edge of the screen to open the taskbar.
OFF	OFF	The taskbar is always visible when you can see the desktop, but it's never visible when a program window is maximized.

If you have a keyboard with the Windows logo key, you may choose to turn off Always On Top. You can quickly see the taskbar using the logo key. You'll also see the Start menu, which may not be what you want. However, you can click one of the program buttons to remove the Start menu and open the program, or click a blank area of the taskbar and then right-click to see the taskbar pop-up menu.

You can also move the taskbar, as well as size it. Point at a blank area of the taskbar, press and hold the mouse button down, and then drag the taskbar to another edge — the top or one of the sides. When you release the mouse button, the taskbar sticks where you leave it. To expand the size (useful if you have many programs running and can't read the program buttons), point at the edge of the taskbar (the edge away from the side of the screen). The mouse pointer turns into a double-headed arrow. Drag the edge out from the taskbar to expand it and in toward the edge of the screen to reduce it in size.

Using the tray

The little "indented" or framed area on the right side of the taskbar is commonly known as the *tray* (although it's more formally named the Notification Area). It's called the tray because it holds things. When you first load NT, the tray holds a digital clock (as you saw in Figure 2-1), but programs that you install may add icons to the tray. Items held by the tray can usually "do" things. You may have programs that run in the background, monitoring system activity. These programs place an icon in the tray indicating that they're at work. In most cases, you can click, right-click, or double-click the icon to perform an action, such as to open a dialog box in which you can configure the program. You can also point at the icon and wait a moment to see a box displaying the icon's name or some useful information.

As an example, you can perform several functions to the clock icon. You can point at it and hold for a moment to see the full date and time (as shown in Figure 2-1). You can right-click the clock icon to see the normal taskbar menu, but with an additional menu option at the top: Adjust Date/Time. Select this option to see the Date/Time Properties dialog box, which you'll learn more about in Chapter 18. (You can also simply double-click the clock to go straight to this dialog box.)

Here's another example:

1. Right-click an empty part of the taskbar, and then choose Task Manager. The Task Manager dialog box pops up. (This dialog box is covered in more detail in Chapter 3.)

2. Click the little button with a horizontal line in the top right corner (■). This minimizes the box.

3. Now look at the tray. A little green box is inside it.

4. Point at the box and hold the mouse pointer there for a moment, and you'll see a message showing the CPU (Central Processing Unit) Usage — how busy your computer is. (See Figure 2-6.)

Figure 2-6 Point at a taskbar icon to see more information, or click, double-click, or right-click the icon.

5. Right-click the box and a small menu opens showing two options: Close Task Manager and Task Manager Always on Top. (By default, Task Manager, if it's open, is always on top of other programs. This option turns that feature on and off.)

Using Folders and Directories

As you learned already, Windows NT uses *folders*. What, exactly, is a folder? Well, it's a type of container used to store things. The term folder is used instead of the old term you may be accustomed to: *directory*.

When you create a file and store it on your hard disk, where does it go? You really can't place all your computer files together on the disk. Modern computers hold thousands, sometimes tens of thousands, of computer files. If all these files sat on the hard disk together, totally disorganized, chaos would ensue. Not only would you have trouble finding files you need, but so would your programs.

Hard disks are organized using what are generally known as *directories*. A directory is a sort of container for holding files — a box, if you will. A directory may contain computer files, but it also may have other directories within it, known as *subdirectories*. Using directories and subdirectories creates a *directory tree*, a hierarchical system in which directories contain directories, which contain yet more directories, all of which may hold files.

Until recently, a directory was a directory, but Microsoft decided to change the terminology a little and now calls hard-disk directories *folders*. Still, you'll often hear folders referred to as directories because that's what so many people are accustomed to. When you look at Windows NT Explorer (Chapter 5) and My Computer (Chapter 6), you'll see that each directory is shown as a folder icon.

You can see folders in different ways in Windows NT, however. You can quickly create a folder on your desktop and store files and shortcuts inside it. You'll learn how to do this in Chapter 4. When you create a folder, you are literally creating a folder — a directory — on your hard disk (inside the Desktop directory I spoke of previously). But you can view the contents of the folder at any time by simply double-clicking the icon on the desktop.

When you opened the Start menu and moved around, you may have noticed that all the options that lead to submenus have icons of folders. Each submenu is a container, and each is literally a folder — or directory — stored on your hard disk. You'll see how to work with the Start menu folders in Chapter 4.

Locking and Closing Windows NT

When you finish working in Windows NT, you can lock it or close it. Windows NT has many built-in security features, which is one reason why so many corporations are buying the system. As you've already learned, you can't get into Windows NT without entering your password. If you are working in a situation in which other users can get to your computer, it's probably not a good idea to leave it running unattended.

If you want to leave your desk for a little while, you can "lock" Windows NT while you are away so that nobody can run any programs or interfere with your open programs. When you return, you can quickly get back to work without rebooting the computer.

Follow these steps to suspend or "lock" operations:

1. Press Ctrl+Alt+Delete. You'll see the Windows NT Security dialog box. If you change your mind, click the Cancel button or press Esc to return to Windows NT.

2. Click the Lock Workstation button. A message appears stating that the computer has been locked. It also shows your username so that others know who has the password to start the computer again.

3. When you are ready to start working again, press Ctrl+Alt+Delete. The Unlock Workstation dialog box opens.

4. Type your Password and click OK. You'll be returned to your work.

TIP Want to run a screen saver while you are away, or automatically lock your computer after a period of inactivity? See Chapter 18 for information about how to do this.

To close Windows NT completely, follow this procedure:

1. Press Ctrl+Alt+Delete. The Windows NT Security dialog box opens.

2. Click the Shutdown button. You'll see a dialog box with two option buttons.

3. If you want to shut down Windows NT and leave it — and even turn the computer off, perhaps — make sure you select the Shutdown option button. To shut down Windows NT and then restart — so that another user can log on, or so that you can boot into the computer's other operating system (if present) — select the Shutdown and Restart button.

4. Click OK. Windows NT shuts down.

5. If you chose Shutdown, you'll soon see a message telling you that you can turn off your computer. If you chose Shutdown and Restart, Windows NT shuts down, restarts, and then displays the message telling you to press Ctrl+Alt+Delete to log on.

TIP You don't have to close your programs before logging off Windows NT. NT automatically closes them for you, but hang around and wait until it's finished because it may ask you if you want to save open documents.

BONUS

More Ways to Shut Down NT

There are a couple more ways to shut down Windows NT:

* Select Start → Shutdown.
* With the desktop selected (click the desktop), press Alt+F4.

Although the method I explained earlier (Ctrl+Alt+Delete) is usually quicker, these two methods provide you with another option: Close All Programs and Log On as Another User. This is a much quicker way to hand over your computer to another user. Instead of completely closing down and then completely restarting, Windows NT simply closes all your programs, removes the taskbar and desktop, and displays the message telling you to press Ctrl+Alt+Delete to log on.

Add Volume Control to the Taskbar

If you want to add a volume control to your taskbar's tray, follow these instructions (assuming you have a properly installed sound card, of course):

1. Select Start → Settings → Control Panel.
2. When the Control Panel folder opens, double-click the Multimedia icon.
3. Click the Audio tab.
4. Check the *Show Volume Control* checkbox on the taskbar.
5. Click OK.
6. You can now operate the volume control by clicking the little speaker icon in the taskbar. Click to see a small volume control (see Figure 2-7). Double-click to open a more detailed control.

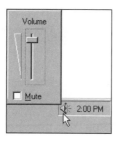

Figure 2-7 Click the volume icon and you see a small volume control slider.

Sort Your Icons

You can sort your icons using a right-click pop-up menu. Right-click a blank area of the desktop (see Figure 2-8). When the pop-up menu appears, click Line Up Icons and the icons move into their invisible "grid" positions.

Figure 2-8 Right-click the desktop to see a pop-up menu.

If you choose Arrange Icons from the menu, you see a submenu. You can sort the icons by Name, by Type, by Size, or by Date created. You can also turn on Auto Arrange from this menu. This feature automatically snaps icons back into position when they are moved or created. It also removes blank spaces between icons, so many users find this option inconvenient. You can't spread the icons around on the desktop if you use this option.

Viewing the Desktop Contents

In Windows 3.1, getting back to Program Manager and starting programs is easy: You simply use Alt+Tab. In Windows NT, however, you have to minimize all open windows to get back to the desktop to start a program using an icon.

There is a way around this problem:

1. Start My Computer by double-clicking the desktop icon.
2. If no toolbar is displayed, select `View` → `Toolbar`.
3. Click the large drop-down list box on the left side of the toolbar, and the list opens.
4. Use the scroll bar to move to the top of the list, and choose the Desktop item.
5. Continue with your work in other programs. You now have a desktop folder that you can swap to using Alt+Tab.

In Chapter 4, you'll learn how to create shortcuts. You could, if you wanted, create a shortcut to the My Computer folder and place it in your Start→Programs menu (you see how to do that in Chapter 4, too). By creating this shortcut, My Computer opens automatically each time you start Windows NT.

Summary

This chapter explained how to start Windows NT and described the different screen elements you see when you enter NT — the desktop, the desktop icons, the taskbar, and so on. Now that you have a good overview of the Windows NT "lobby," so to speak, you are ready to learn how to start working in NT — how to start and use your programs. You'll learn how to do this in the next chapter.

CHAPTER THREE

STARTING PROGRAMS

IN THIS CHAPTER YOU LEARN THESE KEY SKILLS

STARTING PROGRAMS   PAGE 39
MANAGING WINDOWS   PAGE 45
SWITCHING BETWEEN WINDOWS   PAGE 49
FINDING, OPENING, AND SAVING FILES   PAGE 53
CLOSING PROGRAMS   PAGE 56

Now that you've seen how to get into Windows NT, you probably want to start your programs. NT provides many ways to start your programs, and you can add more of your own. In this chapter I cover the various techniques for starting programs, what to do after the programs are running, and a few ways you can customize NT to start your favorite programs quickly.

Starting Programs

Windows NT provides many different methods to start programs. The most common methods include selecting a program from the Start menu and using a desktop icon. I'll begin by explaining the Start menu.

TIP   If you've just rebooted NT, you may find a few windows already open. If you closed NT while Windows NT Explorer was open, for instance, or while a desktop folder was open, NT automatically reopens those windows when you reboot. It won't reopen most other programs, though. For instance, if you had Word for Windows or Excel open when you closed, those programs will not be reopened.

Starting programs from the Start menu

Using the Start menu is the most common way to start a program. When you install a program, it places an option or submenu on the Programs menu, which you get to through the Start menu. (It's rare for a program to place an icon on the desktop, but I'll show you how to do that for yourself in Chapter 4.)

To open a program from the Start menu, follow these steps:

1. Press the Windows logo key on your keyboard, or move the mouse pointer to Start and click. The Start menu opens, as you see in Figure 3-1.

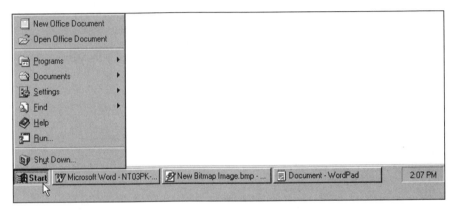

Figure 3-1 Click Start to open the Start menu.

2. If the program you want to open is on the Start menu, click that menu option. Some installation programs place menu options on the Start menu, although most don't. You're going to open a game, so continue to the next step.

3. Point at the Programs menu option and pause for a moment. The Programs submenu opens, as you see in Figure 3-2. Your menu may look different. This one has options for Microsoft Office programs, which yours may not have.

4. Click Accessories to open the Accessories menu, which you see in Figure 3-3.

5. Click Games to see the Games menu shown in Figure 3-4.

6. Click one of the games to start that program.

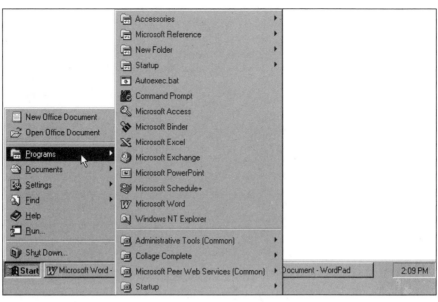

Figure 3-2 The Programs submenu.

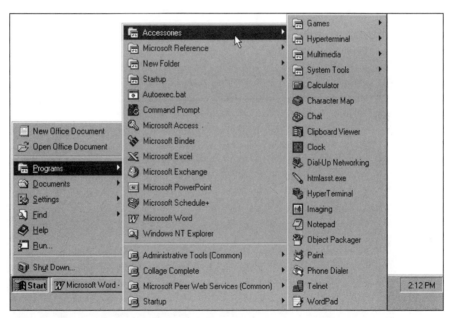

Figure 3-3 Opening the Accessories menu displays more programs.

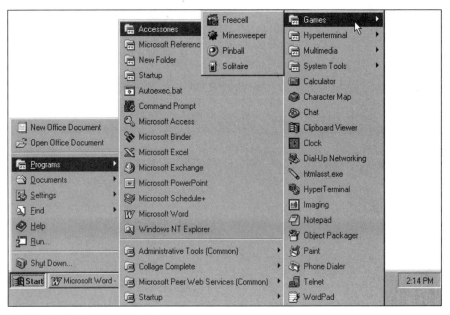

Figure 3-4 Now open the Games menu.

Starting programs using the desktop icons

You can start a program from a desktop icon — whether the icon is a file or a shortcut to a file — simply by double-clicking the icon. Another option is to right-click the icon and choose Open, as shown in Figure 3-5.

Figure 3-5 Right-click an icon and choose Open.

You can also create and modify desktop shortcuts from which you can open programs. You'll learn how in Chapter 4.

Starting programs with the document menu

Many Windows programs have *recall* menus, which enable you to quickly open a document that you've worked on previously. The recall menu is typically placed at the bottom of the File menu. Windows itself has a recall menu. Each time you open a document, the program in which the document is loaded places the name of the document into the Documents menu. (Not all programs place the name in the menu, but many do.)

In order to open a document you've viewed before — even if the program the document requires is not open — simply select Start→Document. You'll see a pop-up menu similar to the one shown in Figure 3-6 showing the files in alphabetical order.

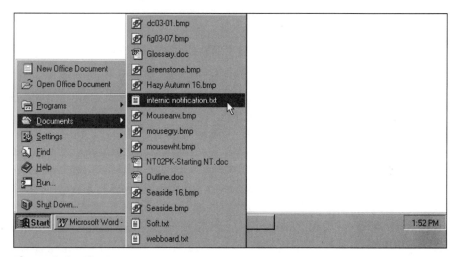

Figure 3-6 The Documents menu.

Click the document you want to open, and the associated program opens and loads the document. Notice that you can use long filenames in Windows NT, so get into the habit of doing so — finding files later becomes easier.

 TIP You already may have noticed that you can clear this pop-up menu:

1. Right-click a blank area of the taskbar.
2. Choose Properties from the pop-up menu.
3. In the Taskbar Properties dialog box, click the Start Menu Programs tab.
4. Click the Clear button.

Starting programs using the Run command

If you want to run a program that has no Start menu option or desktop shortcut, you can use the Run command. Why would you want to use this command? Why not simply *add* a menu option or desktop shortcut? Perhaps you don't plan to use this program often, or perhaps you want to do something fancy, such as open a particular World Wide Web site.

For example, you could open IDG's Web site like this (assuming that you have an Internet connection running; see Chapter 17):

1. Select Start → Run.

2. Type http://www.idgbooks.com and press Enter.

3. Internet Explorer (see Chapter 17) opens and attempts to connect to the IDG Books Web site.

To open a program or document using the Run command:

1. Select Start → Run.

2. Type the name of the program you want to run or the document you want to open (specifying a document opens the associated program). Include the full path — the disk drive letter plus directory names. If you are trying to open or run something on another computer, you have to use the computer name, too. Better still, click Browse to find the file or program. (I'll more fully explain how to use the dialog box that appears under "Finding, Opening, and Saving Files," later in this chapter.)

3. Click OK and the program starts and the document opens (if specified).

TIP   If you are trying to run a program that you know is designed for Windows 3.1, not Windows NT, select the *Run in Separate Memory Space* check box (it's probably already selected). This sets aside a block of memory for the program to run in, thus stopping that program from "crashing" other programs if it has a problem.

After they're running: All about multitasking

I want to quickly mention the differences between Windows NT and Windows 3.1 in the way that they "multitask" programs. If you've been using Windows 3.1, you may already think of that operating system as a multitasking system. And indeed it does let you work with several programs at once. But Windows NT is a true multitasking operating system. Although Windows 3.1 often stops you from doing something while it's working, in most cases, Windows NT allows you to carry out multiple operations.

FEATURE FOCUS

For example, to open more than one program in Windows 3.1, you have to use a command to open the first program and wait until it opens, then use a command to open the second program and wait until it opens, and then use another command . . . and so on.

In Windows NT, you use the command to open the first program, and then immediately — while the program is still loading — use the second command to open the second program, and then the third command, and so on. You may get several programs started before the first finishes loading. Windows NT rarely makes you wait and gives you the capability to perform various tasks at once by using one program while waiting for another program to carry out an operation.

This capability is nice but can create a couple problems. In the early days of NT, new users were often confused because the mouse pointer would change back to a normal pointer so that they could continue working. Users thought that they hadn't clicked the icon properly and would click again and again — ending up with the program opening several times. Microsoft corrected that problem by creating a special pointer — the hourglass. Whenever you see a pointer with an hourglass next to it, NT is doing something for you, but you can carry on and perform another task.

The other problem is that programs you started earlier may suddenly grab "focus" while you are doing something you started later. For example, you start one program, and then another, and then go back to the Start menu to start a third program. As you are about to select something, the first program finishes loading and grabs focus, closing the Start menu. This is irritating but a side-effect of true multitasking.

Managing Windows

Now that you have a window or two open, you need to know how to manage the windows. You can size and move the windows in various ways, so take a look at Figure 3-7 and then at Table 3-1.

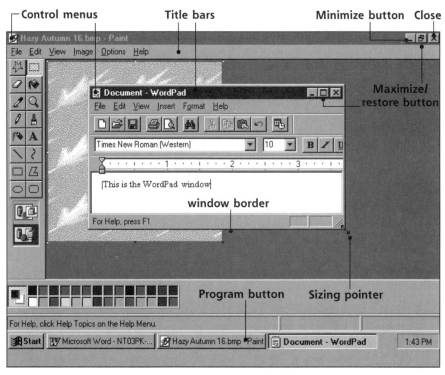

Figure 3-7 Program windows have various size and position controls

TABLE 3-1 Use These Components to Control Your Windows

Window component	Purpose
▬	Click here to *minimize* the program — to make the program window disappear. The program is still running, but you just can't see it.
Hazy Autumn 16.bmp - Paint	A quick way to get the window back is to click the program button on the taskbar. You also can switch back to the window using one of the methods I explain in the section "Switching between windows." Right-click this button to see the program's Control menu.
▫ / ▣	This button has two tasks and two different icons. When the button looks as it does in Figure 3-7 (the first button in the column to the left), clicking the button *maximizes* the window — expands the window to full size and removes the window borders. When the window is maximized, the button changes to show two little squares (the second button). Now you can *restore* the window to its previous size by clicking the button.

Window component	Purpose
✖	Click here to close the program. If you haven't saved your work yet, you're asked if you want to do so. (This may confuse Windows 3.1 users, because that is where the maximize button is located!)
window border	Any time the window isn't maximized or minimized, you can see a border around it. You can drag this border around to increase or decrease the size of the window.
◰	Point at the border and the mouse pointer changes shape. When it looks like this, you can drag the border. You can point at an edge to modify the shape in one direction or point at a corner to change two directions at the same time.
title bar	Double-click the title bar to maximize or restore the window. When the window is not maximized, you can use the title bar to drag the window around.
▤	Click here, or press Alt+Spacebar, to open the Control menu, which has sizing and moving controls. (Each program's Control menu looks different. Most programs use their program icon to represent the Control menu.)

By the way, many programs have *document* windows. Several documents may be displayed within the main program window, each in its own smaller "internal" window, its document window. Although the programs that come with Windows NT don't have this feature, the MS Office programs do, as do many other programs.

TIP **You can quickly control a particular window by right-clicking its program button on the taskbar. The menu that opens enables you to restore, minimize, maximize, move, size, and close the window.**

These document windows work the same way as main windows, except that they don't have title bars when they are maximized. They do have their own Control menus and minimize, maximize/restore, and close buttons. (Minimizing one of these document windows doesn't add a button to the Windows NT taskbar, however; it generally places a small title bar at the bottom of the program window. Double-click the title bar to open the document window, or select it from the program's Window menu.)

Sizing the window

When working in a program, you usually want the program maximized so that it gets all the room available for it. (Remember the taskbar settings, however. As I explained in Chapter 2, in some cases the taskbar takes away space that could be used by the programs.)

Now and again, though, you want to see two windows on your screen at once, or the screen and the desktop. Perhaps you want to drag something from one window to another, or you want something on your desktop.

Follow these steps to size windows:

1. First you have to *restore* the window — the window is neither maximized nor minimized. It's restored to its last non-maximized size. Double-click the title bar or click the restore button.

2. Drag the borders into position using the mouse.

You can also use the Size menu option on the Control menu, but I suspect that this is, to a great degree, an archaeological artifact of an earlier era. Does anyone really use the keyboard, rather than the mouse, to size their windows? Perhaps, but probably not often. (It may be useful in some circumstances for people unable to use a mouse.) Anyway, just in case, to use the Size menu option, restore the window and then click the Control menu and select Size. Then use the arrow keys to move the borders, and press Enter.

Using the taskbar to manage windows

The taskbar has some handy tools for managing your windows. The tool I find most useful is Minimize All. Right-click the taskbar to see the pop-up menu, and then click Minimize All. All your open windows are minimized, leaving your desktop visible.

You quickly can reverse the operation. Choose Undo Minimize All and the windows that were minimized are opened again (only those windows minimized using the Minimize All command, not windows that were already minimized).

In some cases it's not possible to minimize a window. If a dialog box was opened from that window, the window can't be minimized until the dialog box is closed; therefore, you may find that you use Minimize All and still have a window open. (If the Minimize All command is disabled — grayed out on the menu — no windows can be minimized.)

There are four more window-management options on the taskbar:

Cascade Windows This positions all the open windows one on top of the other, in the manner shown in Figure 3-8.

`Tile Windows Horizontally` This stacks the open, non-minimized windows one on top of the other.

`Tile Windows Vertically` This places the open, non-minimized windows next to each other.

`Undo Tile` This reverses the effects of tiling the windows.

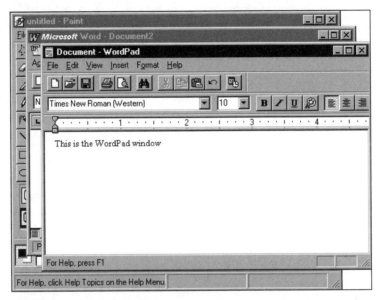

Figure 3-8 Cascaded windows.

You've already seen the Properties option on the taskbar's pop-up menu. You learn about one other option, Task Manager, in the next section.

Switching between Windows

Now that you have a program running — or several programs, perhaps — you'd better learn how to move from one to another. Windows NT is a true multitasking operating system. It enables you to carry out more than one task and to have more than one program running at a time.

That's fine, but what happens when you want to move from one window to another, whether it's a program window or a folder? NT provides many ways for you to do so. Table 3-2 explains.

TABLE 3-2 Switching Between Windows

Method	Explanation
CLICK THE PROGRAM BUTTON	Point at the window's program button (all windows, both program windows and folder windows, have one) and click. I discussed the different ways to set up the taskbar in Chapter 2. The program button may be visible all the time, or you may have to move the mouse to the edge of the screen, or press the Windows logo key on your keyboard, or press Ctrl+Esc to open it.
CLICK A WINDOW	If you've sized your windows such that more than one is visible, you can simply click the window in which you want to work. This selects that window and *brings it to the front* (also known as *moving focus* to the window).
ALT+TAB	Press and hold the Alt key, and then press Tab several times. If you have only one window open, pressing Tab has no effect. If you have two or more windows open, you'll see the bar shown in Figure 3-9. Each press of the Tab key moves the big box from one icon to another, and you can see the name of the selected window below the icon. Release both Alt and Tab when you've selected the window you want to switch to.
SHIFT+ALT+TAB	This key combination works the same as Alt+Tab, except that the box highlighting the icon moves in the opposite direction, which has absolutely no effect if you have only two windows open but can be useful when you have a large number of windows open.
ALT+ESC	Pressing these keys displays another window. This is useful if you have only two or three open windows, but the Alt+Tab method often is easier to use if you have more than that.
OPEN THE TASK MANAGER	Right-click the taskbar and select `Task Manager`, and then double-click the program you want to open.
MINIMIZE ALL WINDOWS	Minimizing all your windows is the most inefficient way to get to the taskbar. You *don't have to do this*, although I've seen people do so. Even if you can't get to the taskbar with the mouse (because you set up the taskbar in such a manner that it's never visible when a program is maximized), you can still get to it using Ctrl+Esc or the Windows logo key.

Figure 3-9 This bar appears when pressing Alt + Tab.

 TIP If you are using Alt+Tab or Shift+Alt+Tab and want to return to the starting window without selecting another, press Esc before releasing Alt.

 TIP Here's an irritating feature that you'll run into. If you open one of NT's properties dialog boxes (such as the dialog boxes opened from the Control Panel or the Taskbar Properties dialog box) and then switch to another program, you can't switch back using Alt+Tab or the taskbar. Rather, you have to minimize windows until you get back to the box. If you have to work in one of these dialog boxes and an application at the same time, size the application window so that you can still see the properties dialog box.

Managing windows with Task Manager

Task Manager provides a number of useful commands for managing your open windows.

To open Task Manager:

1. Right-click the taskbar.
2. Select Task Manager . You'll see the dialog box shown in Figure 3-10.
3. If necessary — if the Processes or Performance pane is displayed — click the Applications tab.

(You can also open Task Manager by pressing Ctrl+Alt+Delete and clicking Task Manager.)

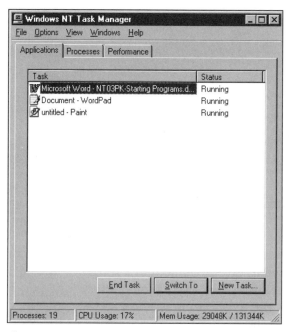

Figure 3-10 The Task Manager.

Table 3-3 explains how to use the Task Manager.

TABLE 3-3 Working with Task Manager

To Do This	Carry Out One Of These Procedures (Your Choice)
TO SWITCH TO ANOTHER WINDOW	Double-click the entry, or click the entry and click the Switch To button, or right-click the entry and select `Switch to`. The Task Manager minimizes and the other window appears.
TO BRING ANOTHER WINDOW TO THE FRONT	Right-click the entry and select `Bring to Front`, or click the entry and select `Windows` → `Bring to Front`. Task Manager remains open (if the `Options` → `Always on Top` menu option is selected), and the chosen window appears below it.
TO CLOSE A PROGRAM	Right-click the entry and select `End Task`, or click the entry and click the End Task button. The program window closes, and Task Manager remains open.
MINIMIZE OR MAXIMIZE A WINDOW	Right-click the entry and choose `Minimize` or `Maximize`, or use the Windows menu. The program minimizes or maximizes (obscuring Task Manager).
CLOSE TASK MANAGER	Click the ✕ button, or choose `File` → `Exit Task Manager`.

You can customize Task Manager in several ways. By default, Task Manager is set to sit on top of all other windows. In other words, as long as Task Manager is open, it obscures another window — even if you click that window to select it. You can change this behavior so that Task Manager acts like a normal window by selecting Options→Always on Top and clearing the check mark from that menu option.

When you switch to another window from Task Manager, the Task Manager window minimizes automatically, even if you selected *Always on Top*. Note also that the *Bring to Front* command makes sense only if the *Always on Top* option is selected. If you *Bring to Front* a window and *Always on Top* is not selected, then that window covers Task Manager — in effect, it's the same as switching to the window.

Here are all the ways to configure Task Manager:

| Options | → | Minimize on Use | When you switch to another program, Task Manager minimizes.

| Options | → | Hide when Minimized | Select this, and when you minimize Task Manager, you won't see a program button on the taskbar, and you won't see Task Manager in the Alt+Tab bar. You'll still see the little green box in the taskbar tray, however.

| View | → | Large icons | Each window is shown as a large icon.

| View | → | Small Icons | Each window is shown as a small icon.

| View | → | Details | Each window is shown as a small icon in a list, with a Status column.

Notice also the New Task button and a File→New Task menu option, which enable you to open a program. Both methods open a dialog box that is exactly the same as the Run dialog box. Also, the Windows menu has various window-management commands, including the Tile and Cascade commands. I haven't yet discussed the Processes and Performance tabs, which you'll learn about in Chapter 19.

Finding, Opening, and Saving Files

Throughout Windows NT you'll see a common form of the Open/Save dialog box. You'll find these dialog boxes in NT's own utilities and in the applications you buy. You'll use these boxes when finding a file on which you want to carry out an operation (for example, when creating a shortcut), when opening files in an application, and when saving files you've been working with. What is basically the same box is used in many different ways, for many different purposes.

Take a look at one of these dialog boxes to see how it works. For an example, right-click the desktop and select New→Shortcut. In the dialog box that appears, click the Browse button. You'll see the dialog box shown in Figure 3-11.

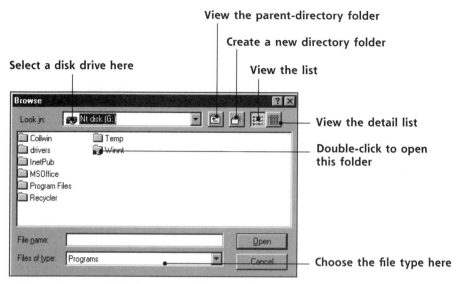

Figure 3-11 A typical Open/Save dialog box.

How does this dialog box work? By providing tools that help you "navigate" around your hard disks. Here's how:

1. Located at the top of the dialog box is the *Look in* drop-down list box. Click inside this box to open the list, and then click the disk you want.

2. In the large list box below the *Look in* drop-down list box, you see a list of directory folders on that disk. You can open one of these folders by double-clicking it or by clicking once to highlight the folder and pressing Enter. When you do this, you'll see that the *Look in* box now shows the folder name.

3. Find your way around the disk by double-clicking folders to open them. You travel down the *directory tree* as you do so, looking in subfolders and in subfolders within subfolders.

4. To move back *up* the directory tree, you can click the 🖿 button, which takes you to the parent folder. You can also open the *Look in* drop-down list box and click any previous folder or another disk drive.

5. When you find the directory you want, you can either select a file (if you're opening a file) or type a filename into the *File name* box (if you're saving a file).

6. If you are opening a file, you may need to select a file type from the *Files of type* drop-down list box. The options you find here vary depending on where you are using this box. In the example, your only choices are Programs and All Files. If you use one of these dialog boxes from a graphics program or a word processor, the file-type options are different.

7. Finally, click the Open or Save button to complete the operation.

There are a few more buttons on the top row of the Browse dialog box. Here's what they do:

Create New Folder. Use this button to create a new folder. Click it, type a folder name, and then press Enter.

List. Click here to see the files and folders listed in multiple columns.

Details. Click here to see the files and folders listed in a single column, along with size, type, date, and attribute information. (Click a column heading to sort the entries in the list by that column's data; click while holding down Shift to sort the list the opposite way.)

You can also right-click files inside this dialog box to carry out various actions (see Figure 3-12). The menu that appears depends on whether you are pointing at a folder or a file. (A different menu appears if you are pointing at blank space. This menu lets you arrange the icons and create new files, as you saw in Chapter 2.)

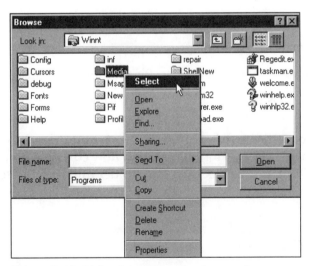

Figure 3-12 Right-click a file to see these options.

Here's what this menu can do for you:

Select Places the filename into the *File name* text box or, in the case of the folder, opens the folder.

`Open` Opens the folder window (if it's a folder) or, in the case of a program file, runs the program. With a data file, this option opens the program that can display the file and then opens the file.

`Quick View` Opens the Windows NT Explorer Quick View application, which lets you quickly view the file contents. (See Chapter 5.)

`Explore` Opens Windows NT Explorer. (See Chapter 5.)

`Find` Opens the Windows NT Find utility. (See Chapter 6.)

`Sharing` Enables you to define how the folder should be shared across the network. (See Chapter 14.)

`Send To` Enables you to send a copy of the file or folder to a disk, e-mail message, Briefcase, and so on. (See Chapter 5.)

`Cut` Removes the file or folder and places it on the Clipboard so that it can be pasted elsewhere. (See Chapter 5.)

`Copy` Places a copy of the file or folder on the Clipboard so that it can be pasted elsewhere. You can use this option to create a copy of a file within the directory, for example.

`Paste` Places a copy of the file or folder into the current directory if you copied a file to the Clipboard using `Cut` or `Copy`.

`Create Shortcut` Creates a shortcut. (See Chapter 4.)

`Delete` Deletes the file or folder.

`Rename` Renames the file or folder. Type a name and press Enter.

`Properties` Opens the file's or folder's Properties dialog box.

TIP Click a file or folder name, wait a moment, and then click the name again. The text will be highlighted. You now can type a new name and press Enter. Or simply click the file or folder and press F2 to rename.

Closing Programs

You have a variety of methods available for closing your open programs:

* Select `File` → `Exit`. Most programs have this menu option.
* Press Alt+F4.
* Right-click the program's taskbar button. Then select `Close` from the pop-up menu.
* Double-click the program's Control menu.

* Open the Task Manager (press Ctrl+Alt+Delete and then click the Task Manager button, or right-click the taskbar and select Task Manager). Then click the program you want to close and click End Task.
* Close Windows NT. It closes all the open programs for you.

TIP Here's a quick way to close several programs at the same time. Open Task Manager, click the Applications tab, and then click each program while you hold down the Ctrl key. Then click the End Task button.

BONUS

Here are a few "extras" intended to help you get into — and around in — Windows NT programs.

The Keyboard Accelerators

You may, if you want, operate the Start menu using the keyboard. That may seem a little odd — most people will use the mouse — but I want to explain it because you'll find that menus throughout Windows NT can be activated using the keyboard. Underlined letters are keyboard accelerators. Pressing that letter carries out the command (pressing **p** selects Programs). What if no letter is underlined? Well, pressing the first letter in the option name moves to the first entry with that first letter. After you open the Programs menu, pressing *a* selects Accessories. Pressing *a* again selects Administrative Tools (Common).

However, what if only one item starts with that letter? Pressing *g* while the Accessories menu is displayed, for example, not only selects Games but also opens the Games menu. This didn't happen for Accessories because there are two choices for a. And pressing *m* in the Games menu not only selects the Minesweeper menu option but also opens the program — something it wouldn't do if there were another menu option starting with g.

A Congested Menu Rx

Your computer may never get into the following mess, but just in case...

A problem develops with the Programs menu and submenus if you load many programs (I'm talking scores of programs, not just a dozen or two). The

Programs menu can get so large that it doesn't work well. If you have many submenus, sometimes a submenu opens over to the left instead of the right. If you move your mouse across to select something from that submenu, the mouse pointer passes over another option that points to another submenu, and the submenu you were trying to reach closes and another opens!

There are two solutions to this problem. First, don't let your menu system get into a mess. In Chapter 4, I explain how to modify the Start menu system so that you can clean it up now and again. If necessary, create several categories within the Programs menu: Graphics Programs, Text Programs, Communications Programs, and so on. Then put all the programs in these categories.

The other fix, an immediate fix, is to use the keyboard in conjunction with your mouse. When one of these submenus opens, and you see that you can't get the mouse pointer to the menu without opening another submenu, simply use the down arrow key to move to the program you want to open (you'll see that the first entry in the menu is selected already) and press Enter. Or press the first letter in the menu-option name.

A Few Quick Tips

Windows NT is full of alternatives. Here are a few different methods for carrying out basic functions.

Closing document windows

Remember the document windows I discussed, the internal windows within some programs that contain individual documents? How can you close these windows? You can generally use the File→Close menu option, or double-click the document window's own Control menu, or press Ctrl+F4.

Running a program

Another way to get to the Run command, which you can use to start a program or connect to an Internet site, is to open Task Manager and click the New Task button. You'll see the Create New Task dialog box, but this is exactly the same as the Run dialog box and works in the same manner.

Opening a file

If you have a file on your desktop and want to open it in a program that's already running, try this:

1. Drag the file icon to the toolbar and hold it over the button representing the program into which you want to place the file, but *don't* release the mouse button.

2. Hold the file suspended over the button, and in a moment the program window opens.

3. Drag the file onto the window and release the button.

Simple, eh? Of course, if the window is already open and not maximized — you can see the file on the desktop — simply drag the file onto the program window. You can also use this method to insert pictures into your word processing or desktop publishing programs.

Reaching the Task Manager

You may want to keep Task Manager running. If you open Task Manager (right-click the taskbar and then choose Task Manager), a small green square appears in the taskbar's tray. Now minimize Task Manager. You can retrieve Task Manager at any time by clicking its program button or double-clicking that little green square. (If you want, you can select Options→Hide when Minimized so that Task Manager has no program button, only the little green square.)

The Task Manager provides a handy way to selectively close programs, minimize or maximize their windows, and switch to them.

Summary

You now have a good overview of using the Windows NT desktop. You can start programs, and you know how to manage the program windows after they're running. You learned how to switch between windows, too, and how to work with the Open/Save dialog boxes that appear throughout Windows NT. You also learned how to close programs.

In the next chapter, you'll learn how to customize the desktop — how to add your own desktop icons, create folders to hold the icons, modify the Start menu, and so on.

CHAPTER FOUR

CUSTOMIZING THE DESKTOP

IN THIS CHAPTER YOU LEARN THESE KEY SKILLS

CREATING YOUR OWN Start MENU OPTIONS PAGE 61

CREATING DESKTOP SHORTCUTS PAGE 65

CREATING FOLDERS PAGE 66

MANAGING SHORTCUTS AND FOLDERS PAGE 67

CREATING DESKTOP FILES PAGE 69

INSTALLING NEW PROGRAMS PAGE 70

I've shown you how to start programs, but, with the exception of the Start→Run command, all these methods use icons and menu options that have been set up by the Windows NT installation program and other installation programs that you've run. How about setting up your desktop and Startmenu to work the way that is most convenient for *you*? That's what I'll cover in this chapter. I'll show you how to move things around in the Start menu, how to add your own options, and how to rename things. You'll also see how to add desktop icons and folders.

Creating Your Own Start Menu Options

All the menu options you see initially were put there by the NT installation program or by some other installation program that you've run. You can add your own options to this menu system and modify the existing ones, but why bother? Well, many small programs don't have installation programs, so they don't add options to the menu. You can add options for these programs. You also may not like the structure of the menu system; you may want to move things around or rename submenus. (I don't like it when an installation program names a submenu after the company name, not the program name; I'm looking for a program when I'm in the Start menu, not a company.)

Follow these steps to add and modify items in the Start menu:

1. Right-click a blank area of the taskbar.
2. Choose `Properties` from the pop-up menu.
3. In the Taskbar Properties dialog box, click the Start Menu Programs tab.
4. To add a new menu option, click the Add button. To remove an option, click Remove. To see the entire menu system in a folder where you can rename, move, remove, and add both menu options and submenus, click Advanced.

Adding menu options

When you click the Add button, you see the Create Shortcut dialog box. You are creating one of the shortcuts we discussed in the last chapter, but this shortcut is not going on the desktop, it's going in a menu. (Each menu and submenu is really a folder inside the Start Menu folder on your hard disk.)

You need to pick the program for which you want to create a menu option. Follow this procedure:

1. Click the Browse button. You'll see one of the new Windows NT/95-style File Open dialog boxes. You'll use this dialog box to find the program file.
2. Click the *Look in* drop-down list box and choose the disk drive the program is on.
3. Double-click the folder icons to move down the directory tree. Click the little folder icon with an arrow on it to move back up the directory tree.
4. When you find the program for which you want to create a menu option, double-click it, or click once and click the Open button. You'll find yourself back at the Create Shortcut dialog box.
5. Click the Next button, and you see the dialog box shown in Figure 4-1.
6. This dialog box shows the menu structure. Click the menu in which you want to place the menu option, and then click Next.
7. Type a name for this menu option. The name shown is the program filename, but you'll probably want to pick a more descriptive name. (You can use a long name, and include spaces, if you want.)
8. Click the Finish button, and that's it! You've just added a menu option. Open the `Start` menu and take a look.

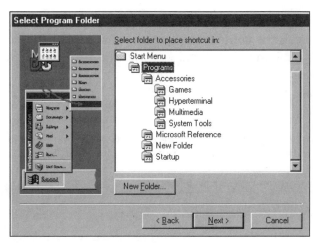

Figure 4-1 The Select Program Folder dialog box.

 TIP   Here's a quick way to add something to the Start menu. Simply drag an icon from the desktop or from Windows NT Explorer (see Chapter 5) and drop it onto the Start button in the taskbar. Windows NT adds the item to the top section of the Start menu. Then you can use the Advanced option to move the item wherever you want within the Start menu hierarchy (see "And all the rest — advanced modifications," later in this chapter).

Removing menu options

Perhaps you were goofing around just now and want to remove what you added. Follow these steps:

1. Click the Remove button in the Taskbar Properties dialog box.

2. Find the item you want to remove. If necessary, click a + sign to open a submenu and see its contents.

3. Click the item you want to remove. You can remove a single menu option or an entire submenu (you can't remove the Programs menu, however), but not multiple items.

4. Click the Remove button to remove the item.

5. Click Close when you've finished.

And all the rest — advanced modifications

If you want to add new submenus, rename or move items, or make all sorts of changes at the same time, you need to click the Advanced button in the Taskbar

Properties dialog box. Click this button and the Windows NT Explorer window opens, showing you the contents of the Start menu folder. You can see the contents in Figure 4-2. Remember, I told you that the Start menu and its submenus are really folders on your hard disk. To perform these advanced modifications, you need to play around with those folders.

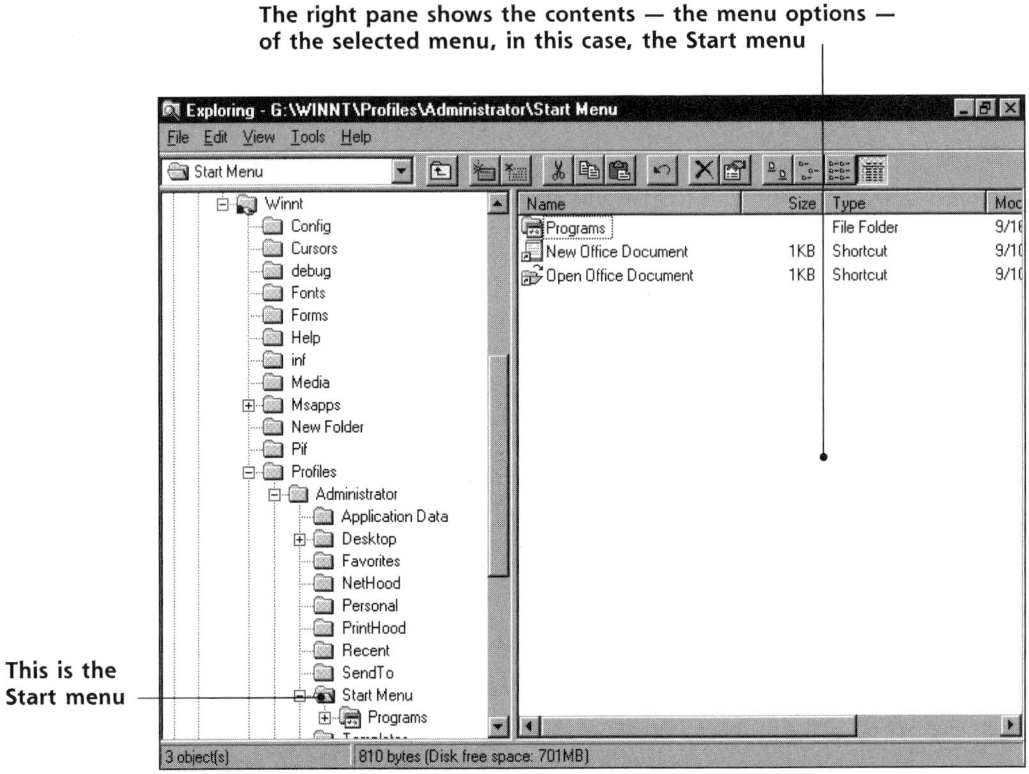

Figure 4-2 Here's where you create new folders, rename items, and more.

We're going to be looking at Windows NT Explorer in detail in Chapter 5, but Table 4-1 contains a quick summary of how to carry out various Start menu operations.

TABLE 4-1 Modifying Your Start Menu in Explorer

To Make This Change	Do This
DISPLAY MORE OF THE MENU SYSTEM	Click the little + signs in the left pane, or double-click folders in the right pane, to open up a submenu. Click folders in the left pane to see their contents in the right pane.

To make this change	Do this
RENAME AN ITEM	Click the item and press F2. Type the new name and press Enter. You can change folder (submenu) names and shortcut (menu-option) names.
CREATE A NEW MENU FOLDER	In the left pane, click the menu folder to which you want to add the new submenu folder. Then select `File` → `New` → `Folder`, and a new folder icon appears in the right pane. Type a name and press Enter.
MOVE ITEMS FROM ONE MENU TO ANOTHER	Click the item you want to move. If you want to move several items, hold down the Ctrl key and click each item. Then drag the items across to the menu folder to which you want to move them.
ADD ITEMS FROM ONE MENU TO ANOTHER	Adding items is the same as moving, except that you must hold down the Ctrl key while you drag the items.
REMOVING ITEMS	Click an item, or hold Ctrl and click several items, and then press the Delete key.
CREATE A NEW MENU OPTION	Click a folder in the left pane and select `File` → `New` → `Shortcut`. Then follow the procedure I explained earlier in "Adding menu options."

Creating Desktop Shortcuts

You can create your own desktop shortcuts so that you can quickly open your favorite programs without digging through the Start menu.

To create your own shortcuts, follow these steps:

1. Right-click the desktop and select `New` → `Shortcut` from the pop-up menu.

2. You'll see the Create Shortcut dialog box.

3. Simply follow the procedure you learned earlier for working in this dialog box (see "Adding menu options"). Rather than add a shortcut (menu option) to the `Start` → `Programs` menu, you'll place it directly on the desktop in the form of an icon.

As you work in NT, you'll start to see the ways in which procedures are similar throughout the system. You are creating a shortcut. A shortcut is a file in a folder. A desktop shortcut is a file in the Desktop folder. A menu option on the Start→Programs menu is actually a shortcut in the \Start Menu\Programs folder, and so on.

Creating Folders

You've just created a desktop shortcut. Creating a folder on your desktop is even easier.

Follow these steps:

1. Right-click the desktop and select New → Folder from the pop-up menu.

2. A little folder icon appears on the desktop, with the name *New Folder* highlighted.

3. Type a folder name, anything you want (up to 250 characters; yes, you can include spaces).

4. Press Enter.

That's it. You've created a folder. To open your folder, simply double-click it (or click once and press Enter, or right-click and select Open). You can then create shortcut icons *within* the folder, or even add subfolders, so that you can create a hierarchy of folders. The first folder may be *My Shortcuts*, for instance. Then inside you may have a folder called *Games*, another called *Business*, and so on.

TIP You can also create shortcuts to folders so that double-clicking the shortcut opens a particular folder (directory) on your hard drive. You have to trick the Create Shortcut dialog box, however. Here's how:

1. Find the folder to which you want to create a shortcut.

2. Look inside the folder and find a file, any file. (In the *Files of type* drop-down list box, select All Files.)

3. Click the file and then click the Open button.

4. In the *Command Line* text box, remove the name of the file, leaving everything else, including \ and " (if present).

5. Continue, and the shortcut is created and linked to the folder.

By the way, you can also create shortcuts to document files, such as word-processing and desktop-publishing files. When you double-click the shortcut, Windows NT figures out which program handles that document, opens the program, and loads the document.

Managing Shortcuts and Folders

A variety of useful commands help you manage your shortcuts and folders. Table 4-2 lists these commands.

TABLE 4-2 Working with Shortcuts and Folders

To do this	Carry out this procedure
SELECT SEVERAL ICONS AT ONCE	Hold down the Ctrl key and click each one. Or rubberband around them — press the mouse button, and then drag diagonally from one point to another. You'll see a dotted-line box appear, and all the icons within the box are selected.
MOVE ONE OR MORE ICONS	Drag the icon (or one of the selected icons if selecting several) to where you want to move it. Drop it onto a folder to place it into the folder. Or right-click the icon (or one of the selected icons) and select `Cut`. The icon (or icons) will appear "fuzzy." Find the folder where you want to place the icon, then right-click in the folder and select `Paste`.
MOVE THE ICONS BACK	Right-click the desktop and select `Undo Move`.
COPY ONE OR MORE ICONS	The same as moving, except that you must hold down the Ctrl key as you drag. A new icon is created. The copy is placed on the desktop (and Copy Of added to the icon name) or inside a folder if you dropped it on the folder. Or right-click the icon and select `Copy`. Then go to the location where you want to place the copy, right-click, and choose `Paste`. This method is handy for copying something to a location that is not immediately visible — several layers down in a folder hierarchy, for example.

(continued)

TABLE 4-2 Working with Shortcuts and Folders (continued)

To do this	Carry out this procedure
CREATE A SHORTCUT	Right-click the icon to which you want to create a shortcut; this may be an icon on your desktop or a file in NT Explorer (see Chapter 5). Select `Copy`. Then right-click the desktop or in the folder where you want to place the shortcut and select `Paste Shortcut`.
COPY AN ICON TO A FLOPPY DISK	Right-click and select `Send To` → `3½ Floppy (A)`. Windows NT copies the item to the disk. If the item is a folder, NT creates a new folder (directory) on the disk and copies the contents of the original to this new folder. If the item is a shortcut, NT copies the shortcut file (actually a small text file with the extension .LNK) onto the disk.
PLACE A COPY IN AN E-MAIL MESSAGE	You can copy the item to an e-mail message. (See Chapter 15.) Right-click and select `Send To` → `Mail Recipient`.
COPY TO OTHER THINGS	You can copy shortcuts and folders to other things, too. The `Send To` menu may contain other options, such as `My Briefcase`. (See Chapter 16.)
REMOVE THE COPY YOU CREATED	Right-click the desktop and select `Undo Copy`.
DELETE AN ICON	Right-click the icon and select `Delete`, or simply click once and press the Delete key.
RECOVER A DELETED FILE	Right-click the desktop and select `Undo Delete`. Also, see Chapter 6 for information about the Recycle Bin.
RENAME ICONS	Click once and then press F2; or click once, pause a second, and then click the icon-label text; or right-click and select Rename. Then type the new name and press Enter.

Here's another way to move and copy icons. Drag an icon, but use the *right* mouse button instead of the left. A *ghost* of the icon is moved, and when you release the button, the menu shown in Figure 4-3 opens. You can then move or copy the item or create a shortcut.

TIP When you learn a technique in one area of Windows NT, try it and see if it works in another area. For example, you've seen how to right-drag icons on the desktop, but you can do this within Open/Save dialog boxes and Windows NT Explorer, too.

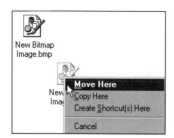

Figure 4-3 Drag with the right mouse button and release to see this menu.

Creating Desktop Files

I've been discussing shortcuts and folders. But remember, you can also have actual files stored on your desktop. For example, right-click the desktop and select New. You've already seen the first two options in the submenu that appears — Folder and Shortcut. But what about the rest of the options?

The other options (which you can see in Figure 4-4) are file types. Choose one of these, and NT creates and stores a new file on the desktop. For example:

1. Right-click the desktop.

2. Select New → Text Document . Windows NT places an icon on the desktop and highlights the name.

3. Type a name for the icon, making sure that you include the file extension shown in the original name.

4. Press Enter.

5. Double-click the new icon to open the Notepad program.

So what do you have? A text file. It's blank, but you can simply double-click the icon to open the appropriate program, which for this file type is Notepad. Then you can start typing.

Note that you can often place files on your desktop when saving from within your programs. Many programs automatically display the Desktop folder when you try to save a file. Don't get into the habit of placing all your work on the desktop, however. It will soon grow too cluttered. Rather, create folders to hold your work. Many programs come with folders — other than the Desktop folder — for holding data files already defined, although you can also create one or two on your desktop and store your work there.

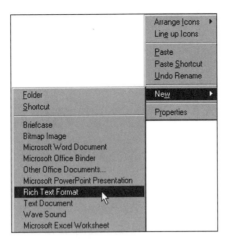

Figure 4-4 You can create new files of various types, and then double-click to open them.

Installing New Programs

Windows NT provides a quick and easy way to install new programs.

Follow these steps:

1. Select Start → Settings → Control Panel .

2. In the Control Panel folder, double-click the icon. The Add/Remove Programs properties dialog box opens.

3. Click the Install button.

4. In the dialog box that opens, click Next. Windows NT begins looking in your disk drives — your floppy and CD-ROM drives — for a disk containing an installation or setup file (INSTALL.EXE or SETUP.EXE, for example). If NT finds such a program, it displays a dialog box with the filename in the text box.

5. If NT is unable to find the program, click Browse and find it yourself.

6. When the installation or setup program you want to run shows in the text box, click Finish and the installation begins.

Look back at the Add/Remove Programs Properties dialog box. Notice that some programs are listed in the large list box. Many programs that you install, though definitely not all, appear in this list box. You can uninstall a program (remove it from your system) or modify the installation (add new components, for example) by clicking it in the list and then clicking the Add/Remove button. The Uninstall or Setup program runs.

TIP   Notice the Windows NT Setup tab. Click here to see information about which Windows NT components have been installed on your system and to add or remove components.

By the way, when you insert a CD into your CD-ROM drive, it may automatically open a window from which you can install or run the program on the CD. This is done using a feature called AutoPlay. Each time you insert a CD, Windows NT looks for a file called AUTORUN.INF, which tells NT what to do with the CD to get started.

BONUS

A Word about User Profiles

I want to quickly mention User Profiles. You're going to be looking at these in Chapter 8, but you may need to understand a little about them now, because they have an effect on your customization efforts.

As you've seen, you have to log into NT each time you boot the operating system. In other words, you have to identify yourself by providing a username, and you have to confirm that you really are who you say you are by providing the correct password. NT can be set up to work with a few, or many, different accounts. In fact, several accounts are set up for you already, including:

* **Administrator account.** The *base* account that is allowed to do anything and everything to NT.
* **Guest account.** A simple account that enables someone to use the computer but not change anything important.
* **Internet Guest account (optional).** An account for someone logging into the computer across the Internet.

You can add more accounts, too. If a system administrator set up your computer, there may be an account restricted for use by the system administrator and a more limited account for you, under your own name. In fact, the system administrator may have set up several accounts for several users, and each account has a different *user profile* (a set of rules that determine how the account may be used).

When you customize the system, *which* account are you modifying? For example, if you add menu options to the Start menu system, which accounts see these new options? Only the one you logged in with. If you add a menu option while logged into the *pkent* account, for example, that menu option isn't visible when logged in using the *jsmith* account. If you log in as the *Administrator* and make changes to the Start menu system and the desktop, those changes aren't visible to the *pkent* and *jsmith* accounts.

How is this accomplished? Remember I told you that the desktop and Start menu system are actually stored in directory folders on the hard disk? The desktop and Start menu system information is stored in the following directory:

```
C:\WINNT\Profiles\
```

Inside the Profiles directory are the following subdirectories:

```
C:\WINNT\Profiles\Administrator\
C:\WINNT\Profiles\All Users\
C:\WINNT\Profiles\Default User\
C:\WINNT\Profiles\pkent\
C:\WINNT\Profiles\jsmith\
```

You can see an example of what this structure looks like in Figure 4-5. Of course, \pkent\ and \jsmith\ appear only if accounts using those names have been created. The other three folders are always there, however. The \Administrator\ folder stores the Administrator's desktop and Start menu, the \Default User\ folder stores the desktop and Start menu that appears if you log in using an account that doesn't have a specific profile set up — if you log in as a guest, for example. What about the \All Users\ folder? This folder provides common setup information — desktop icons and Start menu entries, for example — that appears regardless of the account you use to log in. Only someone logged in as the Administrator (or with the same privileges as the Administrator) can modify the \All Users\ folder.

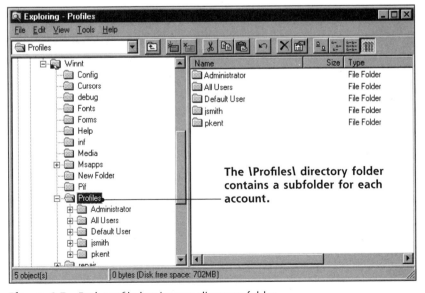

Figure 4-5 Each profile has its own directory folder.

Right-Click the Start Button

A few handy commands are hidden away on a right-click menu that appears when you click the Start button. What do all of these commands do?

Open Opens a folder window, showing the contents of the \Start Menu\ folder. (Remember, the **Start** menu is really a directory on your hard disk. You can now modify things directly from here.)

Explore Opens Windows NT Explorer and shows the contents of the \Start Menu\ folder. This is a shortcut to making advanced modifications to the menu structure.

Find Opens the Find dialog box, which I cover in Chapter 6. This dialog box helps you find a particular file or directory folder anywhere on your hard disk. When you open the Find dialog box from this menu, it's set up to search the **Start** menu folder and its subfolders, but you can modify the settings and search anywhere on your hard disk

Open All Users Opens the \All Users\Start Menu\ directory. This option appears only if you log in with Administrator privileges (you'll learn about this when you look at User Profiles in Chapter 8). This directory stores menu options that appear in the Start menu regardless of the account you use to log in.

Explore All Users Opens the \All Users\Start Menu\ directory folder in Windows NT Explorer. Again, this is available only if you are working in an Administrator account.

TIP **It's a handy thing, the right-click menu. As you have seen, you'll find right-click menus all over the place — not just in NT itself, but in most programs designed to run in Windows NT or Windows 95. When you install a new program or work with one of NT's utilities for the first time, you should right-click everything you see to find out what happens. You'll find all sorts of nice shortcuts.**

Adding Options to the **Send To** Menu

The Send To option on the right-click menu can be handy. It provides a quick way to open a file or send it somewhere. You can use the Send To menu not only on files stored on your desktop but also in any folder. You can use it in Windows NT Explorer, too (which you'll learn about in Chapter 5).

For example, perhaps you want to open a .TXT file. Double-clicking the file automatically opens it in the Notepad text editor (see Chapter 9). But what if you want to open the file in your word processor instead? You have to open the word processor and then use the File→Open command. Wouldn't it be easier if you could choose the word processor from the Send To menu?

Well, you can add things to the Send To menu. You'll use Windows NT Explorer to do so. I'll explain how, although you may want to read Chapter 5 first to learn more about using Windows Explorer.

To add things to the Send To menu, follow these steps:

1. Open Windows NT Explorer.

2. Find the `Send To` menu (it's actually the `\Winnt\Profiles\username\SendTo\` folder).

3. Click the folder in the left pane.

4. Select `File` → `New` → `Shortcut`, and then create a shortcut to the program that you want to add to the `Send To` menu (for example, a shortcut to your word processor).

That's all there is to it. The next time you open the Send To menu, you'll see your new entry.

Summary

In this chapter, you learned how to set up the Windows NT desktop in the most convenient manner. With these techniques, you can create a desktop from which you can start your programs quickly and conveniently. You can also modify the Start menu to keep the programs you use most close at hand.

In the next chapter, you'll learn how to work with Windows NT Explorer. This program is a typical file-management program. If you've used Windows 3.1, you'll find that Windows NT Explorer is similar in some ways to the old File Manager — with significant differences. Windows NT Explorer enables you to carry out a multitude of file operations, from copying and moving files between directories and disk drives to formatting disks and compressing data.

CHAPTER FIVE

WORKING WITH FILES IN NT EXPLORER

IN THIS CHAPTER YOU LEARN THESE KEY SKILLS

OPENING EXPLORER   PAGE 75

MOVING AROUND IN THE DIRECTORY TREE   PAGE 78

CONFIGURING NT EXPLORER   PAGE 79

WORKING WITH FILES   PAGE 81

FINDING FILE AND FOLDER INFORMATION   PAGE 86

USING THE TOOLBAR   PAGE 90

Windows NT contains two critical tools designed to help you find your way around your computer's hard disk: Windows NT Explorer and My Computer. The first is a file-management tool. It replaces the old File Manager program you may have worked with in Windows 3.1. And the second is, well, hard to categorize. It's a folder containing icons that enable you to view the contents of your computer's drives, the Control Panel, the Printers folder, and so on. It works in a similar manner to Explorer, but with fewer tools.

I'll begin with Windows NT Explorer, because after you've seen how it works, you'll quickly understand My Computer.

Opening Explorer

To open Windows NT Explorer, select Start→Programs→Windows NT Explorer}. If the program opens at a reduced size, you may want to maximize it so that you can get a better look. You can see the window in Figure 5-1. Yours may look a little different; if the toolbar isn't visible, select View→Toolbar.

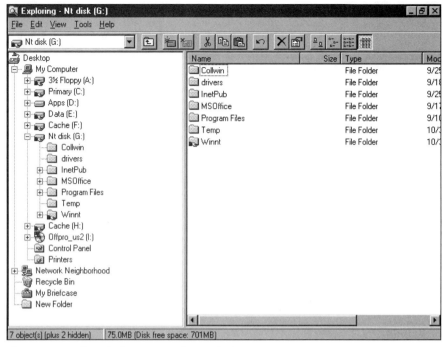

Figure 5-1 The Windows NT Explorer window.

 TIP You actually can open Explorer from anywhere. In many right-click menus you'll find an Explore option. For example, right-click the Start button (or any folder on your desktop) and you'll see one. Explorer was designed to be ubiquitous — wherever you may need it, it's there.

In the left pane is a sort of hierarchy. This is not the same as a normal directory tree hierarchy, however, with directories and subdirectories shown for a single hard drive (which is how the Windows 3.1 File Manager works). In fact, the hierarchy is in some ways a construction of convenience, with no direct relation to any physical structure, as I'll explain.

At the top of the hierarchy is the Desktop. Why? Because the Desktop is intended to be the "starting point" in your exploration of the computer, a sort of home base. The following items are listed in the hierarchy below the Desktop:

* My Computer
* Network Neighborhood
* Recycle Bin
* My Briefcase

These items are shown in the left pane, underneath Desktop. Click the + sign to the left of the My Computer icon to remove all the clutter and view only these items. Then click Desktop itself, and in the right pane you see more items:

Inbox, Internet Explorer, and any shortcuts, files, and folders that you've placed on the desktop.

What's the difference between the left and right panes? The right pane shows everything held by the Desktop. The left pane shows only those items that can contain things. You can see this for yourself by clicking each item in turn.

* Click My Computer to see, in the right pane, your computer's floppy, hard, and CD-ROM drives, along with icons for the Control Panel, Printers, and Dial-Up Networking.
* Click Network Neighborhood to see the network drives available to you.
* Click Recycle Bin to see the files and folders that have been deleted (thrown into the Recycle Bin; see Chapter 6).
* Click My Briefcase to see the files stored in the briefcase for coordination with another computer (see Chapter 16).

This hierarchy is different from a normal file-management program because, as I mentioned, it bears no relation to a physical reality. Although My Computer is shown below the Desktop, and within My Computer you can get to your hard drives, are your hard drives "on" your Desktop? No, of course not. The Desktop is actually a folder held on the hard drive.

This organization doesn't have to be confusing. Don't think of Explorer as a direct replacement for File Manager. Rather, Explorer is a way to find information, in various forms. When you start using Explorer to look at the hard disks, things will appear more familiar — you'll have file folders and subfolders. But in addition to looking at the drives, Explorer also helps you view various software tools, such as My Briefcase, the Recycle Bin, the Control Panel, and so on.

TIP If you really *have* to have the old Windows 3.1 File Manager, you can. It's actually on your hard disk. It's called WINFILE.EXE, and you can start it using the Run command, or you can create a Start option or shortcut to run it.

Table 5-1 shows the icons used in the left pane of NT Explorer and what they represent.

TABLE 5-1 The Windows NT Explorer Left-Pane Icons

Icon	Represents
	The Desktop. Everything else appears below here.
	My Computer contains your disk drives, the Control Panel, and Printers folders.
	A floppy drive.

(continued)

TABLE 5-1 The Windows NT Explorer Left-Pane Icons (*continued*)

Icon	Represents
	A hard-disk drive.
	A shared drive, one that others on the network can use (see Chapter 14).
	A folder on a disk drive on your desktop.
	A CD-ROM drive.
	The Control Panel folder (see Chapter 18).
	The Printers folder (see Chapter 7).
	The Network Neighborhood, where you can find other computers on the network (see Chapter 14).
	The Recycle Bin (see Chapter 6).
	My Briefcase, used to coordinate files used on both your desktop and laptop computers (see Chapter 16).
F	Click here to see more items stored below the item next to the symbol.
F	Click here to close the listing below the item.

Moving Around in the Directory Tree

Open up My Computer again by clicking the + sign next to My Computer. You see a screen similar to Figure 5-1. You may have more disk drives or fewer, more folders or fewer, but it should look similar.

You can click the + signs to expand the directory *tree* for each disk or the - sign to close it. Two types of folders are shown here. The first is a disk directory. (Remember that Microsoft decided to start calling directories *folders*.) The blank folders you can see in Explorer are disk directory folders. But then there are folders with icons such as Printers and Control Panel. These folders are not directory folders but are folders created by Windows NT to hold a group of utilities. You can't use them in the same way as the directory folders. You can't move files from another directory folder into the Printers folder, for example. I'm going to ignore these folders for now and cover them more in detail in Chapters 7 and 18, respectively.

When you click a folder in the left pane (a directory folder, that is), you can see the contents in the right pane. For example, click the Winnt folder. What contents? You may have more directory folders — subfolders (or subdirectories, in the old jargon) of the selected folder — files, or shortcuts. To open the hierarchy — to see the subfolders below the selected one — click the little + sign next to the folder icon.

When you click the Winnt + icon, you see over a dozen subfolders, several with their own + icons. Click these icons to open up the hierarchy even more. Keep clicking these icons and you'll see how the hierarchy is constructed, how the *directory tree,* as it's known (even if Microsoft *does* want to call them folders!), is constructed. Folders, inside folders, inside folders.

You can quickly move down the directory tree, to find a particular folder, by typing the first letter of the folder name. For example, if you want to reach a folder called Navcis, type **n** to move down to the first folder beginning with *n*. (Note that the highlight moves down to only the first n in the open part of the tree — it doesn't open up the tree to find folder names beginning with n at lower levels.) You also can use this method to find particular files while moving around in the right pane.

> **TIP** **Single-clicking a folder in the left pane simply shows the contents of the folder in the right pane. Double-click a folder, and the hierarchy one level below the folder opens in the left pane, too. Double-click a folder icon in the right pane to open that folder's contents.**

Configuring NT Explorer

I personally don't like the way Explorer is set up, but you may not mind. Before you continue, however, you should at least take a look at your options and set up Explorer to display files the way you want them.

Select View→Options and click the View tab. You'll see the dialog box shown in Figure 5-2. Read Table 5-2 for an explanation of your choices.

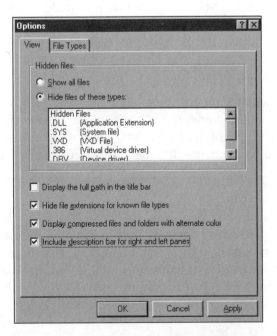

Figure 5-2 Tell Explorer how you want files displayed.

TABLE 5-2 The Explorer View Options

Option	Explanation
SHOW ALL FILES	Explorer shows all the files on your hard disk.
HIDE FILES OF THESE TYPES	Explorer hides some files from your view. In the list box, you can see which ones it hides. You shouldn't normally mess with these files, so perhaps it makes sense to keep them hidden. On the other hand, I like to see what's there, and if you can't see files, you may possibly remove what appears to be an empty folder without realizing that it contains something — NT shows the same confirmation message whether the folder is empty or not!
DISPLAY THE FULL PATH IN THE TITLE BAR	Explorer displays, in the title bar, the full path to the folder in which you are working. With this check box cleared, only the folder name is displayed.
HIDE FILE EXTENSIONS FOR KNOWN FILE TYPES	Check this option to remove any file extensions. The extension is the letters that appear after the period at the end of a filename, such as .TXT, .HTM, .HTML, and so on. The extension identifies the file type. NT is set up to identify many file types (see Chapter 6 for more information). If this check box is checked, NT doesn't bother showing extensions of files that it recognizes. I don't like this, personally, being an old fogey who's accustomed to his file extensions.
DISPLAY COMPRESSED FILES AND FOLDERS WITH ALTERNATE COLOR	Explorer lets you compress files and folders. You'll see how in the section "Compressing drives, folders, and files," later in this chapter. If this check box is checked, Explorer shows the names of compressed files and folders in a different color for quick identification.
INCLUDE DESCRIPTION BAR FOR RIGHT AND LEFT PANES	Immediately below the toolbar is a description bar that displays the folder name on the right. Clearing this check box provides Explorer with a little more room to display the files, at no real expense (the messages aren't terribly useful).

TIP Here's another reason why you shouldn't leave the Hide File Extensions for Known File Types setting the way it is. When you rename a file that has an extension recognized by NT, you can't see the original extension. If you absentmindedly add an extension, you'll end up with *two* extensions, because NT keeps the original one.

Working with Files

What can you do with the files on your hard disks? Well, you can perform certain actions on them — view them, open them, print them, and so on. You can also move and copy them around. Table 5-3 explains how to carry out actions. Note, however, that these actions work only if the file is associated with an application. See Chapter 6 for information about associating files (most are already associated with an application). In Table 5-4, you can learn how to carry out file-manipulation operations such as moving, copying, deleting, renaming, and so on.

 TIP I prefer to use the right-click pop-up menu, but note that you also can carry out many of the commands I mention here from the File and Edit menus on the menu bar.

TABLE 5-3 Carrying Out Actions On Files

To carry out this action	Do this
OPEN THE FILE IN ITS ASSOCIATED PROGRAM	Double-click the file, or right-click the file and select `Open`.
TO VIEW THE FILE IN QUICK VIEW	Right-click the file and select `Quick View`. The file's association must be configured to work with Quick View; see Chapter 6.
TO PRINT THE FILE	Right-click the file and select `Print`. A Print *action* must have been created for the file in its association information.
COPY THE FILE TO A DISK, E-MAIL MESSAGE, AND SO ON	Right-click the file and select `Send To` to see a list of items to which you can copy.
CREATE A SHORTCUT TO THE FILE	Right-click the file and select `Create Shortcut`. Windows NT creates a shortcut file and places it in the same directory, but you can then move that file to another directory or to your desktop. Or, right-click the file and select `Copy`, then right-click the folder where you want to place the shortcut, or on the desktop, and select `Paste Shortcut`.

Note that different file types have different options on the right-click menu. Some file types don't have Quick View and Print, for example. And if a file has no association, it has an Open With menu entry instead of Open. Some file types may have special options, too, such as Test, Install, Unbind, and so on.

TIP When you right-click a folder, you'll see two commands at the top, Explore and Open. Selecting Explore is the same as double-clicking the folder in the right pane; it displays the contents of the folder. But selecting Open displays the contents of the folder in another window, the sort of window used by the My Computer utility. This window is similar to the Explorer window, with a few differences, as you'll see in Chapter 6.

Table 5-4 File Manipulation In Explorer

To carry out this action	Do this
DELETE A FILE	Right-click the file and select Delete, or click once and press Delete.
MOVE A FILE TO ANOTHER FOLDER	Drag the file and drop it onto another folder; or right-click the file and select Cut, and then right-click the other folder and select Paste.
RETURN THE FILE THAT YOU JUST REMOVED	Right-click anywhere in the right pane and select Undo Move.
COPY A FILE TO ANOTHER FOLDER	This is almost the same as moving. Hold the Ctrl key down while dragging, or select Copy from the pop-up menu.
RENAME A FILE	Click the file and press F2 (or right-click and select Rename), and then type the new name and press Enter. (You can also click twice, slowly, on the text itself to highlight it.)
CREATE A NEW FOLDER	Right-click the right pane, anywhere but on a filename or icon. Select New → Folder, type a folder name, and press Enter.
	Or, click a folder in the left pane and select File → New → Folder, type a name, and press Enter.
CREATE A NEW FILE	You can create new files in the same way you saw in Chapter 4. Right-click in the right pane anywhere but on a filename or icon and select New → filetype, or click a folder in the left pane and select File → New → filetype.

The easiest way to move and copy files is by dragging and dropping. You can see this in action in Figure 5-3. Simply click the file you want to move or copy, hold down the mouse button, and then move the mouse pointer. When the pointer is pointing at the folder to which you want to move or copy the file, simply release the mouse button. Generally, you drag files from the right pane onto a folder in the left pane. But you can go the other way, too. You can drag a folder from the left pane and drop it into the right pane to move the entire folder and contents to that folder.

For example, say you want to copy folder 1 into folder A. Click folder A in the left pane so that you can see its contents in the right pane. Then point at folder 1 in the left pane, press and hold down the mouse button, and drag the folder over into the right pane. Because you didn't release the mouse button when you first clicked folder 1, the contents of folder 1 are not shown in the right pane — you can still see folder A, and when you release the mouse button, the contents of folder 1 are dropped into folder A. Try it and you'll see what I mean.

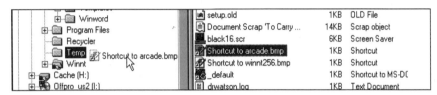

Figure 5-3 Drag and drop files to move and copy them.

TIP   When you drag a file to another folder on the same disk drive, you move the file. If you want to copy the file, hold down Ctrl while you drag and drop. If you drag to a folder on a *different* disk drive, however, you automatically copy the file, even if you don't hold down Ctrl. Notice the mouse pointer while you drag. If you see a little ⊧, you are copying the file.

To *move* a file to a folder on another disk drive, hold down the Shift key while you drag the folder.

Multiple file operations

You can carry out operations on more than one file or folder at a time by first selecting files or folders and then selecting the command. Select multiple files or folders by holding down the Ctrl key while you click each file or folder in the right pane. You can also click one file or folder and then hold down the Shift key and click another; all the file and folders between, and including, the first and last are selected. Then right-click one of the files and folders — all remain selected — and pick the command you want to use.

Here's another way to select icons. As with the desktop, you can drag a "box" around the files or folders you want to select. Hold down the mouse button and drag diagonally to create a box (see Figure 5-4). When you release the button, all the items inside the box are selected.

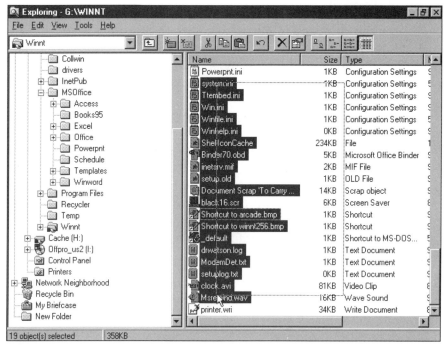

Figure 5-4 Use a "rubber-band" around files to grab them.

You can carry out drag-and-drop operations with multiple files or folders selected, too. Click one of the selected items and hold down the mouse button — all the items remain selected (if you release the mouse button, the one you clicked is selected, and all others deselected) — and then drag.

You also can use the Edit menu. Select Edit→Select All to select all the files and subfolders in the selected folder, or use Edit→Invert Selection to select all the files and subfolders not currently selected. This command is handy when you want to move most, but not all, the files in a folder. Select the files you *don't* want to move, and then select Edit→Invert Selection to select the files you *do* want to move.

Different Explorer views

You can view files and folders several ways in Explorer. Personally, I prefer the way you've seen so far (that's why you've seen it so far!). But you may find one of the other three ways more suitable. In Figure 5-5, you can see the Large Icons view, displayed by selecting View→Large Icons. The advantage? Each file or folder is large and easy to click and drag. The disadvantage? You can't see any details, such as file size and file date, and you can't see many files, as each one takes up a great deal of room.

Figure 5-5 The Large Icons view.

The Small Icon view (View→Small Icons) is similar to the Large Icons view, but, well, the icons are smaller. You see more icons, but you still don't get the details. Then there's the List view (View→List). The icons appear in columns. (In the Icons views, the icons are initially in columns, but you can drag them into new positions; you can't do that in the List and Details views.)

Finally, there's the Details view (View→Details}), which you've already seen and that I prefer. You don't see as many icons on screen as with the List view — you have to scroll down to see them all — but you can see all the information about the files (which is explained later in this chapter).

You can arrange the files and folders in different ways, too. Select View→Arrange Icons to see a menu of sorting options. Select View→By Name, →By Type, →By Size, or →By Date to order the files alphabetically by filename or file type, numerically by the file size, and chronologically by the file-modified date. What does file type mean, by the way? It's not the file extension but the Description of Type given to a file when it's associated with a program (see Chapter 6). If the file isn't associated with any program it simply has the file type *File*.

> **TIP** There's a quicker way to sort files, by the way. If you are using the Details view, you'll see column headers. Click a header to sort by that column. Click the Size header to sort the column according to file size — smallest first, largest last. Click the Size header again to sort the other way — largest first, smallest last.

Finally, I told you that you can drag the icons around in the Icons views. Try it and you'll find that you can arrange them, just as you'd arrange icons on a desktop. In fact, arranging the icons may be a real advantage to this view for many users; you can shuffle through icons, sorting them into different groups, before you carry out an action on them. So there are two commands that you can use to sort the icons again, as you saw when we looked at the desktop — View→Line Up Icons and View→Arrange Icons→Auto Arrange.

> **TIP** You can provide more room in the right pane by dragging the border between the right and left panes to the left.

By the way, you can update a view using the View→Refresh command. This command makes sure that all the files and folders are shown correctly. In most cases, NT Explorer updates the display correctly — if you delete or move a file, for example, the changes are shown. If you're ever unsure as to whether Explorer really has updated the display, you can use this command. You can also use this command to make sure you're seeing the latest on a drive across the network to which you've connected (which I'll discuss in Chapter 14).

Finding File and Folder Information

Windows NT Explorer lets you view information about each file and folder and, in some cases, even change that information. As you've already seen, the Details view has columns of information, showing these five items:

* **Name.** The filename, up to 250 characters. There's also an icon representing the file type. This is an image that is built into the program file or a standard image for that file type. (The icon used for a file type can be modified by clicking the Change Icon button in the Add New File Type dialog box; see the information about file associations in Chapter 6.)

SIDE TRIP

WHAT ABOUT FILTERS?

Many file-management programs have what are known as *filters*, tools that enable you to see only the files you want to see. For example, you may want to see only certain document-type files, such as .DOC, .TXT, .RTF, and .WRI files. The file-management system filters and simply removes from view the files that you don't want to see.
NT Explorer does not have a filter. You can't change the view within NT Explorer to filter out files. However, you can use the Find program to see only the files you want in a particular directory, or even a group of directories. You'll learn about Find in Chapter 6.

- **Size.** The size of the file, expressed in kilobytes (KB).
- **Type.** The file type, as named in the file-associations list.
- **Modified.** The date and time the file or folder was last modified.
- **Attributes.** The attribute letters. Files and folders can have several attributes set, and each has a special letter. These attributes are

    R — Read Only (The file can be used — displayed or played, for example — but not modified.)

    H — Hidden (The file is not visible in Explorer if *Hide files of these types* has been selected in NT Explorer's Options dialog box.)

    A — Archive (The file has not been backed up — archived. Backup programs clear the A attribute. The next time the file is modified, the A attribute is turned back on, so a Backup program knows that it should back up — archive — the file. See Chapter 12.)

    S — System (The file is a special system file, one required by the operating system as a crucial file. The file is hidden if *Hide files of these types* has been selected in Explorer's Options dialog box.)

    C — Compressed (This file has been compressed; more on compression later in this chapter.)

You can see more information about a file or folder by viewing the Properties dialog box. Click the file or folder name and select File→Properties, or right-click the item and select Properties. You'll see the Properties dialog box.

What does this dialog box show us? At the top you see the filename. Then you see the following:

Type. The file type.

Location. The folder in which the file or folder is held.

Size. The size, in MB, KB, or in bytes, of the file. For folders, the size of everything held within the folder.

Compressed Size. If a file has been compressed, you see the compressed size.

Contains. For folders, you see a line showing the number of files and subfolders held by the folder.

MS-DOS Name. Because MS-DOS is stuck with the old, short filename convention, NT gives files and folders *two* names — the long name and an MS-DOS-compatible short name. You see the short name here. If, for example, you copy the file to a disk and give it to someone using DOS or Windows 3.1, that person sees the short name.

Created. The date the file was originally created.

Modified. The date the file was last modified.

Accessed. The date the file was last opened.

Attributes. The attributes that we discussed earlier. You can modify the Read-only, Archive, Compress, and Hidden attributes, if you want, by clicking the check boxes. The System attribute cannot be changed.

TIP   A word about filenames: You can use long names in Windows NT, up to 250 characters long, in fact (well, in theory; 250-character names are too unwieldy to work with in Explorer), so don't worry about the old DOS and Windows 3.1 "8 + 3" restrictions (eight letters in the name, a period, and three letters in the extension). You can use spaces and different case letters, too. Make your filenames actually mean something. Instead of `lettr29.doc` **you can create a file called** `Letter to John Smith about the Internet Project.doc`**, for instance.**

If the file or folder is on an NTFS (NT File System) hard disk, there's also a Security tab, which enables you to protect and track the use of the file, folder, or files within the folder. I'll cover the Security tab in Chapter 8.

If the file is a program or system file of some kind — an .EXE or .DLL file, for example — you find a Version tab, too. Click this tab to see the information shown in Figure 5-6.

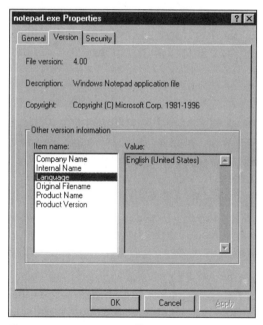

Figure 5-6   A program file's Properties dialog box.

What's all this about? System files often contain identifying information to help you figure out if the file is what you think it is or if it's the latest version. As you see, the information includes a version number, a description, and copyright information (which generally identifies the company that created the file). You can often view more information by clicking entries in the Item name list and viewing the information in the Value box.

You don't often need to use the Version tab, but it can be handy if you run into some kind of problem in which you may be using an old version of a system file or if you're trying to track down a particular program.

> **TIP** Other file types may have different tabs. For example, open an .AVI file's Properties tab, and you find Details and Preview tabs. These files are video files, and the Preview tab enables you to see the file run.

Viewing drive information

Open a Properties dialog box for a disk drive — right-click a disk drive in the left pane and select Properties. You'll find that the box is quite different.

The Properties dialog box contains the following information:

Label. The disk's *label*, a name given to the disk to identify it. You can enter a label yourself, if you want, up to 33 characters.

Type. Indicates whether the disk is a local disk (on your computer) or a network disk.

File system. The file format used on this disk, FAT (File Access Table, the format used by DOS, Windows 3.1, and Windows 95) or NTFS (NT File System, an optional NT file system). Only NTFS disks have all the security features made available by Windows NT.

Used space. The amount of hard-disk space already used.

Free space. The amount of free space on the disk.

Capacity. The total space on the disk.

Compress. Indicates whether the disk has been compressed. See the next section, "Compressing Drives, Folders, and Files."

There's also a Tools tab, which contains utilities that enable you to check for disk errors, to backup data, and to defragment a disk. I'll cover these in Chapter 6. And there's a Security tab, which enables you to set access permissions for the hard-disk drive; see Chapter 8.

Compressing drives, folders, and files

Running out of disk space? Want to free up a little more? You can use Windows NT's compress feature to do so. This feature compresses files but leaves them in a format in which you can still use them. In other words, it's *not* like the compression used in systems such as PKZIP or WinZIP (programs used to create the popular .ZIP format). These programs compress files tightly, and once compressed, the files are unusable; they must be uncompressed before use. Windows NT, however, enables you to compress files to a lesser degree. The files are still usable. Why not have *all* files compressed, then? Well, in theory the files will work a little slower. However, on a fast computer you may not notice any difference.

It's possible to compress the files, on average, around 35 to 40 percent. When I tried, I compressed the files on a drive from 130MB down to about 82MB, a savings of 48MB. You can compress an entire drive or select folders or files.

To compress files, folders, or a drive, follow this procedure:

1. Right-click the item you want to compress, such as a hard-disk icon, a folder icon, or a file icon.
2. Select Properties from the pop-up menu.
3. Check the *Compress* or *Compressed* check box (the actual word depends on what item you are compressing).
4. Click OK. If you compress a disk or folder, you'll see a dialog box asking if you want to compress the contents of all the subfolders held by that disk or within that folder. If so, check the *Also Compress Subfolders* check box.
5. Click OK and the compression begins. If you compress a directory or disk, you'll see a dialog box showing you the progress.
6. Occasionally, you may see a message box telling you that NT is unable to compress a file, perhaps because the file is in use, or maybe because it's a special protected file. Click Ignore All to tell NT to continue compressing without informing you about files that can't be compressed.

TIP You can compress only NTFS (NT File System) drives. NTFS is NT's special disk format. You cannot compress drives formatted using FAT (File Access Table). This format is used by DOS, Windows 95, and Windows 3.1. A computer running Windows NT may have NTFS drives, or FAT drives, or both types. How can you tell which format is used? Look for the File System entry near the top of the disk drive's Properties dialog box. If it's a FAT drive, you won't have a *Compress* or *Compressed* check box.

Using the Toolbar

Windows NT Explorer provides multiple ways to carry out the same command — you can use the menubar commands, the right-click menu commands, or the keyboard shortcuts. To top it all off, there's the toolbar, too.

If the toolbar isn't visible, you can turn it on using View→Toolbar (you can also control the display of the status bar, the message bar at the bottom of the window, using View→Status Bar). Table 5-5 explains what all the toolbar buttons do for you.

TABLE 5-5 The Explorer Toolbar Buttons

Icon	Button	Purpose
	Up One Level	Displays the parent folder of the selected folder in the right pane and highlights the parent folder in the left pane.
	Map Network Drive	Lets you place a network drive in Explorer so that you can access the shared files and folders. See Chapter 14.
	Disconnect Network Drive	Removes a network drive from Explorer.
	Cut	Removes a file or folder and places it in the Windows NT Clipboard so that you can paste it somewhere else.
	Copy	Makes a copy of a file or folder and places it in the Windows NT Clipboard so that you can paste it somewhere else.
	Paste	Places the file or folder in the Clipboard in the selected folder.
	Undo	Undoes the previous operation — returns a recently renamed file or folder to its previous name, for example, or revives a deleted file.
	Delete	Deletes the selected file or folder.
	Properties	Opens the file's or folder's Properties dialog box.
	Large Icons	Displays the right pane in Large Icons view.
	Small Icons	Displays the right pane in Small Icons view.
	List	Displays the right pane in List view.
	Details	Displays the right pane in Details view.

TIP I'm finished in Explorer for now, but I haven't discussed the Network Drive commands in the Tools menu. I'll cover these in Chapter 14.

BONUS

Quickly Open a Folder

There are times when you want to go directly to a directory folder rather than open Explorer and dig through. For example, if someone e-mails me a file, I want to go straight to my e-mail program's download directory.

To put your most-used directories right on your desktop, follow these steps:

1. Open Explorer.
2. Find the folder you want.
3. Right-click the folder and choose Create Shortcut.
4. Look for the new shortcut. It's in the parent-directory folder (the folder that contains the folder for which you're making a shortcut). It's named Shortcut to *filename*.
5. Right-click the new shortcut and select Cut.
6. Minimize Explorer and then right-click the desktop and select Paste.
7. Now, whenever you double-click the desktop shortcut, a folder window opens and shows you the contents of that directory.

You can also drag the shortcut onto the desktop, but if you do, you'll create a copy, not move the shortcut.

Different Explorers for Different Occasions

Setting up special folders is nice, but many users don't much like the folders — they prefer the Windows NT Explorer interface. So how about creating icons that take you to a particular folder, using Explorer to show you what's there?

To create icons, follow these steps:

1. Right-click the desktop and select New → Shortcut .

2. In the Create Shortcut dialog box, type **explorer.exe /e, *path***. For example, to open the contents of a directory called C:\Documents, you type **explorer.exe /e, c:\documents**. You can leave out **/e**, if you want the Explorer to open with only one pane visible (the right pane), omitting the directory-tree view.

3. Click Next.

4. Type a name — the name of the directory (**Documents**, for example) or something more descriptive (**My Word Processing Documents**, perhaps).

5. Click Finish.

Modifying Shortcut Icons

To choose a different icon for the shortcuts you create, follow these steps:

1. Right-click the icon and select Properties.

2. Click the Shortcut tab.

3. Click the Change Icon button to see the Change Icon dialog box.

4. Select the icon you want to use and click OK.

Note that you also can click the Browse button and select another file to see the icons that are held by that file. Many files, particularly program files, contain built-in icon files — you can use any icon from any file for your shortcut icon.

Send To a Common Folder

Remember the Send To option you saw in Chapter 4? When you right-click a folder, file, or shortcut, one of the options you'll see is Send To. And, as you've already learned, you can add items to the menu by modifying the \SendTo\ directory in your Profile.

You can use this system to quickly move files from one place to another. For example, an e-mail program that I often use saves long messages as separate text files. These files are generally from Internet mailing lists, and I want to save them in a particular directory I've set aside for that purpose. I simply can click the text message, choose Send To→Internet Mail, and the file is moved right away — no dragging and dropping.

To add a folder to Send To, follow this procedure:

1. Open Windows NT Explorer.
2. Find the folder to which you want to copy files.
3. Set up Explorer so that you can see that folder and the \SendTo\ folder (\Winnt\Profiles*username*\SendTo\). You may have to select the folder you are going to copy to in the right pane, and then display the \SendTo\ folder in the left pane.
3. Right-click the folder you will be copying to and, still holding down the right mouse button, drag it to the \SendTo\ folder.
4. Release the mouse button and a pop-up menu opens. Select Create Shortcut(s) Here.

That's it. Now, whenever you right-click an icon, you can choose Send To→Shortcut to *directory*. (Rename the entry, if you want.) The file is moved to the directory — not copied — if the directory is on the same hard disk. If the shortcut points to a directory on another disk, the file is copied, not moved.

TIP To use this method to copy a file to the directory if both file and directory are on the same hard disk, hold down the Ctrl key while you select the folder from the Send To menu. To move a file to the directory if they're on different disks, hold the Ctrl key.

Summary

Basic file-manipulation techniques are essential to your mastery of the computer. Once you understand how to shuffle files around — making copies, moving them, deleting them, and so on — you'll be in control of your computer. (It's surprising just how many people work with a computer every day yet don't really understand how to carry out such operations.) If you learn everything in this chapter, you're off to a good start.

There's more, however. In the following chapter, you'll learn how to carry out other important file operations, such as copying and formatting disks, checking for disk errors, associating files with applications, and more. You'll also learn about the My Computer icon, how to search for files and folders, and how to work with the Recycle Bin.

CHAPTER SIX

MORE FILE PROCEDURES — NT EXPLORER AND MY COMPUTER

IN THIS CHAPTER YOU LEARN THESE KEY SKILLS

DISK UTILITIES — FORMATTING, COPYING, AND MORE   PAGE 96

ASSOCIATING FILES WITH APPLICATIONS   PAGE 100

USING MY COMPUTER   PAGE 104

FINDING STUFF WITH FIND AND GO TO   PAGE 105

DELETING (AND RETRIEVING) FILES   PAGE 110

You learned a lot about working with files in Chapter 5, but there's plenty more. In this chapter, you find out about a few utilities that enable you to format and copy disks, check for disk errors, and associate files with particular applications. You also learn about the My Computer icon you've seen on your desktop, how to search for files and folders, and how to work with the Recycle Bin.

Disk Utilities — Formatting, Copying, and More

Explorer provides a number of disk utilities. These are the operations you can carry out:

* Format both floppy disks and hard disks
* Copy floppy disks
* Check for disk errors
* Make backups
* Defragment disks

Formatting disks

Disks must be *formatted* before you can use them. A disk must be set up so that the operating system with which you plan to use the disk can write information to it and read information from it.

You'll rarely format a hard disk; this is generally done only when installing a new hard disk. You may need to format floppy disks now and again, however, so if America Online hasn't sent you any new ones in the mail lately, you'd better buy some. Many floppy disks are sold preformatted, which means you don't need to format them — unless you want to change the format.

Here's another good reason to format floppies: You want to quickly erase a disk so that you can reuse it for something else. For example, you may want to reformat those America Online disks that arrive periodically in your mail; you can't use them *all* for logging onto AOL, and you want to recycle them, don't you? Reformatting a disk is often quicker than to erasing all the files on the disk.

To format a floppy disk, follow these steps (the first step is a little strange, but I didn't program the utility — I'm just reporting!):

1. If you are using Windows NT Explorer, make sure that the floppy is not selected; that is, that the contents of the floppy disk are *not* displayed in the right pane. If necessary, click another disk. If you are using the My Computer folder window (which I'll look at in more detail later in this chapter), you don't have to worry about this step.

2. Now right-click the ▭ icon and select `Format`. You'll see the dialog box shown in Figure 6-1.

3. Make sure the correct capacity is selected in the first drop-down list box. You should format a disk correctly — don't format high-density disks with a low-density format, for example.

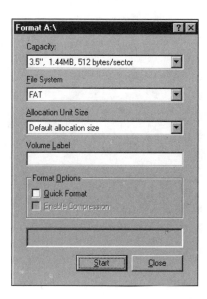

Figure 6-1 Here's where you format a floppy disk.

4. You won't be able to select the File System. It's already set to FAT, and you can't change it. (No, you can't format floppies to use the NTFS file system.)

5. Ignore the Allocation Unit Size setting. This is applicable only for the NTFS format.

6. You can enter a *label* if you want, a name that will appear next to the disk icon in NT Explorer.

7. If the disk is already formatted, but you simply want to clear the contents of the disk, click the *Quick Format* check box. If you want to completely reformat the disk — which you must do if it's a "fresh" unformatted disk — leave this check box clear.

8. Click Start.

9. You'll see a warning box telling you that all the data on the disk will be lost. That's right! Don't accidentally format a disk you need. Click OK and the process begins.

10. When NT has finished formatting your disk, you'll see a message box. Click OK.

If you are formatting a hard disk, you have more options. You can choose between FAT and NTFS in the *File System* box, and if you choose NTFS, you can also select an Allocation Unit Size. And you can turn on compression for the disk by choosing Enable Compression — files that you create on the disk later will automatically be compressed. However, be careful with this dialog box. Whatever you do, *don't accidentally format one of your hard disks when you're trying to format a floppy!* You'll destroy all the data. Use this command only when formatting a new disk or a disk that you have had problems with. Refer to the disk documentation before you take any action.

SIDE TRIP

PROBLEMS?

If the floppy disk's write-protect tab is in the protect position, NT cannot format the disk — the dialog box will probably just flicker for a moment, and nothing more will happen. NT is not very good at letting you know what's going on here.

Remove the disk, turn it onto its front, and move the small tab in the notch in one corner so that it blocks the hole in the disk. Then try again.

Did you miss the first step? If you don't carry out Step 1 in the previous steps, NT can't format the disk. As long as NT is displaying the contents of the disk, it can't format it. If any other window is displaying the disk contents, or if a program is running from the disk, it can't format, either.

By the way, how do you know if a disk is a 1.44MB or 720K disk? The 1.44MB disk has two little rectangular holes in the corners; the 720K disk has only one.

Copying disks

NT has the equivalent of the old DOS DISKCOPY command, which makes an exact copy of a floppy disk's contents onto another. Here's what to do:

1. Right-click a floppy disk and select Copy Disk . The dialog box that opens shows two lists, both containing icons showing all your floppy disks. These days, few NT-capable machines have more than one floppy disk drive, but if yours does, you'll see all the disks here.

2. Click the disk you want to copy *from* in the first list.

3. Click the disk you want to copy *to* in the second list.

4. What if you have only one disk drive? That's okay, because you can copy from and to the same drive. Click the drive icon in both lists.

TIP Both disks must be the same kind. You can't copy from a 3½-inch drive to a 5¼-inch drive, for example. And the disks in both drives must be the same format, too. You can't copy a 720K disk to a 1.44MB disk, either.

5. Click the Start button and the process begins. If you have only one drive, you're prompted to insert the disk that you want to copy into the drive. After the disk has been copied by your computer, you're prompted to place the target disk into the drive. The computer then copies the contents of the first disk onto the target disk.

Checking for disk errors

Disks sometimes contain errors caused by physical problems with the disk or by information being written to the disk incorrectly. For example, if your system crashes for some reason (something that rarely happens with NT), or you get a power cut, a file being written to the disk at that time may not be written correctly.

If you are having a problem with a particular disk — perhaps a program on that disk doesn't run properly anymore, or one of your programs can't read a particular file on that disk — you can quickly check for errors, and in many cases even fix the errors. It's also a good idea to check disks periodically, anyway — once every week or two — and fix errors before they cause problems. The ability to check for disk errors is also handy when you have problems getting data from a floppy disk you've been sent. Sometimes you are able to fix the error and get the data off the disk.

To check and fix a disk, follow these steps:

1. Right-click the disk and select `Properties`.
2. Click the Tools tab in the Properties dialog box.
3. Click the Check Now button.
4. Click the *Automatically fix filesystem errors* check box. This tells NT to look for problems caused by incorrect file writes — files written to the disk, for example, but not properly listed in the tables that your computer uses to find things on the disk.
5. Click the *Scan for and attempt recovery of bad sectors* check box. This tells NT to look for physical problems with the disk and mark the bad sectors of the disk so that they are no longer used.
6. Click the Start button and the process begins — perhaps. You may see a dialog box telling you that NT can't perform the check. In order to fix problems on the disk, NT needs exclusive use of the disk. If you have any open files or are running any programs from the disk, it can't carry on.
7. You have two choices: Click the *No* button, close all the files on that disk, and then try again; or click the *Yes* button to tell NT to check the disk the next time you boot the operating system.

Backing up disks

It's a good idea to back up data from your hard disks periodically. You can see the Backup Now button in the Properties dialog box. It's even present in the box that's opened for a floppy disk, although you'll probably never back up a floppy. Someone, somewhere, may want to archive the contents of a floppy on tape, however, so this button may be useful. Click this button to begin a backup. I'll discuss this in Chapter 12.

Defragmenting disks

Files are not always stored on your disk drives as complete units. Although, when you look in NT Explorer, a file appears to be a single object, in reality it may be split into smaller pieces and stored in separate areas of the disk.

This can create problems, but sometimes it's inevitable. As a disk fills up with data, it becomes difficult to find contiguous space in which to place new files, particularly large ones. So your computer may place part of the file here, part there, and another piece somewhere else. This is known as *fragmentation*.

Now, this is not anything you'll notice directly. Although the file is split physically, NT Explorer (and all other file utilities) still shows the file as a single unit. You may notice, however, that your programs start to slow down because it takes them more time to pull data off a badly fragmented hard disk.

When NT was first introduced, Microsoft said that fragmentation was not a problem with NT, because NTFS saves files in such a manner that fragmentation is avoided. However, it seems that fragmentation *is* a problem for NT, as with other operating systems, and commercial defragmentation tools are now available. If you've installed one designed for NT 4.0, you can click the Defragment Now button to begin the process.

Associating Files with Applications

In Chapter 5 I talked about how file types can be associated with programs in Windows NT. If a file type has an association, it means that NT knows which program can load the file. For example, by default, text files (.TXT files) are associated with Notepad, and .BMP files are associated with Paintbrush. Double-click a .TXT file and Notepad opens, double-click a .BMP file and Paintbrush opens.

But these associations can change. When you install a program, it may modify the associations list. For example, if you install MS Office, it changes the .DOC association from WordPad (NT's own word processor) to MS Word, the word processor that comes with Office. That means if you double-click a .DOC file or try to run it in some other way, instead of WordPad opening and loading the document, Word will do so.

File associations are used in other ways, too. For example, the Internet Explorer Web browser (see Chapter 17) uses the list of associations to figure out what to do with a file that it downloads from the World Wide Web. Some Web browsers, such as Netscape, have an internal list of helpers or viewers. Internet Explorer simply uses the list of file associations already built into NT. If it downloads a .DOC file, for example, it can automatically open WordPad (or MSWord, if you've installed MS Office) and display the file.

You can see a list of these associations, and even modify them. Select View→Options and then click the File Types tab to see the box shown in Figure 6-2. In the Registered File Types list you can see all the files for which NT has an association registered. Click an entry in this list and then look below the list to see the following information about the file:

Extension. This shows the extension, or several extensions, used to identify this file type. For example, .TXT identifies a text file, and .AIF, .AIFC, and .AIFF identify an AIFF Format Sound.

Content Type (MIME). This is an Internet-related item. MIME means *Multipurpose Internet Mail Extensions*, and it's a method used by Internet mail and World Wide Web programs to identify file types. NT can, in some circumstances, use the MIME type to identify a file. The MIME type consists of two parts, a type and a subtype. For example, audio/aiff means that the file is an audio file, specifically of the aiff format.

Opens With. This identifies the program that loads the document if you try to open the document directly — by double-clicking it, for example.

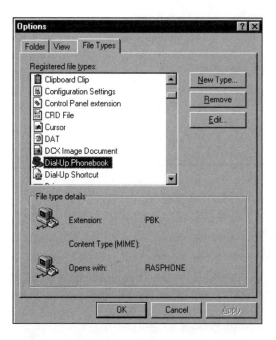

Figure 6-2 The File Types information shows you file associations.

You may never need to do anything in this dialog box. You may never have occasion to set up your own file associations, because most data files are already associated with an application, or will be automatically associated with a particular application by the setup program when you install that application.

Now and again, however, you *may* run into a situation in which you have tried to open a data file — by double-clicking it in NT Explorer, for example — and found that it's not associated with anything. The Open With dialog box, similar to the one shown in Figure 6-3, will open.

Here's how you use the Open With dialog box:

1. From the list, you may simply select a program that you want to use to open this data file.

2. If the program you want to use is not in the list, click the Other button to find the program on your hard disk.

3. If you want to permanently associate the file type with the program you associated — rather than simply open it one time — enter a description of the file type in the top text box.

4. If you associate the file type with the program, also check the *Always use this program to open this file* check box.

5. Click OK.

Figure 6-3 If NT doesn't recognize the file type, it gives you a chance to pick a program.

You can also associate files with programs before you ever need to use them. Here's how:

1. Open the Options dialog box: View → Options .

2. Click the File Types tab.

3. Click the New Type button. You'll see the Add New File Type dialog box (see Figure 6-4).

4. Enter the Description of type — any name or words that describe this file type so that you can recognize it later.

5. Type the Associated extension — the characters that appear after the period in the filename. Type only the characters, not the period. If there are two or more extensions, separate them with spaces.

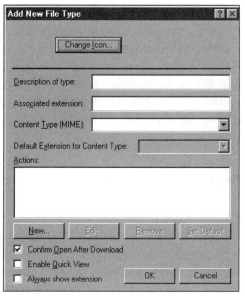

Figure 6-4 You can add file associations to the list.

6. If you know the MIME type, select it from the *Content Type (MIME)* drop-down list box. If you can't find the type in the list, type it into the box. You need this information only for files being downloaded from the Internet.

7. Click the New button to see the New Action box. In the first text box type Open or Print, depending on what you want to do with this file type when you double-click it. Then click the Browse button to find the program that can work with this file type. Close this dialog box when you've finished.

   You can add more than one action, and each action is shown on the right-click pop-up menu for this file type.

8. If you want the Internet Explorer Web browser to ask if you want it to open this file type when it downloads it from the Web, check the *Confirm Open After Download* check box. If this box is cleared, files of this type open automatically.

9. Check the *Enable Quick View* check box if you want to use Quick View to display this file type.

10. If *Hide file extensions for known file types* is checked in Explorer's Options dialog box, you can check the *Always show extension* check box to override that setting for this file type. In other words, even if most file extensions are not shown, this file type's extension will be shown.

11. After you enter all the information, click OK to add the new file type to the list.

TIP The file association list in NT is a little inconvenient. Looking in this list, it's hard to find which program is associated with which file extension. When you add any new associations, you may want to include the extension name as the first thing in the *Description of type* check box so that you can quickly find it while looking down the Registered File Types list in the Options dialog box.

Using My Computer

The My Computer icon provides a quick way to look around your computer. Double-click the icon, and you'll see the My Computer window. At first glance, it looks like an Explorer window without the left pane — look at the toolbar and you'll find the same buttons, and you have the same view options as Explorer, too. For example, in Figure 6-5 I've turned on the Details view.

In fact, the My Computer window *is* similar to Explorer in many ways and has most — but not all — of the same commands. You might think of My Computer as an entry point. Begin looking for things in My Computer. Then, if you need some of the Explorer commands that are not present in My Computer, simply right-click something — a disk drive or folder — and select Explore to open Explorer.

My Computer also provides a quick way to get to the Control Panel (see Chapter 18), Printers Folder (see Chapter 7), and Dial-Up Networking (see Chapter 16). However, you can get to these items from other places, too, sometimes more quickly, and they're also available from within NT Explorer.

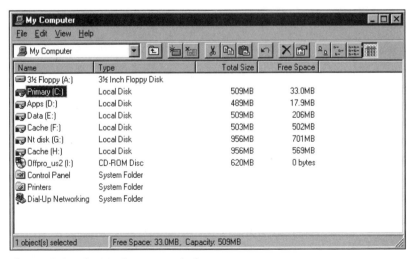

Figure 6-5 The My Computer window.

Setting up the folder windows

There is an important difference between NT Explorer and My Computer. In NT Explorer, everything happens in a single window. However, in My Computer and the other folder windows that can be opened from various places throughout NT, a new window opens each time you open a folder. Personally, I find this rather irritating most of the time — you work your way through the directory tree to find the folder you want, and next thing you know, you have five or six folders cluttering up the place.

To change this behavior, however, follow these steps:

1. In any folder window (opened through My Computer or from some other source, such as a desktop folder), select View → Options .

2. In the dialog box that opens, click the Folder tab.

3. Click the second option button (browse folders by using a single window that changes as you open each folder).

4. Click OK.

Now, each time you double-click a folder to open it, the contents of the window change — another window does *not* open.

> **TIP** Press Ctrl while you double-click, and the *opposite* of whatever is set in the Options dialog box is carried out. In other words, if you select the multiple-window system, holding Ctrl while you double-click a folder causes the contents of the folder to appear in the same window. If you select the single-window system, holding Ctrl while you double-click causes a new window to open.

Finding Stuff with Find and Go To

As programs get bigger and more complicated, and as we spend more time in front of these boxes, more and more data is being stored on hard disks. Little more than a decade ago, a 10MB hard disk was considered ample. Now many single programs need that amount of disk space, and many others need far more, which brings us to a problem: Just how do you *find* stuff in all those thousands of files?

If you've ever wanted to track down a particular file that seemed to have gotten lost — a shareware program you loaded a few weeks ago, or a letter you wrote a month or two back — you'll understand just how useful a search utility can be. Well, NT has such a utility built in, and it's only a few clicks away.

Select Start→Find→Files or Folders and the dialog box shown in Figure 6-6 opens. Or, if you happen to be in NT Explorer when the sudden need to find a file strikes you, select Tools→Find→Files or Folders. This system enables you to search for a file or a folder, and to do so by entering information about the file type, filename, the possible location, and even text inside the file.

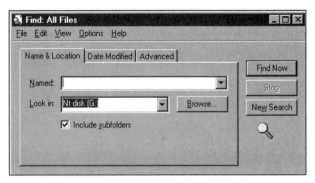

Figure 6-6 Find helps you do just that — find stuff you've lost.

 TIP More ways to open Find: Right-click disk and folder icons in NT Explorer or folder windows, or right-click the Start button.

To use the Find dialog box, follow these steps:

1. If you know the filename, type it into the *Named* text box. If you don't, that's okay; you can enter other information to identify the file. If you know only part of the filename, type that part. For example, perhaps you've created a file called 02FIG01.BMP . . . or was it 01FIG02.BMP? Or 02FIGURE01.BMP? Never mind, type **02**. There's no need to enter a *wildcard,* either. (Some systems require that you enter a & or ? symbol to represent the missing characters.)

2. Next, tell the system where to search. You can select a disk drive from the *Look in* drop-down list box. If you want to search *all* the disk drives at once, select My Computer from the list box, or choose the Local Hard Drives option.

3. You can get more specific if you want. Click the Browse button, and then find the directory you want to search through.

4. Notice the *Include Subfolders* check box. Select this if you want Find to search through the selected directory and all the subdirectories.

5. Click the Date Modified tab if you want to specify a date range — the more information you can provide, the more likely Find will be able to locate what you need. (On the other hand, provide only information that you are quite sure is correct — don't just guess.) The panel in Figure 6-7 shows you the date options.

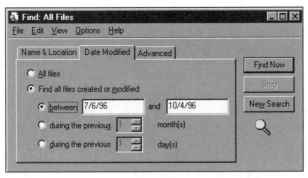

Figure 6-7 Enter information about the date if you are sure you know it.

6. By default, the All Files option button is selected, meaning that Find will ignore file dates. If you want to specify date information, check *Find all files created or modified*.

7. Now choose a method for selecting a date. You can choose *between* — in which case you must enter two dates. You can also choose *during the previous x month(s)* — select or type a number in the little incrementer box. Or choose *during the previous x day(s)* — again, enter a number in the box.

8. Click the Advanced tab to see the panel shown in Figure 6-8.

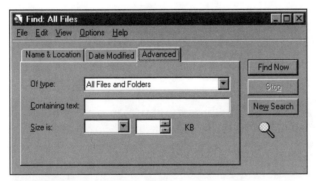

Figure 6-8 Enter information about the file types and text inside the file.

9. In this panel, choose the type of file you want to search for; select from the drop-down list box. You can search for All Files and Folders, Bitmap Images, Clipboard Clips, Internet Documents, MS-DOS Batch files, and so on. There are literally dozens of options.

You can also specify text to look for if you're searching for a text or word-processing file. For example, if you are absolutely sure that the letter you want to find contains the words *Mr. Smith*, type that into the *Containing text* box.

If you want to specify that the text must match the case you entered (for instance, you want Find to ignore any files containing the text *mr. smith* or *MR. SMITH*), select Options → Case Sensitive.

Finally, you can specify a file size (though you probably won't often do so). Choose *At least* or *At most* from the *Size is* drop-down list box, then enter the size, in KB.

10. Click Find Now and away it goes. A blank box opens below the tab that will eventually (we hope) show you the files that Find has found.

11. At any time, you can click Stop and start over. Click New Search to clear all your search criteria and start again.

TIP
You need to enter only one search criteria, by the way. For example, if you simply select *Animated Cursor* from the *Of type* drop-down list box — without entering filename information, dates, or anything else — Find looks for all the animated mouse cursor (.ANI) files. (You'll learn about these in Chapter 18.)

In Figure 6-9, you can see a list of files that Find has discovered for you. Maximize the window to see all the information — the name, location, size, type, and modified date. You can work on the files directly in this box. You'll find menu options that you've seen before in the right-click menu and the File, Edit, and View menus.

You can even create a desktop shortcut from the Find box:

1. Right-click a file.

2. Select Create Shortcut.

3. You'll see a message telling you that you can't place a shortcut here, but you can place it on the desktop. Click Yes and the shortcut is created.

SIDE TRIP

MORE ABOUT FILTERS

In Chapter 5, I told you that you can use Find as a filter system to view only the files you want to see in a particular folder. To do so, you need to use a wildcard, the * character, to represent the filenames. For example, to see all the .DOC files, type *.DOC into the Named text box. To see multiple types — in Chapter 5, I used the example of wanting to view only .DOC, .TXT, .RTF, and .WRI files — separate each file extension with a comma. For example:

    .DOC,.TXT,*.RTF,*.WRI

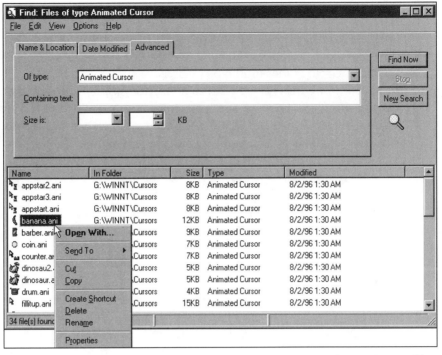

Figure 6-9 The Find box enables you to carry out all the normal operations on files and folders.

 TIP To open the parent folder window, click a file or folder that you've found, and then select File→Open Containing Folder.

Saving a search

You can save a Find operation, if you want, so that you can quickly repeat it. There are two ways to do this. You can save the search criteria, or you can save the search criteria and the list of files that were found. Here's how:

1. Carry out your search, as described earlier.

2. If you want to save the list of files that were found, select `Options` → `Save Results`.

3. Select `File` → `Save Search`. An icon is placed on the desktop.

4. Double-click the icon to open the Find box. If you selected the `Options` → `Save Results` menu option, the box opens and displays the list of files found during the last search.

5. Click Find Now to carry out a new search.

MORE FILE PROCEDURES—NT EXPLORER AND MY COMPUTER **109**

A direct path to a directory

There's another handy utility that you can use to find your way around — the Go To Folder dialog box. This is available in NT Explorer. Select Tools→Go to, and the Go To Folder dialog box opens.

You now can type the path to a directory folder in the text box. For example, if you want to view the \drivers\ folder, you could type **c:\winnt\system32\drivers**. This is a bit of a nuisance, but notice that the text box is actually a drop-down list box. You can to select this entry from the list box next time. Click OK and the directory opens for you.

There are several things to note about this drop-down list box. First, there's a software bug at work here — the list box also contains the programs you've run from the Run dialog box. You'll have to ignore these programs (they won't work if you try them here). Second, if you click the disk drive containing the folder before opening the Go To Folder dialog box, you don't need to include the drive letter when you type the path. However, if you want to select that entry from the drop-down list later, you have to make sure to click the correct disk drive before doing so.

Finally, you can't enter a folder name and hope that Go To Folder finds it, unless it's in the first level. For example, you can't type **drivers** and hope that it finds c:\winnt\system32\drivers; it won't.

Deleting (and Retrieving) Files

You've already seen how to delete files — click a file and press the Delete key, or right-click and choose Delete. But do you know how to get the files back? That's where the Recycle Bin comes in. If you've already tried to delete a file or folder from NT Explorer, the desktop, or a folder window, you saw a message asking if you want to move the file or folder to the Recycle Bin. If you clicked Yes, the file or folder was not actually deleted. Rather, it was stored in a special place on your hard disk.

Why? So that you can get it back, of course, if you later decide that you made a mistake. But don't wait too long. Eventually, the files and folders are removed from the Recycle Bin — as you'll see in a moment.

Take a look at the contents of the Recycle Bin. Here are several ways to open the Recycle Bin:

* The quickest way is to double-click the 🗑 icon on your desktop.
* Right-click the 🗑 icon on your desktop and select `Explore` to open it in NT Explorer.
* If NT Explorer is already open, you can simply click the Recycle Bin icon at the bottom of the left pane.

You can see an example of the contents of the Recycle Bin — shown in NT Explorer — in Figure 6-10.

TIP What's the difference between opening the Recycle Bin in Explorer and opening it by double-clicking the Recycle Bin icon? Open it from the desktop icon, and you get a folder window, like the one you get when you work in My Computer. Open the Recycle Bin in NT Explorer, and you have all the Explorer tools available.

You can use the Recycle Bin just like any other file folder — well, almost. There are a few significant differences between the Recycle Bin and other folders. If you delete a file from the Recycle Bin, it's gone for good — there's no retrieving it! You can't copy a file from the Recycle Bin, either. You can only move it. If you want to retrieve a file, simply move it from the Recycle Bin to another folder. You can drag files *to* the Recycle Bin, too, which is the same as deleting them, of course. But you can't carry out many of the other file operations available, such as creating a shortcut or using Quick View.

TIP The quickest way to retrieve a deleted file is by right-clicking the file in the Recycle Bin window and selecting Restore. The file is moved back to its original location.

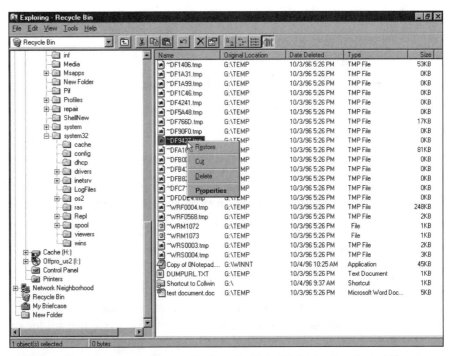

Figure 6-10 The Recycle Bin can be viewed within NT Explorer and used like any other folder.

When you delete a file, it sits in the Recycle Bin. How long does it sit? Until the space is needed by another deleted file. If the Bin fills up (I'll show you how to adjust the size in the next section), the file deleted earliest is removed to make room for the newcomer. And once removed, the file is really gone. There is no recycle bin for the Recycle Bin.

Configuring the Recycle Bin

You can determine how the Recycle Bin works. Right-click the Recycle Bin icon on the desktop and select Properties. Notice that each disk drive has its own tab. If you have multiple hard-disk drives, you can configure each drive's Recycle Bin separately. By default, however, the *Use one setting for all drives* check box is selected. If you want multiple bins, select *Configure drives independently*.

> **TIP** NT sets aside a space on each drive for a Recycle Bin, and each bin works independently of the other. For example, if the bin on drive D is full, when you delete a file, another will have to be removed from the bin to make room, even if the bin on drive C has space. However, you'll see all deleted files, from all drives, in one Recycle Bin window.

Here's how to set up the Recycle Bin:

1. If you want, you may turn off the Recycle Bin entirely (or a bin on a particular drive if you are configuring each drive separately). Check the *Do not move files to the Recycle Bin. Remove files immediately on delete* check box. When you delete a file, it's really deleted — not sent to the Recycle Bin.

2. Use the *Maximum size of Recycle Bin (percent of each drive)* slider to set aside space on the disk drive for the Recycle Bin. By default, this slider is set to 10 percent, which to me seems like a lot of space — but perhaps it's not enough in your case. The more space available for the Recycle Bin, the longer files will stay before being removed. But the larger the Recycle Bin, the less space available for your data and applications.

3. By default, the *Display delete confirmation dialog* check box is checked. If you don't want to see a message asking you if you *really* want to delete a file each time you do so, clear this box.

4. Click OK.

What happens if you do run out of disk space on a particular drive? There are two things you can do. First, you can clear the Recycle Bin to make more room. Right-click the Recycle Bin icon and choose Empty Recycle Bin, or choose File→Empty Recycle Bin while viewing the Recycle Bin folder or the Recycle Bin within NT Explorer. Problem is, this removes *all* files stored in *all* Recycle Bins on *all* the hard-disk drives.

If you want to be more selective, view the Recycle Bin and select only the files you want to remove. As you can see, there's an Original Location column. If you want to clear space on, say, drive D, you can remove files that came from that drive only (and which are stored in that drive's Recycle Bin).

BONUS

What are all these *.TMP Files?

You may have noticed files with the .TMP extension, files with names like ~DF2971.TMP or ~WRS0003.TMP. (Of course, if you left the *Hide file extensions for known file types* setting selected, you won't see the .TMP extension — see Chapter 5.) These files are temporary files created by applications and intended for deletion after a particular operation has been completed. You can think of temporary files as "holding areas" in which programs store information temporarily.

Unfortunately, a temporary file is sometimes not quite as temporary as it should be. Although the files are supposed to be deleted, they are often left behind by a program that crashes, or even when closed correctly, sometimes taking up large amounts of disk space. Take a look in the \Temp\ directory on your hard disk, and you'll probably find a few, perhaps many, temporary files.

To delete temporary files, follow these steps:

1. Click the Modified column heading in NT Explorer to sort the files by date.

2. Select the files that do not have today's date (for example, hold Ctrl while you click the files you want to select).

3. Press Delete.

Some programs also leave behind temporary files in data directories. For example, Word for Windows often creates — and leaves — temporary files with .tmp extensions or files with .doc extensions and names beginning with ~$. Create a file called Letter to John Smith.doc, and later you may find a file called ~$Letter to John Smith.doc. These temporary files can also be deleted, but make sure that you're not trying to delete a temporary file currently in use by the application.

Quickly Open README Files

If you install shareware programs downloaded from the Internet or an online service, you have to place the program in a directory and, in many cases, double-click the program's *archive* file to extract multiple files. (An archive file is a single file that contains other files stored within it.) You'll often notice a file called

README.TXT, README.1ST, or something similar. These files contain information you should read before installing the program.

Double-click README.TXT and Notepad opens so that you can read it. But double-click README.1ST and the Open With dialog box opens (refer to Figure 6-3). You can then find Notepad from the list, but it's way down there. Wouldn't it be nice to put it right at the top of the list so that you can simply double-click it? Well, here's how to do that (you can use this technique to put any often-used program near the top of the list):

1. In NT Explorer, find NOTEPAD.EXE. It's in the \Winnt\ directory.
2. Right-click and select `Copy`.
3. Right-click a blank area and select `Paste`. Explorer creates a copy of the file and names it `Copy of Notepad.exe`.
4. Press F2 to highlight the text, and rename it **_Notepad.exe**. Press Enter.
5. Select `View` → `Options`.
6. Click the File Types tab.
7. Click New Type.
8. Click inside the *Associated extension* text box, and press the spacebar.
9. Click New.
10. In the Action box, type **Open**.
11. In the *Application used to perform action* text box, type **_Notepad.exe**.
12. Click OK.
13. Click Close twice.

That's it, you're finished. Now when you double-click an unrecognized file — such as README.1ST — you'll see the Open With dialog box.

Summary

In this chapter, you learned a few advanced but important file- and disk-management techniques. Some you may never need, and others you'll use all the time. The Find tool, for example, is extremely useful, as you'll discover the next time you mislay a file. The Recycle Bin can be handy, too, the next time you realize that deleting a particular file wasn't such a good idea. If you're lucky, it may still be there waiting for you.

In the following chapter, I'm going to move away from files and disks and onto another important subject, printers. You'll find out how to install and work with printers and how to manage your fonts.

CHAPTER SEVEN

USING PRINTERS AND FONTS

IN THIS CHAPTER YOU LEARN THESE KEY SKILLS

INSTALLING A PRINTER   PAGE 116

USING YOUR PRINTER   PAGE 121

MANAGING PRINTERS   PAGE 123

MODIFYING PRINTER PROPERTIES   PAGE 124

FONT MANAGEMENT   PAGE 129

PICKING SPECIAL CHARACTERS   PAGE 133

A few years ago, back in the days of DOS, each program you bought came with a set of printer drivers. These special programs made sure that the information being sent by the program could be understood by the printer receiving it. You'd install the program and then select the driver for the printer you were using . . . if you were lucky. If you were unlucky, the program didn't have a driver for your particular printer, so you'd have to hope that one of the others would work.

One of the reasons why Windows has been such a success is that it isolates software publishers from the nitty gritty of working with different types of hardware. For example, as long as a program runs in Windows, there's no need for a software publisher to worry about how the program will print. That's handled by Windows itself. All you need to do is install the printer drivers once, and all your Windows programs can use the printer. In this chapter, you'll see how this is done and also find out how to work with fonts.

Installing a Printer

Select Start→Settings→Printers, and the folder shown in Figure 7-1 opens. You may find that you already have a printer installed. In this example, you can see that three printers are installed. The HP LaserJet III is represented by an icon that shows a printer held in a hand. The little hand icon means that this printer is shared on the network — other users on the network can use it by sending data through this computer. There's also an Apple LaserWriter — this icon shows that it is not shared. And there's a LINOTRONIC on 486, which uses an icon to indicate that it's a network printer — a Linotronic printer installed on a computer called 486.

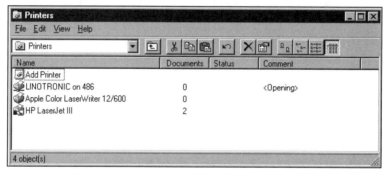

Figure 7-1   The Printers folder.

TIP   There are other ways to get to the Printers folder. In NT Explorer, click the Printers folder at the bottom of the left pane. In My Computer, double-click Printers.

To install a printer, follow this procedure:

1. Double-click the Add Printer icon, or right-click and select Open. The Add Printer Wizard opens.

2. If you haven't installed a printer yet, NT assumes that it should set up the printer as the default printer, the one that your programs will use automatically. But if you already have a printer and want to add another, NT wants to know if you now want the new one to be the default printer. If you select No, then you have to pick the printer each time you want to use it. Click Next.

3. This dialog box is already set up to install a *local* printer, one that is not connected through the network. Click Next to see the dialog box shown in Figure 7-2.

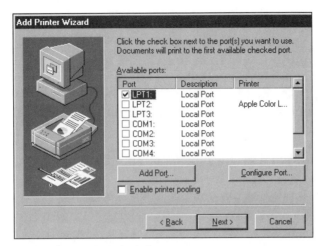

Figure 7-2 Select the printer port.

4. Click the computer port that you used to connect to the printer (usually LPT1).

5. If you want to print to several different printers using a single print driver — for example, you have two identical printers connected to LPT1 and LPT2 — check the *Enable printer pooling* check box. You're then able to select more than one printer port (without this box checked, only one port can be selected). The print driver sends print jobs to the first printer it finds available that is connected to the selected ports.

6. Click Next, and you'll see the information shown in Figure 7-3.

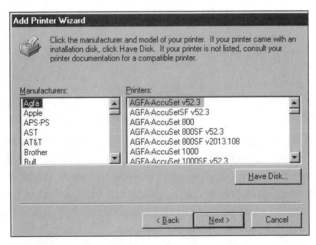

Figure 7-3 Pick the printer.

7. In the left column, select the manufacturer of the printer. The information in the right column changes to show printers sold by that manufacturer.

USING PRINTERS AND FONTS   **117**

8. In the right column, click the printer you have.

TIP Can't find your printer? Then contact the manufacturer and ask for a printer driver. If one is available, you'll then click the Have Disk button and install from the files provided to you by the manufacturer. If no driver is available, the manufacturer should be able to tell you which of the other drivers will work.

9. Click Next. You'll see the dialog box shown in Figure 7-4.

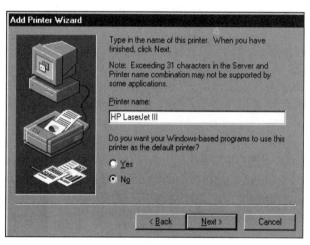

Figure 7-4 Enter a printer name.

10. You can either keep the printer name you have or provide another name. For example, instead of keeping *HP LaserJet III*, you might call the printer *Draft Printer* or *High Resolution*, or whatever. Also, note that if you are installing a printer on a system that already has one installed, you can choose whether to make this the default printer — the one that applications use if you don't pick a different one.

11. Click Next. You'll see the dialog box shown in Figure 7-5.

12. If this printer will be used only from your computer and not across the network, leave the Not Shared option button selected. If you plan to make the printer available to other network users, click the Shared option button. Then click each operating system in the list that is used by the computers on the network that will be using the printer. You can also change the Share Name if you want, the name by which the printer will be identified on the network.

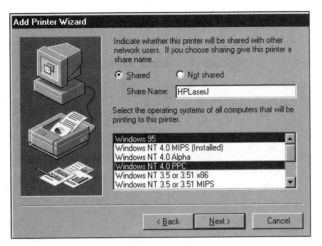

Figure 7-5 Tell NT whether you plan to share the printer.

13. Click Next.

14. In the dialog box that appears, you can choose whether to print a test page on the printer. It's a good idea to do so, although not essential. To print a page, make sure the Yes option button is selected, and click Finish.

15. NT begins copying the print drivers from your installation disks. You may be prompted to insert the Windows NT CD into the drive. If so, click OK and then make sure that the correct drive and directory is shown in the *Copy files from* text box (it's quite likely *not* correct— it may show your floppy disk drive instead of the CD drive). For example, if you are installing onto an IBM-compatible PC, the directory is \i386\. You can use the Browse button to find this directory, if necessary. Then click OK.

16. NT installs the drivers and then prints the test page (if you chose that option). The test page shows information about your printer — the driver filenames, the printer name and share name, and so on. If everything prints okay, click Yes in the dialog box that appears. If not, click No and a Help screen opens. This screen provides a question and answer format to help you make sure that you've connected and installed the printer correctly.

TIP If you set up a printer as a non-shared printer and later want to share it, no problem. Right-click the printer icon, select Properties, click the Sharing tab, and you'll be able to make the changes.

Multiple drivers for one printer?

You can have multiple drivers for a single printer, if you want. In other words, when you print from an application, you'll have several choices, even though you have only one printer. Why would you want to do this? So that you can print to the same printer *in different ways*. For example, you may have one driver set up to print on Letter size paper and another to print on Legal size paper. One driver may use Portrait mode, and another may use Landscape, so you'll see multiple printers in the Printers folder. Each printer will have different names (HP LaserJet III [legal], HP LaserJet [letter], and so on, whatever you choose), and you can set up each one independently of the other. (See "The document properties," later in the chapter.)

TIP You can change printer names the same way you change filenames. For example, click a printer name in the Printers folder and press F2.

What about network printers?

It's easy to connect to a printer across the network. You have the choice of installing a local printer or picking one on the network. If you chose the Network Printer Server option button, you'll see the Connect to Printer dialog box shown in Figure 7-6.

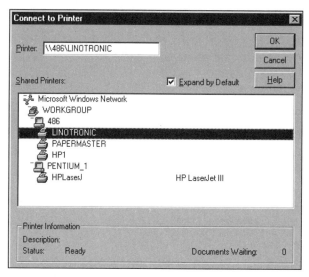

Figure 7-6 You can select a printer elsewhere on the network.

Double-click the entries you see in this dialog box to open up the hierarchy and display the printers. When you find the printer you want to use, click it and then click OK. It's really that simple. The printer is added to your printer folders and will be available to your programs.

TIP In some cases, you may have to install the printer drivers on your own computer. In other cases, NT will be able to use the drivers on the computer connected to the printer you want to use.

That's it. You've installed your printers! Now, how do you use them? I'll explain that next.

Using Your Printer

In most cases, you'll probably use your printer directly from your applications by using the Print command — generally File→Print. However, some programs may have other ways to get to the Print command, such as using a Toolbar button. Some print commands send the document to the default printer immediately, so you have no chance to pick a printer. Notepad works this way (see Chapter 9). In other cases, you'll see a dialog box from which you can select a printer.

TIP Which is the default printer? The one set up in the Printers folder as the default printer. Right-click a printer and look for the Set as De_f_ault menu option. The printer with a check mark next to it is the default printer. If there is no check mark, select the option to make the printer the default.

For example, in WordPad you'll see the dialog box shown in Figure 7-7 when you select File→Print. If you click the Print toolbar button, however, WordPad bypasses the dialog box and sends the file directly to the printer.

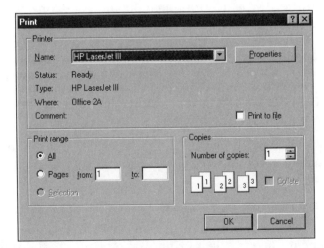

Figure 7-7 A typical Print dialog box.

What can you do with the Print dialog box? That depends on the printer and the application. Each print driver is a little different, and some applications add special features to their Print dialog boxes (such as the ability to specify what sort of items — annotations, summary info, and so on — within the document should be printed and which features should be hidden). However, some features are common to most, if not all, printers. Here's what you'll find in the Print dialog box shown in Figure 7-7:

Name. The printer that will be used. This shows the default printer, but you can select another from the drop-down list box.

Properties button. Click here to see the Printer Properties (I'll cover these later in this chapter).

Status. Tells you if the printer is ready.

Type. The printer type.

Where. The printer port (or network location) being used.

Comment. A comment line that you can add to the Printer Properties, perhaps to further identify the printer.

Print Range: All. Select this if you want to print the entire document.

Print Range: Pages. Select this if you want to print specific pages; enter the range.

Print Range: Selection. Select this if you want to print only the text that has been highlighted within the document.

Copies: Number of copies. Specify how many copies you want to print.

Copies: Collate. If you are printing more than one copy of a multi-page document, you can specify whether you want to collate the document; that is, print all of one copy, then all of the next, and so on (rather than print all the page 1s, all page 2s, and so on).

Print to file. Allows you to create a print file rather than actually printing on paper. The print file can then be taken to another computer and printed from that computer. See "Creating print files," later in this chapter.

When you've made your choices, simply click OK and run to the printer to grab your document as it flies out . . . well, okay, go for coffee while you wait for it to print.

> **TIP** There are other ways to print in NT. Drag a document file from Windows NT Explorer onto a printer in the Printers folder. Right-click on a document file and select Print. Add a printer to the Send To menu (see Chapter 4 for instructions), and then right-click on a document and select Send To→*Printername*.

Managing Printers

You have a degree of control over the print jobs while they are printing. When you send something to a printer, a little icon is placed in the taskbar tray (see Figure 7-8). Right-click this icon and select either the printer name (to open a window for a particular window) or Open Active Printers. You can also simply double-click this icon. The window shown in Figure 7-8 opens and lists all the print jobs going to the specified printer.

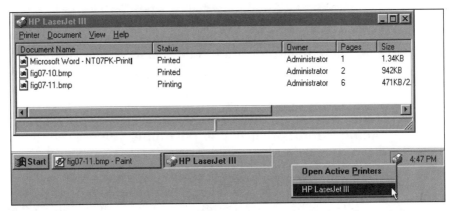

Figure 7-8 The taskbar printer icon provides a way to open the printer window.

What can you do with print jobs? Table 7-1 explains.

TABLE 7-1 Managing Print Jobs

To carry out this procedure	Do this
CANCEL A PRINT JOB	Click the print job and press Delete.
CANCEL *ALL* PRINT JOBS	Select Printer → Purge Print Documents .
PAUSE A PRINT JOB	Right-click the print job and select Pause .
CONTINUE PRINTING	Right-click the print job and select Resume .
RESTART A DOCUMENT FROM THE BEGINNING	Right-click the print job and select Restart .
STOP THE PRINTER FROM PRINTING ANYTHING	Select Printer → Pause Printing .
RESTART THE PRINTER	Select Printer → Pause Printing again.
ADJUST PRIORITY (SO THAT A PRINT JOB PRINTS SOONER)	Right-click the print job and select Properties . Then move the Priority slider to a higher level.

Modifying Printer Properties

You can adjust all sorts of printer properties — characteristics that affect the manner in which the printer operates. You can modify how the print driver *spools* print jobs to the printer, which type of paper to use, how the printer prints graphics, and so on.

There are essentially two forms of properties: the printer properties and the document properties. I'll discuss these two properties in the following sections.

The printer properties

To view the printer properties, right-click a printer in the Printers folder and select Properties. Each panel in the Printer Properties dialog box is discussed in the following section.

NOTE Many printer operations are available to you only if you have Administrator privileges for the printer you are trying to modify.

GENERAL PROPERTIES

Figure 7-9 show the General printer properties, which Table 7-2 explains.

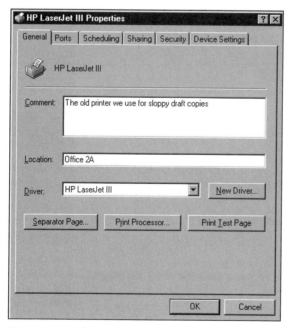

Figure 7-9 The General printer properties.

TABLE 7-2 The General Printer Properties

Item	Purpose
COMMENT	Enter any notes you want in this text box. These can help identify the printer or identify the manner in which you've set up the driver (For example, *Legal paper, Landscape mode,* and so on).
LOCATION	Do you work in a large office building and share many printers with many people? You can let people know where a particular printer is located — an office number, for example.
DRIVER	This shows which printer driver is in use. You can select one of the other drivers from the list, if you want, and then make changes — but you'll lose the settings related to the first driver, and that printer will no longer appear in your list. You can also install a new driver by clicking New Driver.
SEPARATOR PAGE	Click here to select a separator page. This page is printed before each print job to separate them. The seperator page is useful if many people work with the same printer. You can select from PCL.SEP (for printers using the PCL printer language), and SYSPRINT.SEP (for the PostScript language). Both of these files also automatically switch the printer to the appropriate language (if the printer supports that feature). There's also a file called PSCRIPT.SEP that switches the printer to PostScript mode but doesn't print a separator page.
PRINT PROCESSOR	This button provides advanced options for modifying how NT prints on a network, and you should change these options only if told to by the system administrator.
PRINT TEST PAGE	Click here to print a sample page and see information about the printer.

PORTS PROPERTIES

You saw these earlier in this chapter — see Figure 7-2.

SCHEDULING PROPERTIES

Figure 7-10 show the Scheduling properties, which Table 7-3 explains.

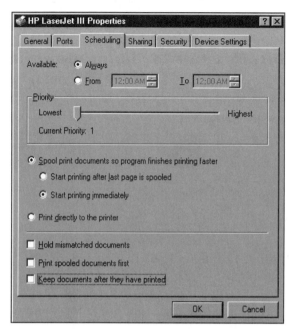

Figure 7-10 The Scheduling properties.

TABLE 7-3 The Scheduling Properties

Item	Purpose
AVAILABLE	You can make the printer available *Always* or specify *From* and *To* times. If you print to a printer that is not available, the document waits and is sent to the printer when it becomes available. This is a great way to schedule big print jobs for after-work hours.
PRIORITY	You can specify the default priority for your print jobs. Each print job is given the priority you specify but can be changed to print sooner or later than other documents, as you saw in Table 7-1.
SPOOL PRINT DOCUMENTS SO PROGRAM FINISHES PRINTING FASTER	Select this option to free up your program more quickly; it creates a print file before sending the data to the printer, which is quicker than printing directly to the printer. If you select this option, you can also specify whether the printer should *Start printing after last page is spooled* or *Start printing immediately*. The first option means that NT will wait until the program has finished printing to the print file and then begin sending data to the printer. The second option means that it will start sending data to the printer as soon as it receives it.

Item	Purpose
PRINT DIRECTLY TO THE PRINTER	This option means that no print spool file is created. Rather, the program prints directly to the printer. This is slightly faster, but it keeps your programs busy longer.
HOLD MISMATCHED DOCUMENTS	This option tells NT to look at a document's properties and, if the properties are set in such manner that they don't match the way the printer has been set up, hold the print job. Other documents in the print queue (the list of documents waiting to print) will continue printing.
PRINT SPOOLED DOCUMENTS FIRST	Select this option to make busy printers work more efficiently. NT starts printing a fully spooled document — one for which the source program has finished creating the print file — before it starts printing a partially spooled document, even if the partially spooled document began first, or if it has a higher priority.
KEEP DOCUMENTS AFTER THEY HAVE PRINTED	Select this option to hold documents in the print queue after they've finished printing. You can then reprint them if you want.

SHARING PROPERTIES

We saw these settings earlier in this chapter — see Figure 7-5.

SECURITY PROPERTIES

You can set permissions — blocking certain users from working with a printer, for example — or keep a record of who uses each printer. See Chapter 8 for more information.

DEVICE SETTINGS

Each printer has different device settings (see Figure 7-11). Click an entry in the list to see the options in the lower half of the dialog box. For more information about your options, see the printer's documentation.

Figure 7-11 The Device Settings properties.

The document properties

Each document can be set up with particular properties — the type of paper you want to print on, the orientation of the paper, the manner in which graphics are printed, and so on. You can modify these properties in two ways: You can modify the default properties — the properties used for every document printed on that printer unless you specify otherwise — or you can specify custom settings for a specific document. Use one of the following procedures for modifying document properties:

* Right-click a printer in the Printers folder and select Document Defaults .
* In the printer window, select File → Document Defaults .
* In a Print dialog box within the application from which you are printing (opened using File → Print), click Properties.
* In the printer window, right-click a particular print job and select Properties . (You'll be able to view the settings, but it's too late to modify some of them.)

The General settings (see Figure 7-12) appear only *after* your program has printed a document. These settings provide a way for you to modify *when* the document will print; as you've seen before, you can modify the priorities. You can also override the printer's schedule settings, which is a good way to print a single document later.

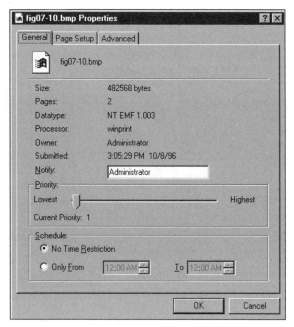

Figure 7-12 The General document settings.

The Page Setup settings are fairly simple. You can choose the Paper Size and Source (the paper tray), the number of copies, and the orientation.

The Advanced options are, well, more advanced. These options also duplicate some of the options shown in the Printer Properties Device Settings. In any case, they are generally dependent on the printer's capabilities, so you should check the printer's documentation if you want to make any adjustments — in most cases, there's no need.

Font Management

One of the really nice things that Windows brought to the world of personal computing was font management, which makes it easy to work with all sorts of different fonts. Whether or not the results are aesthetically pleasing, it's fun to be able to pick and choose fonts at will.

Viewing fonts

Windows NT has a few new features that make it easier still to work with fonts. In particular the ability to quickly view a font by double-clicking the font file is very handy. To view the list of fonts, open the fonts folder. This is the \Winnt\Fonts\ folder, but here's the quickest way to get to it:

1. Select Start → Settings → Control Panel.

2. Double-click the Fonts icon.

You can see in Figure 7-13 what the Fonts folder looks like. It's almost the same as a normal directory folder, but notice the column headings. They start with the Font Name heading, which is a nice convenience. In Windows 3.1, you had to figure out what the font was from the filename.

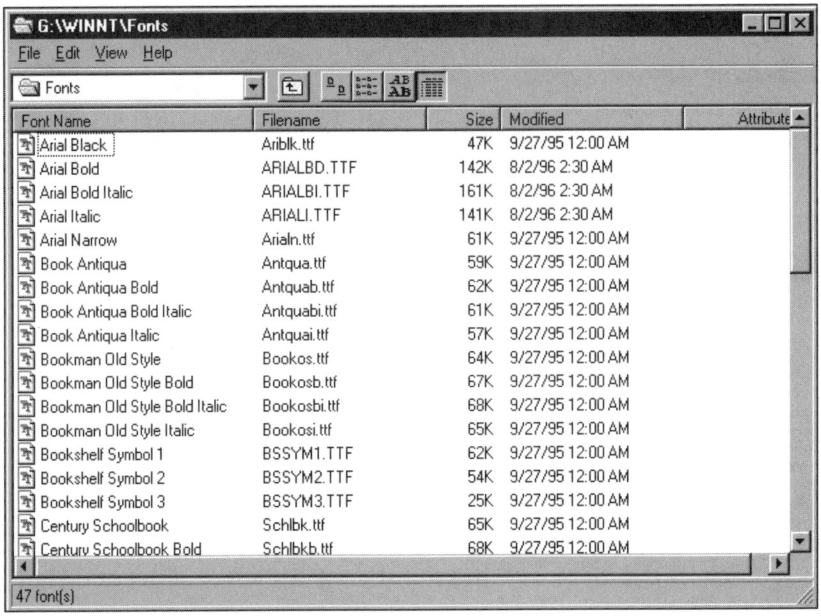

Figure 7-13 The Fonts folder lists all your fonts — and even shows you the font names.

Also, notice the Similarity toolbar button. This helps you search for a particular font by selecting one that is similar to it. Here's how this works:

1. Click the Similarity button.

2. Select a font from the *List fonts by similarity to* drop-down list box. For example, if you are looking for a sans serif headline font, you might select Arial. (*Sans serif* means without the little squiggly pieces — or serifs — at the end of the character strokes; Times New Roman is a serif font, for example, and Arial is a sans serif font.)

3. The Font window sorts the fonts, starting with the font you selected at the top, which it calls *Very similar* (a slight understatement), and working its way down through *Fairly similar* and *Not similar* to *No PANOSE information available*. (There's no font-description information available within the file, so NT has no idea what the font is.)

How can you tell for sure what the font looks like? It's easy — double-click the font (or right-click and select Open) and up pops a font-view window. You can then click the Done button to remove the window, or click Print if you want a hard copy.

These font windows don't show all the available characters in a particular font. If you want to see everything, use Character Map, which you'll look at later in this chapter.

Have you noticed that some fonts seem to be repeated over and over: Arial, Arial Black, Arial Bold, Arial Bold Italic, Arial Italic, and Arial Narrow, for example. The Arial, Arial Black, and Arial Narrow entries represent different — though very similar — fonts. But the Bold, Bold Italic, and Italic entries represent different versions of the Arial font — these are used when you select Bold, Italic, and so on in your word processor. To simplify the picture a little, you can select View→Hide Variations (Bold, Italic, etc.). The Fonts folder changes, and you're now left with Arial, Arial Black, and Arial Narrow.

TIP You can secure fonts, if you want, so that other users cannot delete them — and even so that other users can't use them. Right-click the font, select Properties, click the Security tab, and then click the Permissions button. See Chapter 8 for more information.

Installing new fonts

To install new fonts from the Fonts window, follow these steps:

1. Select 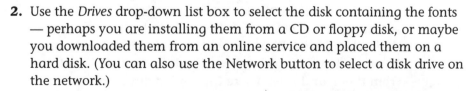 . The Add Fonts dialog box opens (see Figure 7-14).

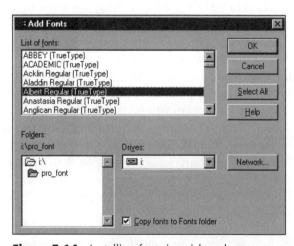

Figure 7-14 Installing fonts is quick and easy.

2. Use the *Drives* drop-down list box to select the disk containing the fonts — perhaps you are installing them from a CD or floppy disk, or maybe you downloaded them from an online service and placed them on a hard disk. (You can also use the Network button to select a disk drive on the network.)

3. Use the *Folders* list box to find the directory folder containing the fonts. Double-click the folder you want to open. When you open the folder, the Add Fonts dialog box will automatically recognize the fonts and display them in the *List of fonts* list box. (This may take a while; you'll see a little progress monitor — *Retrieving font names: xx%* — above the *Drives* drop-down list box.)

4. Select which fonts you want to install. You can click Select All if you want, or click each font while you hold down the Ctrl key. You can also hold down the mouse button and drag the mouse pointer across the fonts you want to select.

5. Notice the *Copy fonts to Fonts folder* check box. This box is checked, and, in most cases, you'll leave it that way. You would clear the box only if the fonts are already on one of your hard disks and will always be available. If you are installing from the network, a floppy disk, or a CD-ROM, you must copy the fonts into the Fonts folder.

6. Click OK and the fonts are installed. They now appear in your applications' Fonts menus and drop-down list boxes, so you can use them in your documents.

Removing fonts

It's easy to build up a huge collection of fonts — and quickly tire of digging through menus and drop-down list boxes looking for the ones you need. How, then, do you get rid of them? Simply delete them. In the Fonts window, select the fonts you want to remove, and press Delete or select File→Delete.

There's a problem with this method, however — what if you want to use the font later? Will you still have the original disk from which you installed the file? Or will the font still be where you found it on the network, online service, or Internet? You can store the fonts somewhere, if you want.

To solve this problem, simply create a directory folder to hold the fonts. You can't make it a subfolder of the \Winnt\Fonts\ directory; you'll have to put it somewhere else. Then move the fonts into the new folder — drag and drop them or Cut and Paste them. Then, when you want to use the fonts again, you can move them back into the Fonts folder. Any font inside the folder is an active font, usable in your programs.

TIP Do you have Windows 95 on your computer and want to install the fonts from that operating system into NT? The Add Fonts dialog box hides the Windows 95 and Windows NT fonts directories, so you can't see the contents of the \Windows\Fonts\ directory in the Add Fonts dialog box. So make a copy of the \Windows\Fonts\ directory (call it \!Fonts\, for example) on the Windows 95 disk, install the fonts into NT from there, and then delete the copied directory.

It's a good idea not to remove any of the original Windows NT fonts. Some of these are needed for displaying text in dialog boxes and windows. Only remove fonts that you've installed yourself.

Picking Special Characters

The font view boxes you looked at don't show you all the characters that are available within a particular font. These boxes are intended to give you an idea of the overall appearance of a font. But many fonts have special characters hidden away within them — characters used in languages other than English, such as accented characters, mathematical symbols, Greek letters, and so on. For example, you may have used the Times New Roman TrueType font, one of the basic sets of fonts provided by NT. And you may think this font has only letters, numbers, and punctuation. But look at Figure 7-15, and you'll see that Times New Roman has much more, if you know how to get to it all.

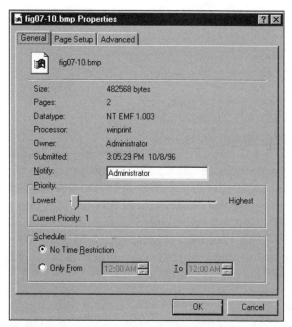

Figure 7-15 Times New Roman — and most other fonts — contain hidden characters.

These characters can be very handy. They allow you to produce professional-looking documents. Instead of using (c) to indicate that a document is copyright, for example, you can use ©. Instead of typing foreign names without all the required accents — and assuming that people won't mind too much — you can use all the correct accents. Some programs come with special utilities that help you pick the correct symbol already built-in. For example, in Word for Windows you can select Insert→Symbol to see one of these utilities. Most programs don't have such a system, but NT itself does. You can use Character Map to select a symbol you want to work with, copy it to the Clipboard, and then paste it into your document.

To open Character Map, select Start→Programs→Accessories→Character Map (see Figure 7-16).

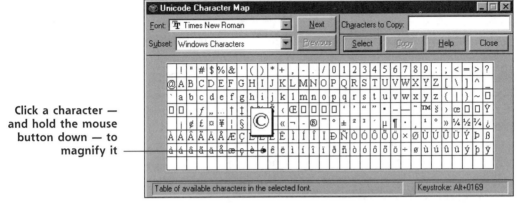

Click a character — and hold the mouse button down — to magnify it

Figure 7-16 Select the symbol you want and copy it to the Clipboard.

To use the Character Map dialog box, follow these steps:

1. Select the font you want to use from the *Font* drop-down list box.

   NOTE There's a *Subset* drop-down list. You can select from different groups of characters within a font set. For example, in Figure 7-15 you saw the main Times New Roman character set. But it has other character sets hidden away, too. Note, however, that only programs that have *Unicode* support are able to use the characters in any but the first subset. Right now, most programs don't have Unicode support, but some do. Windows NT Notepad does, but Windows NT WordPad doesn't. (Unicode is a new system for displaying and printing character sets from different languages.)

2. Use the Next and Previous buttons to quickly move through the Subset options and see what's available. When you find a character you want to use, double-click it, or click once and click Select. The character is placed into the *Characters to Copy* text box. You can continue selecting more characters — each is added to the box.

3. Click Copy. The characters are placed in the Clipboard.

4. Switch to the program in which you want to use the characters.

5. Paste the characters into your document (generally using Ctrl+V or Edit → Paste).

TIP Many fonts have useful symbols, such as the © or ® symbols. But you also have a Symbol font that contains hearts, arrows, Greek characters, and more. And Wingdings has a large selection of useful little characters, too, such as little pictures of phones, mailboxes, floppy disks, numbers in circles, and so on.

BONUS

Creating Print Files

Did you know that you don't have to send a print job to a printer? You can send it to a file, and then give the file to someone else to print for you. For example, if you want to print something on an expensive printer, a Linotronic printer used for book or magazine printing, for example, you can use a Linotronic driver to print to a file, and then send the file to the company department or service bureau that owns the printer. They can print the file directly to their printer.

Or perhaps you are working on a document on your laptop while on the road. You can print to a file and e-mail it to the home office, where someone can print the file.

Printing to a print file is easy. You simply select the FILE "port" while installing the printer. Or carry out the following procedure later to print a single print file:

1. In the Printers folder, right-click the printer and choose **Properties**.
2. Click the Ports tab.
3. Select the FILE check box.
4. Click OK.
5. In your application, select the print command as normal. (The dialog box you'll see depends on the program you are working with. You may see a simple box that enables you to enter a name and nothing more, or you may see a box that enables you to also select a directory to place the print file in.)

6. Type a filename — such as **print1.prn**. It can be anything you want, really. You should generally add .PRN — a typical print-file extension — because the file extension may not be added for you, depending on the program you are working with. (Adding .PRN is not essential, but it helps you identify print files.)

7. Click OK and the document is printed to the file.

You end up with a computer file, probably in the same directory as the file from which you are printing — depending on the program, you may or may not get the chance to specify where to place the file. (If you have trouble finding it, use the Find utility; see Chapter 6.) The next challenge is actually printing the thing.

TIP You can also print to a file using the *Print to File* check box that appears in the Print dialog boxes of most applications.

For example, you're sending the file to someone at the home office, and you want it printed. You'll probably have to explain how to do it. Unfortunately, there is no simple point and click way to print this file. (Windows has been around for a decade, and still this feature isn't built in; don't ask me why!) Here's how to print a print file:

1. Select `Start` → `Programs` → `Command Prompt` to reach the Command Prompt window. This may be considered the MS-DOS window, although, strictly speaking, it's really not DOS. It's a special Windows NT command line mode that incorporates many commands from the old DOS operating system, with others of its own.

2. Change to the disk drive containing the print file. For example, if the file is held on the E drive, type **e:** and press Enter.

3. Change to the directory holding the file by typing **cd** followed by the path and pressing Enter. For example, if the file is held in the E:\DATA\WPROCESSING\ directory, type **cd \data\wprocessing** and press Enter.

4. Type **copy** *filename* **lpty** and press Enter, where *filename* is the name of the print file, and *lpty* is the printer port that the printer is connected to. For example, to print the file PRINT1.PRN to the printer connected to LPT1, type **copy print1.prn lpt1 /b** and press Enter (see Figure 7-17).

5. If you are printing a PostScript print file — a file created using a PostScript print driver — the command is slightly different. Simply omit the **/b** bit at the end.

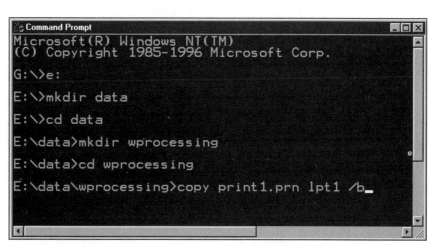

Figure 7-17 To print a print file, use the Command Prompt.

This system is rather clunky, I know, but the one nice thing about it is that it's consistent — the procedure is the same (except for Step 1 — getting to the command line is slightly different) in Windows 95, Windows 3.1, earlier versions of Windows, and in DOS. (The only difference is the **/b** piece, which is not really required in Windows NT, but generally is in other versions of Windows and in DOS.) This means that you can print a file on NT and send it to a colleague who's using, say, Windows 95, and your colleague can print it out.

TIP Here's a handy use for printing to a file — you can send files to people, and they can print the documents, even if they don't own the program that created the documents.

Fonts Come In Different Forms

There are different types of fonts. The most common form these days is TrueType. Windows NT has been optimized to work with these fonts, and, in fact, using TrueType fonts is generally less trouble than working with other forms of fonts. For example, fonts designed for specific printers often don't display well on your screen. TrueType fonts were designed to display the same way that they will print, and TrueType fonts will print on any printer that works with Windows NT.

If you look at the filenames in the Fonts folder, you'll see that many use the .TTF extension — these are the TrueType fonts. Others use the .FON extension, which are a variety of different types of fonts used for such purposes as displaying text in dialog boxes, and old-style vector fonts that have been used by Windows for years.

You can identify TrueType fonts in your applications by looking for the TrueType symbol. As you can see in Figure 7-18, a drop-down list box normally shows which fonts are TrueType and which are not.

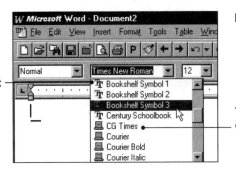

Figure 7-18 Look for T to identify the TrueType fonts. This drop-down list box is from WordPad.

This icon represents a TrueType font

This is a printer font — a font designed for a particular printer

However, just because these fonts are available doesn't mean you should use them in your documents. They often won't print well. You can choose, if you want, to allow only TrueType fonts to be displayed in the Font menus and drop-down list boxes in your programs. Here's how:

1. In the Fonts folder, select View → Options.
2. In the Options dialog box, click the TrueType Fonts tab.
3. Click the *Show only TrueType fonts in the programs on my computer* check box.

Instant Character Map

If you use Character Map often, you'll find that it's irritating to get it each time you need it. You may want to load it automatically each time you load NT. To do so, you need to add it to the Startup folder.

To add Character Map to your Startup folder, follow these steps:

1. Right-click the Start button and select Explore.
2. In Windows NT Explorer, work your way down the folder tree to \Start Menu\Programs\Accessories\.
3. Find Character Map in the right pane.
4. Hold down the Ctrl key and drag Character Map over to the left pane, dropping it into the Startup folder.

The next time you open NT, Character Map will open automatically. You might also consider creating a desktop shortcut, and then adding a keyboard shortcut. Follow these steps:

1. Right-click the shortcut icon and select Properties.

2. Click the Shortcut tab.

3. Click inside the Shortcut Key text box.

4. Press a single key. This is the key you'll use, in combination with Ctrl+Alt, to start Character Map. For example, if you press the = key, you'll use Ctrl+Alt+= to start Character Map. Make sure you pick a combination that isn't already used in your applications, or it *won't* start Character Map.

5. Click OK.

Summary

Now that printing and fonts are out of the way, you've learned some of the most basic information required to work on your applications — you can now get into NT, move around within it, open your programs, and actually produce printed work. From now on, you'll be looking at more advanced information, knowledge you may not need every day, but knowledge that you really need to feel fully at home working in Windows NT.

In the next chapter, you'll look at one of the reasons why so many companies are installing Windows NT: the security features. NT enables you to protect almost everything — from files to fonts. You'll begin learning about how this is done by learning how to create user accounts and how to define what each user may do.

CHAPTER EIGHT

PROTECTING YOUR WORK — PROFILES AND SECURITY

IN THIS CHAPTER YOU LEARN THESE SKILLS

CREATING A USER ACCOUNT   PAGE 142

ALL ABOUT GROUPS   PAGE 144

ASSIGNING A USER TO A GROUP   PAGE 148

DETERMINING OVERALL ACCOUNT POLICIES   PAGE 148

WHAT CAN USERS DO?   PAGE 150

BIG BROTHER'S WATCHING! HOW TO AUDIT   PAGE 154

Windows NT is an extremely secure system. As you'll learn in this chapter, NT provides ways to protect virtually any software component. You can protect files, folders, the Start menu, printers, the desktop — even fonts. By *protect* I mean restrict the use of an item. You can specify exactly who can use an item and what they can do to it — modify it, use it, run it, change the security permissions, and so on.

But how does NT know who is who? At the base of this sophisticated security system lies the user *profiles*. Different accounts are set up for each user, and each account has a profile — a set of rules by which the user's actions are controlled. As you've already seen, a user is identified by logging into the computer. Once logged in, NT assumes that the user is the account owner (that is, that the user has not stolen a password and entered NT illicitly) and provides the type of access allowed for that user.

To begin, you'll learn about user accounts and profiles — what they are and how to create them.

Creating a User Account

I'm going to start by explaining how to create a user account and set up that account's profile. But many readers won't be able to do this. Why? Because they don't have the correct *privileges* or *permissions*. In other words, NT won't allow them to make changes to accounts, because it's been told that they don't have the right to do so.

Follow along as far as you can, though, and then read further to get an idea of how all this links together.

To set up a new User Account, follow these steps:

1. Select Start → Programs → Administrative Tools (Common) → User Manager . You'll see the window shown in Figure 8-1.

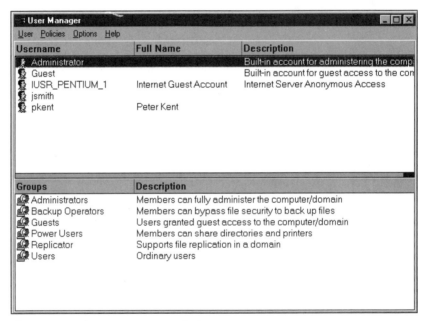

Figure 8-1 The User Manager window.

2. Select User → New User to open the New User dialog box (see Figure 8-2).

3. Type a username. This is the name by which the user is identified when logging into NT.

4. Enter a full name, if you want. This is the user's real name. You may want to create accounts that are shared by several users — if so, you can enter each user's name here.

5. Type a description of the user, if you want. This might be something like *Sales Manager* or, if this account is being used by several people, the name of the department in which those people work.

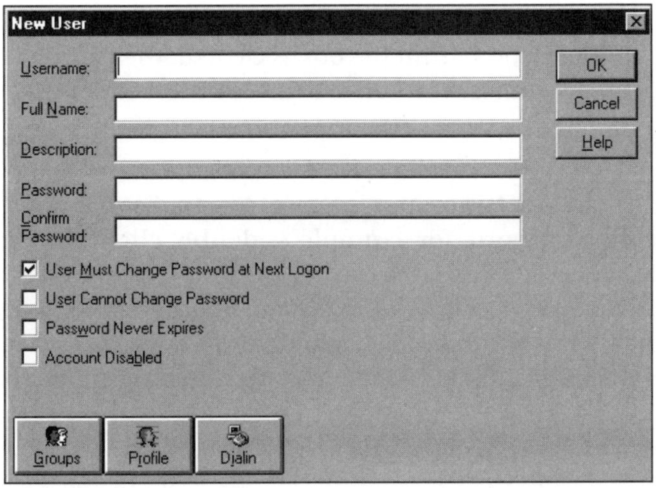

Figure 8-2 The New User dialog box.

6. Type the password that the user or users will need to enter when logging in. You won't see what you type — each character is replaced by an asterisk so that that nobody can peer over your shoulder and steal the password.

7. Because you can't see what you type, you must type the password again in the *Confirm Password* box to make sure you typed what you thought you typed.

8. If you want the user to pick a personal password — one that's easier to remember, for example — check the *User Must Change Password at Next Logon* check box. The user won't be able to enter NT without picking a new password.

TIP Make sure users pick sensible passwords — not kids' names, social security numbers, favorite literary characters, and so on. Often, combining two words with numbers or punctuation characters is a good way to create a password: grunge^mountain or blah%^7oops.

9. If you don't want to allow the user to change the password, check the *User Cannot Change Password* check box. If you are setting up an account that's shared by several users, you'll probably want to use this option (and not use the previous option).

10. As you'll see later (see "Determining Overall Account Policies"), you can make NT periodically ask users for a new password. If you check the *Password Never Expires* check box, however, that option is overridden for this account, and NT will never ask for a new password. Again, this is a good idea for shared accounts.

11. If you are not ready to activate this account, you can check the *Account Disabled* check box. Until the box is cleared, the account cannot be accessed. Of course, you can use this later to temporarily disable an account.

TIP To modify these settings at a later date — to disable an account or change the password, for example — double-click the account name in User Manager, or click once and select User→Properties. You'll find an extra check box: *Account Locked Out*. This check box is used by NT to show that it has disabled the account. You'll see later (see "Determining Overall Account Policies") how and why NT might lock out an account.

12. Click OK and you've created an account.

I haven't looked at the Groups, Profile, and Dialin buttons yet, but I cover these later in this chapter (see "Assigning a User to a Group" and the bonus).

TIP Make sure that you only create usernames that are compatible with the networking system you are connected to.

All About Groups

You've created a new account, but what is the person using the account allowed to do? To a great extent, a user's rights are determined by the group membership. All users are members of at least one group. The following groups are available (you can create more):

✷ **Everyone.** Every user is a member of this group. Being a member of this group means that "these are the rights you have if you aren't a member of any other group."

 NOTE Because everyone is a member of this group and can't be removed (except by having the account locked or disabled, of course), the group name doesn't appear in the list of groups at the bottom of the User Manager window.

✷ **Users.** Ordinary users with, initially, the same rights as Everyone — in other words, there's no difference between someone who is a member of only the Everyone group and someone who is also a member of the Users group. However, you can give the Users group more rights (see "What Can Users Do," later in this chapter).

✷ **Guests.** The Guests group allows you to provide access to occasional users, with restricted rights. Initially, the Guests group has the same rights as Everyone and Users, but you may want to make certain directory folders off limits to guests, for example.

* **Backup Operators.** This group is set up to allow members of the group to back up files and directories (see Chapter 12), even if the user has no right to use those files and directories. In other words, several users may have their own private directories on the hard disk, but a special Backup Operators account can back up all the data from those directories or restore data from backups to those directories.

* **Administrator.** The Administrator can do anything. In addition to all the rights given to other groups, the Administrator can load and unload device drivers (special programs used to work with hardware connected to the computer), manage the auditing system (see "Big Brother's Watching! How to Audit," later in this chapter), and take over system resources from other users. The Administrator can also create, modify, and remove any user account or group, something that other users cannot do.

There are also some specialized groups, only one of which you'll see listed in the Owner Manager window:

* **Power Users.** These users have many of the rights of an Administrator. They have all the rights of the Everyone, Users, and Guests groups, but in addition they can change the system time and shut down the computer from another computer on the network. They don't have the same rights as the Backup Operators, however.

* **Replicator.** This is an account used by Windows NT Server for *directory replication*, the automatic copying of data between computers within a domain.

* **Interactive.** Any user using the computer locally.

* **Network.** Any user using the computer over the network.

* **Creator Owner.** The user who created or owns a resource — a directory folder, file, printer, document sent to a printer, and so on.

* **System.** The operating system itself.

You'll see these groups later, when determining which groups have which rights (see "What Can Users Do?", later in this chapter), and when assigning access to certain resources. You can't assign users to these groups, however. The only groups to which you can assign users are the Administrators, Power Users, Backup Operators, Guests, and Users groups — and any groups that you create. And don't forget that *every user* is a member of the Everyone group!

What's the point?

All this may sound a little confusing right now, but don't worry; it will make sense when you see how these groups are used when assigning access to resources. What NT provides is a flexible way to categorize users. You can then allow certain categories of users to carry out certain functions on the computer. For example:

- You can allow certain groups access to certain data files — the Documentation department can have access to one set of folders and files, the Accounting department access to another set, and so on.
- In order to limit access to some of this information, you have to limit the ability to back up data (otherwise, someone could steal it by simply backing it up and taking it away). So, you can provide one set of users the right to back up data.
- You may want to have more than one Administrator — what happens when the Administrator is sick, on vacation, or gets hit by a bus, after all?
- You may allow network users access to your printers but not to the data on the hard disk.
- Guests may be allowed to open a word processor and work in a folder set aside for guests, but not allowed access to the data owned by the regular users.

You can do a lot with this system. A group might contain a single user or several users. And, as you'll see later, the group system is actually a convenience. You don't have to assign a user to a group — rather, you can provide an individual user with specific rights.

Creating a new group

To create a new group, follow this procedure:

1. Click each user, in the top part of User Manager, that you want to be a member of the new group.
2. Select User → New Local Group . The New Local Group dialog box opens.
3. Provide a group name — Accounting, Documentation, Sales, or whatever — in the Group Name box.
4. If you want, you can include a more detailed description of the group.
5. The users you selected are displayed in the *Members* list box. If you want to see their full names, not just their user names, click Show Full Names.
6. If you want to remove a member, click the member's name and click Remove.
7. To add more members to the group, click Add. The Add Users and Groups dialog box opens (see Figure 8-3).

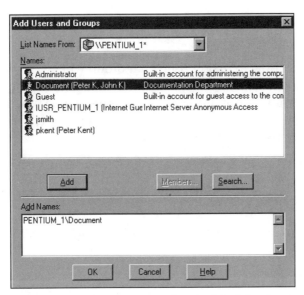

Figure 8-3 Select group members in this dialog box.

8. If you want to add members from another computer in your network domain, select that computer from the *List Names From* drop-down list box.

9. In the *Names* list, double-click each name you want to add, or click once and then click the Add button. The names are added to the bottom text box (*Add Names*).

10. If you want to search for someone in your network domain, and in all domains trusted by the local domain, click Search.

11. When you have all the names you want, click OK.

12. Click OK in the New Local Group dialog box, and you're finished.

13. To modify your settings later, double-click the group name, or click once and select User → Properties .

TIP As you've seen, you can simply create a single account and give several users the account name and password. Why bother creating a new group and assigning individual accounts to the group, then? It's much more secure for all users to have their own private password. And you may want to assign special privileges to individuals within the group, or even assign one user to two or more groups.

PROTECTING YOUR WORK — PROFILES AND SECURITY

Assigning a User to a Group

I just showed you how to assign users to a group when you create the group. Of course, you can also assign new users to an existing group. In Figure 8-2, you saw the Groups button in the User Properties dialog box. You can use this button when creating a new user account or to modify a user account later (double-click the user in the top list). Here's how:

1. Click the Groups button. You'll see the Group Memberships dialog box.

2. Double-click a group name in the *Not member of* list to move that name across to the *Member of* list.

3. You can also select several entries in the *Not member of* list at once, and then click Add.

4. Do the opposite to remove a user from a group — double-click the group in the *Member of* list, or click once and then click Remove.

5. When you finish, click OK.

Determining Overall Account Policies

To determine how Windows NT should manage passwords and how it handles incorrect logon procedures, select Policies→Account in User Manager. The dialog box in Figure 8-4 opens.
These are the options available in this dialog box:

* **Maximum Password Age.** You can select *Password Never Expires*, in which case users can keep the same passwords forever. Or you can select *Expires In* and enter a number of days, in which case users will be forced to pick a new password.

* **Minimum Password Age.** *Allow Changes Immediately* means that users can change passwords whenever they want. *Allow Changes In* means that users can change the password only after the specified number of days.

* **Minimum Password Length.** You can force users to avoid simple passwords by specifying a minimum length, from 1 to 14 characters — enter the number into the *At Least Characters* box. If you select *Permit Blank Password*, users can clear their passwords and log on by typing their account names and pressing Enter.

* **Password Uniqueness.** You can stop a user from reusing passwords, at least for a while. Select *Remember* and then enter the number of passwords that will be stored. The user won't be able to pick a password on this list. This is normally combined with *the Minimum Password Age* setting to stop users from simply changing their passwords several times to force NT to allow them to return to their original passwords.

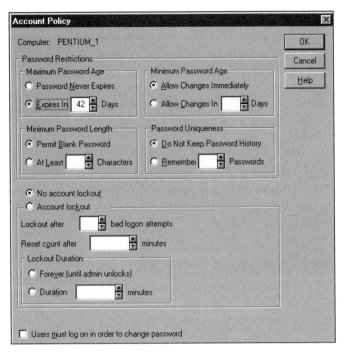

Figure 8-4 The Account Policy dialog box.

* **No account lockout.** If you choose this option button, NT never locks out accounts.

* **Account lockout.** Select this option button if you want NT to lock out accounts for which failed logon attempts — possibly illicit logon attempts — have been made.

* **Lockout after.** Enter the number of bad logon attempts that must be made before NT locks out the account. For example, if you enter 5, the fifth time someone enters an invalid password for an account, the account is locked. This user won't be allowed more attempts.

* **Reset count after.** You can let a user try again later after the number of minutes entered here. (However, this has no effect if the Lockout Duration: Forever option button is selected.)

* **Lockout Duration.** You can select Forever — NT won't reset the account; the Administrator will have to do so (by opening the account's User Properties dialog box and clearing the Account Locked Out check box). Or you can specify a time, after which the account will be unlocked automatically.

* **Users must log on in order to change password.** If this check box is checked, a user can log on to change a password after it's expired. If this button is not checked, as soon as the password has expired the user is locked out and has to inform the Administrator.

TIP When making these settings, consider whether the Administrator will always be available. If so, you can have a strict lockout policy. If not, you may want to be more flexible.

What Can Users Do?

How can you change what a group of users is allowed to do? Two ways: you can modify the User Rights in User Manager, and you can modify permissions linked to specific resources — printers, files, folders, fonts, and so on — throughout NT.

Assigning rights to a group or user

To modify what a user, or the members of a group, is allowed to do, follow this procedure:

1. In User Manager, select   Policies → User Rights . The dialog box in Figure 8-5 opens.

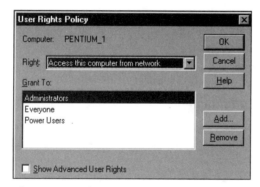

Figure 8-5   The User Rights Policy dialog box.

2. In the *Right* drop-down list box, select the right that you want to assign to a group or user.

3. In the *Grant To* box, you'll see a list of the groups and, perhaps, users who have been assigned the selected right. If you want to assign the right to someone else, click Add to see the box in Figure 8-6.

4. Double-click the groups you want to add, or click once and then click Add.

5. If you want to see individual users, click Show Users.

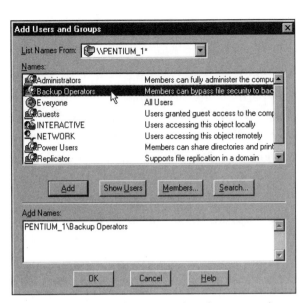

Figure 8-6 Here's where you select the users and groups.

6. If you want to see individual users who are members of a particular group, click the group and then click Members. You'll see a dialog box from which you can select specific members.

7. To find groups and users elsewhere on the network, click Search.

8. When you've added all the groups and members you want to the *Add Names* text box, click OK.

TIP Another quick way to give a user particular rights is to add the user to the group that has those rights.

Restricting access to resources

The other main way to define a user's rights is by specifying which system resources — disks, folders, files, Briefcases, fonts, and printers — the user can work with and what, if anything, he can do.

TIP Whether you'll be able to carry out the following procedures depends on whether the Administrator has allowed you to do so.

The procedure is similar regardless of what item you are working with. As an example, I'll look at how to limit access to a directory folder. Follow these steps:

1. In Windows NT Explorer, right-click the folder for which you want to set permissions, and select .

2. Click the Security tab.

3. Click the Permissions button.

4. In the Directory Permissions dialog box, you'll see two check boxes (if you are setting permissions for a folder or disk drive). Select *Replace Permissions on Subdirectories* to make your changes to all subdirectories, as well as to the selected one.

5. *Replace Permissions on Existing Files* is already checked. This means that the permissions will apply to the files within the folder, not only to the folder itself. Clear this box if you want to work only on the folder.

6. Everyone already appears in the list box. If you plan to restrict access to this folder to a limited number of users, click Everyone and then click Remove.

7. Click Add to add groups and users who will be able to work with this folder. You've already seen the Add Users and Groups dialog box (refer to Figure 8-3). The only difference is that there's a *Type of Access* drop-down list box at the bottom of this one that allows you to specify the access type while adding the people. Don't worry about this for now. I'll explain this list box in a moment.

8. When you've found all the users for whom you want to provide access to the folder, click OK.

9. In the Directory Permissions box, click one of the entries in the list box.

10. In the *Type of Access* drop-down list box, select the type of access the user or group will be allowed. (See Table 8-1 for information about the options you can select.) Repeat for each user and group.

11. If you want to set specific permissions for the folder or file, select Special Directory Access or Special File Access from the *Type of Access* drop-down list box. (The different permissions are explained in Table 8-1.)

12. Click OK.

Notice in the Directory Permissions dialog box that a Type of Access comprises a name (such as Add & Read), followed by two sets of parentheses. The information in the parentheses indicates what the user will be able to do to the directory and what the user will be able to do to the files within the directory. (If you are setting up a printer, for example, you won't have these two sets). The information within the parentheses indicates the specific permissions. Table 8-1 explains what these permissions are.

TABLE 8-1 The Folder and Directory Permissions

Type	Meaning
FULL CONTROL (ALL)	The user can do anything to the folder or files.
CHANGE PERMISSIONS (P)	The user can modify the permissions settings.
DELETE (D)	The user can delete the folder or files.
EXECUTE (X)	The user can execute a program file, read properties, view subfolders, and so on.
NONE	The user can't do *anything*, even read the folder of file properties.
NOT SPECIFIED	This is used to remove permissions from files within the folder. When you create files within the folder, no permissions will be added to them for that user.
READ (R)	The user can view the contents of the folder or files and the properties.
TAKE OWNERSHIP (O)	The user can take ownership of the folder or files (I'll cover this in the next section).
WRITE (W)	The user can modify the folder or files.

Who owns this, anyway?

If a user has Full (All) or Ownership (O) permissions, he can take ownership of a resource. After the user has ownership, he can deny access to all other users — except the Administrator or those in the Administrator group.

Taking ownership of a resource is easy:

1. Right-click the item's icon (such as the folder, file, or printer), and select `Properties`.

2. Click the Security tab.

3. Click the Ownership button.

4. In the Owner box, click Take Ownership.

5. You may also see a message box that asks if you also want to take ownership of all subfolders and files. If you do, click Yes.

Big Brother's Watching! How to Audit

NT has a nifty little tool that may have you spying on other users — the audit tool. It just makes it too easy. (Of course, there are many legitimate reasons to watch what's going on!) There are two main audit levels. You can tell NT to audit particular system events — logging on and logging off, using files, system shutdown, and so on — which are tracked regardless of *who* is causing the system event. You can also tell NT to keep an eye on a particular resource — a single file, a directory, a printer — and specify *who* you want to keep watch on.

TIP Only users with Administrator privileges can turn on the auditing system. Once turned on, other users — depending on their access to specific resources — can audit files, folders, printers, and fonts.

System auditing

To set up system auditing, select Policies→Audit in User Manager. The Audit Policy box opens.

Click the Audit These Events option button, and then select the events you want to watch. In each case, you can tell NT to keep track of processes that finished in success or failure. For example, you may want to track failed logon attempts to find out when someone's trying to break into the computer.

You can watch the following events:

* **Logon and Logoff.** Tracks when users log on or off the system or connect through the network.
* **File and Object Access.** Someone used a folder, file, or printer that has been set up for auditing.
* **Use of User Rights.** A user exercised a special right assigned to him, a right other than the ones assigned to Everyone (logging on and off, for example). If a Backup Operator made a backup, for example, that would be logged.
* **User and Group Management.** A user created, modified, deleted, or disabled a user account, user group, or password.
* **Security Policy Changes.** A user modified user rights or audit policies.
* **Restart, Shutdown, and System.** A user restarted or shut down the system, or some kind of system security event occurred.
* **Process Tracking.** Various program events occurred. These would generally not be of interest to the average user but may be used by a programmer checking program operation.

Watching folders, files, printers, and fonts

You can use the audit system to track the user of particular folders (including the Briefcase), files, printers, and fonts.

 TIP You can audit the use of folders and files only if they are stored on NTFS — NT File System — drives. If some of your hard drives are formatted using FAT, you won't be able to audit them.

To audit your folders and files, follow these steps:

1. In Windows NT Explorer or a folder window, right-click a disk-drive, folder (or Briefcase), file, printer, or font icon and select Properties.

2. Click the Security tab.

3. Click the Auditing button to see the Auditing dialog box (see Figure 8-7).

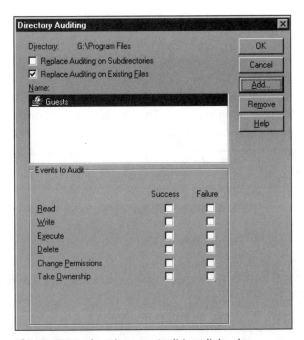

Figure 8-7 The Directory Auditing dialog box.

4. Until you specify *who* you want to watch, this box is mostly disabled. Click the Add button to open a dialog box similar to the one you saw in Figure 8-8. Use this dialog box, as described earlier, to add users and groups.

TIP There's a bug at work here. Although you can select *Everyone* to audit all use of an item, NT won't keep that setting. Instead, you have to select Users. If you removed any individual user from the Users group, you must add that user, too.

5. Click OK and the user's or group's name is placed into the Auditing dialog box.

6. You can now click the following check boxes to determine which events you want to watch:

   Read. The item was used — a document file opened, for example.

   Write. The item was modified — a document file was edited and saved, for example.

   Execute. A program file was run or a file's information was displayed.

   Delete. The item was deleted.

   Change Permissions. Permissions were changed for the item.

   Take Ownership. A user took ownership of the item.

8. If you are setting audit policies for a folder or disk drive, you can select *Replace Auditing on Subdirectories*. This makes your changes to all subdirectories as well as to the selected one.

9. *Replace Auditing on Existing Files* is already checked. This means that the audit policies will apply to the files within the folder, not just the folder itself. Clear it if you only want to audit the folder.

10. Click OK.

TIP In order to audit files and folders, you must turn on *Audit These Events* in the Audit Policy dialog box, and you must select the appropriate check box next to File and Object Access.

By the way, auditing policies affect not only existing files but also new ones created within a folder that is being audited (assuming the files within the folder are also being audited — that the *Replace Auditing on Existing Files* check box is checked). And remember that the higher up the directory "tree" you go, the easier it is to audit a large "area." You can set an audit for an entire disk drive — and all the files and folders within that drive — at once, for example.

Viewing the audit trail

In order to see the results of your audit, you must open Event Viewer. Here's what you need to do:

1. Select Start → Programs → Administrative Tools (Common) . The Event Viewer opens.

2. Select Log → Security to view the Security log. This is where your audit information is stored (see Figure 8-8).

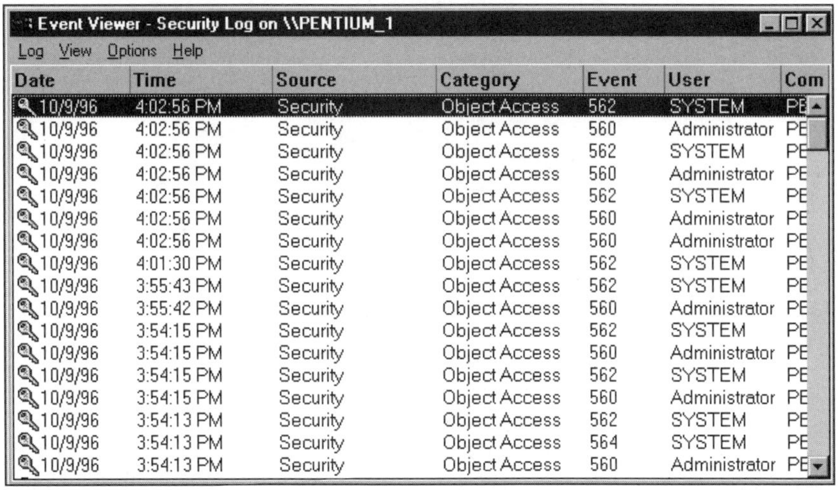

Figure 8-8 The Security Log, shown in the Event Viewer.

3. Double-click an entry to open the Event Detail dialog box.

4. This dialog box often contains information that's pretty hard to decipher. However, you will usually find that there are two related events, one with what appears to be indecipherable nonsense, and the other with information that's closer to real English. Click Next (or Previous) to see the associated entry.

5. Figure 8-9 shows an example of an audit event. You can see from the Category entry, near the top of the box, that an object has been accessed. And you can see lower down that the object is the G:\COLLWIN\readme.txt file. You can also see, from the User entry, that it was the Administrator who used the file.

The log is limited, of course. If you want to make sure that the information you are logging is stored long enough, select Log→Log Settings, and the Event Log Settings dialog box opens.

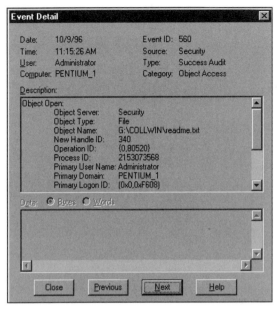

Figure 8-9 The Event Detail dialog box shows information about the event.

Here's how to set up this box:

* **Maximum Log Size.** The more events that you are auditing, the larger the file you'll need. (The security log is stored in a file called \Winnt\system32\config\SecEvent.Evt — you can check the file size and adjust accordingly.)

* **Overwrite Events as Needed.** This ensures that all events are added to the log — but if the log file is full, the oldest events are removed to make room.

* **Overwrite Events Older Than.** This ensures that the events in the log stay there the specified number of days, but if the log fills up, new events can't be added.

* **Do Not Overwrite Events (Clear Logs Manually).** This ensures that the log is not cleared automatically, but if the log fills up, new events can't be added. (You can clear the log manually using Log → Log Settings.

BONUS

Work on Several Users at Once

You can modify settings for several users at a time, if you want. In User Manager, select the users, and then select User→Properties. You'll see a dialog box like that shown in Figure 8-10. As you can see, the users appear in a list box at the top. Make your changes, click OK, and the changes are applied to all the users. Be warned, however, that this can get a little confusing, especially when assigning users to groups.

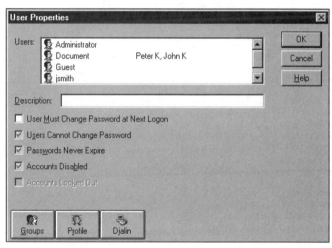

Figure 8-10 If you select several users at once, the dialog box looks a little different.

Copying Profiles and Accounts

You can copy user profiles — to another networked computer, for example, or for a new user. The new profile will contain all the Start menu and desktop settings. Here's how to do this:

1. Select Start → Settings → Control Panel . The Control Panel opens.

2. Double-click the System icon.

3. Click the User Profiles tab. You'll see the information shown in Figure 8-11.

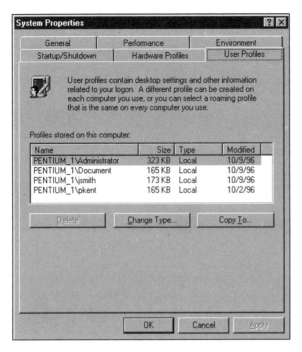

Figure 8-11 The User Profiles information in the System Properties dialog box.

4. Click Copy To.

5. Specify where you want to place the profile. If necessary, click Browse to find the directory or computer where you want to place the new profile.

6. If you are copying the profile so that another user may use it, click the Change button, and pick the user.

7. Click OK to close the Copy To dialog box, and then close the System Properties box.

TIP Note that you can also delete profiles here and change a profile to a *roaming* profile — see the next section for more information.

You can also copy an account. In the User Manager window, select an account, and then select User→Copy. However, this doesn't copy the profile. It simply creates a new account using the same account settings — the same group memberships and password settings, for example. A brand new profile — Start menu and desktop — is created for the new account.

Setting up the User's Environment

You can set up something called the User Environment Profile. This is information related to what happens when the user logs in. It's advanced stuff, things that most users will never bother with. If you want to see what this is all about, however, click the Profile button in the User Properties dialog box. The User Environment Profile dialog box opens.

These are the settings that can be made in the dialog box:

* **User Profile Path.** This allows you to set up a *roaming* profile. If you use several networked computers, you can set up a single profile — Start menu, desktop, and so on — and use that profile from whichever computer you happen to logon from. Enter the network path to the profile you want to use.
* **Logon Script Name.** You can specify a program or batch file to run when you log on.
* **Home Directory Local Path.** You can set up a home directory, one that your applications will automatically use when opening and saving files.
* **Home Directory Connect.** You can use a directory on another networked computer as the home directory. Select a disk drive letter to be used on your computer to identify the directory, and then enter the network name of the directory (see Chapter 14 for more information about networking).

Setting up Dialin Access

If a user is going to use Dialin Access to use the computer (see Chapter 16), you can configure the way in which that will work. Follow these steps:

1. Click the Dialin button in the User Properties dialog box.
2. Check the *Grant dialin permission to user* check box.
3. You can get the computer to call the user; the user dials in, logs on, hangs up, and the computer then dials back and reconnects. (To save the user long distance calls, for example.) If you don't want the user to work with this feature, leave *No Call Back* selected.
4. To enable the user to tell the computer which number to dial back — the computer will prompt for the number — select *Set By Caller*.
5. To make the computer automatically dial a preset number, select *Preset To* and enter the telephone number.
6. Click OK.

Summary

Why are so many companies installing Windows NT, someone recently asked me? There are a variety of reasons, of course — NT is very fast and almost crashproof, for example — but you've just learned about one of the most important motivations. NT has an extremely strong security system that allows a system administrator complete control of the company's PCs. By setting up profiles, an administrator can provide customized user accounts, allowing users all the privileges they need . . . and no more. And even the most technically knowledgeable of users can't fool NT into giving them access to more privileges than they are allowed. The security is built into the operating system at a deep level. The *only* way to fool this security system is to steal a password — so be very careful with yours!

PART TWO
NT'S ACCESSORIES

THIS PART CONTAINS THE FOLLOWING CHAPTERS

CHAPTER 9 TEXT & NUMBERS — WORDPAD, NOTEPAD, CALCULATOR, & MORE

CHAPTER 10 WORKING WITH PICTURES — PAINT AND IMAGE

CHAPTER 11 USING MULTIMEDIA IN WINDOWS NT

CHAPTER 12 KEEPING YOUR DATA SAFE — BACKUP

CHAPTER 13 SIMPLE COMMUNICATIONS — HYPERTERMINAL & PHONE DIALER

Windows NT comes with lots of useful programs, from a text editor and word processor to an audio-CD player (always useful) and a backup program. In Part 2, you'll find out how to use all these programs — how to back up your data onto tape, for example, and how to create pictures or annotate documents you've scanned. Don't buy more software until you've seen what NT can do for you.

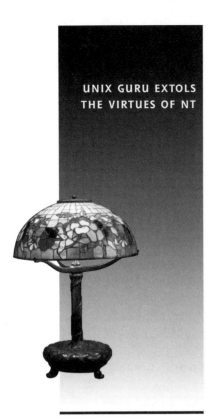

UNIX GURU EXTOLS THE VIRTUES OF NT

When a project team at the Boulder, Colorado-based National Center for Atmospheric Research (NCAR) decided to switch from UNIX workstations to Windows NT to develop software for the National Weather Service 92's radar instrumentation, long-time UNIX guru and software engineer, Joe VanAndel, was concerned. Even for the experienced user, programming on a new operating system can be frustrating. Starting up the application, syntax, commands, development tools, the development environment, and even the user interface often cause confusion.

"Learning UNIX is difficult, at best. You have to search through long manual pages, which don't tell you what you need to learn the system. I didn't want to go through that process again."

But VanAndel quickly found that learning to program with NT was a snap. "NT's online Help was better than anything I've ever seen. I was impressed with the hypertext links, indexing, and examples. With keyword searches, I got everything I needed in short order. I never had to struggle or read a big old manual."

Additionally, he found that, unlike UNIX, "each NT application has integrated help specific to it. The user interface is more consistent — everything has a similar look, everything is intuitive. Unless you examine it really closely, you walk up to NT 4.0 and think it's Windows 95, it's that simple."

The NCAR team needed to build a system that logged data and environmental conditions into a database so that the National Weather Service could see a range of temperatures for a specific location at a particular time. They needed high reliability with a small amount of code.

In that light, VanAndel discovered that NT's development tools for reducing overall code size better than he expected. "NT's operating system uses shared libraries, and the executables are smaller than under UNIX. You can perform more processes in the same memory space in less time."

The tools, he says, are also more robust. For example, "I can remotely give Excel a new set of numbers, and NT updates spreadsheets and graphs them automatically. You can build applications to do numerous things simultaneously, such as programming Visual Basic to take advantage of some functions in Excel. It's slick."

So slick, in fact, that VanAndel is convincing more departments at NCAR to switch from UNIX workstations to Windows NT — something the UNIX veteran never would have done before this project. "I just think it's more productive, more cost-effective, and most of all, more fun to use."

CHAPTER NINE

TEXT AND NUMBERS — WORDPAD, NOTEPAD, CALCULATOR, & MORE

IN THIS CHAPTER YOU LEARN THESE KEY SKILLS

COPYING DATA — USING THE CLIPBOARD   PAGE 166

WORKING WITH A CLIPBOOK   PAGE 169

WORD PROCESSING FOR THE MASSES — WORDPAD   PAGE 171

A SIMPLE TEXT EDITOR — NOTEPAD   PAGE 182

FIGURING NUMBERS — CALCULATOR   PAGE 183

So far, everything you've looked at has been related to what might be thought of as the operating system management — starting and closing programs, working with the Start menu and the desktop, setting up accounts and profiles, and so on. Now you're going to get down to work. In this chapter, you're going to learn about using some of NT's applications, programs that allow you to do real work. We'll look at these items:

* The Clipboard — allows you to copy information from one place to another, within and between programs.
* WordPad — a word processor
* Notepad — a simple text editor
* Calculator — yes, a calculator

★ OLE (Object Linking and Embedding) — an advanced tool for placing the creation of one program in another (see the bonus section)

I'll begin by looking at the Clipboard, something you'll probably use every day you work with your computer.

Copying Data — Using the Clipboard

The Clipboard works quietly in the background. You can use it to copy or move text, numbers, or even pictures. It's so easy to use that most people don't really think much about how it works, or what else it can do. But there's more that the Clipboard can do in conjunction with the ClipBook Viewer — you can create libraries of information, for example. You can then retrieve data from these libraries later.

First, start right at the beginning. How do you use the basic Clipboard commands? Virtually all Windows applications allow you to cut, copy, and paste data to and from the Clipboard. Most programs have menu commands — usually on the Edit menu — that carry out these processes, but there are a number of keyboard shortcuts you can use, too. Table 9-1 shows you what these commands do and how to use the keyboard shortcuts.

TABLE 9-1 The Cut, Copy, and Paste Commands

Command	Keyboard Shortcut	Alternative Keyboard Shortcut	Purpose
CUT	CTRL+X	SHIFT+DELETE	Removes the object and places it in the Clipboard
COPY	CTRL+C	CTRL+INSERT	Makes a copy of the object and places it in the Clipboard
PASTE	CTRL+V	SHIFT+INSERT	Places a copy of the item in the Clipboard into the document
COPY SCREEN	PRINT SCREEN KEY		Makes a copy of the entire screen
COPY WINDOW	ALT+PRINT SCREEN		Makes a copy of the selected window or dialog box

How, then, does all this work? Simple. Select the item you want to copy or move, and use one of the first two commands. Then place the cursor where you want to place the item, and use the last command. What item? It could be text that you've highlighted in a word processor or even in a text box inside a dialog box. It might be numbers in a spreadsheet. It could be a picture in a graphics program.

 TIP The *Alternative Keyboard Shortcuts* shown in Table 9-1 are actually the original Clipboard shortcuts used in an early version of Windows. The first set of shortcuts are now the standard, but you'll find that in most cases, the alternatives work — and in a few rare cases, the programmer writing the program still uses the old shortcuts.

What happens to the object that you copy? It's placed inside the Clipboard. Here's an example you can follow:

1. Press the Print Screen key on your keyboard (it's on the right side of the top row). If you want, hold the Alt key down while you press Print Screen. This "snaps" a picture of the screen or window.

2. Select Start → Programs → Accessories → WordPad to open the WordPad word processor.

3. Press Ctrl+V to place a copy of the screen or window that you "snapped" into the WordPad document (see Figure 9-1).

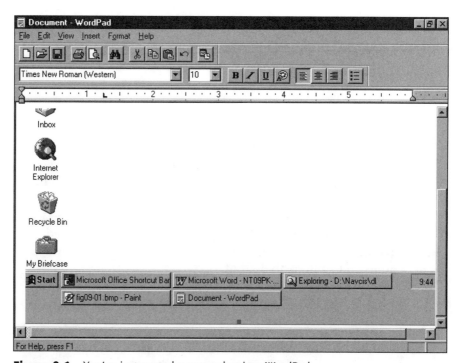

Figure 9-1 You've just pasted a screenshot into WordPad.

4. Select Start → Programs → Accessories → Clipboard Viewer . The Clipboard Viewer program opens.

5. Select Window → 1 Clipboard . You'll see the contents of the Clipboard (see Figure 9-2). (In some cases, you *won't* see a numbered item in the Window menu; try pressing Ctrl+Esc to switch document windows instead.)

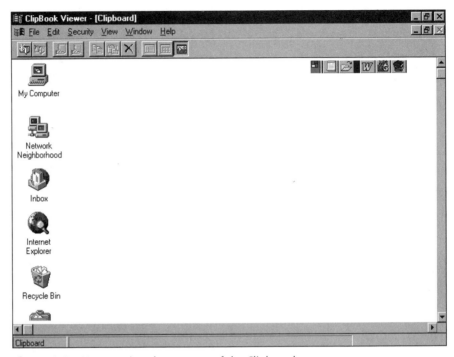

Figure 9-2 You can view the contents of the Clipboard.

In most cases, you don't need to view the Clipboard. You simply cut or copy, and then paste wherever you want to place the item in the Clipboard. There's no need to open the Clipboard Viewer to make sure of what's in there. But there's a problem with the Clipboard. Each time you cut or copy something, you replace whatever is in the Clipboard. So if you now type some text into WordPad, then copy that text to the Clipboard, the picture will be removed. What if you want to save what's there for use later — later today, later this week, later this year? You can use a ClipBook to do that.

Working with a ClipBook

As you saw when you selected Window→1 Clipboard, the ClipBook Viewer can show you the contents of the Local ClipBook. This is a collection of Clipboard images. It's saved on your hard disk, so it's there the next time you open ClipBook Viewer.

To place something into the Local ClipBook, follow these steps:

1. Cut or copy the object — the text, numbers, picture, or whatever — to the Clipboard.

2. Open the ClipBook Viewer.

3. Make sure the Local ClipBook is shown — in the program's title bar, you should see `Local ClipBook`. If not, select `Window` → `2 Local ClipBook`.

4. Select `Edit` → `Paste`, or click the Paste button. You'll see the Paste dialog box.

5. Type a page name — something that will help you find the object when you want to use it later.

6. If you want other users on your network to be able to access this object, click Share Item Now.

7. Click OK and the object is placed into the ClipBook.

Using a ClipBook page

Let's say you saved something into the ClipBook a few weeks ago, and now you want to use it in a document. Here's what you do:

1. Open the ClipBook Viewer and display the Local ClipBook.

2. Find the page you want to use. You can click the Table of Contents button to see a list of all the pages, or click the Thumbnail button to see *thumbnails*. (See Figure 9-3.)

3. When you think you've found the item you want to use, double-click it. It will be shown full size.

4. If you've found the one you want, select `Edit` → `Copy`. The contents of the ClipBook page are placed into the Clipboard.

5. Go to the program in which you want to use the object and paste it into the document.

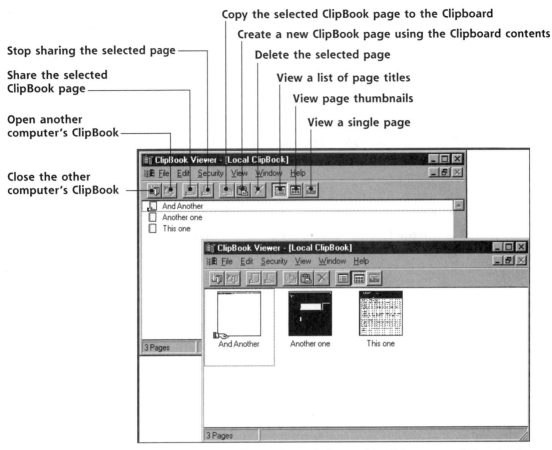

Figure 9-3 Two different ClipBook views: Table of Contents and Thumbnail.

Here's a quick rundown of what else you can do with ClipBook Viewer:

Delete a ClipBook page or clear the Clipboard: Select `Edit` → `Delete`.

Copy the contents of the Clipboard to an existing ClipBook page: Display the ClipBook page and then select `Edit` → `Paste to Page`.

Save Clipboard data or a ClipBook page in a .CLP file (which you can then give to someone else): Select `File` → `Save As`.

Open a .CLP file and view the contents in the Clipboard: Select `File` → `Open`.

View a page or the Clipboard in various different formats: You'll find different options at the bottom of the `View` menu.

Use a ClipBook created on another networked computer: Select `File` → `Connect`.

Allow another network user access to a specific page: Select the page and then select `File` → `Share`.

Stop others from using a specific page: Select the page and then select `File` → `Stop Sharing`.

Make specific sharing & auditing settings, or take ownership (see Chapter 8): Use the `Security` menu.

TIP Individual ClipBook pages can be shared, but not the entire ClipBook itself. You can quickly turn on sharing when creating each page by using the *Share Item Now* check box.

Word Processing for the Masses — WordPad

If you've used Write, the Windows 3.1 word processor, you'll be pleased with its replacement, WordPad. If you never used Write because it just didn't do enough, you may want to take a look at WordPad and see if it has the features you need.

WordPad is a word processing program. It's more sophisticated than the old Write program, yet not as fancy as an expensive program such as WordPerfect or Word for Windows. But you may find that it's plenty powerful enough for many uses — few word processor users work with more than a small percentage of available features, anyway.

While the old Windows 3.1 Write program had its own special file format — .WRI — WordPad works with several different formats. You can see which ones it can handle, and whether it can open or save files on those formats, in Table 9-2.

TABLE 9-2 The WordPad File Formats

Extension	Open?	Save?	Description
.DOC	YES	YES	The Word for Windows Version 6 file format. You can create files in WordPad and use them in Word for Windows.
.RTF	YES	YES	Rich Text Format, a special format used by many different word processors to allow them to share files. Save a file in .RTF format, and it can be opened in most advanced word processors, and it retains all the paragraph and font formatting.

(continued)

TABLE 9-2 The WordPad File Formats (*continued*)

Extension	Open?	Save?	Description
.TXT	YES	YES	A simple text file — no fancy paragraph or font formatting, just letters, numbers, and punctuation. Almost universally readable by text editors and word processors.
.WRI	YES	NO	The old Windows Write format. You can open files that were created using this format, but when you save them, you'll have to select a different format — .DOC, .RTF, or .TXT.

To open WordPad, select Start→Programs→Accessories→WordPad. You'll see the screen in Figure 9-4.

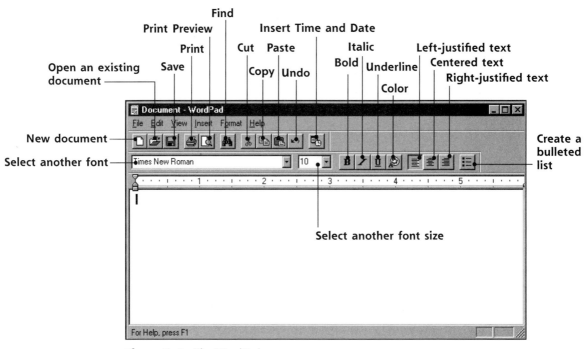

Figure 9-4 The WordPad screen.

SIDE TRIP

TEXT EDITOR VERSUS WORD PROCESSOR

What's the difference between a text editor and a word processor? Text editors came first — they allowed simple manipulation of words on a screen. Later came word processors, which had more sophisticated features, including the capability to use special typographic characters for quotation marks and emdashes, different fonts, various paragraph formats, and so on. A text editor can work with an ASCII text file, but not with one of the special word-processing formats. ASCII — *American Standard Code for Information Interchange* — is a simple format that allows a limited number of different characters.

Opening a document

The following list describes the various ways to open documents:

* When you start WordPad, it automatically opens a new .DOC document. All you need to do is start typing.
* If you've worked in WordPad before, you can quickly open an earlier document. Select `File`, and then select one of the numbered entries near the bottom of the menu.
* Select `File` → `Open` to open an existing .DOC, .RTF, .TXT, or .WRI file from your hard disk.
* Select `File` → `New`. Select the format you want to use, and then click OK.

TIP You don't *really* select a file format until you save the file. In other words, you could select Text Document in the New dialog box, create your document, and then save it as a .DOC document. But if you select Text Document, WordPad assumes that you don't want to use any of the fancy font and paragraph formatting tools, so it removes them from the toolbar; they're still available from the menus, however. And WordPad will use certain options set up for Text Document — see "Setting up WordPad options," later in this chapter.

By the way, if you open a text file, you may discover that you have long lines that shoot offscreen to the right. By default, the lines within a paragraph in text files are not "wrapped" from line to line, so they extend offscreen — you can change this setting, however. See "*Setting up WordPad options,*" later in this chapter.

Working with text

How do you enter text into a document? Just start typing. When you come to the end of a paragraph, press Enter. (Don't press Enter at the end of each line, only at the end of a paragraph.)

TIP There are two typing modes in WordPad and in many other programs — insert and overtype. In insert mode, when you type, the characters to the right of the cursor move to the right to make room for the new characters. In overtype mode, the characters to the right are replaced with the new characters. Use the Insert key to switch between these modes.

WordPad uses all the basic cursor movement keys that you may be familiar with from other Windows programs. Table 9-3 summarizes these movements.

TABLE 9-3 Moving the Cursor in Text

Movement	Keyboard Shortcut
MOVE ONE CHARACTER RIGHT/LEFT	Right arrow/left arrow
MOVE ONE WORD RIGHT/LEFT	Ctrl+right arrow/Ctrl+left arrow
BEGINNING/END OF LINE	Home/End
MOVE TO THE BEGINNING/END OF A PARAGRAPH	Ctrl+up arrow/Ctrl+down arrow
SCROLL UP/DOWN ONE PAGE	PgUp/PgDn
MOVE TO BEGINNING/END OF DISPLAYED PAGE	Ctrl+PgUp/Ctrl+PgDn
BEGINNING/END OF DOCUMENT	Ctrl+Home/Ctrl+End

Note, by the way, that if you press the Num Lock key, turning on the numeric keypad's numeric mode, some of the keys mentioned in the previous table will type numbers, not move the cursor. (Your keypad may have two sets of these keys, one set on the numeric keypad and one in a separate cursor movement group.)

As you'll see in a moment, you'll sometimes need to select text — highlight it, as it's often known — so that you can carry out some operation on it. You may want to copy it to the Clipboard, change its color, set it in a different font, and so on. Table 9-4 shows how you can select text.

TIP Want to quickly insert the date and time into a document? Select Insert→Date and Time, select the format you want to use, and click OK.

TABLE 9-4 Selecting Text in WordPad

To Select This	Do This
A WORD	Double-click the word, or place the cursor in front of the word and press Ctrl+Shift+right arrow.
FROM CURSOR TO START/END OF LINE	Shift+Start/Shift+End
A LINE	Move the mouse cursor to the left column, point to the right at the line of text, and click the mouse button.
MULTIPLE LINES	Drag the mouse pointer across text while holding the mouse button down. Or move the mouse cursor to the left column, point to the right, press the mouse button, and drag the pointer up or down.
A PARAGRAPH	Triple-click a word in the paragraph, or place the cursor in front of the first word and press Ctrl+Shift+down arrow.
ALL TEXT TO START/END OF DOCUMENT	Shift+Ctrl+Home/Shift+Ctrl+End
THE ENTIRE DOCUMENT	Ctrl+A
ANY BLOCK OF TEXT	Hold the mouse button down and drag the pointer across the text.

TIP   To quickly move text around, select the text and drag it to where you want to place it. When you release the mouse button, the text is moved. Holding Ctrl while you do this copies the text.

Changing the look with fonts

You have a number of options available for changing the way your text looks, as you can see in Figure 9-5. You can modify font sizes and typefaces, colors, and styles.

You can either select a font format and then type the text — the typed text will then have that format until you select another format — or you can select existing text and apply a format to it.

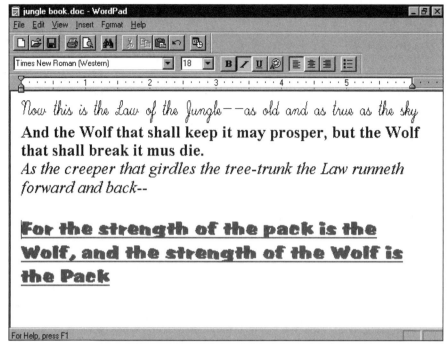

Figure 9-5 Change the font to whatever you want, but don't get carried away.

For example, to change the color of a word that you've already typed, select the text and then click the Color toolbar button. You can now choose a color from a drop-down bar.

You can also do the following to format text:

Change the font. Select a different font from the large drop-down list box.

Increase or decrease size. Select another size from the small drop-down list box.

Make the text bold. Click B

Italicize the text. Click I

Underline the text. Click U

You can change all these features at once, if you want. Select Format→Font to see the dialog box in Figure 9-6. As you can see, you can set the text's font, color, size, and so on. You also have another option, Strikeout, which puts a horizontal line through the middle of the text.

 TIP   There's also a Script option. This allows you to select a specific language, if it's available for that font. You computer must be set up to work with that language in order for the script option to work correctly.

176   NT'S ACCESSORIES

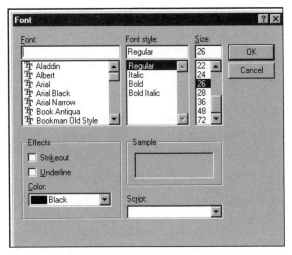

Figure 9-6 Change all the font characteristics at once.

Changing the look with paragraphs

You can also modify the way in which a paragraph appears on the page. In order to do this, you don't need to select any text. Simply place the cursor inside the paragraph you want to modify, and make the changes (or select several paragraphs by highlighting text starting somewhere in the first paragraph and ending somewhere in the last).

Here's what you can do to a paragraph's appearance:

Align the text on the left side of the page	Click
Align the text on the left side of the page	Click
Center the text	Click
Indent the text from edges of the paper	Select Format → Paragraph, make your changes, and click OK.

You can also create bulleted lists quickly. Click the Bullets button and begin typing. Each time you press Enter, you get a new line, starting with a new bullet.

Using tabs

Inexperienced computer users often try to create columns of information by using the Tab key. That's fine, but they try to line up these columns by typing enough tabs to move the text into the correct position. It may take three or four tabs for each column, so you end up with a table created with hundreds of the things.

It's actually much easier to set up the tabs so that all it takes is one press of the Tab key for each column. You can create tabs in the Tabs dialog box. But you can also see the ruler immediately above the dialog box — the ruler is generally the easiest way to create tabs.

Tabs have to be set for each paragraph. If you want to use the same tabs on several existing paragraphs, select all the paragraphs at the same time.

 TIP **To select the entire document — perhaps so you can set tabs for the entire document at once — press Ctrl+A.**

Here's how to use the ruler:

* To place a tab, click inside the ruler at the point at which you want the tab.
* To move a tab, just drag it along the bar.
* To delete a tab, drag it off the bar and release the mouse button.
* To move the left margin, drag ▣ along the bar — drag by the square at the bottom.
* To adjust the first-line indent, drag ▽ along the bar.
* To adjust the left margin, leaving the first-line indent where it is, drag ▣ along the bar — drag by the triangle at the top (see Figure 9-7).
* To adjust the right margin, drag △ along the bar.

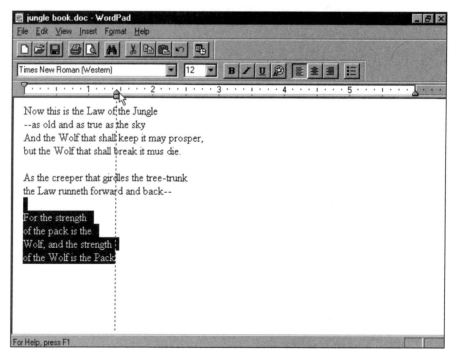

Figure 9-7 Adjust margins by dragging the markers along the bar.

TIP The Undo command is an important tool to remember; you'll find it in most Windows programs. Select Edit→Undo to remove the last change. You can also try Alt+Backspace (which works in virtually all text boxes within program dialog boxes, by the way).

Finding and replacing text

WordPad has tools that help you both find text within a document and quickly replace the text with something else. Here's how to find a word or sentence:

1. Select `Edit` → `Find`. The Find dialog box opens.

2. Type the word or words that you are looking for. You can type just part of a word, if you want.

3. If you type a complete word and don't want WordPad to find words that *contain* the word you typed (for example, you are searching for *Smith*, not *smithy*), click Match whole words only.

4. If you are sure that the word is in the case you typed (you know it's *Smith*, not *smith*), click Match case.

5. Click Find Next. WordPad displays the first occurrence of the word. If it's not the one you want, click Find Next again.

6. When you find the word you want, you don't have to close the dialog box; you can click in the document and work on the word, and then click Find Next to search for another occurrence.

7. When you're finished, click Cancel. Later, you can quickly search again by pressing F3.

Replacing a word or text is similar. Select Edit→Replace. You'll see the Replace dialog box.

Enter all the information as before, but then type something into the *Replace with* box — the text that you want to use instead of the text that you are searching for. Then click Replace All to automatically replace all occurrences, or click Find Next to find them one by one — you can then click Replace to replace a single occurrence.

Printing and previewing

Before you print a document, you may want to preview it to make sure it looks the way you want; that the margins aren't too big or too small, for example. Select File→Print Preview.

Notice the buttons at the top. These allow you to zoom in on the page — to see it a little closer, view different pages if it's a multi-page document; see pages side by side, and, if you're sure it looks okay, start printing the document.

Before you print, however, you may wish to set up the page margins. These are not the same as the indents, by the way. A *page margin* is a space that will remain blank — the document will not print within the margin areas. Paragraph indents are spaces between the edge of the margin and the place where the text begins.

Select File→Page Setup to see the dialog box in Figure 9-8. You can select the paper size to print on and which feeder the printer will use. You can select orientation and enter the margin sizes. When you make these changes, the sample picture will change.

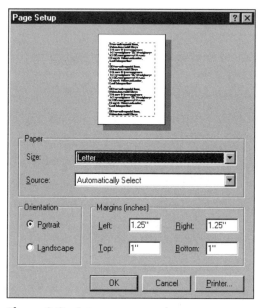

Figure 9-8 Set up your page here.

Saving your work

To save your work in WordPad, simply click the Save button, or select File→Save. If you are working in a document that you've saved previously, and you want to save it with a different name — to create a new document with your recent changes — select File→Save As.

In the dialog box that opens, you can pick the format in which you want to save the file. By default, Word for Windows 6.0 is selected, but you can choose Rich Text Format or Text.

Setting up WordPad options

If you want to modify WordPad's options, select View→Options. Then click the Options tab to see the information shown in Figure 9-9. The *Measurement units* box modifies the units used in the ruler. The *Automatic word selection* check box controls what happens when you drag the mouse pointer over text while holding the button down. If the check box is checked, WordPad automatically selects entire words. In other words, if you stop dragging halfway through a word, WordPad will select the rest of the word for you.

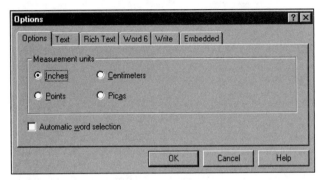

Figure 9-9 The basic WordPad options.

The other panes in the Options box define how WordPad will work with particular file formats: Text (.TXT), Rich Text (.RTF), Word 6 (.DOC), Write (.WRI), and Embedded (a file from another application embedded within WordPad — see "Working With "Objects" and OLE," in the bonus section).

The Word wrap options tell WordPad what to do if a paragraph is more than one line long:

No Wrap. Simply run the paragraph off screen to the right. This is inconvenient.

Wrap to Window. Run the text to the edge of the window, and then start a new line.

Wrap to Ruler. Run the text to the document margins, and then start a new line.

The Toolbar options simply define which toolbars you want displayed while working in certain file types. For example, if you are working in a text document, you don't need the Format Bar and Ruler, as they contain commands to make changes that can't be saved in a text file.

TIP Using e-mail, you can send documents to other people directly from within WordPad and many other applications. Select File→Send. See Chapter 15 for more information.

A Simple Text Editor — Notepad

Notepad is WordPad's little brother. It's a text editor, not a word processor, so it has more limited capabilities and works on simple text documents. Select Start→Properties→Accessories→Notepad to see the window in Figure 9-10.

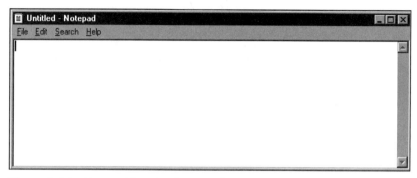

Figure 9-10 Notepad is a simple text editor.

Working in Notepad is simple because there aren't many options. The first thing you should know about is Edit→Word Wrap. With this turned off, long paragraphs will shoot offscreen; with it on, they'll wrap to the next line so that you can read it all.

There are Find and Find and Replace features, almost exactly the same as WordPad's. You can pick a font style and size, too (Edit→Set Font). However, this only changes the way that the text appears in the Notepad window, not how it's saved in the file.

Strangely, there's a more advanced Page Setup dialog box. It lets you create page headers and footers. You have to know the special codes, however (see Figure 9-11).

Table 9-5 lists the codes you can use.

TABLE 9-5 Codes for Creating Headers and Footers

Code	Description
&d	The current date
&p:	The page number
&f	The filename
&l	The text following the code is aligned at the left margin
&r	The text following the code is aligned at the right margin
&c	The text following the code is centered
&t	The current time

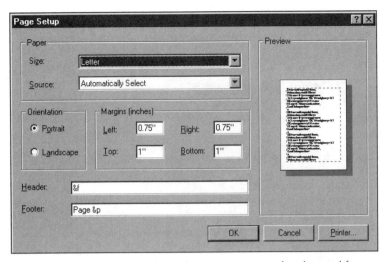

Figure 9-11 If you know the codes, you can create headers and footers.

Finally, there's one unusual feature in Notepad: *Unicode*. This is a new system that is supposed to allow a text font to contain all sorts of different characters, for all sorts of different languages. In effect, it's a universal coding system, usable by anyone using any written language. Unicode is not in wide use currently, but it is possible to save Notepad files in Unicode format.

When you save the file, you'll see a *Save as Unicode* check box; check this to save any special characters you may have entered into your text document. For example, Character Map (see Chapter 7) can be used to paste Unicode characters into Notepad.

FEATURE FOCUS Windows 3.1 Notepad and Windows 95 Notepad both have a limited document size. If you try to open documents that are too large, Write will open instead. That won't happen in Windows NT — Notepad can open documents several megabytes in size.

Figuring Numbers — Calculator

You've looked at words; now it's time for numbers. Select Start→Programs→Accessories→Calculator, and the Windows Calculator opens (see Figure 9-12).

You know how to use a calculator, don't you? Type the numbers into your numeric keypad (with your keyboard's NumLock key turned on), or use the numbers above the text keypad. Or simply click with the mouse on the numbers you want to enter.

You can place numbers into a memory — MS places a number into memory, M+ adds a number to existing contents of memory, MR places the contents of the memory in the text box, and MC clears the memory.

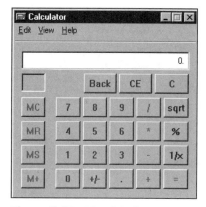

Figure 9-12 The Calculator.

TIP If you can't remember what a button does, right-click the button and select What's This? This is a good way to find the keyboard equivalent, too.

Actually, this calculator will do much more than figure out the price of your pizza order. It's also a scientific calculator. Select View→Scientific to see the calculator in Figure 9-13. This will do all sorts of fancy things, which I've no intention of getting into here, from changing numbers from one base to another, to making complex statistical calculations based on your department's last year's pizza orders. (If you need to know how to use this sort of calculator, you probably already do!)

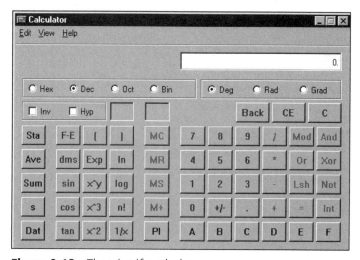

Figure 9-13 The scientific calculator.

TIP To copy a number you've calculated to the Clipboard, press Ctrl+V.

BONUS

Working with "Objects" and OLE

Many Windows programs work with something called *OLE*, Object Linking and Embedding. This system enables you to take information from one program and put it into a document created in another program.

There are both OLE *clients* and OLE *servers* — and some programs are both. A *client* is a program, such as WordPad, that can have data from another program embedded within it. A *server* is a program that can provide data to be embedded within another document. WordPad is also a server program.

So, for example, you might choose to embed information from a paint program, such as Microsoft Paint, into WordPad. Or you might embed a WordPad document into some other program, such as a spreadsheet program, for example.

You'll notice that WordPad has a number of commands that are used for OLE. Table 9-6 lists these commands.

Table 9-6 WordPad's OLE Commands

Command	Purpose
Insert → Object	Insert data from an OLE server into a WordPad document.
Edit → Object Properties	Click the embedded object and select this command to see information about the object.
Edit → Object → Edit	Click the object and select this command to modify the object.
Edit → Object → Edit	Click the object and select this command to view or play the object.

(continued)

Table 9-6 WordPad's OLE Commands (continued)

Command	Purpose
Edit → Paste Special	Copy text from an OLE server into the Clipboard, return to WordPad, and then select this option. Then choose Paste Link and click OK. You've just created a linked object. When the original changes, in the document from which the object was copied, the object in the WordPad document changes, too!
Edit → Links	Click a linked object and select this command to see more information.

Working with these objects can get a little complicated, but here's a quick example of how to insert an object from an OLE server into WordPad:

1. Click inside a WordPad document.

2. Select Insert → Object. The dialog box in Figure 9-14 opens.

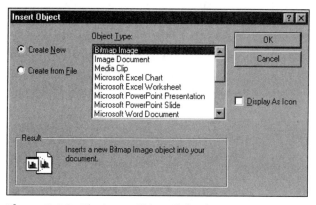

Figure 9-14 The Insert Object dialog box.

3. Make sure *Create New* is selected.

4. Select Paintbrush Picture from the *Object Type* list box.

5. If you want a Paintbrush icon to appear in your document, click the *Display As Icon* box. You won't see the actual picture you're about to create, but you'll be able to open it by double-clicking the icon. If you prefer to see the picture itself, leave this box clear.

6. Click OK and a frame appears in your WordPad document; the WordPad window changes to appear like the Paint windows (which I'll look at in

Chapter 10). See Figure 9-15. If you chose *Display As Icon*, an actual Paint window opens.

7. Draw something — it doesn't have to be fancy. Just hold the mouse button down and drag the pointer across the drawing area.

8. When you're finished, press Esc. (If you chose the *Display As Icon* option, select `File` → `Exit & Return to Document`.

9. That's it. You have your doodle or Paint icon inside your document.

If you want to modify your picture later, just double-click the picture or icon.

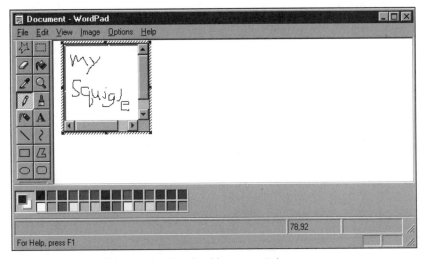

Figure 9-15 As if by magic, WordPad becomes Paint.

> **TIP** Select Start→Programs→Accessories→Object Packager to see the Object Packager window. This special utility enables you to create packages and then copy and paste them into documents. The packages are represented by icons.

Summary

Although Windows NT's own applications are not terribly powerful or sophisticated, they really do come in handy now and again. They also have enough features for many routine computer jobs — so don't think they can't help you. Try them out and see if you like them.

In the next chapter, I'm going to move on to something a little more exciting, the world of pictures. I'll be looking at how to work with Microsoft Paint and Imaging for Windows NT.

CHAPTER TEN

WORKING WITH PICTURES — PAINT AND IMAGE

IN THIS CHAPTER YOU LEARN THESE KEY SKILLS

STARTING MICROSOFT PAINT   PAGE 190

WORKING WITH THE TOOLS   PAGE 192

WORKING WITH COLORS   PAGE 196

OPENING IMAGING FOR WINDOWS NT   PAGE 199

MAKING ANNOTATIONS   PAGE 201

I n Chapter 9, I looked at words and numbers — with a quick side trip into pictures. Now I'm going to look at pictures in more detail. In this chapter, you'll learn about the two NT graphics programs, Microsoft Paint and Imaging for Windows NT. If you've worked with Windows 3.1, you may be familiar with Microsoft Paint. Various versions have been around for a decade or so. Imaging for Windows NT, which is newer, is licensed from Wang and was first released with Windows 95.

What's the difference between Paint and Imaging? Paint is a *paint program*. It enables you to create bitmap images — pictures created by coloring thousands of small dots. (You can see exactly what I mean in Figure 10-7, later in this chapter.) Imaging, however, is an *image-management program*. It does have some tools that enable you to create pictures, although only a few, so you may never actually paint a picture within Imaging. You may, however, scan a picture into Imaging. And you may use the program to add notes to existing pictures, convert them to different formats, highlight parts of them, and so on. In fact, a number of the tools are ideal for adding your own notes to text documents that you've scanned into Imaging.

I'll begin by working with Microsoft Paint.

Starting Microsoft Paint

To open Microsoft Paint, select Start→Programs→Accessories→Paint. You'll see the window shown in Figure 10-1.

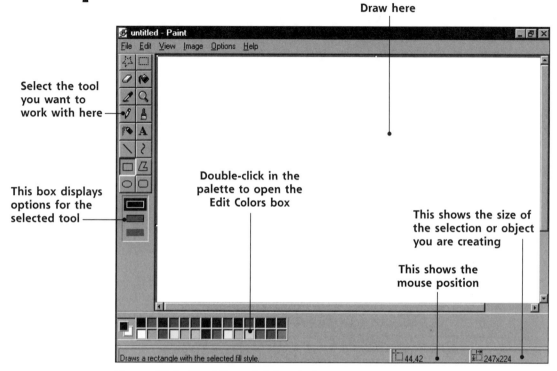

Figure 10-1 The Microsoft Paint window.

When you first open the window, the pen tool is selected. Hold down the mouse button and drag the pointer across the screen, and you'll begin drawing. But the pen isn't the only tool available to you. The tool box on the left side of the window contains all your tools (if the tool box is not visible, select View→Tool Box to turn it on). Table 10-1 explains what each tool does.

TABLE 10-1 The Paint Tools

Tool	Purpose
	Select an irregularly shaped portion of the picture. You can select parts of the picture and then carry out various actions on that part.
	Select a rectangular portion of the picture.
	Fill an area of the picture by "pouring" a color into it. Click with the left button to pour the foreground color, and click with the right button to pour the background color.

Tool	Purpose
⌀	This is sometimes known as the Erase tool, but it's function is a little more complicated. Holding the left mouse button, drag the pointer to replace the area over which you pass with the background color. Hold the right button and drag to replace only those parts of the picture over which you pass that are colored with the foreground color. (For more information about background and foreground colors, see "Working with Colors," later in this chapter.)
🖋	Point at a color and then click to select that color. Click the left button to use the color as the foreground color, and click the right button to use it as the background color.
🔍	Select this tool and then click in the picture to zoom in on the image, making it bigger. Use the tool again to zoom out.
✎	Draw a free-form line. This is like working with a pen or pencil. Drag with the left button to use the foreground color, and drag with the right button to use the background color.
🖌	The brush is similar to the free-form line, with the exception that you can select the brush thickness and shape (the free-form line is simply a one-pixel thick line — a pixel is the smallest dot in a bitmap image). As before, use the left button for foreground color, the right button for background color.
💨	The airbrush or spray can "sprays" dots of color onto the picture. You can pick the size of the spray. Use the left button for the foreground, the right button for the background.
A	You can add text to your picture with this tool (it won't work if you've zoomed in on the picture, however). Create a box using the tool, and then start typing. When you've finished, click another tool. Text is drawn using the foreground color.
\	This tool draws straight lines. Hold the Shift key down while drawing to create horizontal, vertical, or 45-degree lines. (Without Shift held down, you can make the lines go wherever you want.) Use the left button for the foreground color, the right button for the background color.
ʕ	This tool draws curved lines. Draw a straight line, and then click next to the line and drag the pointer to create a curve in the line. Use the Left button for the foreground color, the right button for the background color.
⌂	This tool creates polygons and multi-sided irregular objects. Again, they can be unfilled, filled, or solid. The left button uses the foreground color for the outline, and the right button uses the background color; the fill color is the opposite of the outline color.

(continued)

TABLE 10-1 The Paint Tools (*continued*)

Tool	Purpose
	This tool creates rectangles and squares. You can choose whether to create empty shapes, shapes with border lines and a fill color, or solid-colored shapes. See "The tool options," later in this chapter. The left button uses the foreground color for the outline, and the right button uses the background color; the fill color is the opposite of the outline color. Hold down the Shift key to create squares.
	This tool creates ovals and circles. It works just like the rectangle tool. Hold down the Shift key to create circles.
	This tool creates rectangles with rounded corners. It works just like the rectangle tool. Hold down the Shift key to create squares.

> **TIP** Several tools automatically switch back to the previous tool after you've used them. For example, if you use the color picker, Paint automatically selects the previous drawing tool you were working with immediately after you've used the color picker, so you can quickly use the color you selected.

Opening an existing image

Paint creates Microsoft Windows Bitmap images (.BMP). It can open both .BMP *and* .PCX images, however. The .PCX extension identifies an image saved in the old PC Paintbrush format, the format that Windows Paint used to use a few years ago.

Select File →Open to open an existing file. In the *Files of Type* drop-down list box, select the type of file (Bitmap Files — meaning .BMP files — PC Paintbrush, or All Files).

Working with the Tools

Working with the tools is really quite simple. You point into the workspace and hold down the appropriate button (in most cases, left for foreground color, right for background color, but with a few tools, it makes no difference which button you use).

With some of the tools, all that is required is a single click and the operation is carried out: the Zoom, Fill, and Color Picker tools require just a single click. But some other tools will work with either a click or a drag. For example, click the Airbrush tool to create a splodge of color — or drag to create a series of splodges.

Then there are the tools that require you to drag a shape to create it. With the Rectangle tool, you can drag the mouse to create a rectangle of any size; but remember, hold the Shift key down to create a square.

The tool options

Several tools have special options. If a tool can be modified, you'll see a set of options in a box below the Tool Box. For example, if you select the Rectangle, Polygon, Oval, or Rounded Rectangle tool, you'll see the options shown at the bottom of Figure 10-2.

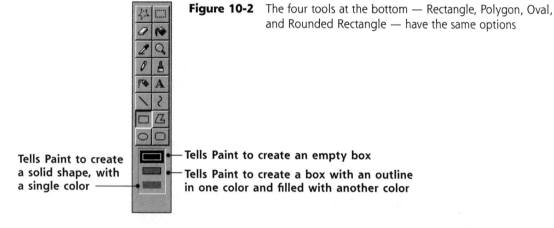

Figure 10-2 The four tools at the bottom — Rectangle, Polygon, Oval, and Rounded Rectangle — have the same options

Tells Paint to create a solid shape, with a single color

Tells Paint to create an empty box

Tells Paint to create a box with an outline in one color and filled with another color

These options enable you to tell Paint how to create the object you want. You can have an empty object — a rectangle, polygon, oval, or rounded rectangle that is empty; no color inside. Or you can create an object with an outline of one color and fill it with another color (left-click to use the foreground color for the outline and the background color for the fill; right-click for the opposite). You can also create a single solid object. (This may seem confusing, but this time it's left-click for the background color and right-click for the foreground color.)

Other tools provide other options:

⬚ & ▫ The box underneath the Selection tools enables you to select opaque or transparent and is used when pasting images. See "Opaque versus transparent," later in this chapter.

▫ The Eraser tool enables you to pick the tool width.

▫ The Zoom tool can be set to different zoom "strengths."

▫ The Brush tool can be different shapes and sizes.

▫ The Airbrush tool can be one of three sizes.

▫ & ▫ The Line and Curved Line tools can be set to different widths.

A The Text tool has the same options as the selection tools — you can use them to appear immediately above the drawing on which you placed it or to give it a special background.

Entering text

If you want to write on the picture, follow this procedure:

1. Click the Text button.

2. If you want to place text on the picture so that you can see the rest of the picture underneath, click .

3. Left-click the color you want to use as the text color. If you are creating a text background, right-click the color you want to use for the background.

4. Click inside the picture, hold down the mouse button, and drag the pointer to create a rectangle in which the text will appear. Release the button when you've got the shape and size you want.

5. The Fonts box will appear (see Figure 10-3). If it *doesn't* appear, select View → Text Toolbar .

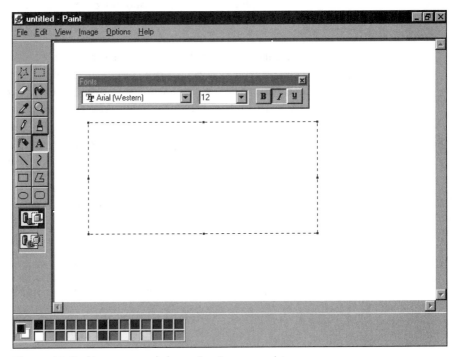

Figure 10-3 You can type information into your pictures.

6. Type the words you want.

7. Use the Fonts box to modify the text. Select the font you want to use, the size, and, if you want, Bold, Italics, or Underline. You can change only *all* the text at once, not individual words or letters.

8. When you've finished, click the Text button or any other tool.

Opaque versus transparent

You've just seen an opaque versus transparent choice in action; you can create text with a background (opaque) or with no background (transparent) so that the picture can be seen below the text. You make this choice by either clicking one of the two choices underneath the toolbar when the Text tool is selected or selecting `Options` → `Draw Opaque`.

You can use this system in some other cases, too. When you create a copy of part of the picture, that copy can be opaque or transparent. For example, try this:

1. Click the Select button.

2. Click the [icon] option underneath the toolbar.

3. Select part of the image — click in the picture, drag the mouse pointer until you've selected the portion you want, and release the button.

4. Hold Ctrl down, point in the middle of the selected area, and then press the mouse button and drag the area. You will be creating a copy of the area (see Figure 10-4).

5. As you drag the selection around in the picture, you'll see that the selection is transparent; you can see the picture below through the areas of the image that have not been drawn.

6. Stop dragging, click the [icon] selection, and try again. This time you'll see that the image is not transparent — you can't see any of the picture below through the selection.

TIP Hold Shift down while you drag a selection to create a strange effect in which the picture is "smeared." Drag without holding any key down to move the selection.

Figure 10-4 You can create an opaque or transparent copy.

Working with Colors

Selecting colors is a simple matter of clicking the color you want to use in the palette. Left-click a color to use that color as the foreground color, or right-click it to use it as the background color (see Figure 10-5).

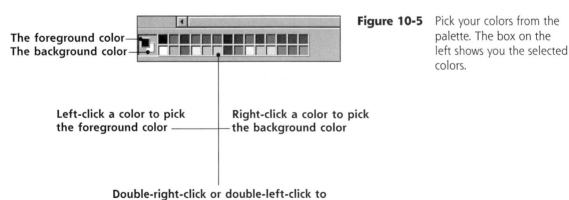

Figure 10-5 Pick your colors from the palette. The box on the left shows you the selected colors.

More colors are available than you can see here, however. Here's how to work with them:

1. Double-click a square in the palette. If you want to select a foreground color, double-left-click. To select a background color, double-right-click. Up pops the Edit Colors dialog box.

2. Click the color you want to use

3. Click OK, and that color is placed into the palette. The original color is replaced with the new one, and the color is selected as the foreground or background color.

Notice also the Define Custom Colors button in the Edit Colors box. Here's how to use it:

1. Click the Define Custom Colors button to expand the box (see Figure 10-6).

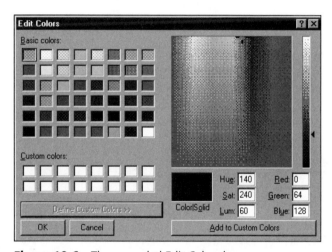

Figure 10-6 The expanded Edit Colors box.

2. Click in the large box to select another color.

3. Click A*dd to Custom Colors* in the Edit Colors box to move the selected color over to the left side of the dialog box.

4. Click OK.

The changes you make are temporary. Close Paint, reopen, and the colors are gone. But you can create special palettes and reload them if you want. Select Options →Save Colors to save a .PAL palette file. Select Options →Get Colors to reload a .PAL file.

Changing views

You can view your image at different resolutions. These are the commands available:

> View → View Bitmap   This displays the picture on the screen alone; you won't see the Paint window. To return to the window, press Tab or Enter, or just click.

> View → Zoom → Large Size   This displays the picture at 400%, four times the normal size.

> View → Zoom → Normal Size   This returns the picture to normal (100%) size.

> View → Zoom → Custom   This displays a box in which you can select from several sizes: 100%, 200%, 400%, 600%, and 800%.

In Figure 10-7, you can see what an image looks like when you zoom right into 600 percent. You can see at this resolution how a bitmap image is created — using thousands of tiny dots. In this case, I've selected View →Zoom → Show Grid and View →Zoom →Show Thumbnail to help me see what's going on. The thumbnail is that little picture in the top left, which shows the picture at a smaller resolution so that I can get a feel for where I am.

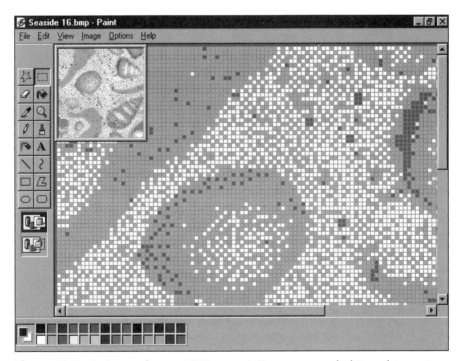

Figure 10-7 An image shown at 600 percent. You can see each dot used to create the picture.

TIP When you zoom right in, you can modify individual pixels. The pencil tool is good for doing this.

Advanced commands

There are a few advanced Paint commands that I haven't covered yet:

`Edit` → `Copy To` Select an area, and then select this command to save the selection in a separate image file.

`Edit` → `Paste From` Paste an image saved in another file into the current image.

`Image` → `Flip/Rotate` Rotate the entire image, or just the selection.

`Image` → `Stretch/Skew` Enlarge or slant the entire image or selection.

`Image` → `Invert Colors` In theory, this switches colors, replacing each one with its complementary color. In practice, it may not work correctly.

`Image` → `Attributes` Displays resolution and color information about the image. You can modify the image to modify the file.

`Image` → `Clear Image` Removes everything in the picture and replaces it with the background color.

TIP Don't forget the right-click menu. You'll find a variety of handy commands, some of which only work while you have a portion of the image selected.

Opening Imaging for Windows NT

To open Imaging for Windows NT, select Start→Programs→Accessories→Imaging. You'll see the window shown in Figure 10-8.

Unlike Paint, you can't begin working in an image right away; you must open an existing image, start a new one, or scan one (if you have a scanner connected to your computer).

To open an existing image, select `File` → `Open`. You can open a variety of different image formats: .JPG, .BMP, .PCX, .DCX, .TIF, and .XIF. You can save only .BMP and .TIF images, however.

To scan a document, select `File` → `Scan New`.

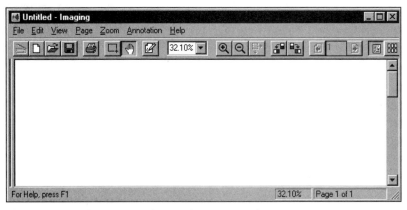

Figure 10-8 The Imaging for Windows NT window

To start a new document, select File → New.

When you create a new document, you have a number of settings that you can specify. Table 10-2 explains what each option does.

TABLE 10-2 The New Blank Document Settings

Setting	Purpose
The File Type tab	
TIF Image Document (TIFF)	A common bitmap format used by many scanning and imaging programs.
Bitmap Image (BMP)	The Windows Bitmap format, which is used throughout Windows. For example, .BMP images can be used for desktop wallpaper.
The Color tab	
Various color settings	You can select the color settings you want to work with. The available settings depend on the file type you selected and the video card and mode you are using. (If your card is not set up to display a certain number of colors, you won't be able to use that many). You can select anything from Black and White (two-color mode) to True Color (almost 17 million colors).
The Compression tab	(See Figure 10-9)
Compression	Image files can often be compressed to take up less disk space. If you select the TIF option, you may be able to select a compression mode — some color choices preclude compression, however. If you select JPEG compression, you can also choose the form of JPEG compression.

Setting	Purpose
The Resolution tab	
Resolution	Select the *image resolution*, the number of dots per inch (dpi). 100 x 100 dpi means that a grid one inch wide and one inch high will contain 100 rows of dots and 100 columns — 10,000 dots. The more dots per inch, the better the image will look, but the more disk space it will take up. You can also select 200 x 200, 300 x 200, or Custom — you enter your own numbers into the X and Y boxes.
The Size tab	
Size	Select the size of the image from the drop-down list box. Consider what size the image will be when printed, if you plan to do so, and select the paper size.
Width & Height	If you select Custom from the Size list, you can enter your own width and height settings.
Units	You can select the units in which the page sizes are displayed.

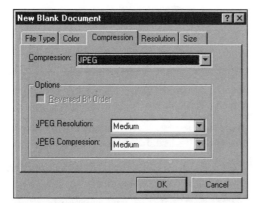

Figure 10-9 The Compression tab.

When you finish setting up your image, click OK. In some cases, it may take a while to create the image you defined, if you set it up to contain many colors and to be very large.

Making Annotations

Imaging for Windows NT has been designed for modifying existing image files. Yes, you can create your own images from scratch, and, in fact, Imaging contains some nice tools for doing so, but the creation tools are actually called *annotation* tools. In other words, the idea is that you will probably be using these tools to make notes on an existing image, such as scanned or faxed documents.

Table 10-3 shows the annotation tools available. They can be selected from the Annotation menu or from the Annotation tool box (select Annotation → Show Annotation Toolbox to turn this on; Figure 10-10 shows this tool box). You'll find that most of the tools are similar to Paint's tools.

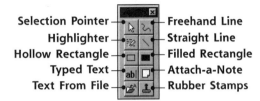

Figure 10-10 The Annotation tool box.

TABLE 10-3 Imaging's Annotation tools

Button	Annotation Menu Command	Purpose
	Selection Pointer	Click an annotation to select it. You can then move it or delete it.
	Freehand Line	Draw squiggly lines.
	Highlighter	Put a yellow "highlight" over part of the image.
	Straight Line	Draw a straight line.
	Hollow Rectangle	Draw a hollow rectangle.
	Filled Rectangle	Draw a filled rectangle.
	Typed Text	Type text directly onto the image (no background).
	Attach-a-Note	Type text with a background.
	Text From File	Insert text from a text file onto the image.
	Rubber Stamps	"Stamp" text across the image. Select from stamps such as *Approved* and *Rejected*, or create your own.

Setting properties

Most of the tools have properties that can be set. In order to do so, you must make sure the Annotation tool box is displayed (select Annotation→Show Annotation tool box). Right-click a tool and select Properties. For example, take a look at the Hollow Rectangle properties shown in Figure 10-11.

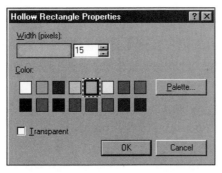

Figure 10-11 The Hollow Rectangle Properties dialg box.

You can do several things here:

* Select the width of the line from the *Width* box.
* Select the line color from the *Color* palette.
* Select *Transparent* if you want to create a "see-through" line that the image below will show through.

TIP   Annotations are temporary. Until you select Annotation→Make Annotations Permanent, you can, in theory, hide the annotations using Annotation→Hide Annotations. (However, that command may not be working — it's available only in .TIF files.) After annotations have been made permanent, they're no longer regarded as annotations, just as bits of the image.

More imaging commands

You're already familiar with many of the commands in Imaging — you've seen some in Paint and in other programs — but before I finish, I want to quickly describe the rest of the special commands in this program:

`Edit` → `Copy From`   If you scanned a document or opened a document, you may have a multi-page file. This command copies the current page to the Clipboard.

`Edit` → `Select`   This command enables you to select part of the image. Remember, there's also the `Annotation` → `Selection Pointer`, but that's used to select only annotations.

`Edit` → `Drag`   You can use this command to drag the image around so that you can view off-screen portions — but it's often easier to use the scroll bars.

`View` → `Zoom Scale to Gray`   Displays black and white documents in grayscales to make them easier to read.

View → One Page Displays a single page at a time.

View → Thumbnails Displays *thumbnails*, small images of each page.

View → Page and Thumbnails Displays thumbnails in one column, the selected page in the other.

View → Full Screen Maximizes the window and then removes the title bar, menu bar, and status bar to give the image more room.

View → Options Genereal Lets you set up general program options.

View → Options Thumbnail Lets you define the size of the thumbnail images.

Page → Insert → Scan Page Inserts a scanned page before the current page in a multi-page file.

Page → Insert → Existing Page Inserts a page from a file before the current page in a multi-page file.

Page → Append → Scan Page Adds a scanned page to the end of the document in a multi-page file.

Page → Append → Existing Page Adds a page from a file to the end of the document in a multi-page file.

Page → Convert Uses the Color, Compression, and Resolution settings that you saw earlier in this chapter (Figures 8 and 11) to convert the image file to another format.

Page → Rescan Replaces the current page with another one from the scanner.

Zoom There are many options for zooming in on the document at different resolutions.

BONUS

Working with Wallpaper

If you've created a picture you want to use in place of your existing desktop wallpaper (the image shown on your Windows NT desktop), follow this procedure:

1. Open the picture in Paint.
2. Select `File` → `Set As Wallpaper (Tiled)` if you want to cover the desktop with the image, repeating it over and over, if necessary, to fill the space.
3. Select `File` → `Set As Wallpaper (Centered)` if you want to place a single image in the middle of the desktop.
4. To change the wallpaper later, repeat the procedure with another image.
5. To replace the wallpaper with one of NT's own wallpapers, right-click the desktop and select `Properties` to see the Display Properties dialog box.
6. Click the Background tab.
7. Select an entry from the Wallpaper list.
8. Select either the Tile or Center option button.
9. Click OK.

If you have a scanner, you can scan an image with Imaging for Windows NT, save it as a .BMP file, and then select that image using the Browse button in the Display Properties dialog box.

Create Your Own Rubber Stamps

If you use Imaging for Windows NT in the manner intended — to annotate scanned documents, for example — you'll find the Rubber Stamps feature very useful. You can create your own stamps to quickly place text messages or small pictures into the document. Here's how:

1. Select `Annotation` → `Rubber Stamps`. You'll see the dialog box shown in Figure 10-12.

Figure 10-12 The Rubber Stamp Properties dialog box.

2. You can see the existing stamps in the list. To create a new text stamp, click Create Text. To create a new picture stamp, click Create Image.

3. Type a name for the stamp in the *Stamp name* box.

4. Type the actual message into the *Stamp text* box — for example, you might create a **Preliminary** message.

5. Click the Date button if you want to include the current date each time you use the stamp, and click the Time button to include the time.

6. You can select a font and font color by clicking the Font button.

7. When you're finished, click OK.

Summary

NT's graphics programs are not top-of-the-line products, but they really are quite serviceable for many uses. Get to know how these products work, and you can use them for most simple graphics tasks.

In the next chapter, I'm going to look at multimedia. You'll learn how to work with CDs — you can play music CDs on your computer, if you want — sounds, and video.

CHAPTER ELEVEN

USING MULTIMEDIA IN WINDOWS NT

IN THIS CHAPTER YOU LEARN THESE KEY SKILLS

PREPARING FOR SOUND   PAGE 208

PLAYING YOUR CDS   PAGE 211

PLAYING SOUNDS WITH SOUND RECORDER   PAGE 215

VIDEO AND MORE WITH MEDIA PLAYER   PAGE 217

CONTROLLING THE VOLUME   PAGE 220

Windows NT comes with four simple multimedia programs:

- **CD Player.** plays your audio CDs through your computer.
- **Media Player.** plays audio CDs, sound files, MIDI music files, and Video for Windows files.
- **Sound Recorder.** records and plays back sounds; you can place the sounds into documents, if you want.
- **Volume Control.** controls system-wide volume settings.

What exactly is multimedia? Just a fancy term for types of information not traditionally associated with computers. Computers have for years displayed words and numbers. Static pictures have been around for some time, in the form of the graphical user interface's icons, buttons, illustrations, and so on. Multimedia generally refers to "other stuff" — sounds, video, and animations.

207

But before you can get started with multimedia, you have to deal with a simple question — Is my computer set up to work with sounds? Here's a quick way to find out. Simply select Start→Programs→Accessories → Multimedia→Volume Control. If you see the message shown in Figure 11-1, then you know your software has not been set up yet.

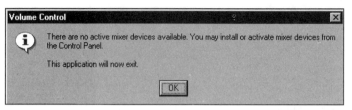

Figure 11-1 Oops! Your sound system hasn't been set up yet.

Preparing for Sound

The problem is not the video. Windows NT is already set up to play Video for Windows files, which I'll look at under "Video and More with Media Player," later in the chapter. But if you want to play sounds through your computer, you need a properly configured sound card. So the first question is: Does your computer have a sound card? If not, you won't be able to use CD Player, Sound Recorder, or Volume Control, and while videos may play, you won't hear the sounds associated with them. (You won't be able to play sounds through the computer itself, but you'll probably still be able to play audio CDs from the CD drive's headset socket, as you'll see under "Playing Your CDs," later in this chapter.)

If you *do* have a sound card, but it's simply not installed, here's what to do to install the drivers needed to run your sound card:

1. Select Start → Settings → Control Panel.

2. Double-click the Multimedia icon to see the Multimedia Properties dialog box (see Figure 11-2).

3. If the settings in the Audio panel of this dialog box are all disabled — "grayed out" — then you know that your sound system isn't set up. Notice in the figure that the *Preferred device* boxes display No Playback Devices and No Recording Devices.

4. Click the Devices tab to see the Multimedia Devices dialog box (see Figure 11-3).

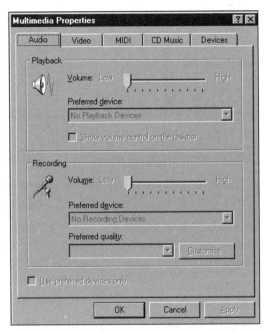

Figure 11-2 The Multimedia Properties dialog box.

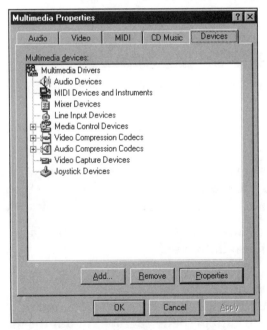

Figure 11-3 Here's where you can see the multimedia devices set up on your computer.

5. To add a sound driver for your sound card, click Add. The Add dialog box opens.

6. Click the entry for the sound card you have in your computer. Unfortunately, not many are listed. If you can't find yours in the list, ask the manufacturer for a disk containing the drivers. You'll then return to this box and select the Unlisted or Updated Driver entry at the top of the list.

7. Click OK and NT begins installing the software.

8. Make sure that the drive letter shown in this dialog box is the correct one for your CD drive and that the disk is in the drive, and then click OK.

9. Depending on the type of sound driver you are installing, you may see a dialog box. This is used to tell NT which I/O (Input/Output) memory setting is used by this card. If you are not sure which setting to use, keep the one NT selected, and click Continue.

10. NT will test the sound card. You may see the message box shown in Figure 11-4. If so, try another memory setting and click Continue again.

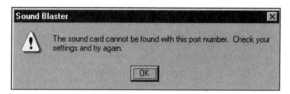

Figure 11-4 Tough luck! you can't set up the sound card.

11. If NT is able to work with the memory setting, it will continue and install the drivers.

12. You may see a dialog box similar to the one shown in Figure 11-5. In this case, there are more choices, but because Auto-Configuration has been enabled, Windows NT makes the choices for you. Click OK to continue.

13. When the drivers have been added, you'll see a message box. Click Restart Now to finish the process.

TIP Windows NT simply doesn't have the degree of hardware support that Windows 95 has. Unfortunately, there's a good chance that you won't be able to get the sound card properly configured! But the manufacturer may have updated drivers that will work. Although the drivers on the NT installation disk didn't work on my system, the new ones from the manufacturer did.

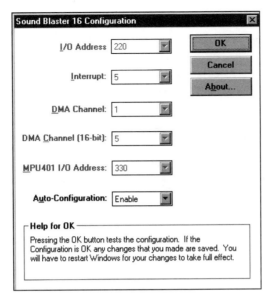

Figure 11-5 This box has more settings, but it also allows you to enable Auto-Configuration to get Windows NT to make the choices.

Playing Your CDs

You can use the Windows NT CD Player whether or not you have your sound card installed and properly configured. With the sound card, the program can play music through your sound card's speakers. Without a sound card, you can still plug headphones into the headphone jack on the front of the CD drive (most computer CD drives have such a jack). You'll then be able to control the volume using the drive's mechanical volume control.

There are two ways to open CD Player (which you can see in Figure 11-6):

* Select Start → Programs → Accessories → CD Player .
* Place an audio CD into the CD drive. In most cases, NT will recognize that the CD is an audio CD, automatically open CD Player, and start playing the music.

When you insert a CD, CD Player takes a look at the CD and figures out what it is — the number and length of the tracks, for instance — and, if you've set up a playlist (which I'll look at in a moment), matches the playlist with the CD. So, it may take a few seconds for the CD to be registered, during which time you'll see the messages *Data or no disk loaded* and *Please insert an audio compact disc* in the Artist and Title boxes. Just wait a few moments for the player to get ready.

Once CD Player is ready, it will normally begin playing the CD. But you can use the controls in Table 11-1 to play the track you want.

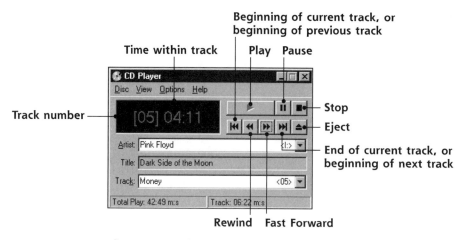

Figure 11-6 The CD Player in action.

TABLE 11-1 The CD Player Controls

Use This	To Do This
▶	Start playing.
‖	Pause playing; click again to resume.
■	Stop and return to the beginning of the CD.
⏮	Return to the beginning of the track. If already at the beginning, go to the beginning of the previous track.
⏭	Go to the beginning of the next track.
⏪	Move back through the current track, second by second.
⏩	Move forward through the current track, second by second.
⏏	Eject the CD from the drive.
ARTIST	If you have multiple CD drives, you can select which CD to play from this drop-down list box.
TRACK	Select the track you want to play. If CD Player was already playing a track, it continues playing the one you select; otherwise, click the Play button to start.

TIP Can't hear the music coming from the sound card's speakers? The volume may be set too low. Open the Volume Control by selecting View→Volume Control. See "Controlling the Volume," later in this chapter.

All about the Play List

Notice in Figure 11-7 that the CD player shows artist, title, and track names. You have to enter the information if you want to see it. It's handy for a couple of reasons — you can pick a track to play without remembering its position on the disk, and you can also create a play list, defining which tracks play in what order. The CD Player *remembers* these play lists. The next time you insert the CD, CD Player will recognize the disk and retrieve the correct play list.

To create a play list, follow these steps:

1. Select Disk → Edit Play List (you must have the CD in the drive to select this option). You'll see the CD Player: Disc Settings dialog box.

2. Type the name of the band or musician into the *Artist* box.

3. Type the album name into the *Title* box.

4. Highlight the text in the *Track 01* text box at the bottom of the dialog box, and replace it by typing the first track name.

5. Press Enter and type the second track name.

6. Continue typing each track name and pressing Enter. Each time you press Enter, the track name is placed into both the *Play List* and *Available Tracks* list boxes.

7. If you want to define the order in which the tracks play when you insert the disk (or even to omit certain tracks), click Clear All to clear the *Play List* box.

8. Double-click the tracks in the order in which you want to play them. The tracks are added to the Play List in that order — you can even add the same track more than once, if you want. (The Reset button returns the Play List to its original state, matching the Available Tracks list.)

9. Click OK.

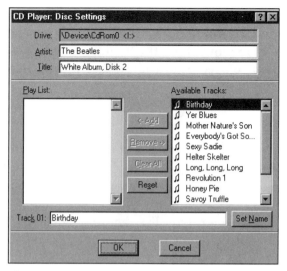

Figure 11-7 Clear the Play List and then start adding the tracks back in.

 TIP Surprise yourself . . . let CD Player pick the tracks for you. You can select Options→Random Order, or play the disk over and over by selecting Options→Continuous Play, or play the beginning of each track so that you can find the one you want by selecting Options→Intro Play. When you hear the track you want, select the option again.

Setting the options

To set CD Player's options, select Options→Preferences. The dialog box shown in Figure 11-8 opens.

Figure 11-8 CD Player's Preferences box.

Here are the available options that you can set:

Stop CD playing on exit. When you close CD Player, the CD stops playing. But if you clear this check box, CD Player will continue playing until it finishes the last track.

Save settings on exit. When you close CD Player, it saves any configuration settings you chose (such as the changes in this Preferences box).

Show tool tips. When you point at one of the CD Player buttons and hold the mouse pointer there for a moment or two, a little box pops up and describes the function of the button.

Intro play length. This is the amount of time that CD Player will play each track if you use the Options → Intro Play feature.

Display font. Select the size of the text in the CD Player "LCD" (the number display panel).

Note that you can also change the information shown in the LCD panel; double-click the panel, or select View→Track Time Elapsed, View→Track Time Remaining, or View→Disc Time Remaining.

Playing Sounds with Sound Recorder

Sound Recorder is a simple recording and playback program. You can listen to .WAV files or create them. These sound files can then be used for a variety of system sounds or even embedded into OLE client documents (see Chapter 9). You can send sound e-mail, for example.

To open Sound Recorder, select Start→Programs→Accessories→Sound Recorder. The window shown in Figure 11-9 opens.

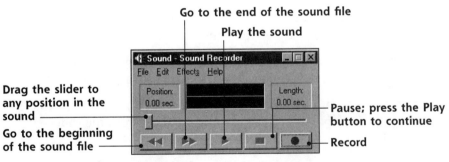

Figure 11-9 The Sound Recorder.

Recording sounds

If you have a sound card capable of accepting microphone input (not all are), you can record music or your own voice. Simply click the Record button, and begin speaking into the microphone or playing the music through the CD Player. This sound is picked up and placed in a sound file by Sound Recorder. To save the file, select File→Save.

To open a sound file, use the normal method: File→Open. You can modify any existing sound file by recording at the end or anywhere within the file, or by using the effects I'll describe in a moment. You can find a sample sound file (Msremind.wav) in the \Winnt\ directory, or use Find (Chapter 6) to search for more.

Editing sounds

Don't like the piece you just recorded? Select File→Revert to remove all the changes since you opened a sound file or since you last saved changes. You can modify your sounds in the following ways:

Make them louder. Select Effects → Increase volume (by 25%).

Make them quieter. Select Effects → Decrease volume.

Make them run faster. Select Effects → Increase speed (by 100%).

Make them run slower. Select Effects → Decrease Speed.

Add an "echo." Select Effects → Add Echo.

Make the sounds play backwards (specially designed for Beatles fans). Select Effects → Reverse.

Copy a sound file into another. Select Edit → Copy. Open another sound file using File → Open, move the slider to the position at which you want to paste the sound, and select Edit → Paste insert. (In some cases the Copy command doesn't work correctly, though.)

Mix a sound file into another. This is the same as copying, but select Edit → Paste Mix. The sound is mixed from the slider position to the end.

Insert another sound file into the current one. Select Edit → InsertFile. The new sound is inserted into the original one at the insertion point.

Mix another sound file in (for example, add background music to a voice). Select Edit → Mix With File. The sound is mixed from the slider to the end of the file.

Delete all of the file from the current point to the beginning. Select Edit → Delet Before Current Position.

Delete all of the file from the current point to the end. Select Edit → Delet After Current Position.

Convert the sound to another format. Select Edit → Properties. In the Properties dialog box, click Convert Now. In the Sound Selection dialog box, select a quality from the *Name* drop-down list box (CD Quality, Radio Quality, or Telephone Quality), and then click OK. See Figure 11-10.

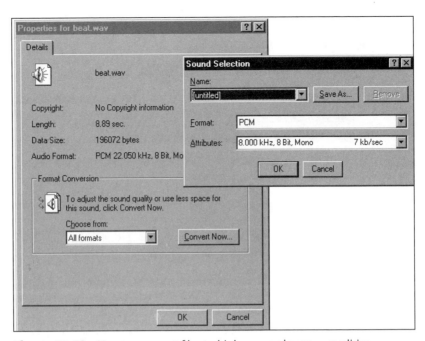

Figure 11-10 You can convert files to higher — or lower — qualities.

TIP You can record sounds then use them as system sounds — sounds played when you open or close programs, encounter errors, and so on. See the information about the Control Panel's Sounds icon in Chapter 18.

Video and More with Media Player

You may think of Media Player as a more advanced Sound Recorder — it's a simple program that plays not only sound files but also MIDI files, CDs, and videos (in the .AVI Video for Windows format).

TIP MIDI means *Musical Instrument Digital Interface.* It's a system used for storing digitally created music (in .MID or .RMI files) and is used by many musicians to digitally store their works. It has a number of advantages over ordinary sound files (such as .WAV files), not the least of which is that MIDI files are much smaller.

To open Media Player, select Start→Programs→Accessories→Media Player. The window shown in Figure 11-11 opens.

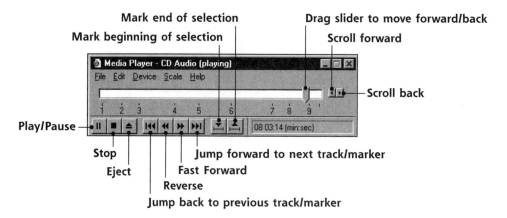

Figure 11-11 Media Player plays .WAV sounds, .MID MIDI files, .WAV videos, and CDs.

There are two ways to open files in Media Player. Here's the first:

1. Select File → Open . In the Open dialog box, select the file type you want to open from the *Files of type* drop-down list box.

2. Double-click the file you want to open.

TIP   You can find loads of sample .WAV, .MIDI, and .RMI files by using the Find system (see Chapter 6) to search for *.mid,*.rmi,*.wav. You may not find many .AVI files, however, but there is one in \Winnt\.

3. If you select an .AVI file, a viewer window opens, as you can see in Figure 11-12. Otherwise, you don't see much happen, except that most buttons are now enabled.

4. Click the Play button to begin playing.

Here's the other way to open a file:

1. Select Device , and then choose one of the top options, such as 1 Sound , 2 MIDI Sequencer , 3 CD Audio , or 4 Video for Windows .

2. If you chose 3 CD Audio , Media Player switches format to show the CD track numbers.

3. If you chose one of the other options, you'll see an Open dialog box, from which you can select the appropriate file type.

4. Click the Play button to begin playing.

Figure 11-12 Media Viewer, playing an .AVI file.

Media Player's options

Media Player has a few options that you can set up. Select Edit→Options to see the dialog box shown in Figure 11-13 (you can make this selection only if you have a file loaded).

Figure 11-13 The Media Player Options dialog box.

You can set many options in this dialog box:

Auto Rewind. Check this to rewind the file to the beginning when you've finished playing it (no, there's no $2 charge for not rewinding your video, but it saves time when you want to play it again).

Auto Repeat. Check this to keep playing the file over and over.

Control Bar On Playback. In "Marking and Copying Selections," later in this chapter, you'll see how to put an object from Media Player into another program, an OLE "client." If you check this box, the object in the client will contain playback controls.

Caption. You can define the caption to be used for the object in the OLE client.

Border around object. Check this to put a border around the object.

Play in client document. Check this to play the file within the client object, rather than opening Media Player to play it.

Dither picture to VGA colors. Check this to change a video's colors to the 16-color VGA palette. Doing so ensures better color quality in some cases (if you are putting the object in a file that you're giving to someone else, for example, and you don't know how many colors their system can display).

Note that you can also select different slider scales from the Scale menu and open the Properties box using Device→Properties. The box you see depends on the file you have loaded — you will be able to modify playback properties for that file type.

Controlling the Volume

The Volume Control is available from a variety of places within Windows NT:

* Select Start → Programs → Accessories → Volume Control .
* Select Device → Volume Control within Media Player.
* Select View → Volume Control within CD Player.
* Left-click the Volume icon on the taskbar's tray.

TIP If you don't see the volume control in the tray, here's how to add it: Select Start→Settings→Control Panel. Double-click the Multimedia icon to see the Multimedia Properties dialog box. Click the Show Volume Control on the Taskbar check box, and then click OK.

If you left-click the tray icon, you get a small volume control (see Figure 11-14) that lets you set the overall system volume. You can click the *Mute* check box to turn sounds off — handy when you get a phone call or hear the boss walking down the corridor.

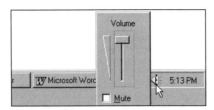

Figure 11-14 A quick and simple volume control.

If you right-click the tray icon and select Open Volume Controls, the full Volume Control program opens (see Figure 11-15). This allows you to set different volumes: Volume Control (overall system volume), Line-In, Midi, CD Audio, and Wave Output. You may find other settings, too, depending on what's chosen in the Properties dialog box (Options→Properties): Microphone, Recording, Voice, and PC Speaker. You can also set Balance and mute each system independently.

Finally, you can right-click the tray icon and select Adjust Audio Properties to see the Control Panel's Audio Properties dialog box.

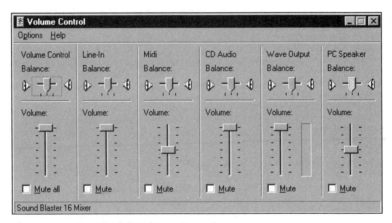

Figure 11-15 The full Volume Control.

BONUS

Marking and Copying Media Player Selections

You can mark a section of a media file within Media Player using the Start Selection and End Selection buttons. When you get to the beginning of the part you want to select, click the Start Selection button. When you get to the end, click the End Selection button.

Why bother? Well, now you can use the Previous Mark and Rewind buttons to move quickly to the beginning and end of the marked section. You can also copy that marked piece into another application. Here's how:

1. Open the media file, or select CD Audio.

2. Use the slider to move to the beginning of the piece you want to copy. Click the Start Selection button.

3. Use the slider to move to the end of the piece you want to copy. Click the End Selection button. You'll see a blue bar marking the selection (see Figure 11-16).

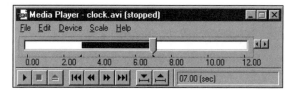

Figure 11-16 Mark your selection.

4. Select Edit → Copy Object . The selection is copied. In the case of CD Audio, a record is made of the selected tracks, though the music itself is not actually copied. (If you made no selection, the entire file is copied, or all the track numbers recorded.)

5. Open an OLE client program, such as WordPad (see Chapter 9 for information about WordPad and OLE).

6. Place the cursor where you want to place the object. Then select Edit → Paste . An object of some kind is pasted into the application.

7. Double-click the object to begin playing (see Figure 11-17).

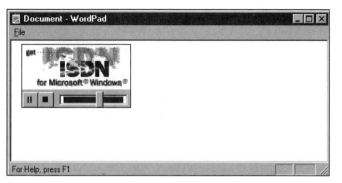

Figure 11-17 You can paste a media object into WordPad and then play it by double-clicking. This is an .avi video.

Note that you can perform something similar from Sound Recorder, too. Select Edit→Copy and then paste the sound into an OLE client. And you can modify the manner in which the OLE object appears and works using the Media Player Options. (See "Media Player's options," earlier in this chapter.)

Don't Be Selfish! Share Your Music!

No doubt by now your system administrator has set up a company-wide CD album network. Yes, you can share your CDs. As long as the CD drive is shared on the network, other users can come in and listen to your music. You can even set permissions for the CD player. In Windows NT, right-click the drive icon, select Properties, and then click the Sharing tab. You can define who's allowed to listen, and how many people at a time may be listening.

Summary

Okay, you've had your fun. Now it's back to work! All this multimedia stuff is fun — the ability to play your CDs while at "work" is especially useful — but there are more important things to do.

For example, when did you last back up all the data on your hard disk? Last week, perhaps? Nineteen eighty-nine, more likely, eh? Well, that's what I'll be looking at in the following chapter — how to back up your work.

CHAPTER TWELVE

KEEPING YOUR DATA SAFE — BACKUP

IN THIS CHAPTER YOU LEARN THESE KEY SKILLS

SETTING UP THE TAPE DRIVE   PAGE 226

MAKING BACKUPS   PAGE 227

PICKING A BACKUP TYPE   PAGE 231

GETTING THE DATA OFF THE TAPE — RESTORING   PAGE 233

TAPE MAINTENANCE   PAGE 235

Have you performed a backup recently? Have you *ever* performed a backup? Backups are like insurance, and they're essential for anyone with valuable data. Sure, if you use your computer only to play games, then you may not care about performing a backup (but then, you're probably not using Windows NT, either). If you do real work and create real data that you save on your hard disk, then you *must* back up your data, or one day you'll regret it.

Consider what happens if your computer is stolen, destroyed in a fire or by lightning, damaged through malicious intent, or if your hard drive dies. How long will it take you to replace the information you'll lose? How much time and money could you lose?

Of course, if you work in an office connected to a network, your system administrator may be performing backups for you. (If you're not sure, check!) But if you are responsible for your own machine, back up your data!

Windows NT has a built-in backup program. Unfortunately, it only backs up to tape drives — it won't back up to removable drives, such as the Iomega Jazz or the Syquest drives — but tape drives are relatively inexpensive these days.

If you've installed a tape drive, you should first make sure that NT is set up to recognize the drive.

Setting Up the Tape Drive

Here's how to set up your tape drive:

1. Select Start → Settings → Control Panel , and then double-click the Tape Devices icon. You'll see the Tape Devices dialog box (see Figure 12-1).

Figure 12-1   The Tape Devices dialog box.

2. In the figure, you can see that the tape drive has not been set up. If yours has not been set up yet, click Detect and Windows NT looks for an attached drive.

3. If NT finds a drive, it will tell you. Click OK to continue.

4. NT now copies the drivers from your installation CD. Follow the instructions.

5. When the drivers have been installed, you must restart your computer before you can use the tape drive.

6. If you return to this dialog box after restarting, you'll see a dialog box similar to the one shown in Figure 12-2 (of course, you may have a different type of drive installed). You can see information about the driver that's being used by clicking the Drivers tab or the Properties button.

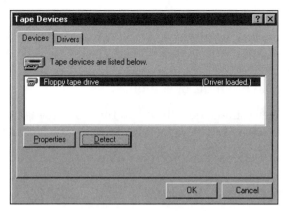

Figure 12-2 The drive is installed and ready to use.

Making Backups

To begin making a backup, follow this procedure:

1. Insert a tape into the drive.
2. Select **Start** → **Programs** → **Administrative Tools (Common)** → **Backup**. After a few moments — while the Backup program checks and starts the tape drive — you'll see the window shown in Figure 12-3.

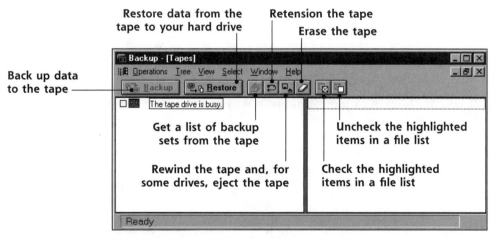

Figure 12-3 The Backup window.

3. You may see a message telling you that the tape must be erased, and the window may show that the tape is a *Foreign Tape*. You may even see this

KEEPING YOUR DATA SAFE — BACKUP

message if you've used the tape with another operating system. Click OK in the message box. (If you don't need to erase the tape, skip to Step 8).

4. Select Opertations → Erase Tape .

5. Click Continue to begin the operation.

6. You may also see a message telling you that the tape is not blank. If you are *sure* that it's okay to erase the data on this tape, click Continue.

7. The erase operation begins; it should be only a minute or two before you see a message telling you that the tape has been erased. Click OK to close the message box.

8. Press Ctrl+Tab or select Window → 1 Drives to see the Drives window (see Figure 12-4).

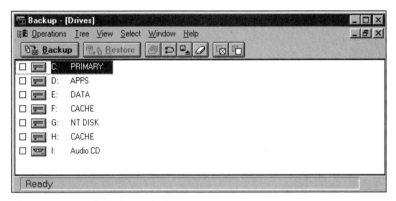

Figure 12-4   The Drives window.

9. If you want to back up an entire disk drive, click the check box next to that drive. Check several drives to back up all of them to the tape at the same time.

TIP   **If you are backing up a lot of data, you may have to use two or more tapes to hold it all.**

10. If you want to back up specific folders or files, rather than everything on the drive, double-click the drive containing the folders or files (or click once and press Enter). You'll see a window similar to the one shown in Figure 12-5.

11. Select the folders and files you want to back up — click in the check boxes. To open the directory tree, use the commands on the Tree menu, or double-click a folder.

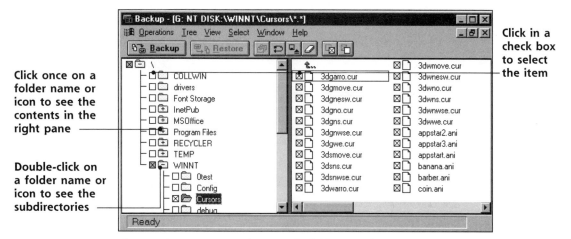

Click once on a folder name or icon to see the contents in the right pane

Click in a check box to select the item

Double-click on a folder name or icon to see the subdirectories

Figure 12-5   You can select specific folders and files.

12. To back up multiple folders or files, hold Ctrl and click the names you want, and then click the button. You can select a contiguous block of names by clicking the first name, holding Shift, and then clicking the last name.

13. Click the Backup button to see the dialog box shown in Figure 12-6. Table 12-1 shows the options in this dialog box.

14. When you've set the backup options, click OK and the procedure begins (see Figure 12-7).

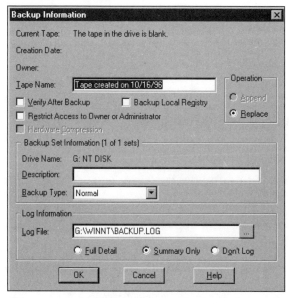

Figure 12-6   Before you can back up, you must set certain options.

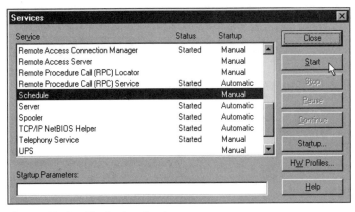

Figure 12-7 The backup begins.

TABLE 12-1 The Backup Information Options

Option	Purpose
TAPE NAME	You can provide a tape name so that you can quickly find the data you want to retrieve later.
VERIFY AFTER BACKUP	Check this to make Backup compare the data backed up on the tape with the data on the disk. Checking this option is a good way to ensure that the data was backed up correctly, though the process will take much longer.
BACKUP LOCAL REGISTRY	If you are backing up the drive that contains your Windows NT Registry — a file with important setup information for NT — you can tell Backup to include those files in the backup... which is a good idea.
RESTRICT ACCESS TO OWNER OR ADMINISTRATOR	Check this if you want to restrict access to this tape. Only the person backing up the tape, or someone with Administrator or Backup Operator privileges, will be able to restore data from the tape or erase or format it.
OPERATION: APPEND	Select this and the data is added to the data already on the tape.
OPERATION: REPLACE	Select this and the data replaces the data already on the tape.
HARDWARE COMPRESSION	Some drives can use hardware compression to "squeeze" the files onto the tape. If your setup allows you to do this, you can check this box. (If you don't have this option, it may simply mean that the drivers you are using don't allow it, not that the drive itself can't compress the files.)

Option	Purpose
DESCRIPTION	Enter a description for this backup set. This is also a way to find what you need later. If you are backing up data from multiple disk drives, you'll see a scroll bar next to the Description and Backup Type options. Use this scroll bar to move through the list of Backup Sets so that you can configure each drive separately.
BACKUP TYPE	Select the backup type that you want to make. I'll discuss these types in "Picking a Backup Type," later in this chapter.
LOG FILE	You can create a backup log file, which records exactly what Backup did. This text box shows the name of the file.
FULL DETAIL	Select this if you want the log to show *everything* that the program did. The file will be large!
SUMMARY ONLY	Select this to get an abbreviated log file, recording just major operations.
DON'T LOG	Select this if you don't want a log file.

Picking a Backup Type

Now, what are these backup types? In Figure 12-6, you saw that you can select from several different backup types. These types vary in the manner in which they handle the archive bit on each file that they back up. You may remember the archive bit from Chapter 5. It's a special indicator attached to each computer file that shows whether the file needs to be backed up. You can see the archive bit in Windows NT Explorer. Display a directory of files, and then make sure you can see the Attributes column in the right pane. If you see an *A* in the column, then the file on that line has been changed and not yet backed up. When a backup program backs up the file, it *may* change the archive attribute (removing the *A* from the Attributes column). But it may not, depending on your backup type choice. The backup types are described in the following list:

Normal. A copy of each selected file, or each file within the selected disk or folder, is placed onto the tape, and the archive bit is cleared; that is, the A no longer shows in the Attributes column.

Copy. A copy of each selected file, or each file within the selected disk or folder, is placed onto the tape, but the archive bit is *not* cleared; A still shows in the Attributes column.

Differential. If you select a disk drive or directory folder, this type of backup copies only the files held by the disk or folder that have the *A* attribute bit set — it doesn't copy *all* files. In other words, NT looks for changed files and copies them. After copying files, the *A* is *not* cleared.

Incremental. If you select a disk drive or directory folder, this type of backup copies only the files held by the disk or folder that have the *A* attribute bit set — it doesn't copy *all* files. A copy of the file is placed onto the tape, and the archive bit *is* cleared

Daily. This type of backup copies only the files created or modified *today*. It doesn't care if the file has the *A* attribute bit set or not; it copies the file anyway. And it won't clear the *A* attribute on those files that do have the *A* attribute set.

TIP   If a program is using a file when the Backup program tries to back it up, that file can't be backed up.

Your Backup Strategy

What these different backup types come down to is what's known as your *backup strategy*. For example, you may do something like this:

* Once a week, select all your disk drives and perform a Normal backup. Everything on the drive is backed up.
* Each evening, select all your disk drives and perform a Differential backup. All files created or modified since the last Normal backup are backed up. If you ever need to retrieve a file, you can check the latest Differential backup. If it's not there, go straight to the latest Normal backup.

That's a pretty good strategy, the only problem being that it uses a lot of tape. The Differential backups get larger each day because they include *everything* that's changed since the last Normal backup. Here's another strategy:

* Once a week, select all your disk drives and perform a Normal backup. Everything on the drive is backed up.
* Each evening, select all your disk drives and perform an Incremental backup. All files created or modified since the last Incremental backup (that day's work) is backed up. If you ever need to retrieve a file, you'll have to check all the Incremental backups one by one, starting with the most recent and working your way back.

This second strategy uses less space on the tape, but it can be inconvenient when searching for a backed-up file. Because the Incremental backup changes the *A* attribute each time it backs up, if you changed a file a couple days ago, then it will be in that day's Incremental set, but not in today's. You may have to dig through sets to find what you need.

TIP Save at least one copy of your tapes away from your computer! Keep one set in a different building, and one set with the computer. If your computer burns or is stolen, it's no good having your tapes go, too!

Getting the Data off the Tape — Restoring

Now and then you'll need to retrieve data from the tape — not too often, one hopes, but backups are a form of insurance, and occasionally you may be happy that you have that insurance.

To restore, follow these steps:

1. Select   Opertations   →   Catalog   to retrieve a list of backup sets on the tape. (I'm assuming that you have just opened Backup and are restoring from a tape you used in an earlier session. If you are just fooling around, backing up and restoring to learn how to do it, Backup already has the list of backup sets, so you can skip this step). In a little while, you'll see a window similar to Figure 12-8.

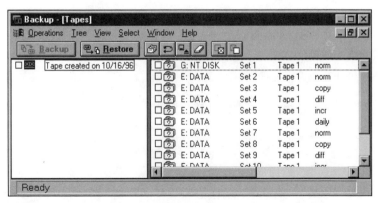

Figure 12-8 You now have a list of backup sets.

2. If you don't see this list of backups (you may see a single backup, with a directory tree in the left pane), select   Windows   →   2 Tapes .

3. Notice that the right pane shows you information about each backup set: the drive from which it was backed up, the series number, the tape number, and whether the backup type was norm (Normal), copy, diff (Differential), incr (Incremental), or daily. Find the set you want to restore.

4. Double-click the set you want to restore, and Backup retrieves information about that set from the tape. A few moments later, you'll see the directory information in a window, similar to Figure 12-9.

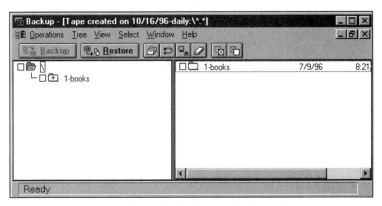

Figure 12-9 Now you have the backup set information.

5. Select the specific files or folders — double-click entries to open up the directory tree — and click the check box to select the files you want to restore.

6. Click the Restore button. You'll see the dialog box shown in Figure 12-10.

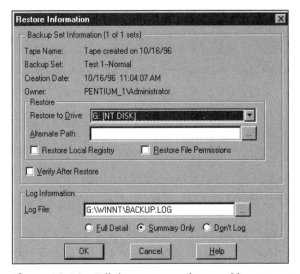

Figure 12-10 Tell the program where and how to restore your files

7. Select the drive to which you want to restore the files in the *Restore to Drive* drop-down list box. You don't have to restore to the same drive that the files came from. In fact, in some cases you won't want to. For example, if you want to keep the latest version of a file but also want an earlier version, don't restore to the same location.

8. Select where on the drive you want to place the restored files by clicking the ▦ button at the end of the *Alternate Path* text box (if you don't enter another path, the original path is used — if you are restoring to a different disk, the original path is reconstructed on that disk).

TIP The directory you select must already exist — you can't create it from within the Backup program. Open Windows NT Explorer and create it there, if necessary.

9. If you want to restore the Windows NT Registry, click the *Restore Local Registry* check box. Doing so wipes out the existing registry, removing any recent changes.

10. Check *Restore File Permissions* if you want the restored files to have the same permissions information as they did when they were backed up to tape. If you *don't* check this, the files will have the same permissions as the directory into which you are restoring.

11. Check *Verify After Restore* if you want the program to check the restored files against the files on the tape to make sure that they were copied correctly.

12. Modify the log information, if you want (see "Making Backups," earlier in this chapter).

13. Click OK and the restore process begins.

14. If a file of the same name as the one you are restoring exists in the directory to which you are restoring, you'll see a message box asking if you want to replace the original file. Click Yes if you do, or Yes to All if you want to tell Backup to stop bothering you with confirmations and just replace all files.

Tape Maintenance

You can carry out a few tape operations:

Erase a tape. To clear a tape's contents, select [Opertations] → [Erase Tape].

Format a tape. To format a tape so that the Backup program can work with it (just like floppies — see Chapter 6 — tapes must be formatted, too), select [Opertations]→[Format Tape]. This option is not available for all types of tape.

Retension a tape. If Backup is having trouble reading from or writing to a tape, you may need to retension it. Doing so tightens the tape, removing loose spots. Some manufacturers recommend retensioning every 20 uses or so. But retensioning is not available for all tape types. Select [Opertations]→[Retension Tape].

Rewind and remove the tape. Select [Opertations]→[Eject Tape] to rewind the tape to the beginning and, if your tape drive can do this, eject the tape.

Get a new catalog. Retrieve a catalog of backup sets from the tape. Select [Opertations]→[Catalog].

BONUS

Scheduling Backups

Windows NT Backup has a serious fault — there's no quick and easy way to schedule a backup. There is a way to schedule, but it's not pretty. Follow this procedure:

1. Select [Start]→[Programs]→[Accessories]→[Notepad] to open Notepad.

2. Type this on the first line: **NTBACKUP BACKUP** *pathnames* **/A /V /B**. The *pathnames* are the disks and folders you want to back up. This command tells Backup to append data to the disk (/A), to verify that the data is correct after backing up (/V), and to back up the registry (/B). Because I haven't specified the *type* of backup, a Normal backup will be performed (all the files are backed up and the archive bit reset).

3. Save the file with a short name — eight characters or less and no spaces in the name — and the **.bat** extension. For example, call it **fullb.bat**.

4. Select [Start]→[Programs]→[Command Prompt] to open the Command Prompt window.

5. Type the name of the file you just created, and press Enter. The command in the file will run (see Figure 12-11), and the Backup program will start and begin work. Check to see that it's backing up the paths you specified.

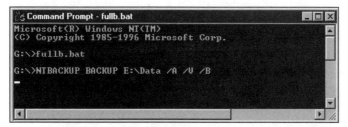

Figure 12-11 You can run the command from the Command Prompt.

6. Return to Notepad and replace the original line with: **NTBACKUP BACKUP** *pathnames* **/A /V /B /T differential**.

7. Save this file as **diffb.bat**. This time, you're performing a differential backup; that's what **/T differential** means.

8. Go to the Command Prompt window and type **diffb.bat**, and then press Enter. Again, the Backup program should run the command.

9. Select Start → Settings → Control Panel .

10. Double-click the Services icon. The Services dialog box opens (see Figure 12-12).

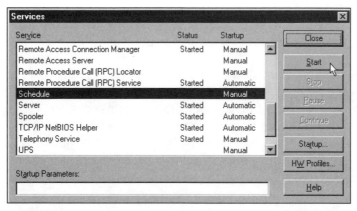

Figure 12-12 Turn on the Schedule service.

11. Click the Schedule service in the list, and then click the Start button. If you have Administrator privileges, the service should start.

12. Click Close.

13. Go to the Command Prompt window. At the command line, type **AT** *time* **/EVERY:***days* **fullb.bat,** and then press Enter. *Time* is the time of day at which you want to run the full backup, and *days* are the days of the week on which you want to run it (M, T, W, TH, F, S, and SU).

14. At the command line, type **AT** *time* **/EVERY:***days* **diffb.bat,** and then press Enter. You can see examples of these commands in Figure 12-21. The AT command schedules batch files to run at specified times.

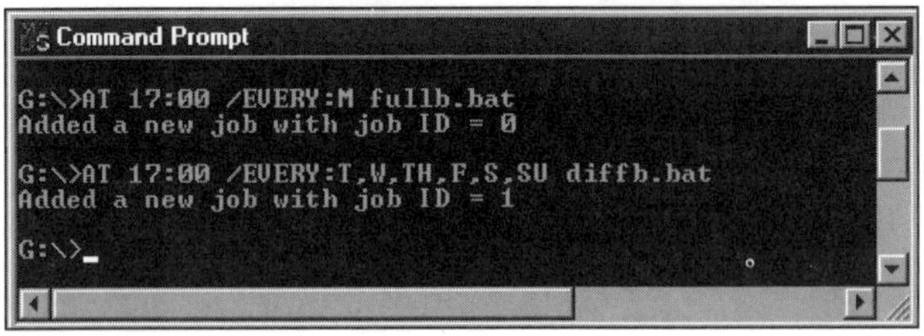

Figure 12-13 Tell NT when to run the backups.

That's it. You've scheduled two types of backup: a weekly full backup and daily differential backups.

TIP   There's a lot more you can do with this backup scheduling system. See the Windows NT help system for more information. In Backup, select Help→Search for Help on, type batch, and press Enter.

Summary

Windows NT Backup is not a great program. (Microsoft knows that, which is why they've hardly changed the program in three or four years.) You should seriously consider a program that is more powerful and more convenient. Backups are extremely important, so you should do everything you can to make performing backups easy.

A good backup program automatically runs backups for you periodically (as you just learned, you can automate backups with Windows NT Backup, but not easily). That's an important feature, because the major stumbling block with backups is forgetting to back up, or simply not being disciplined enough to do it regularly ("Oh, it can wait until tomorrow!").

Good backup programs also enable you to filter out files. Why bother backing up *.tmp or ~$*.* files (which are temporary files accidentally left on your disk drive), for example, or the files in your Web browser's cache? With a filter system, you can easily omit useless files. So, if it's your responsibility to take care of the data on your computer, check into getting a more sophisticated backup program.

CHAPTER THIRTEEN

SIMPLE COMMUNICATIONS — HYPERTERMINAL & PHONE DIALER

IN THIS CHAPTER YOU LEARN THESE KEY SKILLS

PREPARING YOUR MODEM   PAGE 240

WORKING WITH HYPERTERMINAL   PAGE 244

WORKING ONLINE   PAGE 246

SETTING UP A NEW CONNECTION   PAGE 250

USING THE PHONE DIALER   PAGE 250

Windows NT comes with a nice little serial communications program called HyperTerminal. Why? Well, just three years ago or so, most communication between computers that wasn't being carried out across a LAN (Local Area Network) was carried out using serial communications programs. If you wanted to dial into CompuServe, you used one. If you wanted to connect across the phone lines to a friend's, colleague's, or client's computer, you'd use one. Even if you wanted to connect to the Internet, you'd use one.

Things have changed a lot in a short time, and now most communications are carried out using more sophisticated systems, as you'll see in Chapter 16. Still, the serial communications program is in NT and available for use . . . and you may want to use it. There are still thousands of BBSs (bulletin board services) spread around the world, and if you want to connect two computers directly together, well, a serial communication program is a relatively easy way to do that. In this chapter, I'm going to explain how to use HyperTerminal. I'll also quickly describe the Phone Dialer program, something few people use, but who knows, you may want to use it once you know what it does.

TIP If you can't find HyperTerminal or Phone Dialer on your system, then they haven't been installed yet. Double-click the Add/Remove Programs icon in the Control Panel, click the Windows NT Setup tab, double-click the Communications entry, check the boxes on the HyperTerminal and Phone Dialer entries, and then click OK twice.

Preparing Your Modem

Before you can use these communications programs — or Dial-Up Networking, which you'll see in Chapter 14 — you must configure your modem and phone. Here's how:

1. Select Start → Settings → Control Panel.
2. Double-click the Modems icon. The Modems Properties dialog box opens (see Figure 13-1).

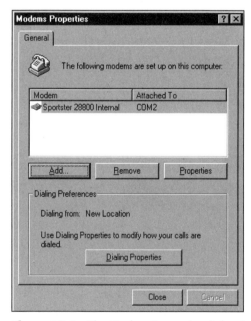

Figure 13-1 The Modem Properties dialog box.

3. Your modem may already be listed in this box (refer to Figure 13-1). If not, click Add to see the Install New Modem dialog box.
4. Click Next and NT starts looking for your modem. Make sure it's turned on if it's an external modem.

5. If you are lucky, NT will eventually find your modem. If you are not so lucky, you'll see a message saying that it has been unable to find the modem, or perhaps it mis-identified the modem. (If so, click Change, click Show All Devices, and select your modem's manufacturer and model. You'll also have to pick the correct COM port.)

6. If the correct modem is shown, click Next. NT installs the drivers for the modem. You're then prompted to insert the NT installation CD.

7. When NT has finished installing your modem, click Finish.

8. To complete the installation, you should restart your computer.

Now you can set up the modem to work the way you want it to. Follow these steps:

1. In the Modems Properties dialog box, click Properties.

2. Choose the speaker volume you want to use. Almost all modems have speakers so that you can hear what's going on while the modem connects. Drag the slider into position.

3. Select the modem's maximum speed. This may already be done for you. Generally, you want to pick a speed that is faster than the modem's rated speed.

   You may be able to select *Only connect at this speed*, if your modem supports it. This option stops the modem from making connections at speeds lower than the one selected. However, this may cause more trouble than it's worth — if you try to connect to a busy system, you may be given a slower modem and lose your connection.

5. Click the Connect tab to see the information shown in Figure 13-2.

6. The first three entries — *Data bits*, *Parity*, and *Stop bits* — define how the modem transmits data after it has connected. You should change these only if told to do so by a service you are having trouble connecting to.

7. Generally, the *Wait for dial tone before dialing* setting should remain checked. This means that the modem listens for the dial tone and then begins dialing. But, if your modem has trouble recognizing the dial tone, or if you have to dial manually before using the modem, you can clear this box.

8. The *Cancel the call if not connected within* setting defines how long the modem should wait before giving up if there's no answer when calling a service. You can leave this as it is for now, or enter a different value.

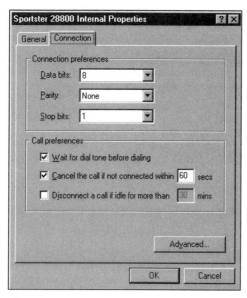

Figure 13-2 The Connection information.

9. The *Disconnect a call if idle for more than* setting is a way to save money, both online charges and toll charges. If you check this box, NT automatically disconnects the modem if you connect to another system but go for more than the specified time without transferring information to or from the other system.

10. Click OK to return to the Modems Properties dialog box.

11. Click Dialing Properties to see the dialog box in Figure 13-3. This box is used to define *how* NT must dial from your location.

12. If you want, you can change the name in the *I am dialing from* text box — change it to **Home**, or **Office**, or whatever you want. You can actually create multiple location settings (using the New button), if you have a laptop, for example.

13. Enter your area code into the *The area code is* box. This helps NT know when you are dialing a long-distance call.

14. Select the country from which you will be calling in the *I am in* drop-down list box.

15. If you must dial a special number to get an outside line, type that number into the *To access an outside line, first dial x for local* box. Also type the number (or another number, if you have to use a different number for long-distance calls) into the *for long distance* box.

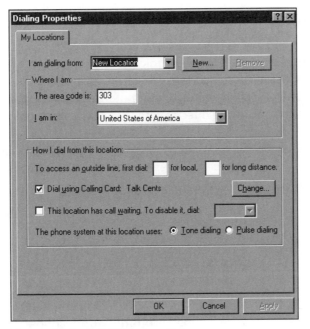

Figure 13-3 Tell NT how to dial.

16. If you want to dial a particular long-distance service to place calls, check the *Dial using Calling Card* check box, and then click Change. (I'll discuss how to work with your long-distance service in "Setting Up Long Distance Services and Calling Cards," later in this chapter).

17. If the line on which you are going to use the modem has call waiting, check the *This location has call waiting* check box. Then select the appropriate code (it varies from area to area) to disable call waiting in the *To disable it, dial* drop-down list box.

TIP If you don't disable call waiting, incoming calls will cause your modem to drop its connections.

18. Select either the *Tone dialing* or *Pulse dialing* option button. Most areas have tone dialing these days. (With tone dialing, when you dial a number, the phone beeps. With pulse dialing, it "click-click-clicks.")

19. Click OK to close the dialog box.

20. Click Close to close the Modems Properties box.

Working with HyperTerminal

HyperTerminal is a serial-communications program. It allows you to connect to bulletin board services and other computers. If a colleague has a Macintosh or Windows 3.1 computer, for example, you can use HyperTerminal to communicate directly with the other person or send files between your computers. (Of course, the other person has to have some form of serial-communications programs set up, too, although not necessarily HyperTerminal.)

There are two ways to open HyperTerminal. You can select the program itself, in which case it will assume that you want to configure a new connection — that is, you are going to tell it which computer you want to connect to. Or you can select a connection that has already been created, and HyperTerminal opens and prepares to connect to the appropriate service.

To open HyperTerminal itself, so that you can set up a new connection, select Start→Programs→Accessories→HyperTerminal, or select Start→Programs→Accessories→HyperTerminal→HyperTerminal.

To open one of the connections that has already been set up for you, select Start→Programs→Accessories→HyperTerminal→ and choose from one of the following: AT&T Mail.ht, CompuServe.ht, HyperTerminal BBS.ht, Microsoft BBS.ht, or MCI Mail.ht. These are different online services. You can get into the Microsoft BBS and HyperTerminal BBS sites for free. You have to be a member of the other services to try them.

To use this system, follow these steps:

1. Select Start → Programs → Accessories → Hyperterminal → Microsoft BBS.ht . You'll see the window shown in Figure 13-4.

2. The dialog box in the middle shows you the number that is about to be dialed. Notice that it includes any extra digits that must be dialed for outside lines or calling cards.

3. Click Dial, and HyperTerminal begins dialing the number.

4. When you are connected to the service (see Figure 13-5), follow the instructions on screen.

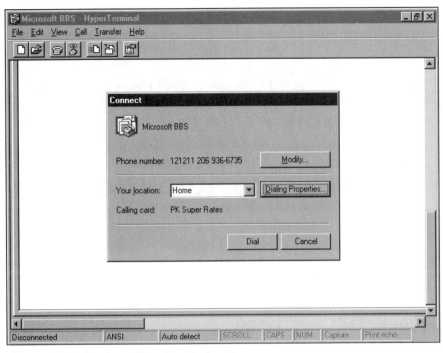

Figure 13-4 Starting a HyperTerminal session.

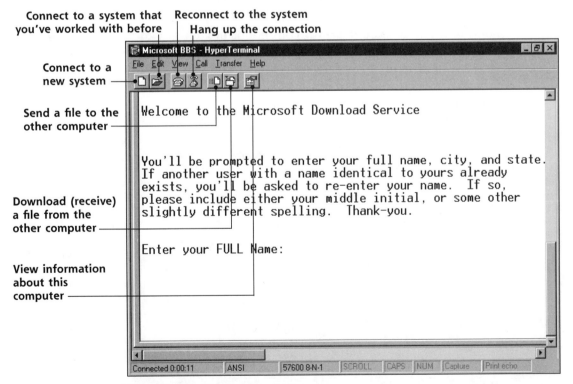

Figure 13-5 You're connected!

SIMPLE COMMUNICATIONS — HYPER TERMINAL & PHONE DIALER

SIDE TRIP

800 Numbers

Oops, here's a problem. What if you are dialing an 800 number? HyperTerminal will treat it as a normal long-distance number. If you have set up a calling card, use your calling card, even though you don't want to use (and perhaps *can't* use) a calling card for a toll-free call. Click <u>D</u>ialing Properties, clear the *Dial using Calling Card* check box, and then click OK. Remember to change the setting back the next time you *do* want to use your calling card.

Better still, create a different "location" for toll-free calls. Call it Toll Free. Then, whenever you are making toll-free calls, you can select Toll Free from the *Your Location* drop-down list box. (To create new locations, click the New button next to the *I am dialing from* text box in the Dialing Properties dialog box.)

Working Online

How do you work online? Each system is different. It may be a bland, black and white text-only system. Or it may be a colorful graphics system. Once connected to a system, your computer becomes a *dumb terminal* of that computer; you'll use the commands provided by that computer. With a little luck, the commands will be easy to use and easy to understand, probably with some kind of menu system from which you can pick. In some cases, the commands will be confusing and obscure, but that's a problem with the program running on the other computer, not with HyperTerminal. All HyperTerminal can do is deliver you to the other computer . . . and provide a few tools to make things a little simpler.

Table 13-1 lists the commands and buttons in HyperTerminal.

TABLE 13-1   HyperTerminal Commands

Button	Command	Description
◻	File → New Connection	Set up a connection for another service. I'll look at this in more detail in "Setting Up a New Connection," later in this chapter.
📂	File → Open	Connect to a different system, one you've worked with before.

Button	Command	Description
☎	**Call** → **Connect**	Reconnect to the system you previously disconnected from.
☎	**Call** → **Disconnect**	Hang up the current connection.
📄	**Transfer** → **Send File**	Upload a file to the other system.
📄	**Transfer** → **Receive File**	Transfer a file from the other system to your hard drive.
🗔	**File** → **Properties**	View information about the current connection setup.
	Edit → **Copy**	Highlight text on the screen, then select this command to copy that text to the Clipboard.
	Edit → **Paste to Host**	Transmits text from the Clipboard to the other computer. You may have written a letter in Notepad earlier, for example, and now you can paste it into the HyperTerminal window to send it quickly.
	Edit → **Select All**	Selects all the text on the screen. You can then copy the text.
	View → **Font**	Modifies the font size and also determines the size of the small terminal window within the main HyperTerminal window. (You can see this terminal window in Figure 13-6.)
	View → **Snap**	Opens up the HyperTerminal window to show the full terminal window within.
	Transfer → **Capture Text**	Tell HyperTerminal to keep a log file — all the text transmitted to or from your computer is saved in a text file.
	Transfer → **Send Text File**	Select this to transmit the text from a file. This is another quick way to upload information.
	Transfer → **Capture to Printer**	Prints the entire session.

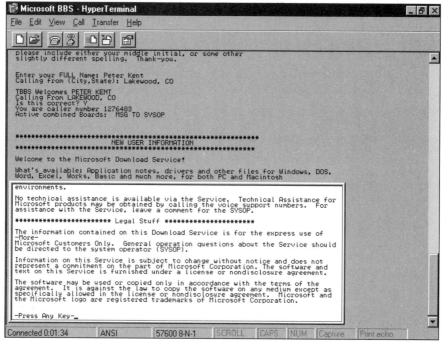

Figure 13-6 Within the HyperTerminal window is a smaller terminal window. The text scrolls off the screen at the top into the gray area.

Downloading files

One of the more common uses of serial-communications programs such as HyperTerminal is to download files from bulletin board services (BBS). For example, say you go to the Microsoft Web site to download Word Viewer, a program that can display Word for Windows files. You find the file. Here's how to download it:

1. Use whatever commands the BBS specifies to download the file. For example, in Figure 13-7, I typed **d** to select the Download mode, then typed the name of the file that I wanted, and then pressed Enter.

2. The BBS will probably ask you what type of download you want to use. There are many different methods. ZMODEM is one of the best types of transfer — it begins the transfer to your system automatically, and if the transmission fails for some reason, you can come back and transfer just the part of the file that wasn't transmitted, not the entire file.

3. Type z and the transmission begins automatically — there's nothing for you to do but sit back and wait.

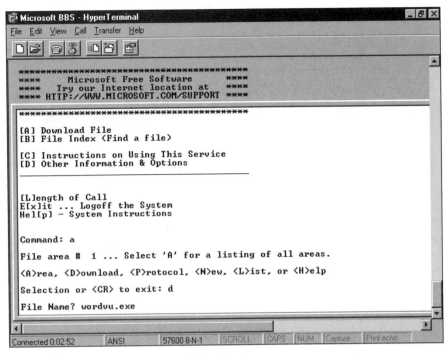

Figure 13-7 Here's how to start a download.

If you select another form of download, you'll have to select the download type. Do that by clicking the Receive button. In the dialog box that opens (see Figure 13-8), you can specify to which directory to download the file and which download type to use.

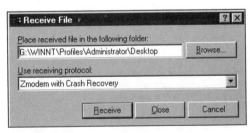

Figure 13-8 You can, if you really need to, specify the download type.

Sending files, which is done far less frequently than downloading files, is similar. You use the Send button to open a similar dialog box, in which you select the file that you want to upload and the upload type.

SIDE TRIP

PROBLEMS?

Sometimes a connection you set up won't work properly. If you find that you can't see what you are typing, try this. Click the Properties button, click the Settings tab, and then click AS<u>C</u>II Setup. In the dialog box that opens, check *Echo typed characters locally* and click OK. Then try again.

Setting Up a New Connection

Here's how to set up a new connection of your own — so that you can connect to a BBS — rather than using the ones provided for by Windows NT:

1. Select Start → Programs → Accessories → Hyperterminal . If HyperTerminal is already open, click the New button.
2. Type the name of the service you are connecting to.
3. Select an icon from the list.
4. Click OK.
5. Type the phone number you have to dial to connect to this BBS, and click OK. You'll now see the Connect dialog box (refer to Figure 13-4).
6. Click Dial to begin dialing.

Using the Phone Dialer

Windows NT contains a simple phone-dialing program that uses your modem to dial the phone for you. You can use this program if you have a modem connected to the same line your phone is connected to. Use the Phone Dialer to make the call, and then, when it starts ringing, pick up your phone.

This program may be too simple to be truly useful, although some users may like it. To open it, select Start→Programs→Accessories→Phone Dialer. You can see the window in Figure 13-9.

Type the number into this box, or select an earlier number from the drop-down list box

Create speed-dial numbers for faster dialing

or press these keys to select the number

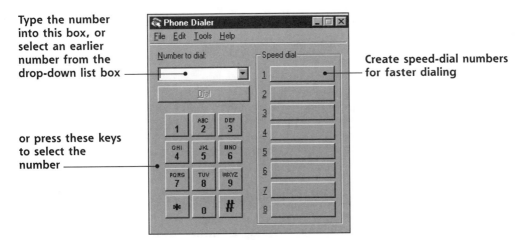

Figure 13-9 The Phone Dialer window.

Here's how to enter a number for the program to dial:

1. Click the number keys to enter the number you want to dial, or click inside the text box and type the number. Remember all the dialing properties and the credit-card calling information you entered? Well, Phone Dialer uses all that information. If you want to call (619) 555-1212, all you need to enter is **6195551212**. Phone Dialer adds the outside-line access code, the long-distance access code, and so on.

2. If you've made calls before using Phone Dialer, you can select an earlier number from the *Number to dial* drop-down list box.

3. Click Dial to begin dialing.

4. Pick up your phone, and then click the Talk button. The modem disconnects and leaves you ready to continue the call.

Well, that's all very nice, but you could dial the phone quicker! The advantage of Phone Dialer is that you can retrieve earlier numbers from the *Number to dial* drop-down list box. You can also set up the Speed Dial buttons. Select Edit→Speed Dial.

Click the button you want to configure, type the person's name, press Tab, and then type the person's phone number. When you're finished modifying numbers, click Save.

TIP Open the Dialer.ini file, in the \Winnt\ directory — double-click the file and it opens in Notepad — and enter speed-dial numbers directly into the Speed dial section. You can also modify the Last dialed numbers section to add or remove numbers from the *Number to dial* drop-down list box.

SIMPLE COMMUNICATIONS — HYPER TERMINAL & PHONE DIALER

BONUS

Setting Up Long Distance Services and Calling Cards

If you want to dial using a particular long-distance service or long-distance calling card, you need to click the Change button in the Dialing Properties box. When you do so, you see the Change Calling Card dialog box (see Figure 13-10).

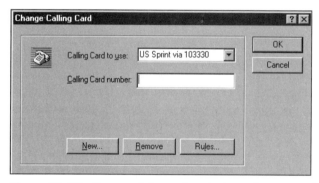

Figure 13-10 You can dial your favorite long-distance service.

Simply select the service you want to use, and then, if appropriate, enter your card number. Although this feature is called the Calling Card feature, it's not only for calling cards. For example, many people dial a special number to get to their long-distance service from home. I have one long-distance service that my phone accesses automatically whenever I dial a long-distance number, another service that I access by dialing a special code (because it gives me good long-distance rates), and a third service, also accessed by a special code (because it gives me good international rates). Unfortunately, you can set up only one long-distance service, although you could set up two or more "locations," one for each long-distance service.

So, you may not need to enter a calling-card number. Take a look at the Sprint service, for example. You have three options:

US Sprint Direct Dial via 103331. This service doesn't require a card number. It's used for calling directly from your home or office, and calls are billed to the number from which you are calling.

US Sprint via 103330. This service is the calling-card service; you do need to enter a calling-card number, or it won't work.

US Sprint via 1-800-877-8000. This service is also the calling-card service; it's simply a different way to access the service. Again, you do need a card number.

You'll find a couple dozen services already set up. If the service you use is not there, you can add your own. Here's how:

1. Click the New button and type the name of the service.

2. You'll see a message box. Click the OK button in this box, and the Dialing Rules dialog box opens.

   Some basic dialing rules are already in this box. Here's what they mean:

Code Box	Code	Meaning
CALLS WITHIN THE SAME AREA CODE	G	When making a local call, simply dial the area number without using the long-distance service.
LONG DISTANCE CALLS	1FG	Dial 1 (in the U.S., that's the long-distance access code), then the area code (F), and then the local number (G).
INTERNATIONAL CALLS	011EFG	Dial 011 (in the U.S., that's the international access code), then the country code, then the area code (F), and then the local number (G).

3. You have to modify these codes to work with your card. Click the question mark button on the title bar, and then click inside any of the text boxes to see a list of these codes (see Figure 13-11). On the other hand, now that you can see the codes in this book, you don't need to open this box (which keeps disappearing, anyway, each time you type something).

TIP   If you know that another card has a similar access system to the one you want to use, or if you want to see some examples of how these codes are set up, click *Copy From* to copy the codes into the Change Calling Card dialog box.

4. Enter the correct codes to carry out the necessary procedures. The following table shows an example:

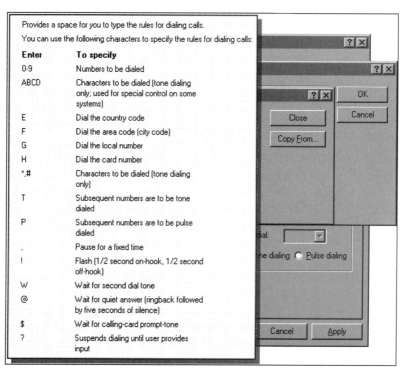

Figure 13-11 The codes you can use while setting up a calling card.

Code Box	Code	Meaning
CALLS WITHIN THE SAME AREA CODE	G	Leave this as it was before, because you won't be using your long-distance service when making local calls, anyway.
LONG DISTANCE CALLS	121211FG	Dial the code that accesses your long-distance service (12121, for example, which I'm hoping is a fake long-distance number!), dial 1, dial the area code (F), and then dial the local number (G).
INTERNATIONAL CALLS	12121011EFG	Dial the code that accesses your long-distance service (12121), dial 011 (the international access code), dial the country code, dial the area code (F), and then dial the local number (G).

The system in the previous table doesn't use a calling-card number — the call is billed to the number of the line on which you make the call. Here's an example of entering a calling-card number:

Code Box	Code	Meaning
LONG DISTANCE CALLS	12121,0FG$H	Dial the code that accesses your long-distance service (12121), pause for a moment (,), dial 0, dial the area code (F), and then dial the local number (G). Finally, wait for the calling-card prompt tone ($), and then dial the card number entered into the Change Calling Card box (H).

5. When you've entered the codes correctly, click Close, and then click OK twice to close the two remaining dialog boxes.

TIP To modify your credit-card and dialing properties later, double-click the Telephony icon in Control Panel.

Summary

Things have changed a lot in the last few years. Just three years ago, most PC communications across phone lines were carried out using serial communications programs such as HyperTerminal. These days, most are carried out using TCP/IP programs, which are designed to work with the Internet. You'll learn more about that in Chapter 16.

Still, there's a wealth of information and software available on BBSs around the world. You'll probably find dozens of these services locally, available with a local phone call — check your local computer newspapers for numbers.

PART THREE

NETWORKING, THE INTERNET, AND INTRANETS

THIS PART CONTAINS THE FOLLOWING CHAPTERS

CHAPTER **14** USING THE NETWORK NEIGHBORHOOD & NETWORK UTILITIES

CHAPTER **15** CORRESPONDING WITH E-MAIL

CHAPTER **16** COMPUTING ON THE ROAD AND ON THE INTERNET

CHAPTER **17** USING THE INTERNET — INTERNET EXPLORER & PERSONAL WEB PUBLISHING

"No man is an island," they say, and it's doubly true of NT workstations. They're designed to be connected together, and they usually are. In Part 3, you'll see how, from working on a local network to working on the Internet. If you have to stay connected, you'll need this information to keep from getting lost.

IMAGINATION IS MORE IMPORTANT THAN KNOWLEDGE

Bruce Hake is a closet techie. Lawyer by day, by night Hake metamorphoses into system administrator of Hake Internet Projects (http://hake.com, also known as HIP). HIP is an Internet service provider primarily serving Immigration Lawyers on the Web (http://www.ilw.com).

Hake wears both lawyer and sysadmin hats in his home office in Silver Springs, Maryland. His office — roughly the size of a walk-in closet — is crammed with a T1 line, five regular phone lines, four computers, a fax and printer, and network hardware hanging on the wall. Observing all is a poster of Albert Einstein, with his eternal words of wisdom, "Imagination is more important than knowledge." Hake's imagination is certainly the driving force behind his NT-powered Web site.

In the early 1990s, when Hake began to envisage running a bulletin board system (BBS) for immigration lawyers, he did background research to find a suitable operating system. Both UNIX and IBM's OS/2 evangelists caught his ear. Technology novice that he was, "I decided on OS/2," Hake says. "I spent a fortune on the OS/2 development package, and I got miles deep in it and on the OS/2 Usenet discussion groups. I became an extremely zealous OS/2 proponent. Showed it off to people all the time."

Hake moved along in his BBS planning. Then early in 1995, Hake got wind of the World Wide Web. "My brother and I called each other up and found out we had both discovered the Web the same day," Hake recalls. "We got so excited about it, we decided to start a company."

Hake set about learning CGI scripting and HTML coding in the OS/2 world. He investigated OS/2-based Web servers. The moment of truth soon arrived. He knew he'd be using a PC, but the fundamental technological uncertainty was the operating system. "I wanted to use OS/2, but when we went searching for the various helper applications for a complete Internet node, the applications simply were not available in OS/2," Hake says.

Hake chose Windows NT over UNIX for a number of reasons. "NT is much more secure," he says. "As a system administrator, I get constant notices about security holes in UNIX systems, but have seen only one issue concerning a security hole in NT. NT requires less ongoing maintenance tweaking, so it saves time. Coming from a PC background, it was more familiar than UNIX. It looked more like the wave of the future."

Furthermore, Hake is impressed with NT's robustness. "NT is solid as a rock, even more so than OS/2, to my amazement," he says. "In 14 months with NT, I've had the 'blue screen of death' only once. With OS/2, it happened every few weeks."

CHAPTER FOURTEEN

USING THE NETWORK NEIGHBORHOOD AND NETWORK UTILITIES

IN THIS CHAPTER YOU LEARN THESE KEY SKILLS

PREPARING YOUR NETWORK CONNECTION PAGE 260

USING NETWORK NEIGHBORHOOD PAGE 262

SHARING YOUR INFORMATION ON THE NETWORK PAGE 267

ACCESSING THE NETWORK THROUGHOUT NT PAGE 269

IMMEDIATE MESSAGING — USING CHAT PAGE 270

A few years ago, if you wanted to share digital information with another person in your company, you'd have to use what's come to be known as the *sneakernet*. You'd copy the information onto a disk, and then walk to the other person's office (perhaps strolling along in your sneakers) and hand over the disk.

These days, millions of offices are networked. The computers are connected by wires, and data flies across those wires between the computers. Need to work on a file on a colleague's computer? You can connect to that computer across the network and open the files. Need to share your information with others? You can do that, too. Want to print on someone else's computer? No problem.

The two roles played on a network are the role of the server and that of the workstation. A *server* is a computer that has a resource — a computer file or printer, for example — that other people want to use. These people can connect to the server and use those resources; the connecting computers are known as *workstations*.

259

Windows NT actually makes it easy for your computer to act as both server and workstation, thus providing resources for other computers to use and using resources provided by other computers. Your computer can be both a workstation and a server at the same time. (This is sometimes known as *peer-to-peer networking*.) And that's what this chapter is all about — how to share resources on an NT network.

Preparing Your Network Connection

Setting up a network connection is not for the faint of heart, nor for the networking neophyte. If you don't understand networking, you may be able to install a network card in a computer and get it running . . . but you may not. To some degree, installation depends on how well the software and installation instructions for the card have been written.

Take a quick look at the network settings, however, to find out if you have a card properly installed and configured. Right-click the Network Neighborhood icon, and then choose Properties. If your networking software *isn't* installed, you'll see a message box asking if you want to install it. Click the Yes button to open the Network Setup Wizard. I'll discuss this in "Installing a Network Card," later in this chapter.

If your software is connected, you'll see the dialog box shown in Figure 14-1. This box shows your computer's name and the name of the *workgroup* of which it is a part. A workgroup is simply a group of computers that have information that needs to be shared within the group. For example, there may be a Sales Department workgroup, an Accounting Department workgroup, a Documentation Department workgroup, and so on. The workgroup name is used to identify the group throughout NT — in the Network Neighborhood and the Printers folder, for example — so that you can connect to other computers in your group and use the resources (files, folders, printers, and so on) that those computers have made available to the other members of the group. However, you cannot connect to computers in workgroups of which you are not a member.

Click the Change button to see the dialog box shown in Figure 14-2. This is where you enter your workgroup information. Your system administrator may have already entered this for you. In any case, don't enter anything here unless your administrator has told you what to enter.

The other options are the domain options. You can be a member of a workgroup or a domain. A *domain* is a sort of super workgroup. You must log onto a domain using a *user name* and *password* provided to you by the system administrator. You can enter this information only after the administrator has set up the domain. As soon as you enter the information and click OK, your computer will contact the domain server. Click the *Domain* option button, and then type the domain name your system administrator gave you.

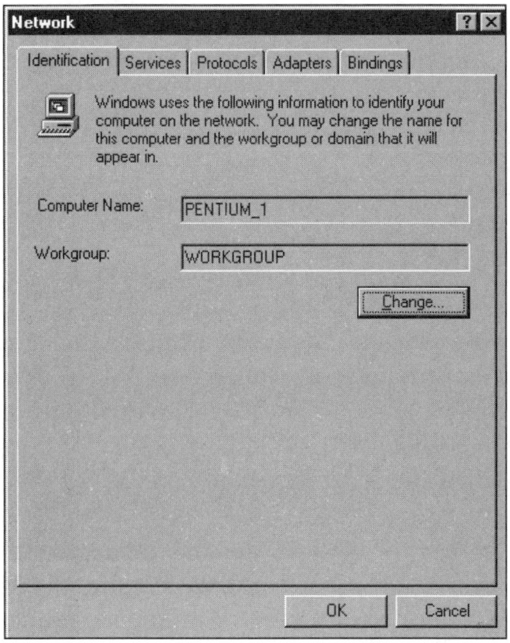

Figure 14-1 Your workgroup information.

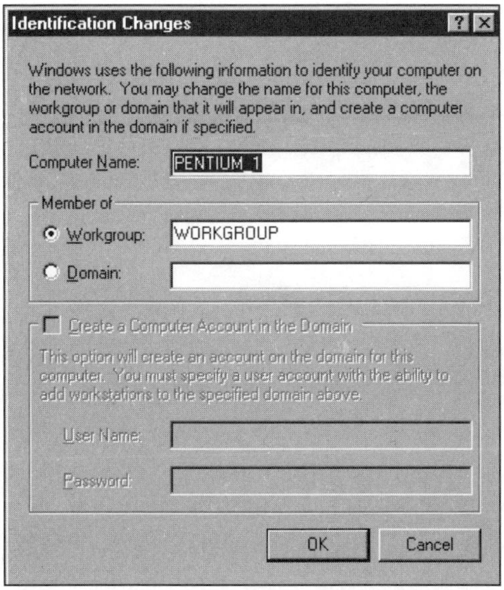

Figure 14-2 Set up your workgroup or domain here.

If you are the system administrator or have the right to add users to the domain, you can click the *Create a Computer Account in the Domain* check box and then enter your *User Name* and *Password*. When you click OK, the computer is added to the domain.

Take a look at the other information in the Network dialog box, if you want — Services, Protocols, Adapters, and Bindings — but don't modify anything in these boxes without help from the system administrator. This stuff is all a little complicated and cannot be configured unless you know how the administrator has configured the network.

Using Network Neighborhood

There are a couple ways to use Network Neighborhood. You'll remember from Chapter 6 that you can view folders and disks two ways. You can view them in simple one-pane folders. For example, double-click My Computer, and you'll see a folder with a single pane. Or you can view them in Windows NT Explorer, which has two panes, folders in the left pane and folder contents in the right pane.

The same goes for Network Neighborhood. You can view the disks and folders on other computers in a single-pane window, or you can open Windows NT Explorer and view the network disks and folders in there, with two panes.

To open Network Neighborhood in a single-pane window (see Figure 14-3), you can

* Double-click the Network Neighborhood icon.
* Right-click the Network Neighborhood icon and select Open .

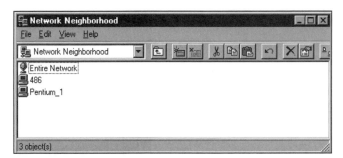

Figure 14-3 Network Neighborhood, in a folder window.

To view Network Neighborhood in NT Explorer, that is, in two panes, you can

* Right-click the Network Neighborhood icon on your desktop and select Explore .
* If you are already in NT Explorer, double-click the Network Neighborhood folder icon.

How do these windows work? Just like the ones you saw in Chapter 6. I won't cover that ground again, so if you need more information about the commands and buttons available in these windows, refer to that chapter. I will, of course, discuss the network-specific commands. I personally find NT Explorer easier to work with than the one-pane folder window, so I'll use that as an example. The principles are the same for the folder window, however.

There are two types of icons below the Network Neighborhood:

🖳 This icon represents another computer in your workgroup.

🌐 This icon represents the network as a whole. Use this to see other resources — other printers and folders — available on the network.

Finding the data you need

To find what you need on another computer, use the same methods you would use if you were digging around on your own hard disk. Treat the computer icons as folder icons. For example, in Figure 14-4 you can see what happened when I clicked the plus sign icon next to the computer named 486. A list of folders appeared below the icon (actually, it took a few moments for the list to appear, as my computer had to grab information about that computer from the network.

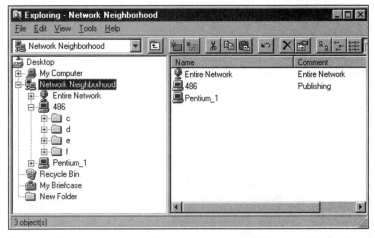

Figure 14-4 I opened up the computer named 486 by clicking the plus sign icon.

What are these folders? They're actually disk drives. That's right, each drive on the other computer is represented by a folder icon. Which drives do you see? The ones that have been shared (see "Sharing Your Information on the Network," later in this chapter).

You can now open these disk drives and see the directory folders within. For example, in Figure 14-5 I clicked the plus sign next to Primary drive C. I can now see the directory folders held by disk C on the computer named 486.

Figure 14-5 Open up a disk drive to see what's there.

A shortcut — mapping a drive

Here's a good shortcut you can use: You can make a directory on another computer's hard drive appear to be a disk drive on your system. That way, instead of digging your way through the other computer's directory tree each time you need something, you can simply open the fake drive. Here's how to create this shortcut from within Windows NT Explorer:

1. Click the Map Network Drive button, or select Tools → Map Network Drive . The dialog box shown in Figure 14-6 opens.

2. The drop-down list box at the top of the dialog box shows all the available disk-drive letters (including any you've already assigned to other network disks or folders). Select the one you want to use for the disk or folder you are about to add, or simply let NT select a disk letter for you.

3. You can type a path to the other computer's disk or folder into the *Path* text box, if you want. But it's usually easier to select the item from the *Shared Directories* list box.

4. If you are connecting to a domain resource, you can log onto the resource using a different domain account name. Enter the domain name, followed by a \, followed by the account name.

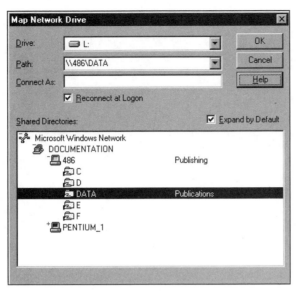

Figure 14-6 Choose the folder that you want to "pretend" is a hard drive on your system.

5. If you want to connect to this disk or directory folder every time you log onto NT, leave the *Reconnect by Logon* check box checked. If you plan to use it only this session, clear the box.

6. The *Expand by Default* check box doesn't do anything for you right now — it determines how this dialog box should act the *next time* you open it. If you clear the check box, the dialog box will show only the first line of the *Shared Directories* list box; it won't automatically show you all the available computers. You may want to clear the box if you are working on a slow or large network.

7. Double-click the computer that has the disk or folder you want to use.

8. Click the shared disk or folder you want to use. You can't actually tell which are folders and which are disks — the same icons are used for both. NT cares only that these are shared resources, disks, and individual directory folders with their subfolders.

9. Click OK and the resource appears in Windows NT Explorer as a disk drive (see Figure 14-7), although using a special icon.

10. To disconnect the drive that you've "created," click the Disconnect Net Drive button, or select Tools → Disconnect Network Drive. A dialog box appears where you can disconnect drives.

11. Click the mapped drive you want to disconnect, and then click OK.

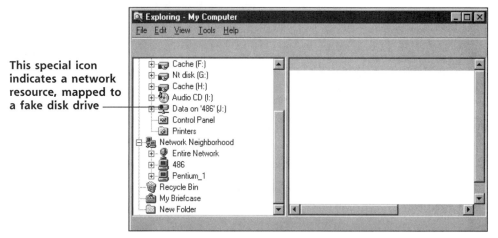

This special icon indicates a network resource, mapped to a fake disk drive

Figure 14-7 You've created a new "disk drive," from which you can access the remote data.

 TIP You can also map drives directly from the Network Neighborhood icon on the desktop. Right-click and select Map Network Drive. Right-click and select Disconnect Network Drive to remove mapped drives.

To quickly map a network drive if you've already opened the other computer's drive or folder in the Network Neighborhood, simply right-click the item, select Map Network Drive, and click OK in the dialog box that opens.

Find the computer you need

Are you looking for a particular computer that you know is on the network, but you don't want to dig through the hierarchy looking for it? If so, then use the Find Computer dialog box. You can open this dialog box several ways:

* Select Start → Find → Computer .
* Right-click the Network Neighborhood icon and select Find Computer .
* In Windows NT Explorer, select Tools → Find → Computer .

Whichever method you use, you'll see the Find Computer dialog box. Simply type the name of the computer you are looking for, and click Find Now. If the utility finds the computer you want, you'll see it in the list box that appears. Double-click the computer to open a folder.

Sharing Your Information on the Network

Okay, you've seen how to get to other people's information, but what about sharing your own? For example, you have a folder containing documents to which everyone in your department needs access. How can you allow them — and only them — to open this folder? Follow this procedure:

1. Right-click the folder or disk and select **Sharing**. The folder's Properties dialog box opens, displaying the Sharing panel.

2. Click the *Shared As* option button to turn on sharing (see Figure 14-8).

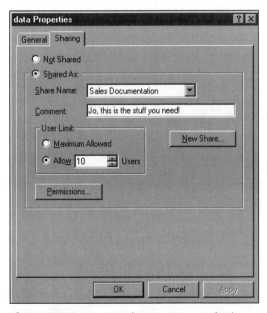

Figure 14-8 Here's where to turn on sharing.

3. The *Share Name* text box contains the real name of the folder or disk drive, but you can modify this name, if you want, to enter something more descriptive. If the folder name is data, for example, you might change it to Sales Documentation.

TIP A long name, such as Sales Documentation, is fine on an NT network, but if you have DOS computers connecting to this network, they won't be able to see the name. If you have DOS users who need to get to your stuff, use a shorter name — eight characters or less.

4. You can also enter a *Comment*. This appears in Windows NT Explorer, and various other places, to help users identify the resource. For example, you could type **Jo, this is the stuff you need!**

5. The *Maximum Allowed* option button is selected by default. This means that as many users as the network will allow can be connected. Or select *Allow* and enter a number between 1 and 10.

6. Click Permissions and the Access Through Share Permissions dialog box opens (see Figure 14-9).

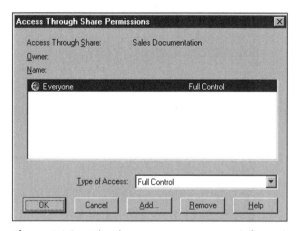

Figure 14-9 Who do you want to use your information?

7. If *Everyone* is shown in this box, click Remove to clear the entry.

8. Click Add and the Add Users and Groups dialog box opens.

9. Double-click the users or groups who you want to give access to your information. (You saw how to use this dialog box in Chapter 8.)

10. In the *Type of Access* drop-down list box, select the type of access you want to provide to these other users: No Access (used to selectively block users — you can provide access to a group and then block particular members), Read (the user can read the files but not modify them), Change (the user can read and modify the files), Full Control (the reader can do anything to the files, including taking ownership — see Chapter 8 — and modifying permissions).

11. Click OK and the selected users and groups are added to the Access Through Share Permissions dialog box.

12. Click OK (twice) to complete the operation.

Now, what happens when users other than those to whom you have granted permission try to access this directory? They'll see a nice little message telling them that they can't get to the information.

On the other hand, if someone is logged onto his or her NT Workstation computer with the correct user name and password, he or she can use the resource.

Accessing the Network Throughout NT

Network Neighborhood is not the only place you can connect to the network. As you've seen throughout this book, you can use network connections from all over the place. When you are installing a font (see Chapter 7), you can click the Network button to connect to another computer and grab a font from there. When you are adding a printer, you can use the Network Printer Server option button to use a printer on another computer (see Chapter 7).

You can even get to the network from within File Open and Save dialog boxes in your applications (see Figure 14-10). Simply select Network Neighborhood from the *Look in* drop-down list box, and then use the computers and folders that appear in the same way you'd use the drives and folders on your own computer.

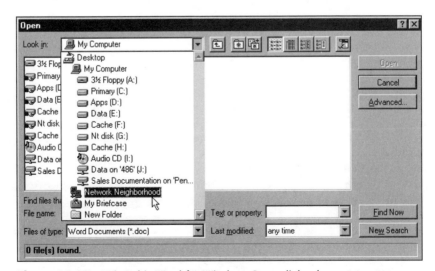

Figure 14-10 Using this Word for Windows Open dialog box, you can open files on other computers.

You can also view other computer's print queues. Double-click a printer in Windows NT Explorer, or even in the Printer's folder. (You can get to a computer by opening Network Neighborhood from the drop-down list box in the toolbar.)

Immediate Messaging — Using Chat

The following application is perfect for figuring out where to go for lunch. Without lifting the phone, without leaving your office, you can "chat" with others in your office using the Chat program. Well, you're not really chatting, you're typing, but never mind, it's still a handy little tool now and then.

Unlike e-mail (see Chapter 15), in which you send a message to someone and then do something else, Chat is an immediate, "real time" form of communication — when you type your message, the recipient reads it immediately, and you can see the response immediately. (Think of e-mail as sending a letter and Chat as making a phone call.) To open Chat, select Start→Programs→Accessories→Chat. The Chat window opens.

Here's how to use Chat:

1. Click the Chat session button, and the dialog box shown in Figure 14-11 opens.

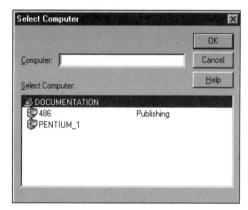

Figure 14-11   Pick the computer you want to call.

2. Double-click the computer you want to call. The Chat window on the other person's computer opens. That user can answer your call by clicking the pick-up icon.

3. Type your message in the top pane. The other person's message appears in the bottom pane.

4. When you're finished, click the Disconnect icon.

Setting up your chat window

You can make a few modifications to the Chat window. Select Options→Preferences to see the Preferences dialog box. You can use this box to change the position of the two panes, and you can select Use Own Font to override the font selection and background color that the other user has made. Then select Options→Font and Options→Background Color to modify the font and background colors.

BONUS

Installing a Network Card

As I mentioned earlier, setting up a network card can be a little tricky. Here's a quick overview of how it's done, but if you run into problems, you'll have to speak with the system administrator:

1. Right-click the Network Neighborhood icon, and then choose Properties . If your networking software *isn't* installed, you'll see a message box asking if you want to install it. Click the Yes button to open the Network Setup Wizard (see Figure 14-12). This enables you to install two types of software: the software needed to connect directly to a network, using an ISDN adapter or network adapter, and the software needed to run Dial-Up Networking, a system that enables you to dial into the network using your computer's modem. Check the appropriate check boxes.

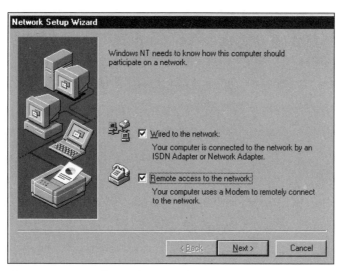

Figure 14-12 Tell NT what sort of network connection you want to set up.

2. Click Next to see the dialog box where you can specify the network adapter card you are using. The easiest way to do this is to click the Start Search button and let the wizard see if it can figure out which card you're working with.

3. If you're lucky, the wizard will find your card. If you're not, you'll get a message telling you to select from a list. Click the Select from list button to see that list (see Figure 14-13).

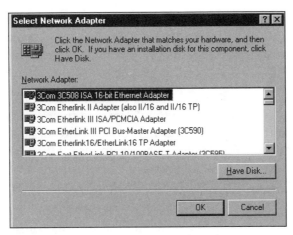

Figure 14-13 Select your network card.

4. Click the network card you have installed.

 TIP If you can't find your network adapter in the list, contact the manufacturer to see if they can send you the software you need. You'll then come back to this point in the procedure and click the Have Disk button.

5. Click OK to place the adapter into the Network Adapter's list inside the Network Setup Wizard box, and then click Next. You'll see a list of protocols (see Figure 14-14).

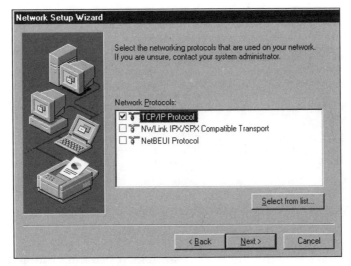

Figure 14-14 Pick your protocol.

6. A *protocol* is a sort of language used by the network. As long as all the computers on the network are using the same language — the same

protocol — they can talk to each other. Ask your system administrator which protocols you should select. Check the protocols you want to use by clicking the check boxes, and then click Next. You'll see a list of network services that you are about to install.

7. You can install more, too, by clicking on the *Select from list* button. You should talk with the network administrator to find out which of these services are appropriate for your network. For example, if you are working with a NetWare network, you can install the Client Service for NetWare service. If you want to set up a Web server on your own computer, you can select Microsoft Peer Web Services (see Chapter 17).

8. Click Next and you'll see a dialog box telling you that the wizard is ready to install. Click Next again, and the wizard begins. You may see a dialog box asking you where the NT files are found. Insert the NT Workstation CD into the disk drive and enter the disk letter (for example, **i:**) into the text box shown, and then click Continue.

9. If your adapter card is properly inserted — an NT-compatible card — and you specified the correct adapter, NT should now display the Adapter Properties dialog box (see Figure 14-15). This box shows the adapter type and configuration information. You can change the card's configuration, by clicking Change, but you shouldn't unless told to do so by the network administrator. Notice also that there's a Test button you can use to verify that NT is working correctly with the adapter (this is enabled only if NT has identified the card). Click OK to continue.

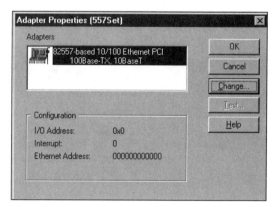

Figure 14-15   The Adapter Properties dialog box.

10. Depending on what protocols you've installed, you may see more messages and questions. For example, if you are installing Dial-Up Networking, you'll see a dialog box (talking about RAS, Remote Access Service, the name of the service to which Dial-Up Networking connects) asking if you want to install the software required to use a modem. If

you are installing the TCP/IP protocol, you'll see a dialog box asking for detailed setup information. This information varies greatly between networks, so you should contact the network administrator (or Internet service provider if you're using Dial-Up Networking to connect to a commercial Internet service) to find out what you need to enter into each box.

TIP Follow the instructions provided, and if you don't know the answers, talk with your system administrator. For more information about Dial-Up Networking, see Chapter 16.

11. After the network adapter and protocol software has been installed, you'll see the dialog box shown in Figure 14-16. This box enables you to modify the *bindings*, the manner in which the protocols, services, and network adapters are linked together. But don't play with this stuff unless your system administrator tells you what to do.

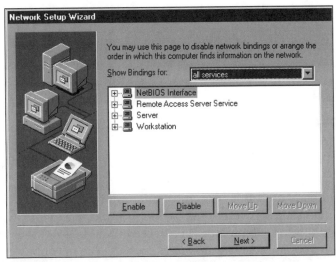

Figure 14-16 Don't change this bindings stuff unless you really know what you are doing!

12. Click Next and you'll see a message telling you that the wizard is ready to start the network. Click Next again, and after a few moments you'll see the dialog box shown in Figure 14-17. This box provides information that identifies your computer on the network. Enter the workgroup name your administrator told you to use. An administrator can also create an account for you in a domain from this dialog box. (That procedure requires an administrator's account name and password.)

13. Click Next, and then click Finish in the next dialog box, and you'll see another dialog box asking if you want to restart Windows NT — you must do so before you can begin working with the network.

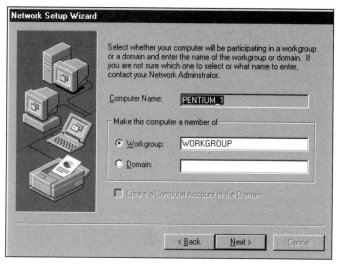

Figure 14-17 Enter the information that identifies your computer on the network.

Summary

Windows NT Workstation 4.0 is a network operating system. That is, it has all the software you need for sharing information across a network already built-in — and most NT computers are connected to networks. NT's networking software is really quite simple. If you know how to use other tools — Windows NT Explorer, the folder windows, the Open and Save boxes, and so on — you'll quickly figure out how to use the network tools, because they were built to work in almost exactly the same way. With a few clicks and double-clicks, you can quickly work with information stored on other computers in the same way you work with information stored on your own computer.

CHAPTER FIFTEEN
CORRESPONDING WITH E-MAIL

IN THIS CHAPTER YOU LEARN THESE KEY SKILLS

SETTING UP WINDOWS MESSAGING   PAGE 277

OPENING WINDOWS MESSAGING AND SENDING E-MAIL   PAGE 282

RETRIEVING AND READING E-MAIL   PAGE 284

USING REMOTE MAIL TO GRAB E-MAIL   PAGE 288

USING THE ADDRESS BOOK   PAGE 289

MUCH, MUCH, MORE   PAGE 292

Windows NT is designed for networking, and a basic component of networking is the capability to send messages between computers. NT uses a system called Windows Messaging to handle Microsoft Mail and Internet mail to and from your computer.

In this chapter, I'll look at how to work with Windows Messaging, from setting up your messaging system to sending and retrieving mail.

Setting Up Windows Messaging

Here's how to set up Windows Messaging:

1. Double-click the Inbox desktop icon. If Windows Messaging is already set up, the Windows Messaging window will open (see "Opening Windows Messaging and Sending E-mail," later in this chapter). If not, you'll see the dialog box shown in Figure 15-1.

Figure 15-1 NT helps you set up Windows Messaging.

 TIP No Inbox desktop icon? If you don't have it, you'll have to install the services. Double-click the Add/Remove Programs icon in Control Panel, click Windows NT Setup, check Windows Messaging at the bottom of the list box, and click OK.

2. The Windows Messaging Setup Wizard is going to configure Microsoft Mail (used across the Network) and Internet Mail (used with an Internet service provider). If you are using only one of these services, clear the other check box, and then click Next to see additional information.

3. In order to use Microsoft Mail, the network messaging system, you need a *postoffice*. This will be set up by the system administrator. The name of the postoffice may already appear in the text box, or you may have to enter it. Enter the path to the postoffice — the computer name and directories — or click Browse to find the computer that contains the postoffice. If you don't know where it is, ask your system administrator.

4. Click Next to see the dialog box with a list of user names that have postoffice accounts.

5. Select your name from the list. You can use the postoffice only if the administrator has set up an account for you. (See "Adding user accounts," later in this chapter.) Click Next and the dialog box with a Password field opens.

6. Simply type your password (which your system administrator set up for you). Click Next for the next dialog box that appears, if you chose the Internet Mail service.

7. You are now going to set up the Internet Mail service and tell the wizard how you are going to connect to the Internet mailbox. Select your

connection type. You can connect to an Internet service via modem, using Dial-Up Networking, or across the network. I'm going to cover how to set up the Internet Mail connection across the network. (See Chapter 16 for information about setting up Internet Mail via a modem.)

8. Click the Network option button, and then click Next. You'll see the dialog box in Figure 15-2.

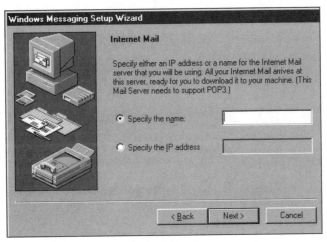

Figure 15-2 Tell NT how to connect to your network's Internet Mailbox.

9. You can enter a mailbox name or an IP (Internet Protocol) address. Your system administrator can provide this information. Click Next and the dialog box in Figure 15-3 opens.

Figure 15-3 Tell NT how to retrieve your mail.

CORRESPONDING WITH E-MAIL **279**

10. In this dialog box, you choose how you want NT to retrieve your messages. If you select Off-line, Windows Messaging retrieves only message *headers*, a line of information telling you what messages are waiting for you. You can then tell Messaging which messages to transfer to your computer. This is useful if you're working with a modem, but it's not so useful over a network. You probably will want to use Automatic, which tells Messaging to send the entire message automatically. Click Next to see the information shown in Figure 15-4.

Figure 15-4 Type your e-mail address.

11. Type in your complete Internet e-mail address, something like jsmith@thiscompany.com. If you're not sure what your e-mail address is, ask your system administrator. You can modify the *Your full name* line if you want. This is simply the name used to identify you in your mail messages. Click Next, and the information shown in Figure 15-5 appears.

12. The information you need to enter now is the account name and password used to log into the Internet mailbox. Again, if you're not sure what yours are, ask your system administrator.

13. Click Next to see additional information about creating an address book file.

14. Tell NT where to find your Personal Address Book. If you haven't used Messaging before, you won't have one, of course, so you can simply let NT create the mailbox.pab file for you. Click Next to create the file and display the next dialog box (see Figure 15-6).

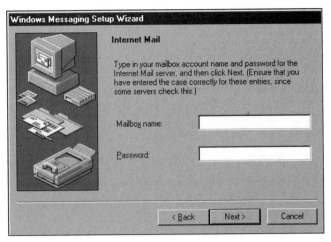

Figure 15-5 Enter your mailbox name and password.

Figure 15-6 NT now creates your personal folders.

15. This time, NT creates a personal folders file, the mailbox.pst file. This is simply a file that holds your e-mail. As you'll see when you work in Windows Messaging, your e-mail messages appear to be stored in folders, but they are really in this file.

16. Click Next, and a message box informs you that you are finished. Click the Finish button.

 TIP You can add (and remove) services later, from within the Windows Messaging window. Select Tools→Services, and then click the Add button.

CORRESPONDING WITH E-MAIL **281**

Opening Windows Messaging and Sending E-mail

Here's how to open Windows Messaging and send a message to someone:

1. Double-click the Inbox desktop icon, or select Start → Programs → Windows Messaging. A little logon box may open (see Figure 15-7). This box appears if you are logged onto your computer as the administrator; otherwise, it doesn't appear.

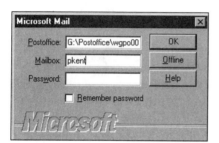

Figure 15-7 Enter your logon information.

TIP Windows Messaging does not work well when more than one user works with Messaging on the same computer. If you really *have* to set up such a situation, make sure that each user has a different .pst file (the personal folders file created during Windows Messaging Setup) and that each user opens Messaging after logging onto his or her own NT account. Separate users shouldn't log on to Messaging from within the Administrator account.

2. This logon box shows the postoffice to which you connect. You usually log onto the same one every time, so you won't have to change this. The Mailbox entry is your account name, and the Password is the password used to access that account. Ask your system administrator if you need (or forget) this information.

3. If you want NT to enter the password for you, check the *Remember password* check box. This means that after you log on to Windows NT, when you start the operating system, NT will assume that you have the right to use this mailbox.

Be careful about walking off and leaving your computer unattended, or others can get to the mailbox, too — without logging on.

4. If you don't want to log on and get messages from your mailbox or send messages — perhaps you are working with a laptop and aren't connected to the network right now — you can click Offline (there's no need to enter a password in this case). Otherwise, click OK. Either way, the Windows Messaging window will open (see Figure 15-8).

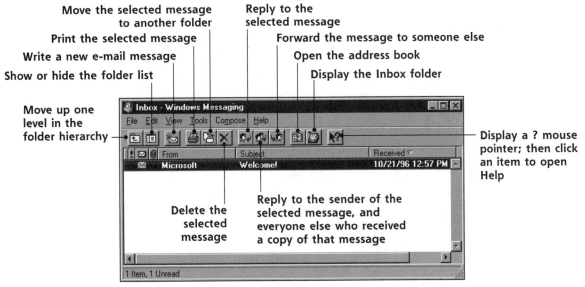

Figure 15-8 The Windows Messaging window.

5. Click the New Message toolbar button, and the New Message window opens (see Figure 15-9).

6. Type an e-mail address into the *To* text box, or click the To button to see the address book (you'll learn more about the address book in "Using the Address Book," later in this chapter). What do I mean by an e-mail address? Either a full Internet address (jsmith@thiscompany.com, for example) or, if using Microsoft Mail, another user name — for example, Peter Kent (not pkent).

7. If you want to send a copy of the message to someone else, type the e-mail address into the *Cc* box, or click the Cc button to open the address book.

8. In the *Subject* text box, type a few words describing the contents of the message. This line will appear in the recipient's Inbox for quick identification of the message.

9. Type your message in the large message area. This is just like a simple word processor. You can use the text-formatting tools to create bold, italic, and colored text. You can choose the font and font size, use bullets, and modify paragraph alignment.

TIP You may want to stick with basic NT fonts — not ones that you've added — or the recipient may not have the font you pick. Another consideration is formatting. You can format text when using Microsoft Mail. But if you are sending e-mail across the Internet, any formatting will be stripped out before the message is sent.

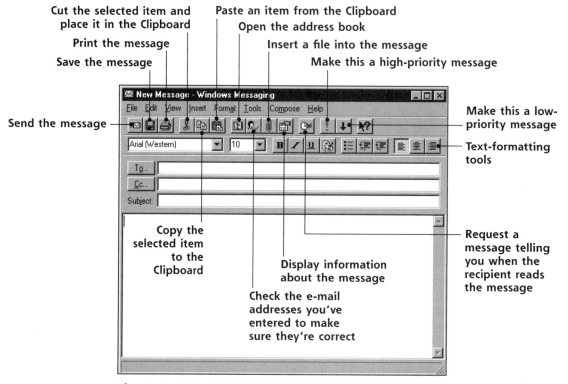

Figure 15-9 Create your message here.

10. When you finish your message, click the Send button. The message is placed in the Outbox and is sent either immediately or the next time you connect to the postoffice or Internet mail server.

 TIP If you want to experiment, send e-mail to yourself.

Retrieving and Reading E-mail

You can view your Windows Messaging window two ways. There's the one-pane view, which you saw in Figure 15-8, and the two-pane view, shown in Figure 15-10. Turn on this view by clicking the Show/Hide Folder List button or selecting View→Folders. With two-pane view turned on, you can see the structure of the folder system.

Figure 15-10 The Windows Messaging folder view, showing the two-pane view.

At the top of the figure, you can see Windows Messaging. This "box" holds two other boxes — the Microsoft Mail Shared Folders and Personal Folders boxes. Initially, Microsoft Mail Shared Folders doesn't contain anything, but you can create folders within this box (see "Much, Much, More," later in this chapter). You can use the Shared Folders to store messages that you want other postoffice users to be able to read. The Personal Folders box contains four folders (and you can add more):

* Deleted Items — Contains messages you've deleted from other folders.
* Inbox — Contains messages you've received.
* Outbox — Contains messages that you've written but haven't yet sent.
* Sent Items — Contains a copy of each message that you've sent.

You can quickly see what the Show/Hide Folder List and Up One Level toolbar buttons do here. Clicking the Show/Hide Folder List button immediately displays the contents of the Inbox folder in the right pane. Clicking the Up One Level button displays the contents of the Personal Folders box. Clicking Up One Level again displays the contents of the Windows Messaging. In other words, the Up One Level button works exactly like in Windows NT Explorer — it moves you up one level in the hierarchy.

So how do you read e-mail? It's easy. You already have a message — every new Inbox has a Welcome! message from Microsoft. Click Show/Hide Folder List to see the Inbox, and then double-click the message to open it. The window in Figure 15-11 opens.

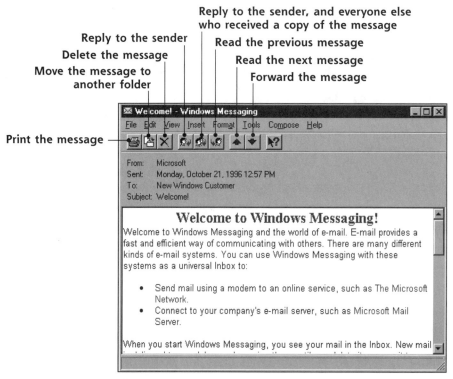

Figure 15-11 Here's where you read your messages.

TIP Now and then, you'll run into the term *Microsoft Exchange*, or simply *Exchange*. For example, some Windows Messaging dialog boxes refer to Exchange, and there's even a Start→Programs→Microsoft Exchange menu option. So what is Exchange? It's simply the original name given to Windows Messaging when it was first released in Windows 95.

How do you actually get your mail? How do you make Windows Messaging retrieve the messages from the postoffice or Internet mailbox? Messaging may be set up to automatically retrieve mail, or you may have to tell it to do so. Here's how to find out:

1. Select Tools → Service. The Services dialog box opens.

2. If you are using Internet Mail, select the Internet Mail entry and click Properties.

3. In the dialog box that opens, click the Connection tab. You'll see the information shown in Figure 15-12.

4. Notice the *Work off-line and use Remote Mail* check box. If this is checked, Windows Messaging will never automatically check for mail — you'll have to use Remote Mail, which I'll look at later in this chapter.

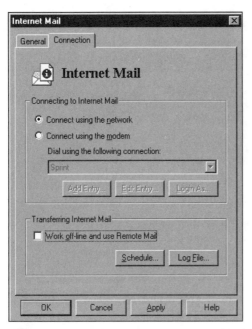

Figure 15-12   Here's where you set up the delivery options for Internet mail.

5. If you want Windows Messaging to grab mail automatically, make sure the check box is clear, and then click Schedule. Up pops a dialog box.

6. Enter a number into the incrementer box to tell Windows Messaging how often to check for mail.

7. Click OK twice to return to the Services dialog box. If you have Microsoft Mail, click the Microsoft Mail entry, and then click Properties. In the dialog box that opens, click the Delivery tab to see the dialog box in Figure 15-13.

8. Enter the retrieve interval into the *Check for new mail every X ___ minute(s)* box. Note that unless you are connected via a modem and Dial-Up Networking (see Chapter 16), there is no option for remote retrieval of Microsoft Mail. And the *Enable incoming mail delivery* and *Enable outgoing mail delivery* check boxes simply turn the e-mail system on and off.

9. Click OK twice to close the dialog boxes.

TIP   You can override the settings, and retrieve and send e-mail between normal scheduled times, by selecting Tools→Deliver Now Using→All Services.

Figure 15-13 Tell Messaging how often to check for Microsoft Mail.

Using Remote Mail to Grab E-mail

If you set up Windows Messaging to retrieve Internet e-mail via Remote Mail, or even Microsoft Mail via Remote Mail if you are using a Dial-Up Networking connection (Chapter 16), mail won't automatically come to or be sent from your mailbox.

To use Remote Mail, follow these steps:

1. Select Tools → Remote Mail . The Remote Mail window opens.

2. Click the Data on '486' icon and Remote Mail connects to the postoffice or Internet mail server. It sends any mail waiting in your Outbox and checks to see if any mail is waiting for you.

3. If you have messages waiting for you, a list of message headers appears in the window. You'll see the sender's name, a message subject, the date it was received, and, in some cases, how long it will take to retrieve it (see Figure 15-14).

4. Click a message that you want to retrieve and click . If you want to retrieve the message but also leave the message at the postoffice or Internet Mail server, click . This is useful if you want to retrieve the message again later, perhaps from a different computer.

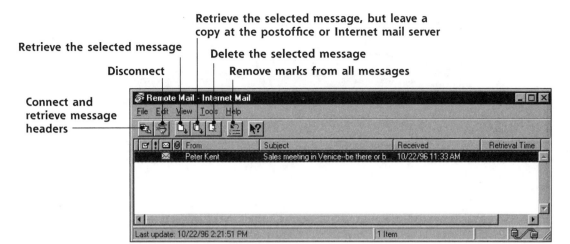

Figure 15-14 The Remote Mail window.

5. Click the data on '486' icon again, and Remote Mail connects to the postoffice or Internet Mail server and carries out your instructions — transferring any mail that you have marked for download. It also displays the headers if more mail has arrived for you.

Using the Address Book

As I mentioned earlier, Windows Messaging has an address book from which you can select people's addresses — not only addresses that you've entered into the book, but system-wide address books, too.

Sending e-mail to an existing address

To use the address book while creating an e-mail message, follow these steps:

1. Click the To button in the New Message window. The Address Book opens (see Figure 15-15).

   In this example, you can see that several names are already in the Address Book. Where did they come from? Notice the *Show Names from the* drop-down list box at the top of the window. This box says Postoffice Address List, which is a list of the addresses held by the postoffice itself; in other words, the addresses of the postoffice's own accounts.

2. If you want to use a name from your own address book — you'll see how to add names later in this chapter — select Personal Address Book from the *Show Names from the* drop-down list box.

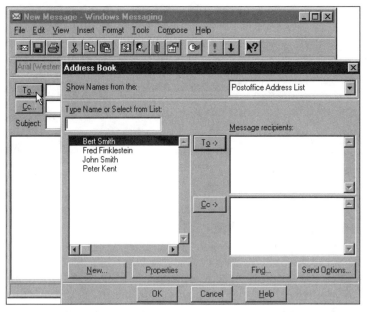

Figure 15-15 Using the Address Book to insert an address into the message.

4. Double-click the name of the person to whom you want to send a message, or click once and click To. The name is added to the top *Message recipients* box.

5. If you want to send a copy of the message to someone else, click that person's name and click Cc.

TIP To see information about someone, click that name in the left box, and then click Properties. If you've already placed the name in one of the right list boxes, you can double-click the name in that box. To remove a name from the To or Cc boxes, click once in the name and press Delete.

6. Click OK and the names are placed in the To and Cc boxes in the New Message window.

Adding names to the address book

Here's how to add names to the address book:

1. In the Windows Messaging window, click the Address Book button to open the Address Book window (see Figure 15-16).

2. Click the New Entry button, and the New Entry dialog box opens (see Figure 15-17).

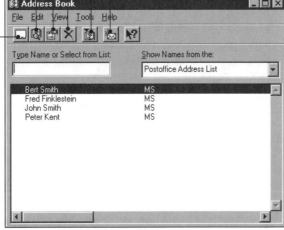

Figure 15-16   Viewing the Address Book.

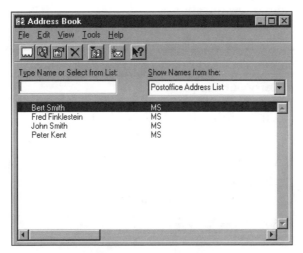

Figure 15-17   The New Entry dialog box.

3. Click the sort of address you want to add: Internet Mail Address, Microsoft Mail Address (don't click the bold Microsoft Mail text — it's just a header and can't be used), Other Address (maybe you want to add someone's mail information to the address book and won't be sending e-mail to the person), or Personal Distribution List (you are going to create a mailing list that allows you to send one message to multiple recipients).

4. Click OK, and a Address Properties dialog box opens.

5. The dialog box you see depends on the sort of entry you are adding. The box in the figure appears when you are creating an Internet Mail entry. Type a *display name* — the name under which the entry should appear in the Address Book — and the person's e-mail address (such as jsmith@thiscompany.com).

6. The *Always send messages in Microsoft Exchange rich text format* tells Windows Messaging to keep any special text formatting that you've used (colors, bold, italic, special fonts, and so on). That's generally okay with Microsoft Mail, but not with Internet E-mail.

7. You can click the other tabs to enter more information — notes, phone numbers, company name, department, and so on.

8. Click OK to add the person to the Address Book.

Much, Much, More

I could devote several chapters to Microsoft Messaging — there's so much to cover, way too much to cover here. So, to help you find your way around, Table 15-1 provides a few directions:

TABLE 15-1 A Few More Windows Messaging Procedures

To do this	Carry out this procedure
CREATE A NEW FOLDER	Click within the folder in which you want to place the new folder, and then select `File` → `New Folder`.
MOVE MESSAGES BETWEEN FOLDERS	While reading a message, click the Move Item button. Or click a message in the Windows Messaging window and click the Move Item button.
SEARCH FOR A PARTICULAR MESSAGE	Select `Tools` → `Find`.
MODIFY THE WINDOWS MESSAGING OPTIONS	Select `Tools` → `Options`.
ADD, REMOVE, AND MODIFY SERVICES	Select `Tools` → `Services`.
MANAGING MICROSOFT MAIL	Select `Tools` → `Microsoft Mail Tools`.
MODIFY THE WINDOWS MESSAGING TOOLBAR	Select `Tools` → `Customize Toolbar`.

To do this	Carry out this procedure
MODIFY THE WINDOWS MESSAGES COLUMNS	Select View → Columns.
CHANGE THE MESSAGE SORT ORDER	Select View → Sort.
TO SEND COMPUTER FILES IN E-MAIL	Click the Insert File button.

TIP If you ever have problems opening your inbox and reading messages, use the Inbox Repair Tool. Select Start→Programs→Accessories→System Tools→Inbox Repair Tool.

BONUS

Setting Up a Postoffice

In order to function, Windows Messaging requires a postoffice. Messages are stored by the postoffice, and each time a user starts Windows Messaging, the program connects to the postoffice to see if any new messages have been delivered. Messages that you send to others are stored in the postoffice until the recipients retrieve them.

A postoffice has to be set up for a network or workgroup by the system administrator. Here's how it's done:

1. Double-click the Microsoft Mail Postoffice icon to see the dialog box in which you can create a new postoffice, or administer an existing one.

2. Click *Create a new Workgroup Postoffice* and then click Next. The dialog box in which you tell NT where to place the postoffice appears.

3. You can type a path to a directory or click the Browse button and select a directory. You can pick a directory on your hard drive or on another computer, but the directory must be available to everyone using the postoffice, of course. If you want to create a directory to hold the postoffice — **\PostOffice**, for example — do so in Windows NT Explorer, and then return to this box. Click Next and the dialog box opens where you can confirm the desired location of the postoffice.

4. This dialog box shows you the location you selected. Click Next and NT opens a dialog box in which you can enter administrator-account information (see Figure 15-18).

Figure 15-18 Tell NT how you plan to access your administrator account.

5. Enter your name, your mailbox account name — a shortened version of your name, for example, something like *jsmith* — and the password you'll use to access the administration features. If you want, you can also enter additional information that will help other users contact you, such as your phone numbers, office and department names, and notes.

6. Click OK and a message box appears, reminding you to provide full access to the postoffice directory to all users. Click OK and you're finished — the postoffice has been created.

Adding User Accounts

Remember from earlier in the chapter that users can use Microsoft Mail only if the administrator has already set up an account for them. Here's how to do that:

1. Double-click the Microsoft Mail Postoffice icon.

2. Click Administer an Existing Workgroup Postoffice, and then click Next. A dialog box opens where you tell NT which postoffice to use.

3. Select the postoffice you want to work in. If the correct postoffice is already displayed, simply click OK.

3. Enter your mailbox name and your password in the dialog box that appears, and then click Next. Postoffice Manager opens (see Figure 15-19).

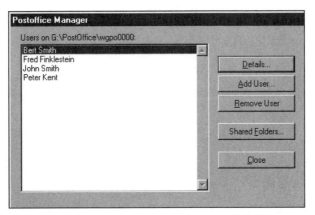

Figure 15-19 Here's where you'll manage postoffice accounts.

4. Click Add User to create another user account. You'll see the Enter Your Administrator Account Details dialog box (refer to Figure 15-18).

5. Use the other buttons to manage the accounts: *Details* to view and modify a user's information (such as change a password), *Remove User* to delete a user account, and *Shared Folders* to see a dialog box showing you how much disk space is used by the postoffice.

Summary

I've given you a quick overview of Windows Messaging, perhaps as much as you will ever need to know. Still, there's much more involved if you really want to learn. For example, you can modify the manner in which Windows Messaging handles incoming e-mail, or how it sends files via the Internet. Play around with the settings and options, and see what's available to you.

In the following chapter, I'll move onto something more advanced: working with Internet Explorer. This is a Web browser, a program that lets you view documents on the Internet's World Wide Web or on your corporate intranet.

CHAPTER SIXTEEN

COMPUTING ON THE ROAD AND ON THE INTERNET

IN THIS CHAPTER YOU LEARN THESE KEY SKILLS

SETTING UP DIAL-UP NETWORKING   PAGE 298

DIALING INTO YOUR NEW CONNECTION   PAGE 303

TAKING FILES ON THE ROAD WITH BRIEFCASE   PAGE 307

WORKING WITH HARDWARE PROFILES   PAGE 311

In this chapter, I describe a few tools that help you work at a distance — at a distance from a computer containing information you need — and even work with your office computer while you are out of the office. I'll start with *Dial-Up Networking*, a tool that enables you to connect your computer to another one across the phone lines. The other computer may be a server on your company's network, a friend's or colleague's computer, or a computer owned by an Internet service provider. You'll use Dial-Up Networking to work with an NT service known as Remote Access Service. You can call in and work with the network resources as if you were in your office. Grab your e-mail, log onto the Internet, and surf the World Wide Web.

I"ll also explain a couple things specifically designed for business travelers. *Briefcase* is a simple utility that helps you keep track of the files you take with you, so updating the originals on your desktop computer's hard disk is easier when you return to your office. And *Hardware Profiles* are a way to make a single computer work with different hardware in certain situations. For example, if you have a laptop connected to the network in your office, you can automatically disable the network hardware and software when you travel.

Setting Up Dial-Up Networking

Installing and configuring a Dial-Up Networking connection can be complicated. I could spend a quarter of this book explaining how to do it, and you still wouldn't have all the information you need, because each connection is a little different.

The only way to be sure you are setting up the connection correctly is to get all the information you need from your system administrator or Internet service provider. You need to know exactly what to enter in each text box and which options to select in each area.

I'm going look at how to set up Dial-Up Networking, but if you plan to do this, make sure you get *detailed* information before you start. Preferably, you need a snapshot of each dialog box showing all the selections and entries. (Your system administrator can use Alt+Print Screen to copy each dialog box to the Clipboard and paste them into a word-processing document.) If you run into problems, you'll have to ask your system administrator for more information or for help. But who knows, you may be lucky and find that your particular Dial-Up Networking installation is a breeze.

Installing Dial-Up Networking

To begin, see if you have Dial-Up Networking installed on your system. To do so, follow these steps:

1. Double-click the My Computer icon on your desktop. The My Computer folder opens.

2. Double-click the Dial-Up Networking icon in My Computer. If Dial-Up Networking is not installed, you'll see a message box telling you. Click Install to install the service. (If you do have the service installed, you'll see the Dial-Up Networking dialog box — see Figure 16-7. Skip forward to the next section, "Setting up your first connection.")

3. NT installs the service. You may be prompted to insert the Windows NT Installation CD.

4. You may see a dialog box asking if you want to install a modem. Follow the instructions. Installation is quite straightforward. (For more information, see Chapter 13.)

5. Then you'll see the Add RAS Device dialog box. This shows the *RAS Capable Devices* drop-down list box, which lists the modem or modems that you can use for Dial-Up Networking.

6. If you have multiple modems, select the one you want to use from the list, and then click OK to add it to the Remote Access Setup dialog box (see Figure 16-1).

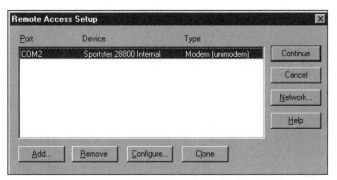

Figure 16-1   The Remote Access Setup dialog box.

7. With the modem you plan to use selected, click Configure. This pops up a dialog box where you define the sort of sessions you want to have with Dial-Up Networking. The *Dial out only* option button is already selected, which means you can dial from your computer to another one — to your company's system, for example, or to an Internet service provider. That setting is the most common. Or, you can select *Receive calls only* — other computers can dial into yours. You can also have both types of session if you choose *Dial out and Receive calls*.

8. Make your selection and click OK. Then click Network in the Remote Access Setup dialog box. This time, you'll see a dialog box that defines the network protocols that will be used (the "languages" used by the computers to communicate with each other), and, if you have set up your computer to allow other computers to dial in, how sessions will be run (see Figure 16-2). You normally don't need to modify these items, unless told to do so by your system administrator.

9. Click OK in the Network Configuration dialog box to close it. (If you are setting up the system to allow computers to dial into your computer, and perhaps through your computer to the network, you'll see more dialog boxes. This is complicated stuff that you can't do without detailed information from the system administrator.)

10. Click Continue in the Remote Access Setup dialog box, and NT finishes installing the Dial-Up Networking files. You may see a dialog box. Again, you need to know what the system administrator wants you to do with this option.

11. NT has almost finished installing Dial-Up Networking. Click OK to complete the process.

12. When you see a dialog box telling you to restart your computer, click Restart.

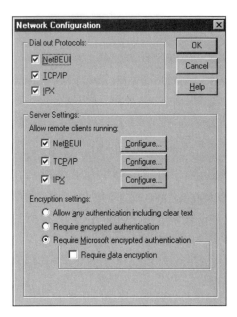

Figure 16-2 This Network Configuration dialog box shows options for both dialing out and dialing in. (Yours may show only one or the other set.)

Setting up your first connection

Okay, you've installed Dial-Up Networking. You have the software you need, and now you have to tell it how to connect to another computer. In the following example, I look at how to connect to an Internet service provider:

1. Double-click the My Computer icon on your desktop. The My Computer folder opens.

2. Double-click the Dial-Up Networking icon in My Computer. You may see the New Phonebook Entry Wizard box (see Figure 16-3). If you already have other Dial-Up Networking connections set up, you'll see the Dial-Up Networking dialog box instead (see Figure 16-7); click New to see the New Phonebook Entry Wizard.

3. Type a name that identifies this Dial-Up Networking connection — the name of the Internet service provider, the name of the company department, or whatever. Then click Next and the Server dialog box opens (see Figure 16-4).

4. Check all the check boxes that are appropriate for this connection. If you are not sure about any of these options, ask your system administrator or the technical support people at your Internet service provider. In this example, I'm checking all three boxes. (If you don't check all three, you won't see all the boxes and steps I'm about to describe.)

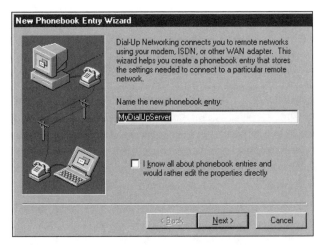

Figure 16-3 The New Phonebook Entry Wizard.

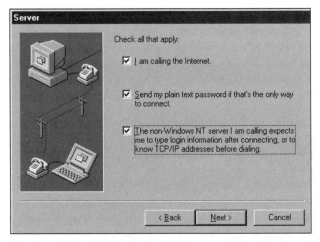

Figure 16-4 The Server dialog box.

5. Click Next and the Phone Number dialog box opens. Type the phone number you must call to connect to the other computer. If you want to use the dialing options you specified when setting up your modem (see Chapter 13), click the *Use Telephony dialing properties* check box. These options might include, for example, dialing a number required for an outside line or using your credit-card account. Also note the Alternates button. This allows you to store several different numbers for this connection and make Dial-Up Networking dial each number in sequence until it finds a free one.

6. Click Next and the Serial Line Protocol dialog box opens. You must select the type of protocol that will be used to communicate with the other computer. In most cases, it's PPP, although some old systems still use

COMPUTING ON THE ROAD AND ON THE INTERNET

SLIP. Check with the system administrator if you're not sure. SLIP (Serial Line Interface Protocol) and PPP (Point to Point Protocol) are two common protocols used by computers dialing into the Internet and other computer networks.

7. Click Next and the dialog box opens that tells Dial-Up Networking how to log on. Dial-Up Networking can log on to some systems automatically, with no assistance from you. In some cases, however, you may need to log on manually, typing an account name and password. If so, select *Use a terminal window*. Or, better still, obtain a script from your system administrator or service provider, place the script (it's a .scp file) into the \Winnt\System32\Ras\ directory, and then click *Automate with this script* and select the .scp file from the drop-down list box. (Click the Refresh list button if you can't see the script file you just added.)

8. Click Next and the IP Address dialog box in Figure 16-5 opens. If your system administrator or service provider has told you to enter an IP address (an *Internet Protocol* address, a number that identifies your computer), enter it here.

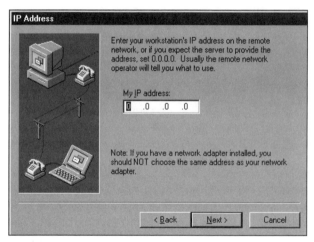

Figure 16-5 Your Internet Protocol address, if you have one, goes here.

9. Click Next to see the Name Server Addresses dialog box, shown in Figure 16-6. Your system administrator or service provider may also have given you numbers that identify *name servers,* computers used to help other computers on the network find addresses. Enter these numbers here.

10. Click Next to see a dialog box telling you that you're finished. Click Finish and the Dial-Up Networking dialog box appears, showing you your new connection.

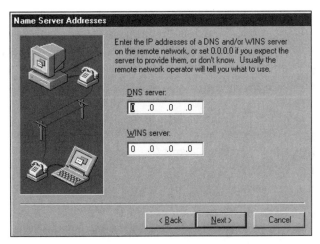

Figure 16-6 Now enter the name server addresses.

Dialing into Your New Connection

In Figure 16-7, you can see the Dial-Up Networking dialog box. At the top is a *Phonebook entry to dial* drop-down list box. This shows your Dial-Up Networking connection. If you have more than one connection, you can select the one you want to use from this list.

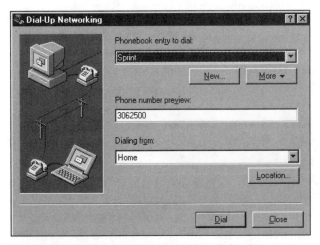

Figure 16-7 The Dial-Up Networking dialog box.

The *Phone number preview* text box displays the number that will be dialed — it shows all the digits that will be dialed. Remember, however, that if you want to use the special numbers (outside lines, calling cards, and so on) you configured when you set up your modem (see Chapter 13), you should have selected *Use Telephony dialing properties* in the Phone Number dialog box.

TIP If you didn't select *Use Telephony dialing properties* when you set up this connection, you can do so now. Click the More button, and a menu opens. Select Edit entry and modem properties, click the Basic tab, and check the *Use Telephony dialing properties* check box.

The *Dialing from* entry (refer to Figure 16-7) shows which of the Telephony Dialing Properties you plan to use. Chapter 13 explains how to set up these locations, and again, unless you've selected *Use Telephony dialing properties*, this entry has no effect on the number dialed.

Ready to dial? Follow this procedure to watch a session in action, right from the start:

1. Double-click the My Computer icon on your desktop. The My Computer folder opens.

2. Double-click the Dial-Up Networking icon in My Computer. You'll see the Dial-Up Networking dialog box.

TIP You can also select Start→Programs→Accessories→Dial-Up Networking to see the Dial-Up Networking dialog box.

2. Select the connection you want to use from the *Phonebook entry to dial* drop-down list box.

3. Click Dial. The dialog box in Figure 16-8 opens.

Figure 16-8 Enter your username and password.

4. Type your username, the name by which you are identified on the other computer. If you are not sure of this name , ask your system administrator.

5. Type the password you've been given.

6. In some cases, you may need to enter a domain name, but generally not when connecting to an Internet service provider. Ask your system administrator.

7. If you want NT to save this password for you so that you don't have to enter it each time you connect, click *Save password*.

8. Click OK and the system begins dialing. You'll see a message box showing you the progress of the call.

9. When you see the Connection Complete dialog box, you know that you've connected to the service.

TIP So what happens if you *can't* connect? Talk to your service provider or system administrator. Maybe one of the many different settings wasn't entered correctly, or maybe there's a problem with the modem speed (you can connect at a lower speed, perhaps), and so on.

10. Notice that the *Close on dial* check box is selected. As soon as you close this message box, the Dial-Up Networking dialog box will close. There's a *Hang up* button in that box, but that's okay; you probably don't need it anyway. And as you'll see in a moment, you can use the Dial-Up Networking Monitor to disconnect your call.

11. Click OK and you're connected to the remote computer.

If you are connecting to a company's NT server, you can now use your programs as if you were connected at work on the LAN. You can use Windows Messaging to grab your e-mail (see Chapter 15), work with Windows NT Explorer, and so on. If you are connected to an Internet service provider, you can now use your Internet programs (such as Internet Explorer, see Chapter 17), and you can use Windows Messaging to grab e-mail.

Closing your connection

When you're finished with your connection and want to close it, you can choose a couple ways to do so:

* If the Dial-Up Networking window is open, click the *Hang up* button.
* Right-click the Dial-Up Networking Monitor in the taskbar's tray, select Hang up , and then click the name of the connection you want to close (see Figure 16-9).

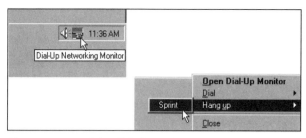

Figure 16-9 Right-click the Dial-Up Networking Monitor to open the menu.

Keeping the monitor handy

If you use Dial-Up Networking frequently, you may want to keep the Monitor's icon in the taskbar's tray. Here's how:

1. If a connection is active, double-click the Monitor icon in the taskbar. If not, double-click the Dial-Up Monitor icon in Control Panel. The Dial-Up Networking Monitor window opens.
2. Click the Preferences tab.
3. Click the *Include a Dial-Up Networking Monitor* button in the Task List.
4. Click OK.

Now you'll always see the icon in the tray. You can use it for these purposes:

* **To dial a connection** — Right-click and select Dial → Connection name .
* **To hang up a connection** — Right-click and select Hang up → Connection name .
* **To open the Dial-Up Networking window (so you can add, modify, or remove connections)** — Right-click and select Dial → Open Phonebook .
* **To open the Monitor** — Double-click the icon, or right-click and select Open Dial-Up Monitor .

If you prefer, you can have a small Monitor window, rather than a tray icon. This is chosen with the *As a Window on the Desktop* option button in the Preferences area of the Monitor.

The Status and Summary panes of the main Monitor window are not terribly useful to most users because they contain fairly advanced information. However, you may need to use this information when reporting problems to the system administrator.

Taking Files on the Road with Briefcase

If you have ever traveled with a laptop and had to coordinate data stored on the laptop with data stored on your desktop machine, you know what a headache it can be. You have to remember which files are the up-to-date ones, as well as which files were changed most recently. If you travel frequently, it's not an easy matter.

Windows NT can help out, using Briefcase. This is a special utility for managing files that you swap between computers. You "carry" files in the Briefcase when you go away; when you return, you can quickly update the original files.

You can use the My Briefcase icon on your desktop, if you want, although it may be easier to use it within Windows NT Explorer, where you can quickly drag files from anywhere on your hard disks. You can also create multiple briefcases and put them wherever is most convenient. You might use different briefcases for different collections of files, different types of trips, and so on.

To open My Briefcase, follow these procedures:

- Double-click the My Briefcase icon on your desktop. A folder window opens.
- Right-click the My Briefcase icon and select Open. A folder window opens.
- Right-click the My Briefcase icon and select Explore. Windows NT Explorer opens (see Figure 16-10).

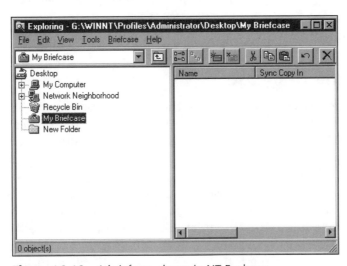

Figure 16-10 A briefcase, shown in NT Explorer.

Packing files in the briefcase

Starting is simple. Just drag files from a directory onto the My Briefcase icon. Files are always copied, never moved, into My Briefcase, regardless of which disk they are coming from or which key you hold while you drag. Another way to copy is to right-click the file you want and select Send To→My Briefcase. (As you saw in Chapter 4, you can add other briefcases to this menu, too.)

TIP Put a briefcase wherever you need one. To create one, click in the folder where you want to place the briefcase, then select File→New→Briefcase. Then click the new briefcase in Window's NT Explorer's right pane, press F2, and rename it.

Now take the briefcase with you. If the briefcase is small, you can move it onto a floppy disk. If it's large, you can move it to another computer across a network connection. For example, if you have a laptop, you can connect the laptop to the network and then transfer the briefcase to the laptop.

Note, however, that you can't drag a briefcase (or rename it) from the left pane of the Windows NT Explorer window. If you click the briefcase in the left pane, NT regards the briefcase as "open," so it can't be moved or renamed. You have to click the briefcase in the *right* pane before you can carry out either operation.

By the way, note that you're not copying the briefcase — you're moving it. When you drag the briefcase to a floppy disk or to another network computer, the briefcase will actually be moved off your hard disk and onto the other disk. And if you are using floppies, when you move the briefcase to the other computer's drive, it's also moved, not copied. To avoid problems, the Briefcase system doesn't want unnecessary copies lying around!

Using the briefcase

Now that you have the briefcase on the other computer, how do you use it? You work directly on the files within the briefcase. Use the briefcase just like any other file folder. Open a File Open dialog box, for example, and you'll see that you can open files that are held within the briefcase. (Not all programs will be able to do this, however; some programs written for Windows 3.1 may not be able to work with the briefcase. On the other hand, many Windows 3.1 programs will see the briefcase as a simple directory and *will* be able to use it.)

Don't take files out of the briefcase. If you do, they lose their original settings. For example, you copy a file into a directory, work on it, and then copy it back. Briefcase now regards the file as a copy of the file in the directory in which you just modified it — not a copy of the file on the original computer. Thus, when you transfer the briefcase back to the original computer, it's shown as up-to-date, even though it's not.

> **TIP** You can use a briefcase to move files from your Windows NT computer to a Windows 95 computer (Windows 95 uses the same briefcase system).

Checking your files

Okay, you've taken a few files on a trip with you. You transferred the files to the original computer, but you don't remember which ones you changed and which you haven't. How do you find out? Simple. Open the briefcase, and you can see which files have changed (see Figure 16-11).

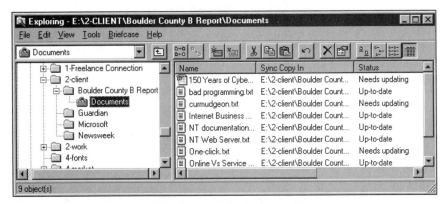

Figure 16-11 The briefcase shows you what's changed.

You can see two important pieces of information in the briefcase. There's the Sync Copy In column, which shows you where the original files came from. Then there's the Status file. This may show *Up-to-date*, meaning the file is the same as the original, or *Needs updating*, which means it's not.

To update files, follow these steps:

1. Right-click the name of a file that needs updating and select Update . Or right-click the briefcase name and select Update All . The Update Documents dialog box opens (see Figure 16-12)

    This dialog box shows you the changes that have been made: files modified in and files deleted from the briefcase, files modified in and files deleted from the original directory, and files modified or deleted in both the briefcase and directory. Here's what the icons mean:

    ⇒ The briefcase file has changed, while the original was unchanged. The original will be changed.

    ⇐ The original file has changed, while the one in the briefcase was unchanged. The one in the briefcase will be changed.

↘ Both files have changed. (You've got a problem, and the briefcase can't help you figure it out!) Nothing will be done to these files unless you choose another option.

✘ A file has been deleted (look at the text in the left or right column to figure out which). If the file in the briefcase was deleted, the original will now be deleted. If the original was deleted, the one in the briefcase will now be deleted. So be careful!

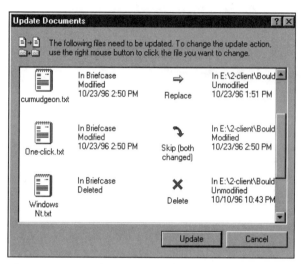

Figure 16-12   The Update Documents dialog box shows you which files have been modified.

2. If you want to specify what happens to a particular file (for example, a deleted file or one of the Skip files), right-click the file. You'll see a pop-up menu (see Figure 16-13).

3. Select the option. For example, if you clicked a file marked as Skip, because both files have changed, you can select one of the Replace menu options to define which file should be replaced.

4. When you've made all your changes, click the Update button, and the modifications are made.

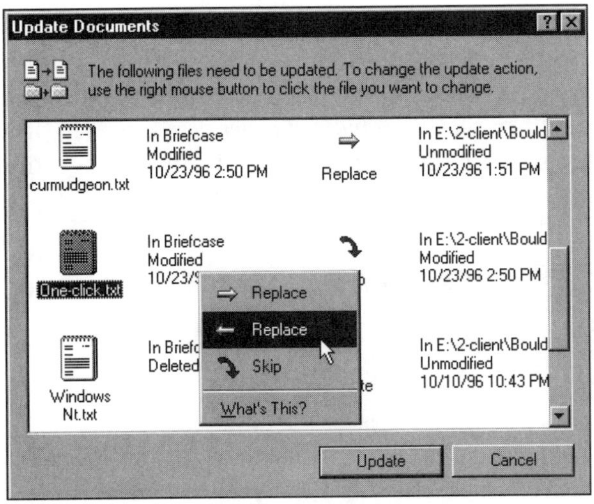

Figure 16-13 Right-click to update a particular file.

Working with Hardware Profiles

Another handy tool that can be useful for people who travel with their computers is the *hardware profile*. The idea behind this feature is that if you have a computer that you use in more than one location, you may have hardware that you use in one location but not the other. In particular, you may have a laptop that uses a network card in the office — but not while you're traveling, of course — or a laptop that uses a docking station while in the office. Hardware profiles provide a way to automatically turn off the software used to run the hardware that you don't need while traveling.

To create a hardware profile, follow these steps:

1. Open the Control Panel (Start → Settings → Control Panel) and double-click the System icon.

2. In the System Properties dialog box, click the Hardware Profiles tab. You'll see the information shown in Figure 16-14.

3. Specify how you want NT to handle hardware profiles. It may be able to figure it out, if you are using a dockable computer — a portable computer that has a docking station. If you create a hardware profile linked to a particular docking state, and if NT can recognize that state, then it automatically picks the hardware profile for you. Otherwise, you have to select a profile from the Hardware Profile menu (see "Working with Harware Profiles," later in this chapter).

You can select *Wait indefinitely for user selection* after entering the Hardware Profile menu. In other words, NT won't continue the boot process until you pick a profile. Or you can select *Wait for user selection for X seconds, then select the highest order preference*. In other words, NT waits for the specified number of seconds, then selects the hardware profile at the top of the list.

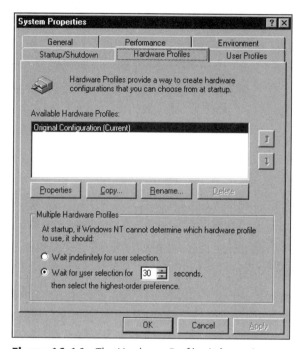

Figure 16-14 The Hardware Profiles information.

TIP The little up-arrow and down-arrow buttons on the right side of the dialog box enable you to move the order of the hardware profiles. And if you don't want to go into the Hardware Profiles menu automatically, because you are not currently using an alternative hardware profile, you can set the *Wait for user selection for* number to 0.

4. Click Copy to copy the original configuration. Type a new name into the Copy Profile dialog box (**Travel**, for instance), and click OK.

5. With the new configuration selected, click Properties. The dialog box in Figure 16-15 opens.

6. If your computer is a dockable portable computer, click the *This is a portable computer* check box.

7. Select the computer's docking state. If NT recognizes the computer's docking state, it selects it for you.

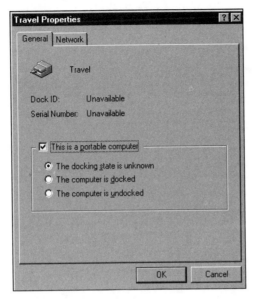

Figure 16-15 Tell NT whether this is a portable computer.

8. Click the Network tab, and you'll see another dialog box.

9. If your laptop has network hardware installed, you can click the *Network-Disabled hardware profile* check box to disable all the networking hardware and software while using this profile.

10. Click OK twice to close the dialog boxes.

That's it, you've created a hardware profile. You may also have disabled all the networking. Now you can disable other devices and services for that profile... if you really know what you are doing. Double-click the Devices or Services icon in Control Panel. You can see an example in Figure 16-16.

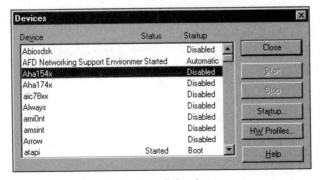

Figure 16-16 The Devices dialog box.

COMPUTING ON THE ROAD AND ON THE INTERNET **313**

If you are sure you know what you are disabling, you can select a device or service that you want to disable, and then click the *HW Profiles* button. You see the Device dialog box. For example, if you have a dockable laptop, you could disable equipment that is in the docking station. Simply click the profile for which you want to disable the device or service, then click *Disable*, and click Close to close the dialog box.

To select your hardware profile during the boot process, follow these steps:

1. Start your computer.

2. You go straight into the Hardware Profile menu — you won't see the usual Press spacebar NOW to invoke Hardware Profile/Last Known Good menu message. The following screen appears:

   ```
   Hardware Profile/Configuration Recovery Menu
   This menu allows you to select a hardware profile
   to be used when Windows NT is started.

   If your system is not starting correctly, then you may switch to a
       previous system configuration, which may overcome startup
       problems.
   IMPORTANT: System configuration changes made since the last
       successful startup will be discarded.

       {Original Configuration}
        Travel
   ```

3. Use the arrow keys to select the hardware profile you want to use, and then press Enter. NT boots using that profile.

BONUS

MultiLink Connections

NT has a great new utility that can really speed up connections. Using the *MultiLink* feature, you can use several modems at the same time to transfer to the same computer. For example, if you had two 57,600 bps modems installed in your computer, and two installed in the computer you were calling, you could use both at the same time to connect your computers. Instead of sending data at a speed of 57,600 bps, you could transfer at 115,200 bps. (You need two phone lines, also.) You can also link ISDN devices together — to get *very* fast connections — or even mix and match — use both ISDN and modems.

Data sent across each individual line is regarded as part of the same single transmission. NT will split a file into pieces, for example, and send bits of it on each line, instead of all over one line. The computer at the other end then gathers together the individual pieces and pastes it all together again.

Here's how it's done:

1. Open the Dial-Up Networking dialog box (from My Computer or by right-clicking the Monitor icon on the taskbar and selecting `Dial` → `Open Phonebook`).

2. In the *Phonebook entry to dial* drop-down list box, select the connection you want to modify.

3. Click More and select Edit Entry and Modem Properties. The Edit Phonebook Entry dialog box opens

4. Click the Basic tab to see the information in Figure 16-17.

5. In the *Dial using* drop-down list box, select Multiple Lines, and then click Configure. The Multiple Line Configuration dialog box opens (see Figure 16-18).

6. Select the devices you want to use, and then click OK.

7. Now, when you dial this connection, all the devices will dial at the same time. The receiving computer must have MultiLink turned on.

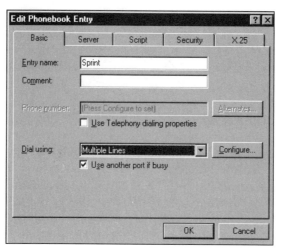

Figure 16-17 Here's where you select multiple line connections.

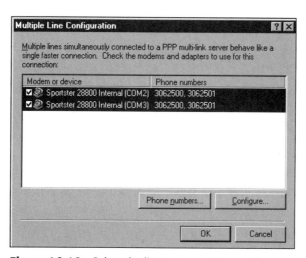

Figure 16-18 Select the lines you want to use for a single connection.

Briefcase too Big for a Floppy?

If the files you placed in the briefcase take up more room than a floppy disk can hold, that's okay; you can still get by with a bit of fiddling around. If necessary, NT will copy the briefcase onto multiple floppy disks (it displays a message box — insert a new floppy and click Retry). Here's what to do when you transfer the briefcase to the other computer:

1. Copy the briefcase from the first disk. You'll see the My Briefcase icon — drag it to the location you want it on the computer's hard disk.

2. NT copies the briefcase, then stops when it finishes (no, it won't prompt for the rest of the briefcase).

3. Insert the next disk, and you find that there's no My Briefcase icon. Instead, there's a normal folder icon, with the same name as the briefcase.

4. Drag that folder icon to the same location as the briefcase (not into the briefcase itself, but into the folder that's holding the briefcase). The Confirm Folder Replace dialog box appears

5. Click *Yes to All*, and NT will copy all the files from the folder into the briefcase.

6. The folder remains on the floppy disk — you can delete it.

7. Work with the briefcase as normal.

8. When you want to transfer the briefcase back to the original computer, use the same process.

Yes, this is a little clunky . . . but it does work.

Summary

Dial-Up Networking can be a little tricky sometimes. Remember, if you can't get it to work, you should talk with the person responsible for the computer you are dialing. After it's up and running, it's almost like magic. You can use computers hundreds, maybe thousands, of miles away as if they're in the next room. Well, almost . . . you'll find it's a bit slower over phone lines.

After you have Dial-Up Networking running, you can also connect to the Internet, and that's the subject of the next chapter. You'll learn how to work with Internet Explorer, NT's built-in Web browser.

CHAPTER SEVENTEEN
WORKING ON THE WEB — USING INTERNET EXPLORER

IN THIS CHAPTER YOU LEARN THESE KEY SKILLS

GETTING STARTED WITH INTERNET EXPLORER   PAGE 320

UPGRADING INTERNET EXPLORER   PAGE 321

MOVING AROUND ON THE WEB   PAGE 323

SEARCHING FOR WHAT YOU NEED   PAGE 326

FINDING YOUR WAY BACK   PAGE 327

In this chapter, I'll take a quick look at working on the World Wide Web and the Internet using Internet Explorer, Microsoft's Web browser. Before I start, however, I should explain a few terms.

What's the *Internet*? It's a huge system of interconnected computers, spanning the entire globe. It's used by millions of people in scores of countries to communicate with e-mail, find information on the World Wide Web, "discuss" different subjects in over 40,000 internationally distributed discussion groups, and more. When your computer is connected to the Internet — either through your corporate network or by dialing into an Internet service provider — you are able to take part in all these activities.

Well, what's the World Wide Web, then? Aren't the Internet and the World Wide Web the same thing? Many people think the terms *Internet* and *World Wide Web* are synonymous, but they're really different things. You can think of the Internet as the hardware — the computers, cables, satellite links, and so on — connecting all these millions of computers together. The World Wide Web is software running on the Internet. Although it's just one of the software systems using the Internet, it is the most popular today.

The World Wide Web is a giant *hypertext* system. If you open a Windows Help file — select an option from the Help menu in any Windows program — you're viewing a hypertext system. You click a *link,* and related information pops up. (Hypertext systems are collections of electronic documents linked to each other. A link is generally specially formatted text, usually underlined and colored, that references another document. A user clicks the link with the mouse to open the referenced document.)

The Web is the same sort of thing, except it's spread across the Internet. When you click a link in a Help file, the information that's retrieved comes from another part of the Help file, or maybe from another Help file on your hard disk. When you click a link in a Web document, the information that's retrieved may come from another part of the world!

Getting Started with Internet Explorer

To start the Internet Explorer Web browser, simply double-click the Internet Explorer icon on your desktop. You *may* see a message saying that Explorer is not your default browser. That means that .htm and .html files are associated with a program other than Explorer (see Chapter 16 for information about file associations). This may be because another browser has been installed on your computer. You can click Yes to modify file associations, if you want.

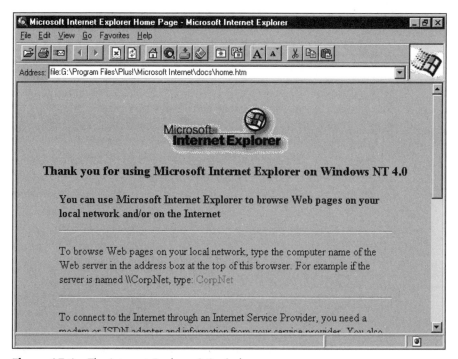

Figure 17-1 The Internet Explorer 2.0 window.

When Explorer opens, you see a window similar to that shown in Figure 17-1. This is actually Internet Explorer 2.0, the version that was shipping with Windows NT at the time of writing. You may find that your version of NT has a different or later version of Internet Explorer installed. Internet Explorer 4.0 is due to be released sometime in 1997.

TIP To find out which version you are using, select Help→About Internet Explorer.

I recommend that you upgrade to the latest browser. It will have more features and will work better with the pages you are likely to come across on the World Wide Web.

Upgrading Internet Explorer

You can download the latest version of Explorer from Microsoft's Web site. First, make sure your connection to the Internet is running. Start your Dial-Up Networking connection to your service provider (see Chapter 15), or make sure your network connection to the Internet is working. (See your system administrator for details on how to set up Explorer to work with the network *proxy servers* that may be required. Proxy servers provide a "path" between the Internet and a private network, allowing the Web browser to obtain information from the World Wide Web.). Then follow these steps:

1. If you are using Internet Explorer 2.0, click the button. If you are using Internet Explorer 3.01, click the Product News button. (Can't see that button? It should be below the Address text box; if you can't see it, try dragging the lower border of the Address bar down.) Explorer begins transferring a Web page to your computer and displaying the contents.

2. At the page that Internet Explorer now displays, you should find a link that will take you to an upgrade area. For example, Figure 17-2 shows what this page currently looks like. (Depending on the speed of your connection and how busy the Microsoft site is, it may take a little while to display all the pictures on the page.)

3. Click the link to the upgrade area, and a new page appears.

4. Follow the instructions for the download. You can select the version you want to download. There are different versions for the different types of computer that can run Windows NT.

Type the Web address (URL) of the page you want to view

Pictures are often links, too; if the mouse pointer changes to a little hand, than the picture is a link

The underlined and colored text are links; click to see related information

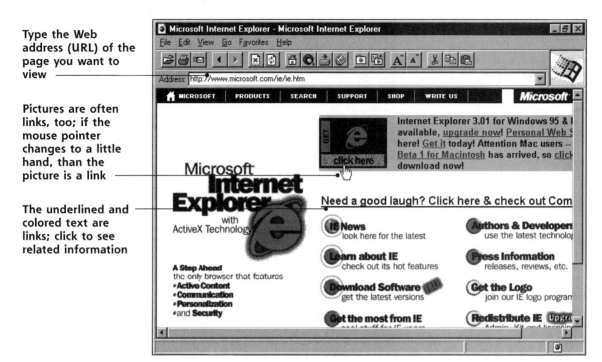

Figure 17-2 Click the *upgrade now* link.

5. After selecting the version and language, you see a list of links to the upgrade file. These are links to download sites throughout the world. You can select a site close to you or one in an area that is currently at night, so it may not be busy. Click one of the links to begin the file download.

6. If you are using Internet Explorer 2.0, the file is transferred to your computer and a dialog box is displayed that allows you to save the file. Internet Explorer 3.01 performs differently. If you're using that program, you can specify a download directory, and *then* the file is transferred. Either way, place the file in a new directory, such as C:\Winnt\IE Install. (The file transfer may take a long time, especially if you have a dial-up connection to the Internet. The file is currently over 8MB.)

 TIP Internet Explorer 2.0 has a bad file-transfer system — one good reason to upgrade to the latest version. If you want to be sure that it's actually transferring (there's no progress monitor in the browser itself), double-click the 🖥 icon in the taskbar's tray. Then look at the Bytes In value in the Dial-Up Networking Monitor. The value changes as the data is transferred.

7. When the file has transferred, close Internet Explorer and use Windows Explorer to find the file you transferred (which will probably be called something like **msie301mnt.exe**). Double-click the file to begin the installation program.

322   NETWORKING, THE INTERNET, AND INTRANETS

TIP You should also download and install any Windows NT Service Packs that the Web page tells you that you need.

When you've installed the program, connect to the Internet, and start Internet Explorer again. You're taken to a page that allows you to register the program and download additional components.

In effect, I've thrown away Internet Explorer 2.0 and am now working with Explorer 3.01. That's the program I use from now on in this chapter.

Moving Around on the Web

There are a number of ways to move around on the Web or a corporate intranet. I"ll describe these ways in the following sections.

Click a link

A *link* is an item in a document that references another document. When you click the link (see Figure 17-3), the referenced document is transferred. A link may be on a word, a block of text, or a picture. When you see the little hand icon, you know you're pointing at a link.

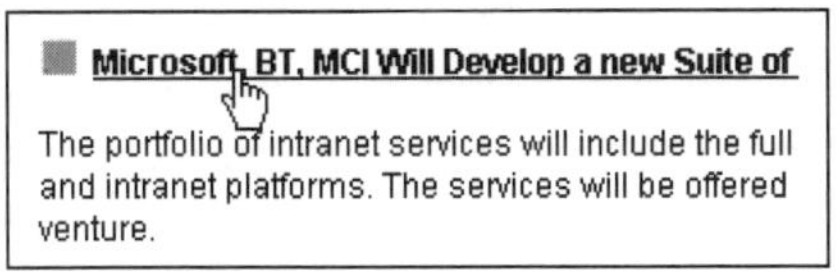

Figure 17-3 Point at the link and a hand appears. Click to see the referenced document.

Where do you find links to click? All over the place. The home page displayed when you open Internet Explorer has a few links. And you can find links when you search for information (see "Searching for What You Need," later in this chapter).

 TIP The *home page* is the page that appears when you start your browser. The term is often also used to mean the main page at a Web site — the IDG home page, the CNN home page, and so on.

Type a URL

You can type a URL into the Address box (or press Ctrl+L to see a box in which you can type the URL). Press Enter, and the browser finds the referenced page (see Figure 17-4).

Figure 17-4 Type a URL and press Enter.

But what is a URL, and where do you find them? URL means *Uniform Resource Locator*, and it's a sort of Web "address." It tells the browser where to find the page you want to view. Here's a typical URL: **http://www.microsoft.com/ie/**, which means, "go to the www.microsoft.com Web server, and load the main page in the /ie/ directory." Now, notice that all these slashes are *forward* slashes, not the normal backslashes used when describing a path on your hard disk. That's because the Internet was originally run by computers using the UNIX operating system, and UNIX uses forward slashes, not backslashes. The convention is to use forward slashes for all URLs. However, if you forget and use backslashes, don't worry. Explorer figures it out for you.

You can find URLs all over the place. They're mentioned in magazine articles, on TV news shows, in advertising, in Internet directories, and so on.

TIP In most cases, you don't need to type the http:// piece. Internet Explorer adds it for you. However, a number of URLs don't start with http://. Some start with gopher:// and ftp://, for example, and in these cases, you may have to type the complete URL.

Select from the Favorites

The Favorites list contains the addresses of places on the Internet that you want to return to. (This sort of system is often known as a *bookmarks* system — the original term used on the Web.)

To add things to the Favorites list, follow these steps:

1. When you reach a page that you think you may want to return to, select `Favorites` → `Add to Favorites`. (You can also open this menu by clicking the Favorites button.) The Add to Favorites dialog box opens.

2. You can click OK and place an entry to the Favorites folder and menu, or click *Create in* to place it in a subfolder. You see the dialog box in Figure 17-5.

3. Click New Folder to create a new folder in which to store the entry.

4. Click the name of the folder into which you want to place the entry, and then click OK.

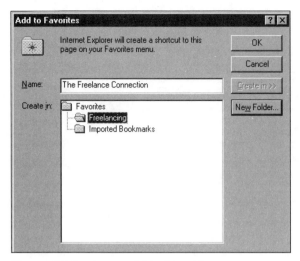

Figure 17-5 Create a folder hierarchy to store your Favorites entries.

That's it. You've added something to the Favorites. Now how do you use it? Well, later on, in the current session or any time in the future, you can open the Favorites menu and find the entry. If you placed the entry directly in the Favorites folder when you created it, you'll find it at the bottom of the menu. If you placed the entry into a subfolder, you'll find a submenu corresponding to that folder, and you'll find the entry there. Simply select the entry and you'll go there.

 TIP When you have created loads of Favorites, the menu won't be able to display them all. Select Favorites→More Favorites. The Favorites folder opens (it's actually a real directory folder on your hard disk). Go to an entry by double-clicking it.

Select from the history list

A *history list* is a list of Web pages that you've seen before. Internet Explorer has a history list that is better than it's rival, Netscape Navigator. The history list not only keeps track of documents you've been to during the current session, but it stores the entries so that you can use the history list in subsequent sessions, too. You can go back hundreds of pages to something you viewed days or even weeks before.

There are a couple ways to use the history list. If you've recently seen the page — within the last five or six pages — you can select it from the Go menu. You'll see the page's title or, in some cases, its URL. Simply click the page to go there. If the page you want to go to isn't in the menu, select Go→Open History Folder. The history folder opens, and you can double-click the page you want to return to.

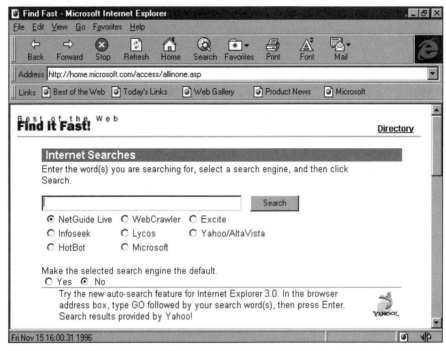

Figure 17-6 Whatever you're looking for, you can probably find it here.

Searching for What You Need

The Web is huge. How do you find what you need . . . or what you *want*, anyway? (Much Web content is better classified under the *Stuff You Might Want to Goof Off With* than under the *Essential Stuff You Really Need* heading.) Explorer provides a quick way to search for what you're looking for:

Click here to use Web *search engines* to find exactly what you need.

Best of the Web. Click here to see a list of links to sites that Microsoft believes rate as some of the best stuff out there.

Today's Links. Click here to see a list of links that the folks at Microsoft have found for you today.

The most useful is the Search button. When you click this, you see something similar to the page in Figure 17-6. This is what the page looks like right now, but these things change so quickly that it will look a little (perhaps a lot) different by the time you see it.

Type a word or phrase into the text box, click the option button next to the name of the search engine you want to use, and then click OK. Within a few seconds, you should see a list of links to Web pages matching what you're looking for.

I know this is an Internet heresy, but the World Wide Web really can be an incredible productivity sinkhole. It's quite easy to start reading, following interesting-looking links here and there, and find yourself way off-track a few hours later. For example, I've just been looking at a "photograph" of Michael Jackson's baby. Admittedly, it hasn't been born yet, but that's no problem for the staff of the National Enquirer Web site (http://www.nationalenquirer.com/), which I had no idea existed until I read the Today's Links page.

 Scroll down this page to find links to all sorts of useful reference and search sites.

Finding Your Way Back

Here's the big problem with hypertext: it's easy to get lost. Luckily, there are a few ways to find your way home again:

🏠 Click here to return to your browser's home page.

 Want to pick a different page as your home page? Display the page in the browser, select View→Options, click the Navigation tab, and then click the Use Current button.

 Click here to return to the http://www.microsoft.com/ page.

⇐ Click here to return to the page you just saw; continue clicking to move back through the history list, page by page.

⇒ This is the Forward button; it takes you to the page you just returned from.

Here are a couple more buttons that are handy, too:

✖ This stops the current page from being loaded.

↻ This reloads the current page; you can use this button if you think the page may have changed.

BONUS

More Internet and Intranet Stuff

There are many features of Internet Explorer that I haven't covered. Table 17-1 provides a few pointers to those features.

TABLE 17-1 More Internet Tools

Feature	More information
OPTIONS	There are *lots* of program options. You can modify the way that Explorer displays colors and backgrounds, the toolbar, fonts, and so on. You can also modify the way in which a variety of program functions operate — where the temporary files are saved, for example. To modify options, select View → Options .
SECURITY	Explorer has a sophisticated security system. There's a *ratings system*, intended to enable you to block certain "offensive" sites, and a *certification system* designed to allow Web sites to "prove" that they are genuine and not impostor sites. However, note that neither system is yet in wide use on the Web. To modify the settings, select View → Options and click the Security tab.
MAIL PROGRAM	Internet Explorer has a good Internet-mail program that you can use instead of Windows Messaging (it's much easier to work with). Select Go → Read Mail , or use the Mail button.
NEWSGROUPS	Newsgroups are discussion groups. There are well over 20,000 internationally distributed newsgroups, on subjects both serious and flippant. Internet Explorer has a built-in newsgroup program. Select Go → Read News , or use the Mail button.
PERSONAL WEB SERVER	Windows NT Workstation comes with a product called Personal Web Server that you can use to set up your own mini-Web site on the corporate intranet or even the World Wide Web. You can find more information about the product at http://www.microsoft.com/IESupport/content/mspws/. In order to use it, you must install the Microsoft Peer Web Services from the Network dialog box (see Chapter 14). After doing so, select Start → Programs → Microsoft Peer Web Services (Common) → Product Documentation for more information.

Feature	More information
EXTRANETS AND PPTP	*Extranet* is the new term being given to private networks running on the Internet. They're also known as *Virtual Private Networks* (VPNs). Using something called PPTP (Point to Point Tunneling Protocol), a company can build an intranet on the Internet. All the users connect through the Internet, yet the Web sites they connect to are private, accessible only to authorized users. This provides a low-cost way for companies to build private, international corporate networks. In order to use this system, you must load PPTP from the Protocol tab of the Networks dialog box (right-click the Network Neighborhood icon on your desktop and select `Properties`). When you do, you have to configure Remote Access Service to work with PPTP. You connect to the network by dialing into the Internet, then using Dial-Up Networking to "dial" again, this time using the host name of the computer that's hosting the private network instead of a phone number. See your system administrator for more information.
TELNET	Telnet is a system that enables you to log onto other computers across the Internet. It's not used much these days, but if you *do* want to use it — for example, you might want to log onto your Internet service provider in order to change your password — select `Start` → `Programs` → `Accessories` → `Telnet`.

Summary

I've given you a *very* quick overview of working on the Web with Internet Explorer. There's much more to tell, far more than I can squeeze into the space available, so if you spend any time on the World Wide Web, find a book to help you, or spend some time reading the Help files. Also, select Help→Microsoft on the Web→Frequently Asked Questions. This takes you to the Microsoft Internet Explorer support page, where you can find detailed information — from a list of questions and answers to the MS Knowledge Base, a huge collection of technical information about Microsoft Products.

PART FOUR

GETTING UNDER THE HOOD

THIS PART CONTAINS THE FOLLOWING CHAPTERS

CHAPTER **18** CUSTOMIZING YOUR SYSTEM

CHAPTER **19** MAINTAINING AND FIXING WINDOWS NT

One size most certainly doesn't fit all in the computer world. You don't want a cookie-cutter operating system; you need to be able to modify it to suit your needs. In Part 4, you'll look at scores of little ways you can get NT to work just the way you want, from the Accessibility options that help the disabled work with the keyboard and mouse, to crazy color schemes and moving mouse pointers.

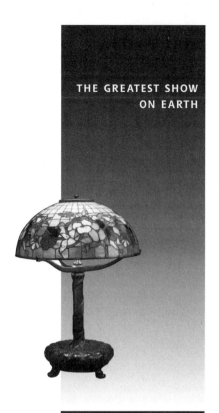

THE GREATEST SHOW ON EARTH

Ladies and gentlemen and children of all ages! Welcome to *Jumbo!*, the biggest single site on the World Wide Web!

Shareware leviathan Jumbo! (http://www.jumbo.com) leads the pack with over 200,000 pages and more than three million hypertext links to ftp (file transfer protocol) repositories all over the planet. This behemoth attracts 1.5 million visits per month. Jumbo! users can find 60,000 shareware and freeware programs at the site and download over 30,000 programs every day.

It's a three-ring circus juggled by three 200MHz Pentium computers fully loaded with 140MB megabytes of RAM and 10GB gigabyte hard drives. And it all runs on Windows NT.

"Economics was the reason," says Will Margiloff, Vice President of Business development of the New York City-based firm. "We started out as a pretty small company. With less than $100,000 to develop and run until our first client was signed, we couldn't afford a huge SPARC platform." SPARC is Sun's mammoth workstation with a sweet tooth for the operating system monster, UNIX.

In March 1995, company founders Dick and Anne Firestone thought finding online software had to be easier and dreamed up the idea of an ftp catalog on the Internet. They purchased the Pentiums and NT for relative peanuts. With the programming elan of 16-year-old Bronx High School of Science student, Jon Conlon, Jumbo! was up and running by July.

"NT works for a young Web site," Margiloff continues. "Somebody can put together a really good package that doesn't cost tens of thousands of dollars and can get it up and running in days."

With 16 subject areas — from business and utilities to multimedia and games — available in every operating system, Jumbo! offers a carnival of software. Given the dearth of NT software archives on the Internet, NT aficionados are especially delighted to find 12,000 programs alone for their favorite flavor of Windows. Users take a look at 8,000 pages a day, says Margiloff. "The number one section accessed for Windows NT is Internet and intranet software, followed by business applications and games. Most NT usage is coming from networks, specifically from the technical folks who are most interested in applications for their intranet or business."

In fact, between the server software, HTML markup software, sounds, clip art, Java, and multimedia, Jumbo! has everything an entrepreneur needs to run an entire Web site, says Margiloff.

The only thing missing is the operating system. "You gotta buy it from somebody," says Margiloff.

CHAPTER EIGHTEEN
CUSTOMIZING YOUR SYSTEM

IN THIS CHAPTER YOU LEARN THESE KEY SKILLS

SETTING ACCESSIBILITY OPTIONS PAGE 336

MODIFYING THE DATE AND TIME PAGE 340

RESOLUTIONS, COLOR, AND WALLPAPER PAGE 341

CONFIGURING THE KEYBOARD AND MOUSE PAGE 346

AUDIBLE COMPUTING — MODIFYING SOUNDS PAGE 349

In the old days (a decade or so ago), when you loaded an operating system, you didn't expect many choices. What you got was what you got. You didn't expect to be able to make many changes to the way in which the operating system functioned.

All that has changed dramatically. Windows NT has so many configuration settings that few people understand them all. You have settings to make the operating system look nice (whatever *you* think is nice, anyway), to allow for the fact that you're not in the Pacific Standard Time time zone (MS-DOS assumed that everyone lived in California), to allow for difficulties you may have in using a mouse or keyboard, and so on. In this chapter, you'll be looking at these things — ways to modify your computer.

Most customization options are available from the Windows NT Control Panel, a folder containing more than two dozen icons leading to dialog boxes and folders with hundreds of different options. To open the Control Panel, select Start→Settings→Control Panel. You can see the Control Panel in Figure 18-1. Refer to Table 18-1 to see what each icon does.

333

Figure 18-1 The Control Panel.

TABLE 18-1 The Control Panel Icons

Icon	Name	Purpose
	ACCESSIBILITY OPTIONS	Settings designed to make it easier for disabled computer users to work with Windows NT. You can modify the way in which your keyboard, sounds, and mouse work.
	ADD/REMOVE PROGRAMS	Used to install and uninstall programs (see Chapter 4) and add and remove NT components.
	CONSOLE	Determines what the Command Prompt window will look like (you saw an example of this in Chapter 12).
	DATE/TIME	Modify your date, time, and time zone settings.
	DEVICES	Used to start and stop a variety of "devices." This is only for experts!
	DIAL-UP MONITOR	Monitors Dial-Up Networking connections and controls the monitor icon in the toolbar. See Chapter 16.
	DISPLAY	Modifies your screen colors, resolution, screen savers, wallpaper, and so on.
	FONTS	Replaces the Control Panel folder with the Fonts folder. See Chapter 7.
	INTERNET	Sets the proxy server used for accessing the Internet through your network. See Chapter 17.
	KEYBOARD	Modifies a variety of keyboard settings.

Icon	Name	Purpose
	MAIL	Sets up Windows Messaging options. See Chapter 15.
	MICROSOFT MAIL POSTOFFICE	Administers the Microsoft Mail postoffice. See Chapter 15.
	MODEMS	Sets up modems. See Chapter 13.
	MOUSE	Sets mouse speed, buttons, pointers, and motion.
	MULTIMEDIA	Sets up multimedia devices. See Chapter 11.
	NETWORK	Adds and modifies network services. See Chapter 14
	PC CARD (PCMCIA)	Manages PC Cards (those little credit-card size computer cards that many laptops — and some desktop computers — use).
	PORTS	Used to add and modify serial communications ports.
	PRINTERS	Replaces the Control Panel folder with the Printers folder. See Chapter 7.
	REGIONAL SETTINGS	Sets up the way in which your computer should display numbers, money, times, dates, and so on, depending on the region in which you are located.
	SCSI ADAPTERS	Used to install and manage SCSI adapters, computer cards used to connect a range of different devices, from hard disks to tape drives and scanners.
	SERVER	Enables you to watch traffic between your computer and the network. You can use this utility to disconnect specific users from your computer.
	SERVICES	Enables you to start and stop a variety of NT software services. This is another utility for experts.
	SOUNDS	Sets up the manner in which NT will work with sounds.
	SYSTEM	Manages virtual memory, hardware profiles (Chapter 16), user profiles (Chapter 8), startup and shutdown options, and overall system performance.
	TAPE DEVICES	Adds and configures tape drives. See Chapter 12.
	TELEPHONY	Sets up your telephone-dialing parameters. See Chapter 13.
	UPS	Configures an uninterruptible power supply, a device that provides power to your computer even if the power company's power is cut.

Setting Accessibility Options

The Accessibility options were really designed for people who have difficulty using the keyboard and mouse, or who are unable to hear computer sounds. However, even if you feel you have no such problems, you may want to take a quick look at these settings. I use ToggleKeys, for example, to let me know when I accidentally hit the Caps Lock key.

To set Accessibility options, double-click the Accessibility Options icon in Control Panel. You see the dialog box in Figure 18-2.

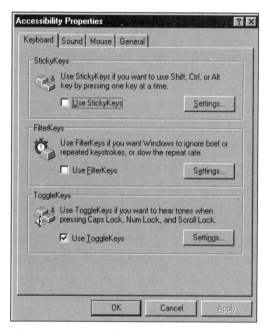

Figure 18-2 The Keyboard Accessibility settings.

Keyboard settings

You can turn on three different keyboard settings, and modify the manner in which each setting works, using the Settings buttons:

> **StickyKeys.** If you have trouble pressing two keys at once, turn on StickyKeys. For example, if you need to press Ctrl+I to make a word italic in a word-processing document, you can press Ctrl and then I. You don't have to hold them down at the same time. Or, to type a capital C, press Shift and then press C. (StickyKeys works with Shift, Ctrl, and Alt.) The StickyKeys settings allow you to turn the feature on and off by pressing the Shift key five times, press any of the three keys twice to turn it on and keep it on (you could press Ctrl twice, then press the arrow keys to jump from word to word in your

word processor, for example), turn the feature off if two keys are pressed at the same time, and make a sound whenever on of the three keys is pressed.

FilterKeys. FilterKeys can be used to ignore keys that are pressed accidentally — keys that are pressed quickly or that are repeated quickly. Use the Settings button to select the FilterKeys shortcut (you can turn the feature on and off by holding down the Right-Shift key for eight seconds), ignore repeated keystrokes if they are typed more quickly than the speed you specify, turn off or slow down keyboard repeat (keyboard repeat is when a character is typed over and over when the key is held down), define how long a key must be held down for it to be accepted by the computer, and make the computer sound a "blip" each time a key is pressed.

Note that there's a bug in these Settings dialog boxes. There are test boxes in which you can type and see what happens, but these boxes don't work unless you make your settings, leave the boxes, click the Apply button in the Accessibility Properties dialog box, and then reopen the dialog boxes.

TIP You can also set keyboard repeat rates in the Control Panel's Keyboard box. FilterKeys overrides those settings.

ToggleKeys. Turn this on to hear a beep when you press Caps Lock, Num Lock, or Scroll Lock. The turn-on and turn-off beeps are different. The only Setting you can make is to allow you to turn the feature on and off by holding down Num Lock for five seconds.

Sound settings

Click the Sound tab to see the two option in the Sounds area:

Use SoundSentry. If this is turned on, each time one of your programs "beeps" at you, you see a visual indicator. You must click the Settings button and select the type of indicator you want to see. Experiment with these indicators — some don't seem to work well. You can make programs indicate a beep by flashing the title bar, the window, or the "desktop" (which actually seems to be a random block of your screen).

Use ShowSounds. Turn this on to tell Windows NT programs that you want to see captions instead of sounds. This works only if the program has the capability of displaying such captions — and most currently don't.

Mouse settings

Click the Mouse tab to see the information shown in Figure 18-3.

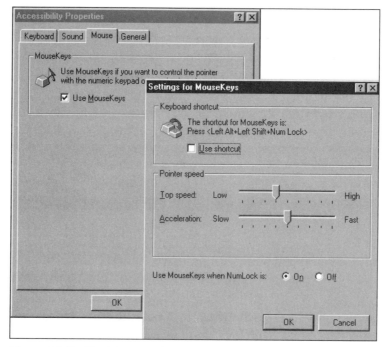

Figure 18-3 The Mouse settings.

The only setting here is *Use MouseKeys*. This enables you to move the mouse with the keyboard's numeric keypad. As you can see in Figure 18-3, you can modify how all this works. You can set up the shortcut so that you can quickly turn the feature on and off from the keyboard (by pressing Left Alt+Left Shift+Num Lock — of course, you may need StickyKeys to do this!).

You can also adjust the speed and the acceleration of the mouse pointer. And, in theory, you can choose to have the feature function when Num Lock is turned on or off. However, you may find that it works only if you set *Use MouseKeys when NumLock is* to Off. Make sure that the Num Lock key is indeed turned off.

Table 18-2 explains how to use the numeric keypad. The items in the left column are the mouse actions. In the right column are the keystrokes you use to simulate those mouse actions.

TABLE 18-2 Moving the Mouse Pointer with the Keyboard

This movement	Uses this keystroke
MOVE POINTER	Use the arrow keys
MOVE POINTER DIAGONALLY	Use Home, End, Page Up, Page Down
CLICK	Press 5

This movement	Uses this keystroke
DOUBLE-CLICK	+
HOLD THE MOUSE BUTTON (SO YOU CAN DRAG)	Insert
RELEASE THE MOUSE BUTTON	Delete
RIGHT-CLICK	press - and then 5
RIGHT DOUBLE-CLICK	press - and then +
CLICK BOTH MOUSE BUTTONS	press * and then 5
DOUBLE-CLICK BOTH BUTTONS	press * and then +
RETURN TO NORMAL CLICKING (AFTER PRESSING - OR *)	press /

General settings

Click the General tab. Under the General Settings tab, you'll find these options:

Automatic Reset. You can tell NT to turn off all the accessibility features if the computer isn't used for a specified time.

Notification. Turn this on to sound a tone each time you turn a feature on or off using one of the shortcuts.

SerialKey Devices. If you have a special device used to input information to the computer — an *augmentative communication device* or *alternate input device* — you should turn on SerialKey and use the Settings button to specify which port the device is connected to.

TIP If you are logged in as the administrator when you close the Accessibility Properties dialog box, you see a message box asking if you want to save the new settings as the default for new users. Click Yes and the settings will be used for all new profiles.

By the way, there are other settings that may be of use to the visually impaired. The Display settings (see "Resolutions, Colors, and Wallpaper," later in this chapter), allow you to modify colors, fonts, the size of certain components (including icons), and so on.

Modifying the Date and Time

Double-click the Date/Time icon in Control Panel. Before you set your clock, set your time zone (modifying the time zone changes the clock's time). Click the TimeZone tab to see the dialog box in Figure 18-4. (This is one of the things you won't be able to set unless you have System Administrator privileges. If you don't, you'll see a message box saying *You do not have the proper privilege level to change the System Time.*)

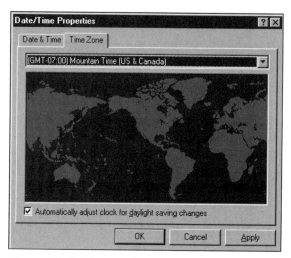

Figure 18-4 Get your time zone right... we're living in a networked world now.

Unlike Windows 95, you can't just click your area of the world in this dialog box. You must select it from the drop-down list box. Notice also the *Automatically adjust clock for daylight saving changes* check box. If you check this, the computer changes the time when the clocks are moved forward or back, *if* you've selected the correct time zone. Some areas of the world don't use daylight savings time. For example, if you live in Indianapolis, you should select Indiana (East), *not* Eastern Time (US & Canada).

 TIP   In many cases, perhaps most, having the correct time zone really doesn't matter much. But if you are on an international network, or you send information across the Internet, you may want to make sure the time zone is correctly set.

Click the Date & Time tab to see the information shown in Figure 18-5. This dialog box sets the computer's system date and time, which is used whenever you save a file. Select the correct month and year, then click the day in the calendar. The quickest way to set the time is to double-click the hour, type a number and press Tab, type the minutes and press Tab, type the seconds and press Tab, then press **p** or **a** to select PM or AM.

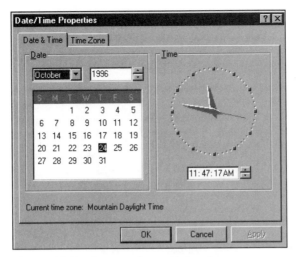

Figure 18-5 Set your date and time here.

Resolutions, Colors, and Wallpaper

You can open the Display Properties dialog box in a couple ways. You can double-click the Display icon in the Control Panel, or you can right-click the desktop and select Properties.

Background

The Background pane of this dialog box enables you to modify your desktop. You can select a pattern from the list on the left — you can even click Edit Pattern to modify or create patterns. You can also select a wallpaper from the list on the right. These are bitmap files, so you can create your own, if you want, in Paint (see Chapter 10) or in any other graphics program. You can even scan photos, save them as bitmaps, and use them for your wallpaper.

When you select a wallpaper, choose either *Tile* (the wallpaper image will be repeated over and over, to completely cover the desktop), or *Center* (one image appears in the middle). But see the *Stretch desktop wallpaper to fit the screen* setting in the "Plus!" section, later in this chapter.

TIP You don't have to close the dialog box to see your pattern or wallpaper. Simply click the Apply button to instantly make your changes.

Screen Saver

Click the Screen Saver tab to see the dialog box shown in Figure 18-6. The screen saver is a special display that appears after your computer has been idle for a specified period — no keyboard or mouse activity. If you walk away from the computer, the screen saver will eventually appear, blocking your work from view.

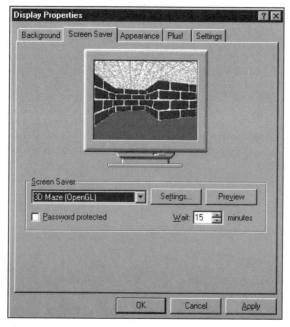

Figure 18-6 Set up your screen saver here.

Select the screen saver you want to use in the *Screen Saver* drop-down list box — you'll see the screen saver in the sample window. If you want to see it's full size, click *Preview* (be careful to keep your mouse completely still after clicking, or you'll immediately turn it off).

Click Settings to modify your selected screen saver. You can enter the text that appears on the screen, modify the type of motion, the speed, and so on. You can also enter a *Wait* period, the number of minutes that the computer will wait after keyboard and mouse activity stops before starting the screen saver.

Then there's the *Password protected* check box. After the screen saver has started, you can't re-enter NT without entering your password. NT will use the Lock Workstation command (which you saw in Chapter 2).

Appearance

Click the Appearance tab to see the dialog box in Figure 18-7. This is where you set up your screen colors. The large box at the top, with the simulated windows and message box, shows you what a color scheme looks like. You can select the scheme from the *Scheme* drop-down list box. There are all sorts of strange color schemes, so experiment a little.

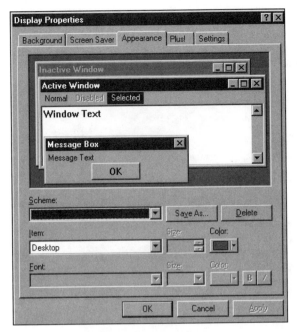

Figure 18-7 Pick a color, any color.

You can also modify a particular screen element. Click an item in the top box — a menu bar, title bar, the desktop, or whatever — to select it, or choose an item from the *Item* drop-down list box. Then you can modify the item using the following elements:

Item Size. If you selected something that can be enlarged or reduced in size, you can enter the size into the incrementer.

Item Color. If the item's color can be changed, click the Color box to see a little pop-up color selector, and then click the color you want to use.

Font. Some of the items are text — text in windows or message boxes, for example. Use the *Font* drop-down list box to select the font that you prefer.

Font Size. Select the font size.

Font Color. Select the color.

B. Click this to make the text bold.

/. Click this to make the text italic.

TIP After you've set all the colors, sizes, and fonts just the way you want them, click Save As to save your color scheme.

Plus!

Click the Plus! tab to see the options in Figure 18-8. These allow you to modify a few basic desktop and window settings.

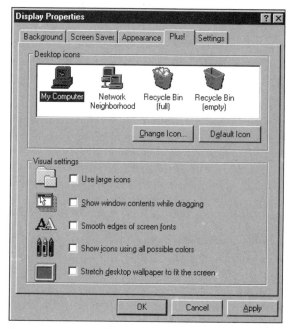

Figure 18-8 Modify icons and other general settings.

Here are the changes you can make:

Desktop icons. Select an icon and click Change Icon to choose a different icon.

Use large icons. Select this to expand the size of the icons on your desktop and in folders.

Show window contents while dragging. When you drag a window in Windows NT, you see an outline of the window; the window actually moves when you release the mouse button. Check this box, however, and the actual window moves with the mouse.

Smooth edges of screen fonts. Checking this box smoothes the edges of fonts on your screen. You may not notice much difference, however. And you may have to select a video-mode with more colors.

Show icons using all possible colors. If you are using a video mode with many colors (High- or True-Color mode), you can check this box to make the icons use more colors and look less grainy.

Stretch desktop wallpaper to fit the screen. If you have a small bitmap set as a centered wallpaper, checking this box will stretch the bitmap to cover the entire desktop.

Settings

Click the Settings tab to see the area in which you modify the monitor's video mode (see Figure 18-9).

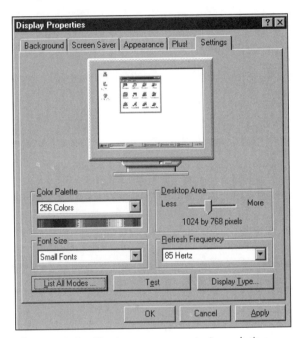

Figure 18-9 Change your computer's resolution and colors here.

These are your options:

Color Palette. Choose the number of colors you want to use from this drop-down list box. The more colors you use, the more memory your video card will need, and the slower NT is likely to operate.

Desktop Area. Drag the slider to modify the screen resolution. The left side of the slider provides a low-resolution — everything looks big. The right side provides a high-resolution — everything looks small. Remember that you can use other settings in the Display Properties dialog box to adjust icon, text, and other component sizes — so you could use a high-resolution and still have readable icons and menus.

Font Size. Some video modes allow you to select a font size. So if you have a high-resolution mode, you can use large fonts in order to read icon labels and menus. When you close the dialog box, you're prompted to install a new set of fonts from the NT installation disk.

Refresh Frequency. Refresh frequency is how often the monitor "flickers," how often it repaints the monitor's screen. The larger the number, the better, because it's less tiring to look at a high-refresh screen than a low-refresh screen.

List All Modes. Click here to see a list box showing dozens of different permutations of resolutions, colors, and refresh rates. You can click one and then click OK to quickly set the other options automatically.

Test. Once you have the settings you want to use, click Test to make sure they work. If you get a blank screen for five seconds, they don't! If they do work, you see a screen showing colors, text, and arrows for five seconds.

Display Type. Click here to see more information about your video card and to install new video drivers.

Apply and OK. Don't click these buttons until you've used the Test button! If you selected a video mode that doesn't work, you get a blank screen!

TIP Didn't take my advice, eh? Selected a mode without testing and now have just a blank screen? Reboot (if you press Ctrl+Alt+Delete, you may see the Windows NT Security dialog box; otherwise, just press the computer's reset button). Then, when you see the first boot screen, select `Windows NT Workstation Version 4.00 [VGA mode]`. When you log into NT, you'll see the Display Properties dialog box and can reset your screen.

Configuring the Keyboard and Mouse

You can modify the manner in which you use both your keyboard and your mouse — which buttons carry out operations, how fast things move, and which cute little walking dinosaur to use for your mouse pointer.

Keyboard settings

Double-click the Keyboard icon in Control Panel to see the dialog box in Figure 18-10.

Here are your options:

Repeat delay. This setting defines how long you must hold down a key before it starts repeating. For example, hold down a key in a word processor, wait for the specified delay, and the key repeatedly types the character.

Repeat rate. This setting defines, in theory, how quickly the characters are typed. You can test the setting in the text box, but you may find that the setting doesn't actually do anything!

Cursor blink rate. You've seen your cursor blink in a word processor . . . well, this setting defines how quickly it blinks.

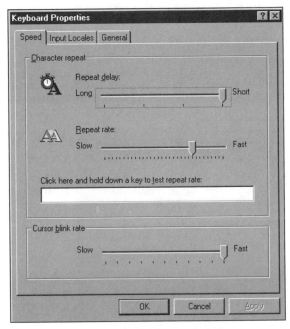

Figure 18-10 Set your keyboard speed here.

 TIP Remember, these settings are overridden by the Accessibility Options you saw earlier in this chapter.

Clicking the Input Locales tab pops up a dialog box that enables you to use different keyboards, set up for different areas of the world and different keyboard styles. Click an entry in the list box, and click Properties to see a list from which you can select a particular type of keyboard. For example, perhaps you have two keyboards, a QWERTY keyboard and a Dvorak keyboard, for two different users. You can add another keyboard locale and then set that locale to a particular type of keyboard. Here's how:

1. Click Add. The Add Input Locale dialog box opens.
2. Select the keyboard type from the list, and click OK. If there's already one keyboard of this type in the list, you'll see the Input Locale Properties dialog box.
3. Select the keyboard type from the list.
4. Click OK and the keyboard is added to the list.

Notice that you can also select a keyboard shortcut — Left Alt+Shift or Ctrl+Shift — to quickly switch between keyboard settings. And you can put a keyboard indicator into the taskbar's tray; clicking the indicator opens a menu showing the keyboards from which you can select.

TIP The General tab, both here and in the Mouse Pointers box, enables you to install a different device.

Mouse settings

To modify the mouse, double-click the Mouse icon in Control Panel. The dialog box in Figure 18-11 opens.

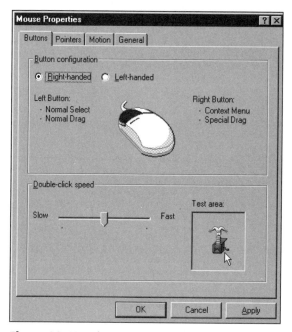

Figure 18-11 The Mouse Properties dialog box.

At the top of the box, you can swap the mouse buttons. By default, the left button is the primary one, but you can click Left-handed to make the right button primary, if you want. Below the *Button configuration* is the *Double-click speed* setting. This defines how fast you must click the mouse button to carry out a double-click action. You can test the speed, to find the one most comfortable for you, by double-clicking the jack-in-the-box — jack pops out if you click at the correct speed.

Click the Pointers tab to get to the best part of the dialog box . . . where you can select those little dinosaurs I was talking about (see Figure 18-12).

You can select a preset scheme of mouse pointers, if you want, from the *Scheme* drop-down list box. Or click a mouse pointer type and then click Browse. You can choose from scores of different mouse pointers, from the cute to the mundane. There are two types of mouse-pointer files: .cur files (just plain old mouse pointers), and .ani files (*animated* mouse pointers). Yes, you really can use a moving metronome, horse, or drum as a mouse pointer. If you ever want to return to the normal settings for the selected scheme, however, click Use Default.

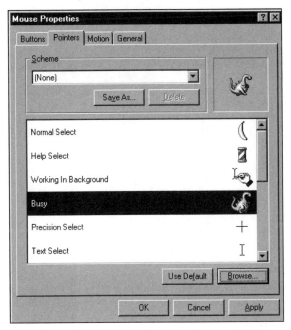

Figure 18-12 Pick your dinosaur, banana, hand, barber's pole...

Click the Motion tab, and you'll get to a tab that allows you to set the "speed" at which the pointer moves. This isn't really the speed, though, it's the distance moved across the screen for a given hand motion. The faster the setting, the further the mouse moves. You can also turn on *Snap mouse to the default button in dialogs*. This great little tool automatically moves the mouse pointer to the selected button when you open a dialog box in most, though not all, applications.

Audible Computing — Modifying Sounds

If you double-click the Sounds icon in Control Panel, you see the Sounds Properties dialog box (see Figure 18-13), in which you can define the sounds that should play for particular events.

As with the mouse pointers, you can pick a scheme (from the *Schemes* drop-down list box near the bottom of the dialog box) and get a set of matching sounds. There are jungle sounds, robot sounds, funny little musical instrument sounds, and something called Utopia, which is an odd little mixture. To test the sounds, click an event in the large list box, and then click the Play button to the right of the preview window.

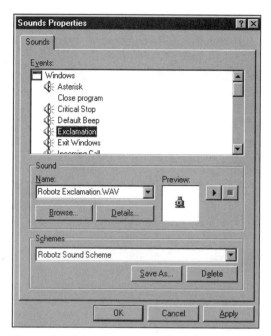

Figure 18-13 You want jungle sounds? Robot sounds? Weird stuff?

The little preview window, by the way, shows you if the sound is part of a particular set (you see a little robot, frog, instrument, or smiley face) or one of the default sounds (you see a speaker icon).

You don't have to stick with the schemes, of course. You can mix and match. Click the event in the list, then select a sound from the *Sound Name* drop-down list box, or click Browse and select a sound from any list of .WAV sounds. You can even use Sound Recorder (see Chapter 11) to create your own sounds.

BONUS

What Happens During Startup?

You can modify what your computer does during the startup procedure in the System Properties dialog box. Here's what to do:

1. Double-click the System icon in Control Panel. The System Properties dialog box opens.

2. Click the Startup/Shutdown tab to see the panel in Figure 18-14.

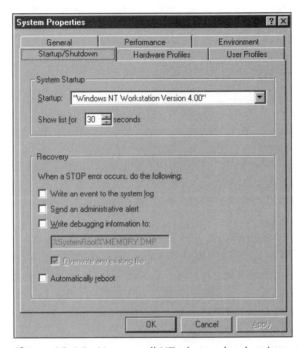

Figure 18-14 You can tell NT what to do when it starts.

3. The *Startup* drop-down list box contains a list of possible operating systems. It may only show *Windows NT Workstation Version 4.00* and *Windows NT Workstation Version 4.00 [VGA mode]*. It may also show another operating system if you are using a "multi-boot" system. Select the one that you want to appear at the top of the list during boot. (See Chapter 1.)

4. In the *Show list for* box, enter the number of seconds that the list should appear on your screen before the entry at the top of the list is automatically selected. If you want the screen just to appear momentarily, enter **1**.

5. If you want NT to boot without displaying the operating system options screen, enter **0**. (Instead, the first option in the list is selected automatically.)

If you want, you may modify the text that appears in the *Startup* drop-down list box. Open the BOOT.INI file — it's in the root directory of your C drive — in Notepad, and modify the text between quotation marks. For example, you'll see something like this:

```
[boot loader]
timeout=0
default=multi(0)disk(0)rdisk(1)partition(1)\WINNT
[operating systems]
multi(0)disk(0)rdisk(1)partition(1)\WINNT="Windows NT Workstation
    Version 4.00"
multi(0)disk(0)rdisk(1)partition(1)\WINNT="Windows NT Workstation
    Version 4.00 [VGA mode]" /basevideo /sos
C:\="Microsoft Windows"
```

You could change it to this:

```
[boot loader]
timeout=0
default=multi(0)disk(0)rdisk(1)partition(1)\WINNT
[operating systems]
multi(0)disk(0)rdisk(1)partition(1)\WINNT="Windows NT 4.00"
multi(0)disk(0)rdisk(1)partition(1)\WINNT="Windows NT—VGA mode"
    /basevideo /sos
C:\="Windows 95"
```

Be careful to change nothing but the text within quotation marks; don't modify anything else. Then go to Windows Explorer, find the BOOT.INI file, and clear its Read-only attribute (right-click the file and select Properties, then click the *Read-only* check box). Save your changes to BOOT.INI from Notepad, then turn Read-only back on.

By the way, the Shutdown part of the tab name (Startup/Shutdown) is a euphemism. As you can see, the information at the bottom of the box defines what NT should do if the system *crashes*, which actually doesn't happen very often with NT.

Summary

There are so many ways to modify the manner in which your computer operates... there's something for everyone. Spend a little time experimenting with what works best for you, and you're bound to come across something useful. Simply choosing the best screen resolution and then setting icon and text sizes appropriately can make working in NT much easier, and ensuring that your keyboard and mouse are set up properly will be a real help, too.

CHAPTER NINETEEN

MAINTAINING AND FIXING WINDOWS NT

IN THIS CHAPTER YOU LEARN THESE KEY SKILLS

A QUICK LOOK AT THE SYSTEM — TASK MANAGER PAGE 355

TRACKING SYSTEM PERFORMANCE PAGE 357

VIEWING EVENT LOGS PAGE 360

FINDING SYSTEM INFORMATION PAGE 361

Windows NT has a variety of programs that are used to manage the operating system and its network connections. I won't look in detail at most of these, as they're advanced and, in some cases, quite complicated, but a few have some useful features for the average user. The administrative utilities are shown in Table 19-1. (You may not have all these, unless you've installed the appropriate options).

TABLE 19-1 Windows NT's Administrative Utilities

Utility	Purpose
Opened from the Start → Programs → Administrative Tools (Common) menu:	
DISK ADMINISTRATOR	Enables you to partition and format hard drives and specify drive letters. You shouldn't play around in here unless you are sure you know what you're doing.
EVENT VIEWER	Displays system messages concerning program errors, devices that were unable to start, auditing (see Chapter 8), and so on.

(continued)

TABLE 19-1 Windows NT's Administrative Utilities *(continued)*

Utility	Purpose
PERFORMANCE MONITOR	Shows you more details than you ever wanted to know about how well your system is performing — from how busy your hard disk drives are to how many phone calls have been made to your computer.
REMOTE ACCESS ADMINISTRATOR	Used to manage incoming calls using Dial-Up Networking. Remember, RAS (Remote Access Service) is the NT service that allows other systems to call into an NT computer.
TASK MANAGER	You saw the task-switching part of Task Manager in Chapter 3. But you can also use Task Manager to view basic system-performance information and the software "processes" that are running.
WINDOWS NT DIAGNOSTICS	This service is really not "diagnostics." Rather, it's used to display system configuration information, such as memory use, version information, network statistics, and much more.

Opened from the Start → Programs → Microsoft Peer Web Services (Common) menu:

Utility	Purpose
INTERNET SERVICE MANAGER	Used to manage Internet connections to your computer.
INTERNET SERVICE MANAGER (HTML)	Also used to manage Internet connections to your computer, but it's in HTML (HyperText Markup Language) format. In other words, it's a series of Web pages, so it can be used from within your Web browser.
KEY MANAGER	Used for generating public/private key pairs to encrypt data that is being transmitted across the Internet or an intranet.
PEER WEB SERVICES SETUP	Enables you to set up the Peer Web Services, a system used to set up a mini Web site that others on your intranet or on the Internet can use to view your Web pages (see Chapter 17).

In addition to these utilities, you also have all the utilities in Control Panel, which I covered in Chapter 18.

A Quick Look at the System — Task Manager

In Chapter 3, you saw how to use Task Manager to switch between programs or close programs, but there's another use for the program. You can use it to get a quick look at your CPU and memory use.

Right-click the taskbar and select Task Manager. Click the Performance tab, and you'll see the information shown in Figure 19-1. At the top of the box, you see your CPU usage. In this example, you can see spikes when programs were being loaded, with a fairly low background level. If your computer was working as a server that many other people were using, you might see higher CPU levels.

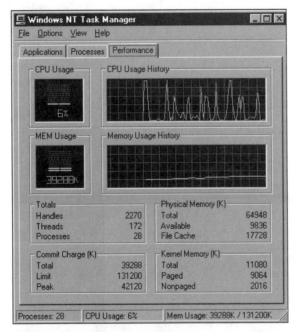

Figure 19-1 The Task Manager shows CPU and memory usage.

The lower part of the box shows memory usage. Again, as the programs are loaded, the memory is increasing. If the number in the MEM Usage box is often close to the Total value under Physical Memory, you may want to consider adding memory to your computer.

SIDE TRIP

How Much Memory Do You Need?

Most computers are sold with insufficient memory. (It's a way for the computer vendors to keep their prices low and competitive, but it means that the computers don't work as well as they could.) True, there's something called a *paging file*. This is an area on the hard disk that works as *virtual memory*. That is, when your computer has filled all the RAM chips with data, the hard disk can act as simulated memory — when the computer needs to put something else into memory, it goes into the paging file. But this means that retrieving data from memory will be *much* slower.

Microsoft recommends 16MB of memory for a computer running NT, but that's a bare minimum, really. (They also say you can run it with 12MB, but you wouldn't want to.) 32MB of memory is a more reasonable amount, and more than that is better. Take a look at the Task Manager's MEM Usage box to see how much memory you commonly use, and how much you use when you have many programs open. You may find that you are often using more than 32MB.

Want to see what all that memory is used for? Click the Processes tab, then click the Mem Usage column at the top of the list box you see (see Figure 19-2). The list is sorted with the programs that take up most memory listed first.

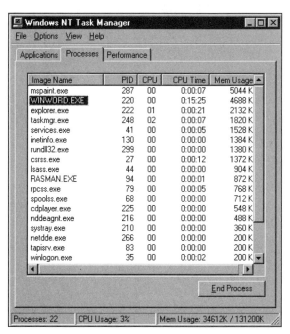

Figure 19-2 You can see which programs are using the most memory.

It's not always clear what these programs are, however, because many are started in the background by various NT processes. You know what mspaint.exe and winword.exe are (MS Paint and Microsoft Paint). There's explorer.exe (NT Explorer), cdplayer.exe, and so on. But others, such as csrss.exe and inetinfo.exe, are not so obvious.

Tracking System Performance

Performance Monitor is a more advanced version of the Task Manager's Performance and Processes panes. Select Start→Programs→Administrative Tools (Common)→Performance Monitor. You see the window in Figure 19-3. This program not only shows you what's going on (with dozens of obscure system processes), but you can actually get the program to store the information for later viewing.

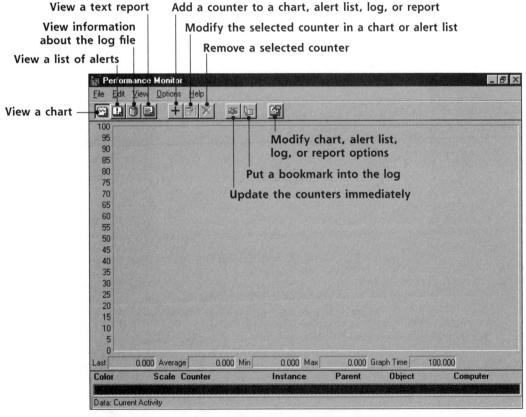

Figure 19-3 Performance Monitor; not much happening yet.

Here's how to get Performance Monitor to monitor something:

1. Click the toolbar button, or select **Edit** → **Add to Chart**. The Add to Chart dialog box opens (see Figure 19-4).

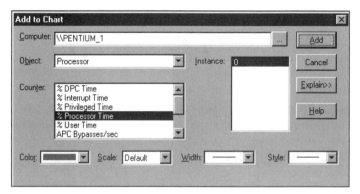

Figure 19-4 The Add to Chart dialog box.

2. Your computer is shown in the *Computer* box, but you can click the button at the end of the box to select another computer on the network, if you want.

3. From the *Object* drop-down list box, select the category from which you'll select an item to monitor. You can select Processor, Memory, Logical Disk, Physical Disk, Telephony, Server, and so on.

4. The *Counter* box now changes to show you the specific items that you can monitor for the object you picked. Select one or more of these counters. (Hold Ctrl while you click, or drag the mouse pointer over the counters while holding the button down.)

5. If you're not sure what all these things are, click the Explain button. The dialog box adds a *Counter Definition* text box at the bottom. Click a counter to see its explanation in the text box.

6. In some cases, you may see entries in the *Instance* box. That happens when more than one of the selected items can be counted. In this box, you can select which of them to count. For example, if you select Physical Disk, and you have two hard disks in your computer, you can monitor Disk 0, Disk 1, or Total (both).

7. Now define how you want this item to be shown on the chart. You can use the drop-down list boxes to select the color, scale, width, and style. (If you select multiple counters, Performance Monitor picks the colors for you.)

8. Click Add to add the counter to the chart. You can now add another counter.

9. When you are finished, click Done (see Figure 19-5).

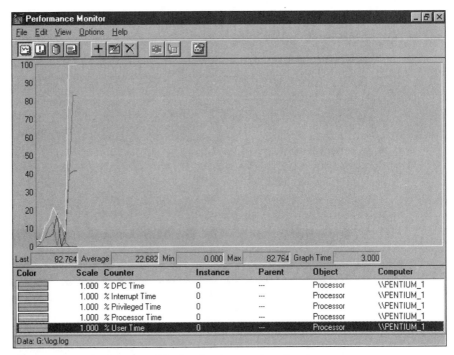

Figure 19-5 Performance Monitor begins creating the chart.

Alerts, logs, and reports

There are actually four basic modules in Performance Monitor. You can create charts, as you've just seen, but you can also set up alerts, logs, and reports.

The alerts are simply a way to track potential problems. For example, you might track disk space usage or memory so that you know if your system is close to being overloaded. Each time the particular counter crosses a threshold that you set, an alert line is added to an alert log.

The log enables you to store all sorts of performance information in a text file that you can examine later. And the reports are instantaneous displays of information — not a log of activity over a particular period, but rather a series of lines containing continually changing data.

Adding items to the alerts and reports is similar to adding them to charts, although particulars vary a little. With an alert, you have to specify when it should show — the threshold that must be crossed, for example. With logs, however, you select an entire process and later examine the log using the chart, alert, and report modules. You must select Options→Data From to open the log, and then set up the chart, alerts, and reports as normal.

Viewing Event Logs

Event Viewer displays a variety of system, application, and security messages, from general event messages that are added to the viewer when you log on and log off to error messages and messages from the audit system (which you saw in Chapter 8). Now and then, you may even see an error message box open when you start NT. This box tells you to look in Event Viewer for a description of a problem that has occurred, perhaps because a software driver hasn't loaded correctly for some reason, or a piece of hardware is not functioning.

To open Event Viewer, select Start→Programs→Administrative Tools (Common)→Event Viewer. See Figure 19-6.

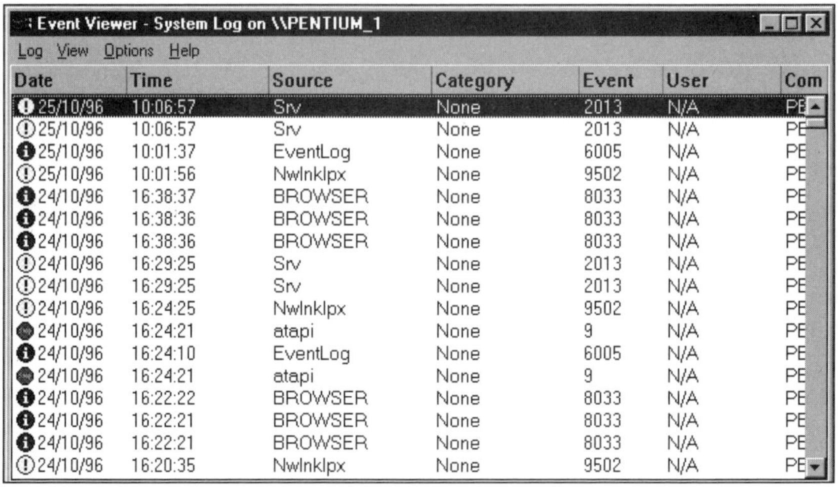

Figure 19-6 The Event Viewer, showing System events.

Figure 19-6 shows the System messages. If you want to see the other sets of events, select Log→Security and Log→Applications. To see an event's details, double-click an event in the list (they are generally sorted with the most recent at the top, so if you've just seen an error message telling you to view Event Viewer, double-click the one at the top). You see a box similar to that shown in Figure 19-7.

You can click Next to see the details of the next item in the list, or Previous to see the one before this. The message in Figure 19-7 is easy to understand: disk D is almost full. Unfortunately, many of these messages are not so clear and are generally intended for system administrators.

TIP See Chapter 8 for information on setting up the Log Settings.

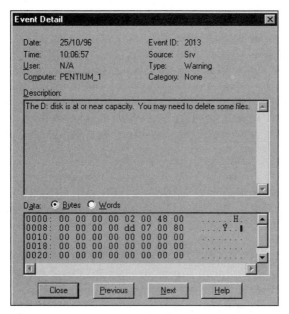

Figure 19-7 An event's details.

Finding System Information

The Windows NT Diagnostics box is not really a diagnostics utility. It doesn't diagnose problems for you; it simply displays lots of information about your system (most of which has little to do with problems). Still, you may find it handy now and again when you need to know something about your computer and the NT configuration. In particular, it may be handy when talking with technical support people who are helping you to diagnose problems.

Select Start→Programs→Administrative Tools (Common)→Windows NT Diagnostics. You see a box with nine tabs:

Version. Your NT version number and serial number, along with the Registered To name and company name.

System. Your computer type, BIOS information, and CPU type.

Display. Detailed information about your video card: the BIOS, chip type, amount of memory, and so on.

Drives. A list of floppy, hard, and CD drives in your system.

Memory. Detailed information about your computer's memory: how much it has, how much is available, and all sorts of arcane memory statistics (handles, threads, kernel memory, and so on).

Services. This tab displays two lists, one showing system services and the other showing system devices available to your computer (these are the services and devices controlled by the ![] Services and ![] Devices icons in Control Panel). It shows which are running and which are stopped.

Resources. Handy stuff for fixing hardware configuration problems. You have five lists here: IRQ (Interrupt Requests), I/O Port (Input/output), DMA (Direct Memory Access) channels, Memory addresses, and Devices. (See Figure 19-8.)

Environment. Displays environment variables, such as the number of processors used (Windows NT can run on computers that have multiple processors), temporary-file directory names, the Windows NT directory, and more.

Network. Shows network information, such as your access level, the computer name, your domain name, and so on. There are four lists here, including Transports, Settings, and Statistics, that contain plenty of advanced network information.

Figure 19-8 The IRQ and DMA lists can be useful when installing new hardware.

There's a Properties button in this dialog box. You can select an item in one of the lists, and then click Properties to open a box showing more information. For example, the dialog box in Figure 19-9 shows details about a disk selected under the Drives tab.

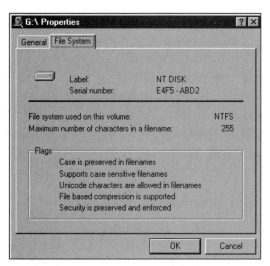

Figure 19-9 Select an item and click Properties to see more information.

BONUS

Your Basic Maintenance Schedule

What sorts of things should you be doing to keep your system running smoothly? There are a few basic procedures you should carry out:

* You *must* perform backups (see Chapter 12). Okay, it won't keep your system running smoothly, but it will help you recover when it doesn't.

* It's a good idea to check all your hard disks for errors periodically (see Chapter 6). Every week or two is probably a good idea. This is especially important if you have a dual-boot computer, a computer on which you are running Windows 95 or Windows 3.1, for example, in addition to Windows NT. Those operating systems are rather messy and often create file problems that the NT error-checking system can fix.

* Defragment your hard disks periodically (see Chapter 6). NT doesn't have a built-in disk defragmenter, so if you want to do this, you need to buy an add-on utility. Run the utility periodically — every couple weeks, perhaps — and it will tell you if you need to defragment.

* Clear the ~*.tmp files from your \TEMP\ directory (see Chapter 6). This will free up disk space. And look for those temporary files stored by some other programs, files such as MS Word's ~$*.doc files.
* Check your memory use occasionally to see how often you use more memory than is available in RAM (at which point the computer has to use virtual memory). If it's often, get more RAM! At $5 or $6 per megabyte, you soon make the money back in increased productivity.

Summary

Windows NT comes with far more management and maintenance tools than the average user will ever be able to work with. Much of the information provided is advanced and not intended for the average user. It's intended for system administrators, technicians, programmers, technical-support staff, and other such technical personnel. However, there is useful information among all this detail, and it's also worth learning how all these things work. The next time someone in technical support asks you for some strange technical information, you know where to find it.

DISCOVERY CENTER

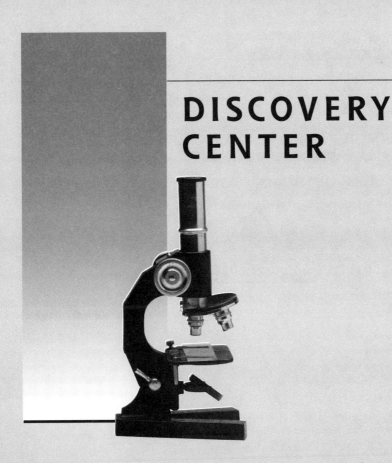

Like all books in the **Discover** series from IDG Books Worldwide, *Discover Windows NT Workstation 4.0* includes a feature called (hold your breath, now) the Discovery Center. The Discovery Center acts as a visual guide to the most commonly performed actions in Windows NT Workstation. Turn to the Discovery Center when you want concise, step-by-step instructions for completing a task — especially when you aren't quite sure which NT feature you use to perform that task. (If you already know the name of the NT feature, you can easily find the information you need by using the book's index.) The Discovery Center also shows you where to turn in the book for more details about the task. Think of the Discovery Center as just one more method you can use to quickly accomplish your goals when using Windows NT Workstation 4.0.

To Start Windows NT (page 20)

If the computer is off, turn it on and the boot procedure begins. If there's a dialog box on the screen that says *It is now safe to turn off your computer*, then click the Restart button.

If You Have Multiple Operating Systems (page 20)

You see a list of operating systems that you can use.

1. Choose Windows NT Workstation.
2. Press Enter.

The Windows NT "Desktop" (page 23)

To Start Programs (page 39)

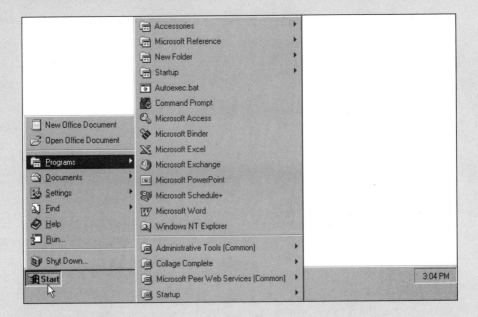

1. Click the `Start` button.
2. Click the `Programs` option to see a list of programs and program submenus.
3. Click the program you want to start.

To Configure the Taskbar (page 30)

1. Right-click the taskbar.
2. Choose `Properties`.
3. Use the first two check boxes in the Taskbar Properties dialog box to configure the taskbar.

To Switch to a Program (page 29)

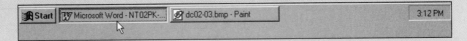

Click the appropriate taskbar button. Every running program has a button.

To Start a Program from the Start Menu (page 40)

1. Click the Start button (or press the Windows logo key) or press Ctrl+Esc.
2. Click the menu options you want to select.

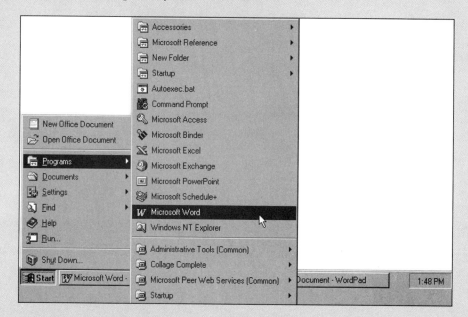

To Start a Program from an Icon (page 42)

Double-click the desktop icon.

To Open a Document You've Used Before (page 43)

1. Select Start → Documents.
2. Click the document you want.

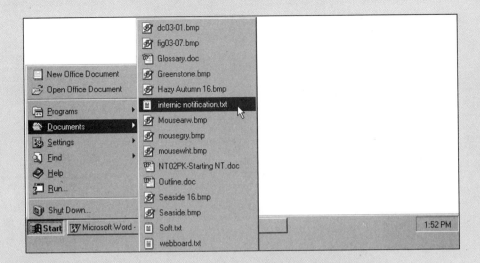

To Open a Program by Path and Filename (page 44)

1. Select Start → Run.
2. Type the path and filename.
3. Press Enter.

To Move from One Window to Another (page 49)

Press Alt+Tab or click the taskbar program buttons.

To Close a Program (page 56)

Press Alt+F4. or select File → Exit.

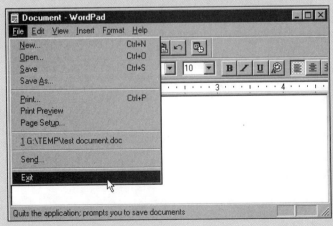

To Modify the Start Menu (page 61)

1. Right-click the taskbar.
2. Select **Properties**.
3. Click the Start Menu Programs tab.
4. Click Add, Remove, or Advanced.

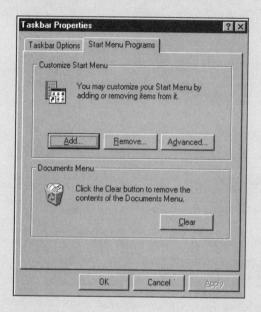

To Add a Program Directly to the Start Menu (page 62)

1. Find a program or shortcut to the program on the desktop or within Windows NT Explorer.
2. Drag the icon onto the Start button and release.

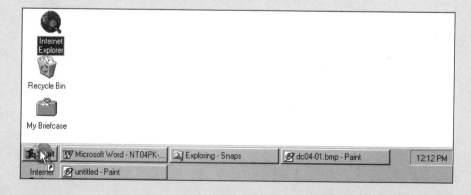

To Create a Desktop Shortcut (page 65)

1. Right-click the desktop.
2. Select New → Shortcut .

To Create a Desktop Folder (page 66)

1. Right-click the desktop.
2. Select New → Folder .

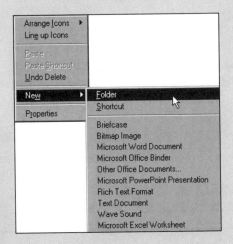

To Open Windows Explorer (page 75)

Select Start → Programs → Windows NT Explorer .

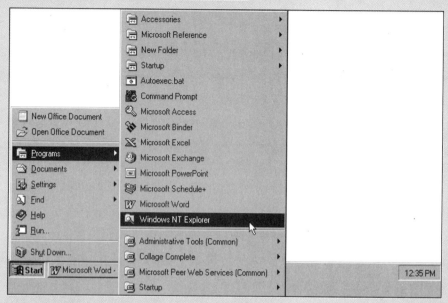

To Set Up NT Explorer Options (page 79)

Select View → Options , and then click the View tab.

To Copy a File to a Folder on the Same Hard Disk (page 83)

Press Ctrl while dragging the file.

To Copy a File to a Folder on Another Hard Disk (page 83)

Drag the file — don't press any key.

To Carry Out Various Operations on Files (page 81)

1. Right-click the file.
2. Select the operation from the menu.

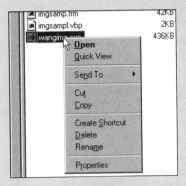

To View Information about a File, Folder, or Disk (page 87)

1. Right-click the icon.
2. Select **Properties**

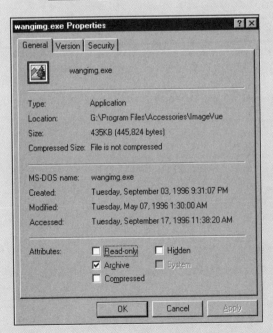

DISCOVERY CENTER

To Format a Floppy Disk (page 96)

Right-click the 3½ Floppy [A:] icon and select Format .

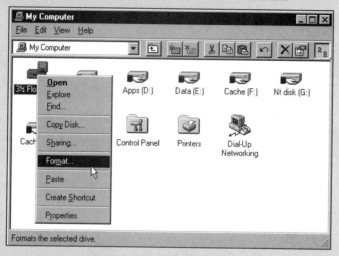

To Duplicate a Floppy Disk (page 98)

1. Right-click the 3½ Floppy [A:] icon and choose Copy Disk .
2. If you have only one floppy drive, click Start.
3. If you have multiple drives, select the one to copy from and the one to copy to (both must be the same type), and then click Start.

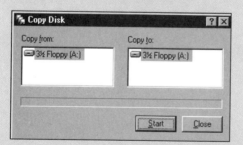

To Check Disks for Errors (and Fix Errors) (page 99)

1. Right-click the disk and select Properties .
2. Click the Tools tab in the Properties dialog box.
3. Click the Check Now button.

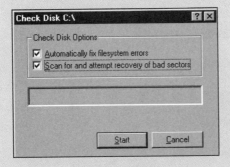

4. Click the Automatically fix filesystem errors check box.
5. Click the *Scan for and attempt recovery of bad sectors* check box.
6. Click the Start button and the process begins.

To Find File-Association Information (page 102)

1. In Windows NT Explorer or a folder window select View → Options .
2. Click the File Types tab.

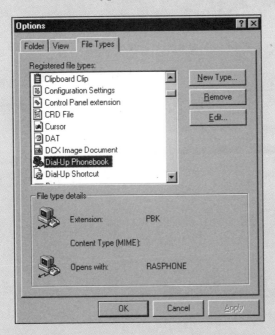

To Find a File You've Lost (page 105)

1. Select Start → Find → Files or Folders.

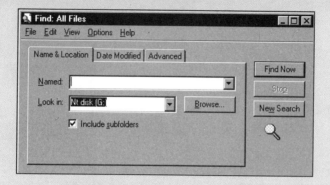

2. Enter identifying information — part of a name, a location, date, and so on.
3. Click Find Now.

To Install a Printer (page 116)

1. Select Start → Settings → Printers.
2. In the Printers folder, double-click the Add Printer icon.
3. Follow the Add Printer Wizard instructions.

To View the Print Queue (page 123)

Right-click the printer icon in the taskbar tray while a document is printing.

To Cancel a Print Job (page 123)

Click the print job and press Delete.

To Cancel All Print Jobs (page 123)

Select Printer → Purge Print Documents.

To Pause a Print Job (page 123)

Right-click the print job and select Pause .

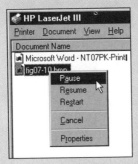

To Continue Printing a Print Job (page 123)

Right-click the print job and select Resume .

To See What a Font Looks Like (page 130)

Double-click the font in the Fonts folder.

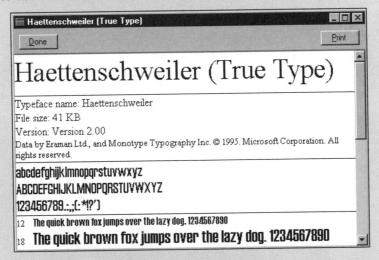

Finding a Special Character (page 133)

1. Select **Start** → **Programs** → **Accessories** → **Character Map**.
2. Select the font you want to work with from the *Font* drop-down list box.
3. View the symbols in the main area of Character Map.
4. Click a character to magnify it.

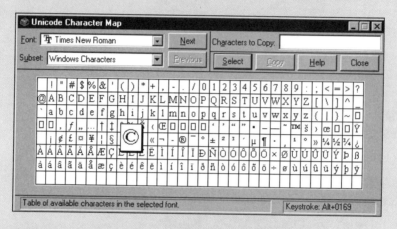

To Create a New User Account (page 142)

1. Select **User** → **New User** to open the New User dialog box.

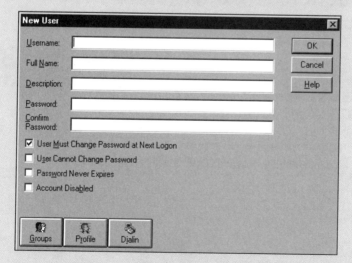

2. Type a username.
3. Enter the user's full name, if you want.
4. Type a description of the person, if you want.
5. Type the password that the user will need to enter when logging in.
6. Type the password again in the *Confirm Password* box.
7. If you want the user to pick a personal password — one that's easier to remember, for example — check the *User Must Change Password at Next Logon* check box.
8. If you don't want to allow the user to change the password, check the *User Cannot Change Password* check box.
9. You can make NT periodically ask users for a new password. If you check the *Password Never Expires* check box, that option is overridden for this account.
10. If you are not ready to activate this account, you can check the *Account Disabled* check box.
11. Click OK.

To Create a New Group (page 146)

1. Click each user that you want to be a member of the new group.
2. Select [User] → [New Local Group].

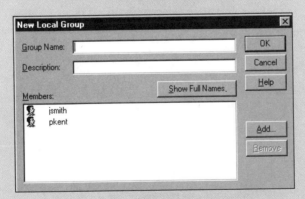

3. Type a group name in the *Group Name* box.
4. Type a more detailed description in the *Description* box.
5. To add more members to the group, click Add.

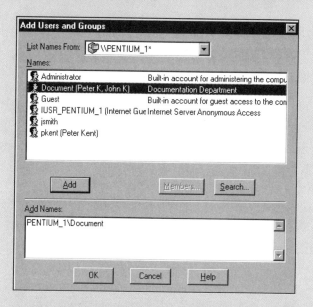

6. In the Names list, double-click each name you want to add.
7. Click OK.
8. Click OK in the New Local Group dialog box.

Assigning a User to a Group (page 148)

1. Click the Groups in the User Properties box.

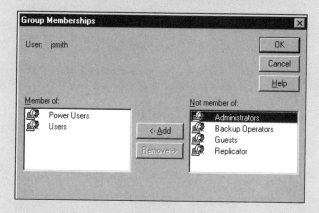

2. Double-click a group name in the *Not member of* list to move that name across to the *Member of* list.
3. Click OK.

To Assign Rights to a User or Group (page 150)

1. In User Manager, select Policies → User Rights .

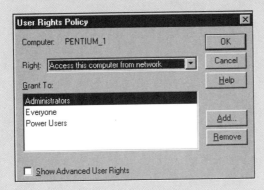

2. In the *Right* drop-down list box, select the right that you want to assign to a group or user.
3. Click Add.
4. Double-click the groups you want to add, or click once and then click Add.
5. Click OK.

To View the Contents of the Clipboard (page 168)

1. Select Start → Programs → Accessories → Clipboard Viewer .
2. Select Window → 1. Clipboard .

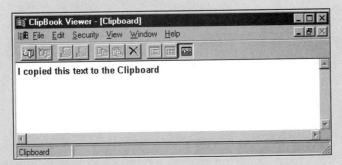

To Save an Object in the ClipBook (page 169)

1. Cut or copy the object to the Clipboard.
2. Open the ClipBook Viewer.

3. Select Window → 2. Local Clipbook.
4. Select Edit → Paste.

5. Type a Page Name.
6. Click OK.

To Open WordPad (page 172)

Select Start → Programs → Accessories → WordPad.

To Place a Tab in the Ruler (page 177)

Just click in the ruler.

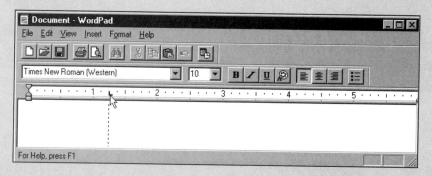

To Search for Text (page 179)

Select Edit → Find.

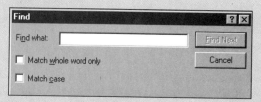

To Open Notepad (page 182)

Select Start → Properties → Accessories → Notepad.

To Open Microsoft Paint (page 190)

Select Start → Programs → Accessories → Paint .

To Set a Paint Tool's Options (page 193)

1. Click the tool in the tool box.

2. If the tool has options, you'll see an additional box below the tool box.

To Set an Imaging Tool's Options (page 202)

1. Open the Annotation tool box: Annotation → Show Annotation Toolbox .
2. Right-click the tool you want to modify.

3. Select Properties.

DISCOVERY CENTER

To Create Your Own Rubber Stamps (page 205)

1. Select [Annotation] → [Rubber Stamps].

2. Click Create Text or Create Image.
3. Type a name for the stamp in the *Stamp Name* box.
4. Type the message into the *Text Message* box. If you're creating an image file, use the Browse button to select the image you want to use.
5. Click the Date button if you want to include the current date, and the Time button to include the time.
6. Click OK.

To Install Sound Drivers (page 208)

1. Select [Start] → [Settings] → [Control Panel].
2. Double-click the Multimedia] icon.
3. Click the Devices tab.
4. Click Add.
5. Click the entry for your sound card. If yours isn't there, contact the manufacturer.
6. Click OK and NT will begin installing the software. Follow the instructions.

To Open CD Player (page 211)

Select Start → Programs → Accessories → CD Player. Or simply place an audio CD into the drive and NT will start CD Player automatically.

To Create a Play List (page 213)

1. Insert a CD.
2. Select Disk → Edit Play List.
3. Type the name of the band or musician into the *Artist* box.
4. Type the album name into the *Title* box.
5. Highlight the text in the text box at the bottom of the dialog box and type the first track name.
6. Press Enter and type the second track name. Repeat for each track. The track name is placed into both the *Play List* and *Available Tracks* list boxes.
7. Click Clear All.
8. Double-click each track in the order you want to play them. The tracks are added to the Play List in that order.

9. Click OK.

To Open Sound Recorder (page 215)

Select Start → Programs → Accessories → Sound Recorder .

To Open Media Player (page 217)

Select Start → Programs → Accessories → Media Player .

To Open the Mini Volume Control (page 220)

Left-click the Volume icon on the taskbar's tray.

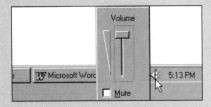

To Set Up a Tape Drive (page 226)

1. Select Start → Settings → Control Panel, and then double-click the Tape Devices icon.

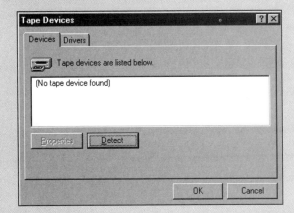

2. Click Detect and Windows NT looks for an attached drive.
3. If NT finds a drive, it displays a message box letting you know. Click OK to continue.
4. NT will now copy the drivers from your installation CD. Follow the instructions.

To Open Windows NT Backup (page 227)

1. Insert a tape into the drive.
2. Select `Start` → `Programs` → `Administrative Tools (Common)` → `Backup`.

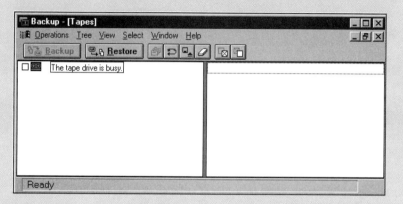

To Back up Data (page 228)

1. Select `Window` → `1. Drives` to see the Drives window.

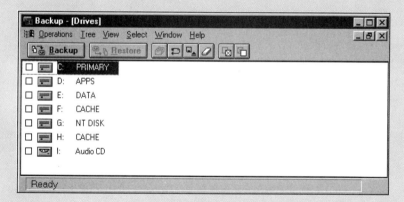

2. To back up an entire disk drive, click the check box next to that drive.
3. To back up specific folders or files, double-click the drive containing the folders or files.

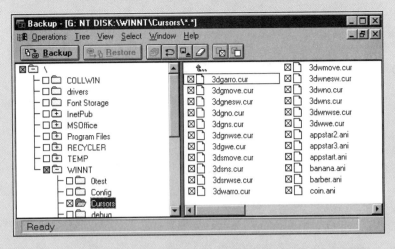

4. Select the folders and files you want to back up — click in the check boxes. To open the directory tree, double-click a folder.

5. Click the Backup button to see the Backup Information dialog box.

6. Make your selections, and then click OK.

To Restore Data (page 233)

1. Open the Backup program.
2. Select `Operations` → `Catalog` to retrieve a list of backup sets on the tape.
3. If you don't see the list of backups (you may see a single backup, with a directory tree in the left pane), select `Window` → `2. Tapes`.
4. Double-click the set you want to restore, and Backup retrieves information about that set from the tape.

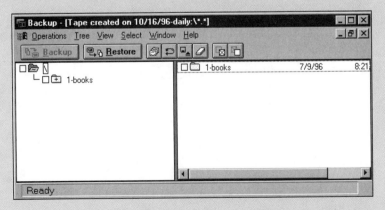

DISCOVERY CENTER

5. Select the specific files or folders — double-click entries to open up the directory tree — and click the check boxes to select the files and folders you want to restore.

6. Click the Restore button.

7. Make your restore-option selections and click OK to begin the restore process.

To Install a Modem (page 240)

1. Select Start → Settings → Control Panel.
2. Double-click the Modems icon.

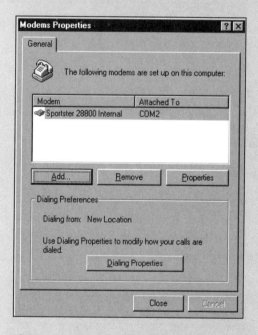

3. If your modem is not listed, click Add to see the Install New Modem dialog box.

4. Click Next> and NT starts looking for your modem.

To Set up a New Connection (page 244)

1. Select Start → Programs → Accessories → HyperTerminal.

2. Type the name of the service you are connecting to, and select an icon from the list.
3. Click OK.

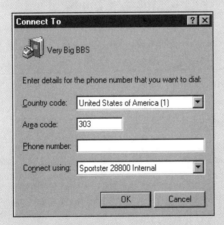

4. Type the phone number you have to dial to connect to this BBS, and click OK.
5. Click Dial to begin dialing.

To Start Phone Dialer (page 250)

Select Start → Programs → Accessories → Phone Dialer .

To Dial a Call (page 251)

1. Click the number keys to enter the number you want to dial, or type the number.
2. If you've made calls before using Phone Dialer, you can select an earlier number from the *Number to dial* drop-down list box.
3. Click Dial to begin dialing.

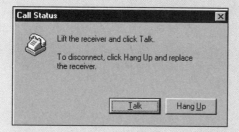

4. Pick up your phone, and then click the Talk button. The modem disconnects and leaves you ready to continue the call.

To Enter Your Network Identification (page 260)

1. Right-click the Network Neighborhood icon.
2. Choose Properties .
3. Click the Change button.

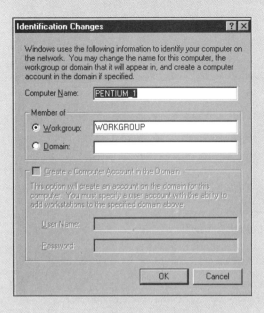

4. Enter the information provided by your system administrator.

To Share Your Data (page 267)

1. Right-click the folder or disk and select `Sharing`.
2. Click the *Shared As* option button to turn on sharing.

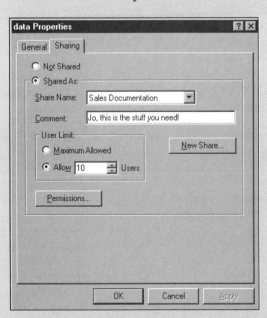

3. Click Permissions and the Access Through Share Permissions dialog box opens.

4. If *Everyone* is shown in this box, click Remove to clear the entry.
5. Click Add.
6. Double-click the users or groups that you want to give access to your information.
7. In the *Type of Access* drop-down list box, select the type of access you want to provide to these users.
8. Click OK three times to complete the operation.

To Open Chat (page 270)

Select 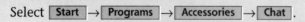.

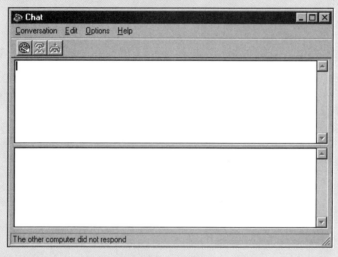

To Send E-mail (page 282)

1. Double-click the Inbox desktop icon, or select Start → Programs → Windows Messaging. You may see a logon box (if you are logging on as an administrator).

2. Enter your mailbox account name and your password, and click OK.

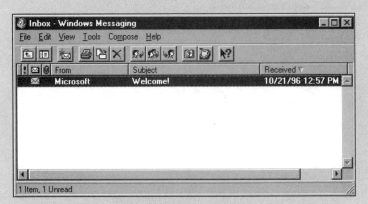

3. Click the New Message button.

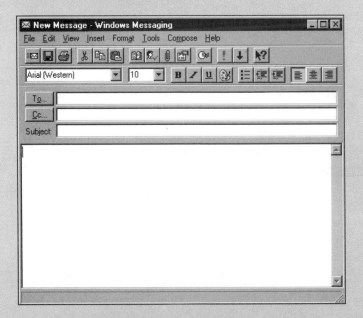

4. Type an e-mail address in the *To* text box.

5. In the *Subject* text box, type a few words describing the contents of the message.

6. Type your message in the large message area.

7. When you've finished your message, click the Send button, and the message is placed in the Outbox. The message may be sent immediately or the next time you connect to the postoffice or Internet mail server.

To Read E-mail (page 284)

1. Click the Inbox button to see the Inbox.
2. Double-click the message to open it.

To Retrieve Remote Mail (page 288)

1. Select Tools → Remote Mail .
2. Click the Transfer Mail button and Remote Mail connects to the postoffice or Internet mail server.

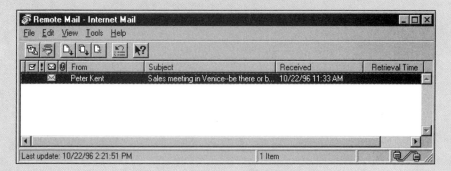

3. Click a message that you want to retrieve and click the Mark to Retrieve button.
4. Click the Transfer Mail button again, and Remote Mail again connects to the postoffice or Internet Mail server and transfers any mail that you have marked for download.

To Use the Address Book (page 289)

1. Click the To button in the New Message window.

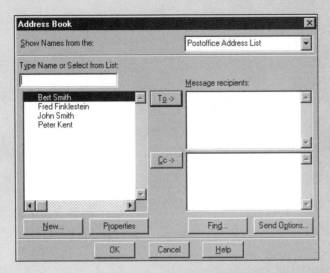

2. Double-click the name of the person to whom you want to send a message. The name is added to the *Message recipients* box.

3. If you want to send a copy of the message to someone else, click that person's name and click Cc.

4. Click OK and the names are placed into the *To* and *Cc* boxes in the New Message window.

To Install Dial-Up Networking (page 298)

1. Double-click the My Computer icon on your desktop. The My Computer folder opens.

2. Double-click the Dial-Up Networking icon in My Computer. If Dial-Up Networking is not installed, you'll see a message box telling you. Click Install and NT begins installing the service.

3. You may see a dialog box asking if you want to install a modem. Follow the instructions.

4. Select the modem you want to use for Dial-Up Networking. Play around with the settings and options to see what's available. Then click OK.

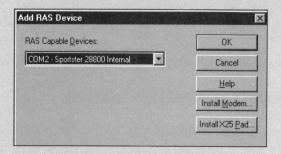

5. If you are only dialing out from the computer (no computers are dialing in to yours), than no changes are necessary in the Remote Access Setup dialog box. Click Continue and NT finishes installing the Dial-Up Networking files.

To Create a New Connection (page 300)

1. Double-click the My Computer icon on your desktop. The My Computer folder opens.

2. Double-click the Dial-Up Networking icon in My Computer. You may see the New Phonebook Entry Wizard dialog box. If you already have other Dial-Up Networking connections set up, click New in the Dial-Up Networking box to see the New Phonebook Entry Wizard.

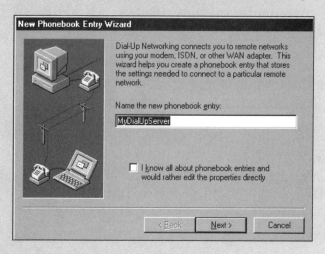

3. Type a name that identifies this Dial-Up Networking connection, and click Next.

4. Check all the check boxes that are appropriate for this connection (ask your system administrator).

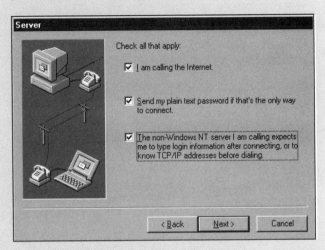

5. Click Next and enter a phone number.

6. Click Next and select the type of protocol that will be used to communicate with the other computer.

7. Click Next and tell Dial-Up Networking which logon method to use.

8. Click Next and enter the IP address given to you by your system administrator.

9. Click Next and enter the name — server numbers given to you by your system administrator.

10. Click Next. You'll see a dialog box telling you that you're finished.

11. Click Finish and the Dial-Up Networking box appears, showing you your new connection.

To Dial a Dial-Up Networking Connection (page 304)

1. Select Start → Programs → Accessories → Dial-Up Networking .

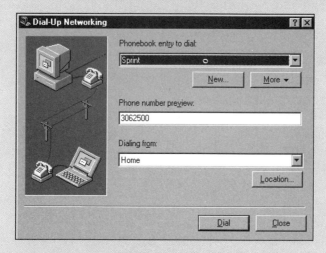

2. Select the connection you want to use from the *Phonebook entry to dial* box.
3. Click Dial.

4. Type your user name and password.
5. In some cases, you may need to enter a domain name. Ask your system administrator.
6. Click OK and the system begins dialing to connect to the service.

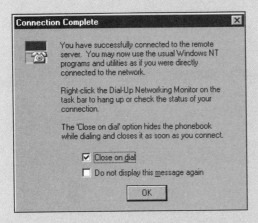

7. Click OK to connect to the remote computer.

Ways to Move Around on the Web (page 323)

* Click a link (underlined and colored text, or some pictures).
* Type a URL into the Address box and press Enter.
* Select from the Favorites list (click the Favorites button).
* Select a previously viewed page from the history list (open the `Go` menu).

To Add to the Favorites (page 324)

1. When you reach a page that you think you may want to return to, select `Favorites` → `Add to Favorites`.

2. Click OK to add an entry to the Favorites folder, or click Create In to place it into a subfolder.

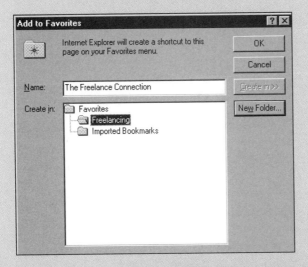

DISCOVERY CENTER **401**

3. Click New Folder to create a new folder in which you can store the entry.

4. Click the folder into which you want to place the entry, and then click OK.

To Modify Most Settings (page 333)

1. Open the Control Panel: Select Start → Settings → Control Panel .

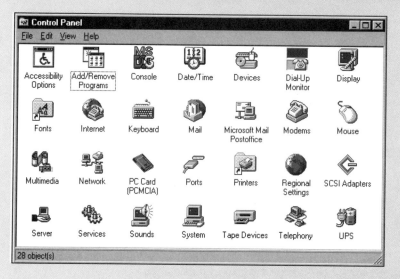

2. Double-click the appropriate icon.

To Make the Computer More Accessible (page 336)

Modify the Accessibility Settings (double-click the Accessibility Options icon):

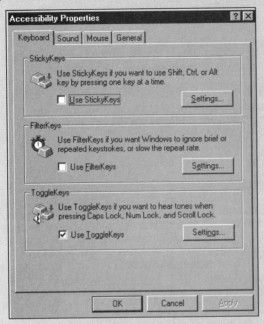

* StickyKeys holds the Shift, Ctrl, and Alt keys down for you.
* FilterKeys can ignore accidentally repeated keystrokes and keys held down too long.
* ToggleKeys sounds a tone when you press Caps Lock, Num Lock, or Scroll Lock
* SoundSentry and ShowSounds use visual indicators instead of sounds.
* MouseKeys allows you to move the mouse with the numeric keypad.

To Change Your Desktop Wallpaper (page 341)

1. Double-click the Display icon in the Control Panel, or right-click the desktop and select Properties.

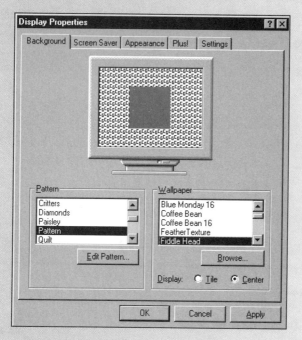

2. Select an item from the Wallpaper list.
3. Select Tile, to fill the desktop with the image, or Center, to put one image in the middle of the screen.
4. Click Apply or OK.

To Set Your Monitor's Resolution and Colors (page 345)

1. Open the Display Properties box, then click the Settings tab.

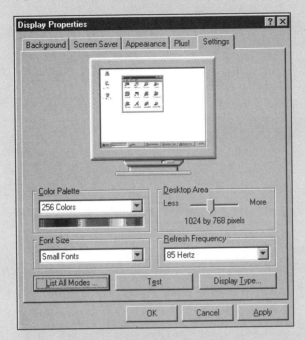

2. Choose the number of colors you want to use from the *Color Palette* drop-down list box.
3. Drag the Desktop Area slider to modify the screen resolution.
4. Click Test to make sure the settings work. The settings are tested for five seconds; if you get a blank screen, they don't work. If the settings do work, you see a screen showing colors, text, and arrows.
5. Click OK.

To Pick Your Mouse Pointers (page 348)

1. Double-click the Mouse icon.
2. Click the Pointers tab.

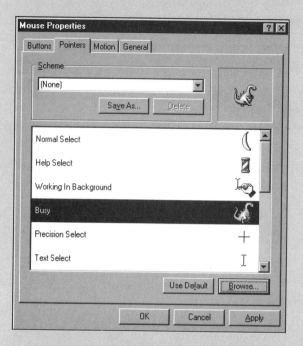

3. You can select a preset scheme of mouse pointers, if you want, from the *Scheme* drop-down dialog box. Or click a mouse pointer type and then click Browse. You can pick from scores of different mouse pointers, static and animated.

To See Your Computer's Memory Use (page 355)

1. Right-click the taskbar and select Task Manager .
2. Click the Performance tab.
3. Look in the MEM Usage box.

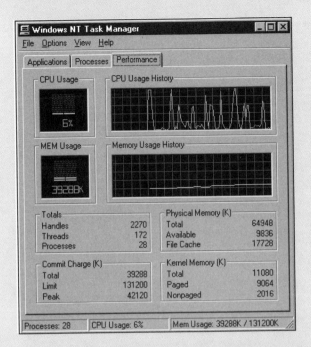

To See Which Programs are Using the Most Memory (page 356)

1. Right-click the taskbar and select Task Manager .
2. Click the Processes tab.
3. Click the Mem Usage bar at the top of the list box. The processes are sorted with the biggest memory hog at the top.

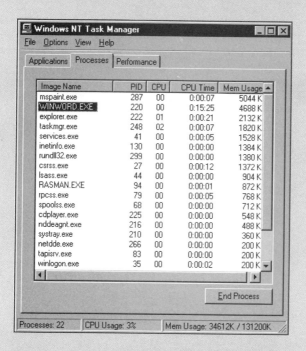

To Open Performance Monitor (page 357)

Select Start → Programs → Administrative Tools (Common) → Performance Monitor.

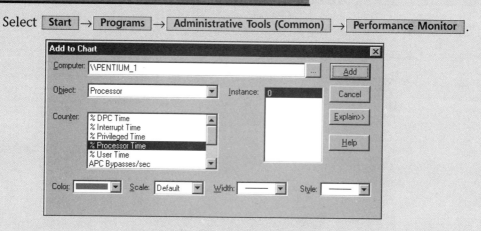

To Open the Event Viewer (page 360)

Select Start → Programs → Administrative Tools (Common) → Event Viewer.

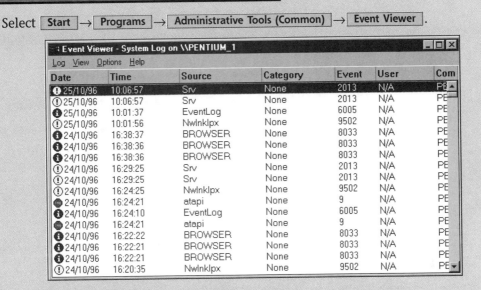

To View an Event's Details (page 360)

Double-click an item in the list.

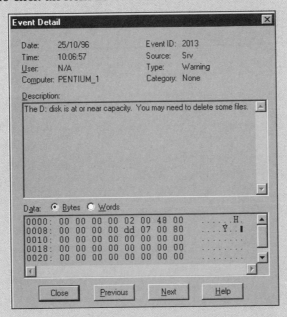

To View General System Information (page 361)

Select Start → Programs → Administrative Tools (Common) → Windows NT Diagnostics. Then click the appropriate tab (Version, System, Display, Drives, Memory, Services, Resources, Environment, or Network).

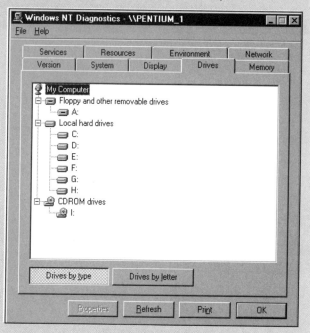

VISUAL INDEX

The Windows NT Desktop

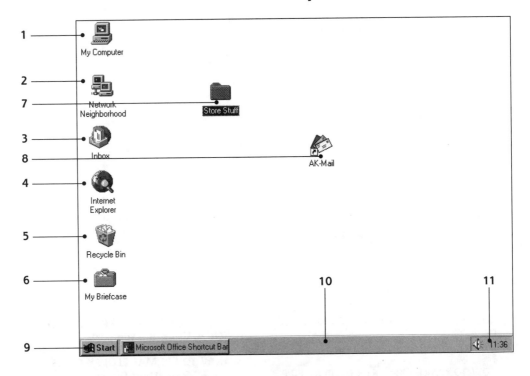

1. **HOW TO USE "MY COMPUTER" TO FIND YOUR WAY AROUND**
   [Ch 6, Using My Computer]

2. **HOW TO CONNECT TO COMPUTERS ON THE NETWORK**
   [Ch 14, Using Network Neighborhood]

3. **HOW TO SEND AND RECEIVE E-MAIL**
   [Ch 15, Opening Windows Messaging and Sending E-mail]

4. **HOW TO WORK ON THE WORLD WIDE WEB**
   [Ch 17]

5. **HOW TO RECOVER DELETED FILES**
   [Ch 6, Deleting (and Retrieving) Files]

6. **HOW TO TAKE FILES WITH YOU WHEN YOU TRAVEL** [Ch 16, Taking Files on the Road With Briefcase]

7. **HOW TO CREATE YOUR OWN FOLDERS TO STORE FILES** [Ch 4, Creating Folders]

8. **HOW TO CREATE SHORTCUTS TO YOUR PROGRAMS**
   [Ch 4, Creating Desktop Shortcuts]

9. **HOW TO USE THE START MENU** [Ch3, Starting Programs From the Start Menu]

10. **HOW TO USE THE TASKBAR**
    [Ch 4, Using the Taskbar to Manage Windows]

11. **HOW TO USE THE TRAY** [Ch 4, Managing Windows with Task Manager]

Windows NT Explorer

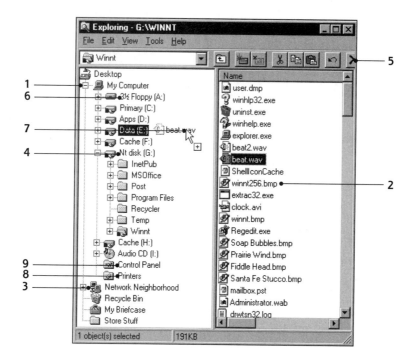

1 **HOW TO MOVE AROUND THE DIRECTORY TREE** [Ch 5, Moving Around in the Directory Tree]

2 **HOW TO MAKE EXPLORER DISPLAY FILE EXTENSIONS** [Ch 5, Configuring NT Explorer]

3 **HOW TO CONNECT TO NETWORKED COMPUTERS**
   [Ch 14, Using Network Neighborhood]

4 **HOW TO SHARE YOUR DATA ON THE NETWORK** [Ch 14, Sharing Your Information on the Network]

5 **THE WINDOWS NT EXPLORER TOOLBAR** [Ch 5, Using the toolbar]

6 **HOW TO FORMAT FLOPPY DISKS** [Ch 6, Formatting Disks]

7 **HOW TO MOVE FILES AND FOLDERS** [Ch 5, Working With Files]

8 **HOW TO SET UP PRINTERS** [Ch 7, Installing a Printer]

9 **HOW TO CUSTOMIZE YOUR SYSTEM** [Ch 18]

Working with Programs

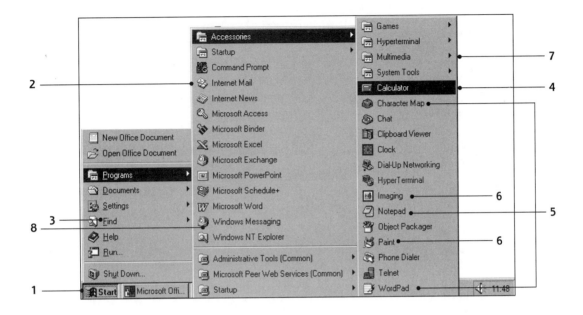

1 **HOW TO USE THE START MENU** [Ch 3, Starting Programs From the Start Menu]

2 **HOW TO ADD YOUR OWN MENU OPTIONS** [Ch 4, Adding Menu Options]

3 **HOW TO FIND FILES, DIRECTORIES, AND MORE ON YOUR COMPUTER** [Ch 6, Finding Stuff With Find and Go To]

4 **USING THE CALCULATOR** [Ch 9, Figuring Numbers — Calculator]

5 **WORKING WITH TEXT ACCESSORIES** [Ch 9, Word Processing for the Masses — WordPad]

6 **WORKING WITH IMAGE ACCESSORIES** [Ch 10]

7 **USING THE MULTIMEDIA ACCESSORIES** [Ch 11]

8 **WORKING WITH E-MAIL** [Ch 15, Opening Windows Messaging and Sending E-mail]

VISUAL INDEX **413**

Customizing Your System

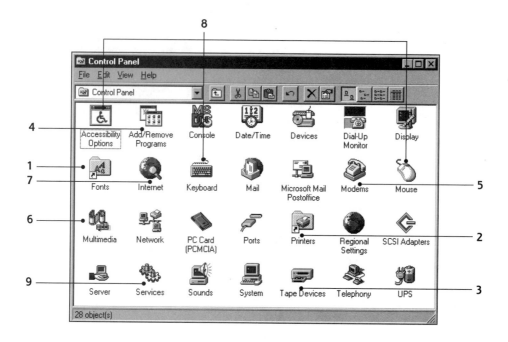

1. **HOW TO WORK WITH FONTS**
   [Ch 7, Viewing Fonts]

2. **HOW TO INSTALL PRINTERS**
   [Ch 7, Installing a Printer]

3. **HOW TO WORK WITH BACKUP TAPE DEVICES** [Ch 12, top]

4. **HOW TO INSTALL NEW PROGRAMS**
   [Ch 4, Installing New Programs]

5. **HOW TO CONFIGURE MODEMS**
   [Ch 13, Preparing Your Modem]

6. **HOW TO WORK/CONFIGURE MULTIMEDIA DEVICES** [Ch 11, Preparing For Sound]

7. **HOW TO WORK ON THE INTERNET**
   [Ch 17]

8. **HOW TO CUSTOMIZE THE WAY YOU INPUT DATA** [Ch 18, Setting Accessibility Options, and Ch 18, Configuring the Keyboard and Mouse]

9. **HOW TO CUSTOMIZE VARIOUS SYSTEM OPTIONS** [Ch 18]

Making Your System Secure

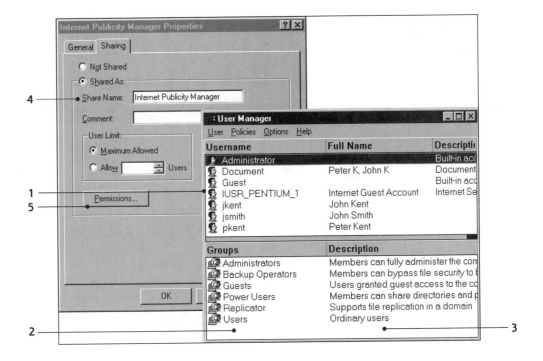

1 **CREATING USER PROFILES (ACCOUNTS)**
  [Ch 8, Creating a User Account]

2 **WORKING WITH USER GROUPS**
  [Ch 8, All About Groups]

3 **DEFINING WHO CAN DO WHAT**
  [Ch 8, What Can Users Do?]

4 **SHARING FILES AND DIRECTORIES ON THE NETWORK** [Ch 14, Sharing Your Information on the Network]

5 **DEFINING WHO CAN USE YOUR DATA ON THE NETWORK** [Ch 8, Restricting Access to Resources, AND Ch 14, Sharing Your Information on the Network]

Working on the Internet

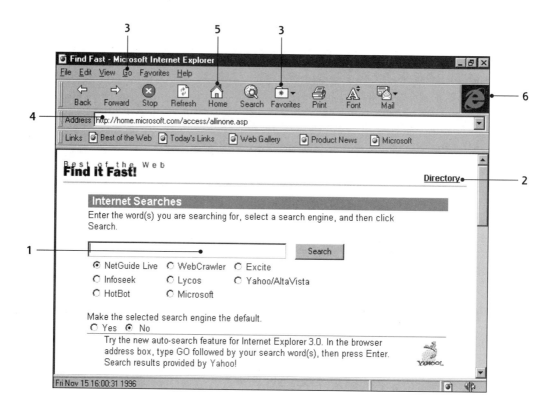

1. **HOW TO FIND THINGS ON THE INTERNET** [Ch 17, Searching For What You Need]

2. **USING LINKS TO MOVE AROUND THE WORLD WIDE WEB** [Ch17, Moving Around on the Web]

3. **USING "FAVORITES" TO FIND PAGES YOU'VE VISITED BEFORE** [Ch 17, Select From the Favorites]

4. **HOW TO WORK WITH URLs (WEB ADDRESSES)** [Ch 17, a URL]

5. **HOW TO GET "HOME"** [Ch 17, Finding Your Way Back]

6. **HOW TO GET THE LATEST INTERNET EXPLORER** [Ch 17, Upgrading Internet Explorer]

7. **HOW TO USE THE HISTORY LIST** [Ch 17, Select From the History List]

INDEX

A

Accessibility options, 334
Accessories menu, 40–41
Add/Remove Programs, 26, 334
address books, 289–293
administrator accounts, 71–72
alerts, 359
Always on Top option, 31–33, 53
annotations, 201–204
Appearance tab, 342–343
associating files, 100–104
auditing, 13, 154–158
Auto hide check box, 31–32
Automatic Reset option, 339

B

backup systems, 14, 97, 99, 225–238, 363
    making backups, 227–231
    restoring data from, 233–235
    scheduling for, 236–238
    selecting backup types, 231–232
    strategies for, 232–233
bindings, 275
bookmarks, 324–325
booting, 1, 20–23
    automatically opening programs upon, 39
    dual-boot computers and, 20–22
    hardware profiles and, 314
    modifying the procedure for, 350–352
Briefcase, 15, 307–314
    checking files in, 309–311
    icon, 23, 24
    opening, 307
    packing files in, 308
Browse dialog box, 53–54

C

Calculator, 14, 165, 183–185
Calling Card feature, 252–255
Cascade Windows command, 48
CD Player, 14, 207, 211–215, 223
certification system, 328
Character Map, 14, 133–135, 138–139
Chat, 15, 270–271
clicking, 20
Clipboard, 14, 165–168
ClipBook, 14, 169–171
clock, 23–24, 29, 33–34
Close button, 46, 47
Close command, 56
closing
    document windows, 58
    programs, 52, 56–57
    Windows NT, 35–36
colors
    Control panel settings for, 340, 342–345
    Paint and, 196–198
compression, 89–90
CompuServe, 239
control menus, 46, 47, 48, 56
Control Panel, 15, 24, 26, 51, 333–350
Copy command, 55, 166–168
copying
    the briefcase, 216–217

(continued)

417

copying *(continued)*
    disks, 96, 98
CPUs (central processing units), 9–10, 34, 332,
361 crashes, 9–10
Create New Folder button, 55
Create New Task dialog box, 58
Create Shortcut command, 55
customization, 331, 333–352
Cut command, 55, 166–168

D

date/time settings, 33, 334, 340–341
Date/Time Properties dialog box, 33
default systems, 21
defragmentation, 100, 363
deleting
    files, 110–112
    fonts, 132–133
Desktop. *See also* Desktop shortcut icons
    basic description of, 2, 23–28
    contents, viewing, 38
    customizing, 61–74
    files, creating, 69–70
    switching back to, 27
Desktop shortcut icons, 13, 25
    basic description of, 27–28
    Control Panel settings for, 344
    creating, 27, 34, 65–66, 93–94
    managing, 67–68
    sorting, 37–38
    starting programs with, 42
Details button, 55
device settings, 127–128
diagnostics tools, 16, 331, 353–364
Dialin Access, 161
Dial-Up Networking, 15, 24, 288, 297–303
    closing connections with, 305–306
    dialing into new connections with, 303–306
    installing, 298–300
    Internet Explorer and, 321, 322, 329
    monitoring, 334
    setting up connections with, 300–303
directories, 34–35, 110. *See also* folders
    in Explorer, 78–79
    finding files in, 54
    permissions for, 152–154
disk(s)
    backing up, 97, 99
    copying, 96, 98
    copying My Briefcase on, 216–217
    defragmenting, 100, 363
    errors, checking for, 99
    formatting, 96–98
Disk Administrator, 16, 353
Document menu, 42–43
document properties, 128–129
Documents option, 30
domains, 260
double-clicking, 20
drive(s)
    compressing, 89–90
    information, in Explorer, 89
    list of, 361
    mapping, 264–266
    tape drives, 226–236

E

e-mail. *See also* Windows Messaging
    address books, 289–293
    Internet Explorer and, 328
    retrieving/reading, 284–288
    sending, 282–284, 289–290
    setting up, 277–281
    using remote mail to grab, 288–289
errors, 99, 363
event logs, 359, 360–361
Event Viewer, 16, 353, 360–361
Excel, 39
Exchange, 286
Exit command, 56
Explore All Users command, 73
Explore command, 55, 73

Explorer, 13, 26, 28, 90–91
  basic description of, 95–114
  compressing data with, 89–90
  configuring, 79–80
  creating icons with, 92–93
  drive information in, 89
  finding file/folder information in, 86–90
  moving around the directory tree in, 78–79
  multiple file operations with, 83–84
  opening, 75–78
  views, 84–87
  working with files in, 75–94
extranets, 329

F

Favorites lists, 324–325
file extensions, 101
file icons, 28
File Manager, 26
FilterKeys, 337
Find, 13, 27, 55, 105–110, 179
folder(s). *See also* directories
  auditing, 155–156
  basic description of, 27, 34–35
  compressing, 89–90
  creating, 34, 66–67, 292
  e-mail, 292
  icons, 28
  information in Explorer, 86–90
  managing, 67–68
  opening, 92
  permissions, 152–154
  Send To option and, 93–94
  windows, 13, 105
footers, 182–183
fonts
  basic description of, 115–139
  Control Panel settings for, 343, 345
  installing, 131–132
  management, 129–133

  Paint and, 194–195
  removing, 132–133
  special characters, 133–135
  viewing, 129–130
  WordPad and, 176–177
Fonts folder, 13, 334
formatting disks, 96–98
FTP (File Transfer Protocol) sites, 11

G

Games menu, 40, 42
General printer properties, 124–125
General Settings tab, 339
Go To command, 105–110
group membership, 144–140
Guest accounts, 71–72

H

hard disks, maintaining, 363. *See also* disks
hardware. *See also* disks; memory; printers
  hard disks, 363
  installing, 21, 116–121
  the Internet as, 219
  modems, 240–243
  mouse, 335, 337–339, 346, 348–349
  Profiles, 15, 21–22, 297, 311–314
headers, 182–183, 280
Help, 30
HIP (Hake Internet Projects), 258
history lists, 325–326
home pages
  basic description of, 323
  returning to, 327
HyperTerminal, 15, 239–256
  downloading files with, 248–249
  setting up new connections with, 250
  working online with, 246–260
hypertext, 320

I

IDG Books WorldWide Web site, 44
Imaging, 14, 189
   making annotations with, 201–204
   opening, 199–201
Inbox icon, 23, 24
installing
   Dial–Up Networking, 298–300
   fonts, 131–132
   hardware, 21, 116–121
   new programs, 70–71
   printers, 116–121
Internet, 257–276, 297–318
   Guest accounts, 71–72
   use of the term, 319
Internet Explorer browser, 15, 23–24
   basic description of, 319–330
   e-mail program, 328
   getting started with, 320–321
   navigating with, 327
   searching for what you need with, 326–327
   upgrading, 321–323
Internet Service Manager, 354
intranets, 257–276
IP (Internet Protocol) addresses, 279, 302

K

keyboard
   accelerators, 57
   designed for Windows 95, 30, 33
   settings, 336–337, 334, 346–348
Key Manager, 354

L

Last Known Good configuration, 21
licenses, software, 17
links
   basic description of, 320, 321
   bookmarks, 324–325
   in history lists, 325–326

images as, 322
List button, 55
locking Windows NT, 35–36
logging
   off, 27
   on, 1–2, 22–23
logo key, 30, 33, 50
logs, 359, 360–361

M

maintenance, 353–364
Media Player, 207, 217–220
memory
   information, 361
   requirements, 356
   usage, 355–357, 363
menu(s)
   adding options to, 62–63
   advanced modifications to, 63–65
   basic description of, 29
   control menus, 46, 47, 48, 56
   removing options from, 63
microprocessors, 9–10, 34, 332, 361
MIDI (Musical Instrument Digital Interface), 217
MIME (Multipurpose Internet Mail Extensions), 101
Minimize All command, 48
Minimize button, 46
minimizing/maximizing windows, 46–49, 50, 52
modems, 240–243
Monitor icon, 306
mouse settings, 335, 337–339, 346, 348–349
MultiLink connections, 315–316
multimedia, 14, 207–224
Multimedia Player, 14
multi–platform support, 9
multitasking, 44–45, 49–53
My Briefcase, 15, 307–314
   checking files in, 309–311

icon, 23, 24
opening, 307
packing files in, 308
My Computer, 13, 95
basic description of, 104–105
Dial-Up Networking and, 298, 300
directories and, 34
icon, 23, 24
viewing Desktop contents and, 38

N

NCAR (National Center for Atmospheric Research), 164
Netscape Navigator browser, 325
networking, 9, 10, 257–276. *See also* Network Neighborhood
accessing networks through NT, 268–270
connections, preparing, 260–262
multiLink connections and, 315–316
network cards and, 277–276
Network Neighborhood, 15, 259–279. *See also* networking
finding computers with, 266
finding data with, 263–264
icon, 23, 24
mapping drives with, 264–266
sharing information with, 267–269
Network Setup Wizard, 260–262
newsgroups, 328
Notepad, 14, 165, 182–183
Notification option, 339
NTFS (NT File System), 12

O

Object Packager, 14
Office, 30, 47
OLE (Object Linking and Embedding), 166, 185–187

Open All Users command, 73
Open command, 55, 73
opening
files, 27, 53–56, 59
folders, 27
Open Office Document option, 30
Open/Save dialog box, 53–56
operating systems, 11–12
ownership permissions, 153

P

Paint, 14, 189
advanced commands for, 199
changing views in, 198–199
colors and, 196–198
creating wallpaper with, 205
opening images with, 192
starting, 190–192
tools, 192–196
paragraphs, 177
passwords, 35, 141–144, 148–150, 260–261, 302
Paste command, 55, 166–168
PC cards, 335
Peer Web Services, 15, 354
Performance Monitor, 16, 354
permissions, 13, 152–154
Performance Monitor, 357–359
Personal Web Server, 328
Phone Dialer, 15, 239, 250–251
play lists, 213–214
Plug and Play, 18
Plus! tab, 344–345
pointers, sizing, 46, 47, 48
postoffice, 293–294
PPTP (Point to Point Tunneling Protocol), 329
printer(s), 115–139

INDEX **421**

(continued)

printer(s) *(continued)*
   creating print files and, 135–137
   device settings, 127–128
   installing, 116–121
   managing, 123
   multiple drivers for, 120
   network, 120–121
   properties, modifying, 124–129
   WordPad and, 179–180
Printers folder, 13, 24, 335
processors, 9–10, 34, 332, 361
program buttons, 29, 46, 50
Program Manager, 25, 27, 38
Programs menu, 25, 40–41, 57–58
Properties command, 55
Properties dialog box, 55
protocols, 273–275, 301–302, 329

Q

QuickTour, 1–6
Quick View command, 55

R

RAM (random-access memory), 364
   See also memory
ratings system, 328
README files, 113–114
recording sounds, 215–216
Recycle Bin, 23, 24, 110–112
regional settings, 335
remote mail, 288–289
Rename command, 55
reports, 359
right-clicking, 20
Rubber Stamps, 205–206
Run command, 23, 43–44, 58
Run dialog box, 23
Run in Separate Memory Space
     check box, 44

S

saving files, 27, 53–56, 180
scheduling properties, 126–127
screen savers, 35, 341–342
SCSI adapters, 335
search. *See also* Find
   criteria, saving, 109
   engines, 326–327
security, 9, 11–12, 141–162
   auditing, 154–158
   assigning rights, 150–153
   creating user accounts, 142–144
   determining account policies, 148–150
   group membership and, 144–149
   Internet Explorer and, 328
   locking Windows NT, 35–36
   passwords, 35, 141–144, 148–150,
     260–261, 302
   permissions, 13, 152–154
   properties, 127
   restricting access to resources, 152–154
Select command, 55
Send To command, 55
Send To menu, 73–74
Send To option, 93–94
SerialKey Devices option, 339
server(s)
   definition of, 259
   monitoring, 335
   name, 302
   proxy, 321
Server (Windows NT), 16–17
service packs, 11
Settings option, 30
Settings tab, 345–346
Shareware Leviathan Jumbo! Web site, 332
Sharing command, 55
ShowSounds, 337
shutdown, 6, 30, 35–36
sizing pointers, 46, 47, 48

sneakernet, 259
sorting icons, 37–38
sound(s)
    Control Panel settings for, 335, 337, 349–350
    editing, 216–217
    recording, 215–216
    sound cards and, 208–211
Sound Recorder, 14, 207, 215–217
SoundSentry, 337
special characters, 133–135
stability, 9, 10
Start button, 3, 13, 24–25
    basic description of, 24, 28–29
    location of, 28
    rightclicking, 73
    starting programs with, 29–30
starting, 19–38
    programs, 29–30, 39–60
    Windows NT, 1–2, 6
Start menu, 3, 25, 58
    options, 29–30, 61–65
    starting programs from, 40–42
StickyKeys, 336–337
system
    auditing, 154
    information, finding, 361–364
    performance, tracking, 357–359
System Properties dialog box, 350–352

T

tabs, 177–179
tape drives, 226–236
Taskbar
    basic description of, 28–34
    clock, 23–24, 29, 33–34
    controlling windows with, 46–49
    customizing, 30–33, 37
    location of, 23–24
    tray, 23, 28, 29, 33–34
    Volume Control, 14, 37–38, 207, 220–222

Taskbar Properties dialog box, 30–33, 51
Task Manager, 16, 26, 58, 354
    basic description of, 49–53, 355–357
    closing, 52
    customizing, 53
    managing windows with, 50, 51–53
    opening, 51, 56, 59
Task Manager dialog box, 33
telnet, 15, 329
text, entering, with Paint, 194–196
Tile Windows Horizontally command, 49
Tile Windows Vertically command, 49
title bars, 46
TMP files, 113
ToggleKeys, 337
toolbar, 90–91
tray, 23, 28, 29, 33–34
troubleshooting, 353–364
turning off, your computer, 6, 20, 36
turning on, your computer, 1, 20

U

underlined letters, 57
Undo Tile command, 49
UNIX, 164, 332
updates, 11
UPS (uninterruptible power supply), 335
URLs (uniform resource locators), 322, 323–324
US Sprint, 252–253
user
    accounts, 142–144, 294–295
    names, 260–261
    profiles, 71–72, 141, 159–161

V

version numbers, 361
video
    cards, 21, 361
    drivers, 21, 345
Volume Control, 14, 37–38, 207, 220–222
VPNs (Virtual Private Networks), 329
VxDs (Virtual Device Drivers), 17

W

wallpaper, 25, 205, 341
Welcome to Windows NT dialog box, 22–23
window(s)
    borders, 46, 47
    managing, 45–49
    minimizing/maximizing, 46–49, 50, 52
    switching between, 49–53
Windows 95, 1, 9, 17, 19, 44–45
    booting and, 20–21
    keyboards designed for, 30, 33
    Plug and Play, 18
    Windows NT and, comparison of, 25–27
Windows Messaging, 15, 24. *See also* e-mail
    opening, 282–284
    retrieving/reading messages with, 284–288
    sending e-mail with, 282–284
    setting up, 277–281
Windows NT FTP site, 11
Windows NT Workstation Web site, 10
Word for Windows, 39
WordPad, 4, 14, 165, 171–181
workstation, 12–16, 259
World Wide Web, use of the term, 319–320